Anonymus

United States Catholic Historical Magazine

Volume 2

Anonymus

United States Catholic Historical Magazine
Volume 2

ISBN/EAN: 9783742809162

Manufactured in Europe, USA, Canada, Australia, Japa

Cover: Foto ©ninafisch / pixelio.de

Manufactured and distributed by brebook publishing software (www.brebook.com)

Anonymus

United States Catholic Historical Magazine

UNITED STATES

CATHOLIC

HISTORICAL MAGAZINE.

PUBLISHED UNDER THE AUSPICES OF THE UNITED
STATES CATHOLIC HISTORICAL SOCIETY.

VOLUME II.

NEW YORK:
PRESS OF THE SOCIETY,
1888.

CONTENTS.

POPE DAY IN AMERICA. By John Gilmary Shea. Read before the U. S. Catholic Historical Society........ 1

THE ACADIANS BEFORE THEIR DISPERSION. By the Abbé, H. R. Casgrain. Paper read before the U. S. Catholic Historical Society.... 8

HOW FATHER HARDINGS' DEED OF ST. MARY'S CHURCH PROPERTY CAME TO BE RECORDED By BISHOP EGAN. 31

NOTES ON PARKMAN'S "CONSPIRACY OF PONTIAC," By Oscar W. Collet.............................. 35

SOME LANCASTER CATHOLICS AND OTHER NOTES, By S. M. Sener..... 49

THE ORIGIN OF THE MISSION TO THE FLATHEAD INDIANS. Paper read before the U. S. Catholic Historical Society, By Edmond Mallet...................... 55

SIR JOHN JAMES OF CRISHALL, ESSEX, Bart. The benefactor of the Pennsylvania Missions. By John Gilmary Shea..... 86

CATHOLIC AND ANTI-CATHOLIC ITEMS FROM NEW YORK PAPERS, 1765—1778.......... 93

MEETINGS OF THE U. S. CATHOLIC HISTORICAL SOCIETY... 99

NOTES.—Sketch of a Silver Cross found near Montpelier, Iowa, 48; When was St. Genevieve founded? 101; Rev. R. Molyneux's Memoir of Rev. Ferdinand Farmer, 103; Early Priests at Albany, 103; Priests at Frederick, Md., 103; An Early Priest at Princeton, 104; Rev. Raphael Fitzpatrick, 104; Anecdote of

Prince Gallitzin, by Rt. Rev. Michael O'Connor, 104;
Reminiscences of Rev. John Shanahau, 105; A Heme
Catechism 105

QUERIES.—What College did the Holy Man of Tours attend? Dr. O'Fallon's Colonies; N. Dame de Guiaudet.. 106

NOTICES OF RECENT PUBLICATIONS.—Ecclesiastical History of Newfoundland, by Very Rev. M. F. Howley, 108; A History of the Rise and Progress of Catholicism in Wallingford, Conn., by John G. Phelan, 108; The Iowa Historical Record, 109 ; The Church in Northern Ohio, and in the Diocese of Cleveland, 109; Church and State in the United States............. 110

ANNOUNCEMENT.—Dr. Shahan's History of the Catholic Church in the Diocese of Hartford.... 112

HISTORY OF THE CATHOLIC CHURCH IN MONROE CITY AND COUNTY, Mich. By Rt. Rev. Camillus P. Maes, D.D. Bishop of Covington 113

CHRISTOPHER DAVENPORT. The Brother of New Haven's Founder, a Franciscan Friar. By Rev. T. J. Shahan, D.D 153

COLUMBUS AND THE MEN OF PALOS. By John Gilmary Shea 164

MAJOR GOSSELIN, U. S. A. By Edmond Mallet 176

LE GARDEUR DE ST. PIERRE. (A Foot-Note.) By Edmond Mallet... 180

FATHER PETER MILET'S CAPTIVITY AMONG THE ONEIDA INDIANS, 1689-1694........................ 183

CATHOLIC AND ANTI-CATHOLIC ITEMS FROM NEW YORK AND PENNSYLVANIA PAPERS, 1775-1782....... ... 199

SUMMARY ON THE CATHOLIC RELIGION IN THE ENGLISH COLONIES IN AMERICA. Communicated by Very Rev. Charles A. Vissani, O. S. F 206

ADVENTURES OF A JESUIT LAY BROTHER, WHO SET SAIL FOR
MARYLAND IN 1657. 212

FURTHER NOTES ON POPE-DAY. By Rev. T. J. Shahan,
LL. D........ 214

LETTER OF RT. REV. JOHN CARROLL, DD., to Hon. Sam.
Dexter, Esq., Secretary of War, on the Indian
Missions.... 217

FIRST DIOCESAN SYNOD OF BALTIMORE. (From a contemporaneous manuscript)............... 218

NOTES.—Silver Chalice found in Pennsylvania; Early
Notice of Catholics at Boston; Maryland Catholics
during the Revolution; Madame Montour and her
Family; The Old Bell of the Kaskaskia Church... 220

QUERIES.—Rev. Francis Valley; Priests in Virginia in 1678 221

NOTICES OF RECENT PUBLICATIONS.—The Iowa Historical
Record. Life, Journals, and Correspondence of
Rev. Manasseh Cutler, D. D., by William Parker
Cutler and Julia Perkins Cutler. Biography of
Lieut. Col. Julius P. Garesché, Asst. Adjt.-Gen. U.
S. A., by his son...... 222

ANNOUNCEMENT...... 224

A MEMOIR OF THE LIFE AND LABORS OF THE RIGHT REV.
AMADEUS RAPPE, D.D., first Bishop of Cleveland.
By the Rev. G. F. Houck 225

HISTORICAL SKETCH OF THE REV. JOHN THAYER, Boston's
first native-born priest. By the Rev. Arthur T.
Connolly, of Roxbury, Mass 261

EARLY CATHOLICS IN CONNECTICUT. By the Rev. T. J.
Shahan, D.D...................... 274

THE BEGINNINGS OF THE CAPUCHIN MISSION IN LOUISIANA.
By J. G. S.................................... 295

ROBERT WALSH. By Henry C. Walsh............ 301

PETITION OF THE ROMAN CATHOLICS OF MARYLAND TO
THE UPPER HOUSE OF ASSEMBLY IN 1756............ 314

GENERAL DESCRIPTION OF THE METROPOLITAN PROVINCE
OF BALTIMORE IN THE UNITED STATES OF NORTH
AMERICY. By Archbishop Maréchal............... 318

THE CATHOLIC LAITY'S DIRECTORY TO THE CHURCH SER-
VICE, with an Almanac for the year 1817........... 320

MEETINGS OF THE UNITED STATES CATHOLIC HISTORICAL
SOCIETY............. 322

NOTES.—Advertisement of the first Catholic Bible, 260;
Bishop Carrol in Boston; Church at Vincennes in
1816, 273: A Flemish History of Canada; Indians on
the English Coast in 1508, 294; Notes on old Churches near Washington, 313; The Poor Clares at
Georgetown, 317; Bancroft's False Charges against
the Catholics of 1776, 328; New Mexican Antiquities,
by A F. Bandelier......... .,................... 330

QUERIES—History of Church Organs; Chronology of
Catholic Churches; Catholic Newspapers and Periodicals; San Miguel de Guandape; Pope's Absolution 333

BOOK NOTICES.—History of the Catholic Church, by
Brueck—Birthday of the State of Connecticut.—His-
tory of the Equestrian Statue of Israel Putnam.—
Church History, by Professor Kurtz......... 334

MEMORANDA....................................... 336

HISTORY OF ANCIENT VINLAND, OR PART OF NORTH AMER-
ICA. By Thormod Torfason. Translated by Charles
G. Herbermann, PH. D., LL. D.

Google

Google

WE, Catholics of the United States, have been lamentably neglectful in regard to the history of our Church, having done little to preserve material from which hereafter writers may be able to record what has been done by the Church, her bishops, priests, religious, and people. Here and there a few have labored with but little encouragement, and even what they painfully collected has too frequently been scattered or destroyed.

A better feeling seems to be awakening. Exertions in the right direction are now made at Philadelphia, Notre Dame, and elsewhere. In New York the only institution specially devoted to the task is "The United States Catholic Historical Society."

Every Catholic gentleman should feel it an honor and a duty to aid the Society by active co-operation as members or by subscribing to its magazine, or increasing its collections. In a great city like ours there ought to be a library where all books, magazines, newspapers, pamphlets, and documents relating to the Catholic Church and her children in the past should find a place. With a little zeal and interest a great collection can be made. Many families, churches, and institutions every year destroy material that would be regarded as of great value by historical scholars.

The Society has no reason to complain of its past or of any indifference or lack of promptness in its members, yet we may say that our membership ought to be greatly enlarged, and we feel assured that all our present members will promptly and cheerfully pay the annual dues to enable the Executive Council to continue the Quarterly Magazine which has been printed this year and sent to all our members, as well as to meet the expenses of a room, meetings, etc.

The Magazine has been very favorably received by historical students at home and abroad, and has already awakened much interest.

We call upon all to co-operate heartily in the good work. If you are already a member, endeavor to enlist others in the cause, and do not rest satisfied with mere payment of dues, but send contributions to the Library of books, pamphlets, magazines, newspapers, engravings, portraits, letters of bishops, priests, and others.

If not a member, apply for information as to the Society and its work.

THE EXECUTIVE COUNCIL OF THE U. S. CATHOLIC HISTORICAL SOCIETY,

P. O. Box, 2078.   20 WEST 27th STREET,
NEW YORK.

CONTENTS.

	PAGE
POPE-DAY IN AMERICA. By John Gilmary Shea. Read before the U. S. Catholic Historical Society, January 19, 1888.	1
THE ACADIANS BEFORE THEIR DISPERSION. By the Abbé H. R. Casgrain. Read before the U. S. Catholic Historical Society, February 21, 1888.	8
HOW FATHER HARDING'S DEED OF ST. MARY'S CHURCH PROPERTY CAME TO BE RECORDED BY BISHOP EGAN	31
NOTES ON PARKMAN'S "CONSPIRACY OF PONTIAC." (Tenth Edition, 1882.) By Oscar W. Collet.	35
SKETCH OF A SILVER CROSS FOUND NEAR MONTPELIER, IOWA. By Rev. John F. Kempker.	48
SOME LANCASTER CATHOLICS, and other Historical Notes. By S. M. Sener.	49
THE ORIGIN OF THE MISSION TO THE FLATHEAD INDIANS. By Edmond Mallet.	55
SIR JOHN JAMES, OF CRISHALL, ESSEX, BART., the Benefactor of the Pennsylvania Missions. By John Gilmary Shea.	86
CATHOLIC AND ANTI-CATHOLIC ITEMS FROM NEW YORK PAPERS, 1765-1778.	93
MEETINGS OF THE UNITED STATES CATHOLIC HISTORICAL SOCIETY.	99
NOTES.—When was St. Genevieve Founded? By O. W. Collet, 101; Rev. R. Molyneux's Memoir of Rev. Ferdinand Farmer; Early Priests at Albany; Priests at Frederick, Md., 103; An Early Priest at Princeton, N. J.; Rev. Raphael Fitzpatrick; Anecdote of Prince Gallitzin, by Rt. Rev. Michael O'Connor, 104; Reminiscences of Rev. John Shanahan; A Heme Catechism	105
QUERIES.—What College did the Holy Man of Tours attend? —Dr. O'Fallon's Colonies—N. Dame de Guiaudet	106
NOTICES OF RECENT PUBLICATIONS.—Ecclesiastical History of Newfoundland, by Very Rev. M. F. Howley, D.D., 106; A History of the Rise and Progress of Catholicism in Wallingford, Conn., by J. G. Phelan, 108; The Iowa Historical Record; The Church in Northern Ohio and in the Diocese of Cleveland from 1817 to September, 1887, by Rev. George F. Houck, 109; Church and State in the United States, by Philip Schaff, D.D.	110
ANNOUNCEMENT.—History of the Catholic Church in the Diocese of Hartford, by Rev. T. J. Shahan, D.D.	112

THE first volume of THE UNITED STATES CATHOLIC HISTORICAL MAGAZINE is now ready, neatly bound in cloth. Price $2.75. Subscribers returning the Numbers for 1887 in good condition by mail or express, prepaid, with a P. O. order for 75 cents, will receive a copy in cloth. Cases for binding sent postage free on remitting 50 cents. J. G. S.

UNITED STATES CATHOLIC
HISTORICAL MAGAZINE.

POPE-DAY IN AMERICA.

BY JOHN GILMARY SHEA.

[Read before the United States Catholic Historical Society, January 19, 1888.]

THE present Pope has recently had a day—a day of Jubilee, commemorated in all parts of the world. The faithful testified their joy at the celebration of his sacerdotal Jubilee, and renewed the protestation of their heartfelt allegiance to the See of Unity, to the one whom Christ has set to govern His kingdom. Princes and rulers of all lands, Mohammedan and heathen, as well as Christian, sent their courteous offerings and congratulations to His Holiness, Pope Leo XIII.

The Pope has just had a day, and a glorious day. But is this my topic? No, I am going back into the past.

There was a time when, in New England and other colonies, the Pope had his day, which was very enthusiastically celebrated. This, as a matter of history, will doubtless be new to most of my hearers, for it is not brought into prominence in the current histories of the country, and few would trace the only remnant left of the old-time celebration,—the Fourth-of-July firecracker—to its real origin.

The celebration of Pope-Day arose in a curious way. After the overthrow of the English commonwealth, and the restoration of Charles II., New England was in a dilemma.

The English Crown was asserting its rights over New England, and State holidays had to be observed. But how were the Puritans to keep Guy Fawkes' Day, the 5th of November? A few misguided Catholics, driven to desperation by the penal laws, had plotted to blow up King James I. and his Parliament, led on by government detectives, in all probability. But how could the Puritans, who, as a body, drove the son of James from the throne, and sent his head rolling from the executioner's block—how could they hold up Guy Fawkes to public execration for an unaccomplished crime, when their own hands were reeking with royal blood?

The case was indeed a puzzling one. But New England shrewdness saw a way out of the difficulty. A clergyman of the Established Church in England, when he found his flock growing listless and indifferent, or, what was worse, inclined to criticise him, used to give them what he called "Cheshire Cheese"; he began a series of philippics against the Pope. This always roused them to zeal and friendly feeling.

New England, in the same way, resorted to "Cheshire Cheese," and by a happy device pleased Court and people. They would celebrate the 5th of November with all due noise and honor; but they had the Pope carried around in effigy, instead of Guy Fawkes, amid the noise of firecrackers, and finally committed it to the flames amid loud huzzas.

Thus, though they sang

"Let's always remember
The fifth of November,"

the day became, on this side of the Atlantic, not Gunpowder Treason, but Pope-Day. The contrast between that annual insult of the last century, and the recent ovation of all loyal hearts, the tributes paid by the rulers of English-speaking lands, is striking enough. "Viva il Papa-re!"

Boston, being a city of great cultivation and refinement, took the lead in celebrating Pope-Day. An effigy of the Pope was made, and generally one of the Devil; these were placed on a platform, and carried by the crowd, who kept firing crackers, home-made at first, but when New England enterprise opened intercourse with China, the Chinese firecrackers were imported for use on Pope-Day.

On the front of the stage was a huge transparency, with inscriptions suited to the temper of the times. Boys below the platform worked strings, causing the figures to face toward the houses and make gestures.

At the head of the procession went a man ringing a bell, and bawling a song, which ended:

> "Don't you hear my little bell
> Go chink, chink, chink?
> Please give me a little money,
> To buy my Pope some drink."

Every house on the route of the procession was required to contribute to the expense of the show, under penalty of having the windows broken, or being otherwise damaged.

The procession passed through the Common, past the State House, and often ended on Copp's Hill, where the effigies were consumed in a bonfire.

Such was Pope Day in Boston, which never dreamed in that day of the Old South Church existing to see Boston ruled by a Catholic mayor, the see of a Catholic archbishop, or its celebrating with loud acclaim an anniversary of a Pope.

The newspapers of the day sometimes described these processions on Pope-Day as being carried on "with great decency and decorum"! But it was not always so. In the course of time, one quarter of Boston thought itself badly treated in the arrangements for the procession. Then North End and South End each had a Pope, and the processions generally met on Union Street, where a fight took place for the possession of all the figures, the North Enders burning them on Copp's Hill if they won the day, while their antagonists, when successful, burned the Pope on the Common.

In 1745, the celebration of Pope-Day was especially disgraceful. A paper of the time says:

Tuesday last being the Anniversary of the Gunpowder Plot, two Popes were made and carried thro' the Streets in the evening, one from the North, the other from the South End of the Town, attended by a vast number of negroes and white servants, armed with clubs, staves and cutlashes, who were very abusive to the Inhabitants, insulting the Persons and breaking the windows, &c., of such as did not give them money to their satisfaction, and even many of those who had given them liberally; and the two Popes meeting in Cornhill, their followers were so infatuated as to fall upon each other with the utmost Rage and Fury. Several were sorely wounded and bruised, some left for dead, and rendered incapable of any business for a long time to the great Loss and Damage of their respective Masters.

And he prints a letter from a subscriber, condemning the supineness of the authorities. This letter was as follows:

I hope you will not suffer the grand fray, not to say bloody, that happen'd before your Door last Tuesday evening to pass off without a public rebuke; and such an one as becomes a person zealous as well for the Peace and Good Order of the State as the Church. What a scandal and Infamy to a Protestant Mob, be it of the rudest and lowest Sailors out of Boston, or even of the very negroes of the Town, to fall upon one another with Clubs and Cutlashes in a Rage and Fury which only Hell could inspire or the Devil broke loose from chains there could represent! Is this a meet or sufferable show of Protestant zeal against Popery? Is this to honor the Protestant religion to the few French prisoners of war that are left among us? Or can our children or servants be safe in the streets at such a time if such Rioters be permitted? Or in a word, what madness must seize the two mobs, united Brethren, as they would appear against Popery, to fall upon each other, break one another's Bones or dash one another's Brains out?

Why this enormity above all others should be winked at, and the Inhabitants of the Town with their Dwellings left to the mercy of a rude and intoxicated Rabble, the very Dregs of the People, black and white, and why no more has been done to prevent or suppress such Riotous proceedings, which have been long growing upon us, and as long bewailed by all sober Persons, must be humbly left to our betters to say.*

But the voice of "decency and decorum" could not stop the celebration of Pope-Day. As politics grew fierce, first the Pretender, then obnoxious English statesmen, were burned in effigy with the Pope.

In 1755, "the Devil, the Pope, and the Pretender, at night were carried about the city on a bier, their three effigies hideously formed, and as humorously contrived, the Devil standing close behind the Pope, seemingly paying his compliments to him, with a three-pronged pitchfork in one hand, with which at times he was made to thrust his Holiness on the Back, and a lanthorn in the other, the young Pretender standing before the Pope, waiting his commands."

The newspaper which gives these details adds: "In their route through the Streets, they stop't at the French General's Lodgings,"—this was General Dieskau, then lying wounded and a prisoner in Boston,—"where a guard was ordered to prevent mischief by the Mob. The General sent down some silver by the carriers, with which after giving three huzzas, they marched off to a proper place, and set fire to the Devil's tail, burning the three to cinders." †

The passage of the Quebec Act, by which Catholics in Canada and the country northwest of the Ohio were maintained in the exercise of their religion, as it was under French rule, excited a bitter feeling in the Thirteen Colonies. This revived the Pope-Day celebration, and gave it new zest.

We have accounts of the observance of the day in several places in the year 1774:

The last public celebration of "Pope Day," so called in Newbury and Newburyport (Mass.), occurred this year. To prevent any tumult or disorder taking place during the evening or night, the town of Newburyport voted October 24, 1774 "that no effigies

---

* "Weekly Post-Boy," Nov. 18, 1745.
† "Annapolis Gazette," Dec. 4, 1755.

be carried about or exhibited on the 5th of November, only in the day-time." Motives of policy afterwards induced the discontinuance of this custom which has now become obsolete. This year (1774) the celebration went off with a great flourish. In the day-time companies of little boys might be seen in various parts of the town, with their little popes dressed up in the most grotesque and fantastic manner, which they carried about, some on boards and some on little carriages for their own and others' amusement. But the great exhibition was reserved for the night, in which young men as well as boys participated. They first constructed a huge vehicle, varying at times, from 20 to 40 feet long, 8 or 10 wide, and 5 or 6 high, from the lower to the upper platform, on the front of which they erected a paper lantern, capacious enough to hold in addition to the lights, five or six persons. Behind that as large as life sat the mimic Pope and several other personages, monks, friars and so forth. Last but not least stood an image of what was designed to be a representation of old Nick himself, furnished with a pair of huge horns, holding in his hands a pitchfork and otherwise accoutred, with all the frightful ugliness that their ingenuity could devise. Their next step after they had mounted their ponderous vehicle on four wheels, chosen their officers, captain, first and second lieutenant, purser and so forth, placed a boy under the platform to elevate and move around at proper intervals the movable head of the Pope.*

This same year, the two rival factions in Boston united in one celebration of what they called a Union Pope.

Even down in the Carolinas the day was observed, feeling being very strong there, as we may see by the fact that South Carolina alone, of all the States, made Protestantism the established religion in her first Constitution.

A letter from Charleston in November, 1774, says:

> We had great diversion the 5th instant in seeing the effigies of Lord North, Governor Hutchinson, the Pope and the Devil, which were erected on a moving machine, and after having been paraded about the town all day, they were in the evening burnt on the common with a large bonfire, attended by a numerous crowd of people.†

---

* "History of Newburyport," p. 249.
† "New York Journal," Dec. 15, 1774.

General and enthusiastic as was the celebration of Pope-Day in 1774, it was the last occasion of that crafty means to excite the ignorant and brutal to hatred and violence against Catholics, though it needs no philosopher to see in Pope-Day the genesis of some events in our own time.

Pope-Day ended with 1774.

The next year the din of arms sounded through the land. Protestant and Catholic alike shouldered their muskets, and marched side by side in the cause of America. Yet in the very camp of Washington, in the army where Catholic soldiers from Maryland and Pennsylvania were gallantly facing the foe, it was proposed to celebrate Pope-Day. But from the headquarters of the Army of Freedom came the words of George Washington, already strong in the attachment of his fellow-citizens:

> November 5th.—As the Commander-in-Chief has been apprised of a design formed for the observance of that ridiculous and childish custom of burning the effigy of the Pope, he cannot help expressing his surprise that there should be officers and soldiers in this army so void of common sense as not to see the impropriety of such a step at this juncture; at a time when we are soliciting, and have really obtained the friendship and alliance of the people of Canada, whom we ought to consider as brethren embarked in the same cause,—the defence of the Liberty of America. At this juncture and under such circumstances, to be insulting their religion, is so monstrous as not to be suffered or excused; indeed, instead of offering the most remote insult, it is our duty to address public thanks to these our brethren, as to them we are indebted for every late happy success over the common enemy in Canada.*

This was the funeral oration on the celebration of Pope-Day. It was heard of no more.

It would be presumption in me to continue, after George Washington has spoken.

But I will merely add that the firecrackers of Pope-Day have been transferred to the Fourth of July.

---

* Washington's Works, iii., p. 144.

THE ACADIANS BEFORE THEIR DISPERSION.

By the Abbé H. R. Casgrain.

[Read before the United States Catholic Historical Society, February 21, 1888.]

The muse of Longfellow in depicting the history of Evangeline invested with undying interest the terrible crime against humanity and law committed by the English authorities, when in 1755 they seized seven thousand inhabitants of Nova Scotia, destroyed their houses, farms, and stock, sent the unfortunate people on vessels without regard to the ties of blood or affection, separating husband from wife, and children from parents; and then scattered them along this coast from Massachusetts to Georgia to be treated as paupers.

The sympathy awakened by the poem of Evangeline deepened the stigma on the cruel perpetrators of the wrong. It has caused writers to spring up, who seek to justify the crime by endeavoring to show that it was made necessary by the conduct of the Acadians in giving aid to the French. But Governor Lawrence, whose proclamation is the indictment, trial, and sentence of seven thousand Catholic men, women, and children, puts it upon no such ground; he states distinctly that they were punished as Popish recusants, and he cites an Act, under which he professed to act, but which is not to be found on the statute-books of England.

To meet the new perverters of history, the Abbé R. A. Casgrain, of Quebec, has prepared for us the following paper, which his voyage to Europe prevents his reading before us.

To understand properly the position of the Acadians in Nova Scotia at the time of their expulsion, we must go back to the treaty of Utrecht, in 1713. By this treaty France ceded

Acadia to England, and the French settled in that province, which then definitively assumed the name of Nova Scotia, passed under the English rule. By a special clause of the treaty the free exercise of the Catholic religion was guaranteed to the Acadians, and a year's delay was granted to those who preferred to leave the province.* A few days after the signature of the treaty (April 11, 1713) Queen Anne removed this restriction and prolonged the period indefinitely.†

The oath of allegiance administered to them by one of the first Governors of Annapolis, Gen. Richard Phillips, contained the express condition that they were not to bear arms against the French or Indians. This condition seemed necessary to induce the Acadians to remain attached to the province, of which they were the sole inhabitants. This gave rise to the name of "French Neutrals," by which they were subsequently known.

It was easy to foresee that such a system could not fail to entail disastrous results on the little growing population, thus placed between two rival powers, always ready to open hostilities, and who would be sure to dispute their neutrality. They were fatally destined to be victims; but their misfortune exceeded all that could have been anticipated.

Although the yoke of the English governors was not, in general, severe, yet some of them molested the Acadians, and provoked discontent by arbitrary acts, especially by hampering their missionaries in the lawful exercise of their ministry. Thus they endeavored to force them to throw off the authority of the Bishop of Quebec, on whom they depended, and so violate the most fundamental rules of the Catholic hierarchy. They went so far as to wish to dispose of parishes by

---

* "Nova Scotia Archives," p. 12.

† Ib., p. 15. Even if Queen Anne's letter cannot be interpreted as meaning an indefinite stay, as some maintain, it cannot be gainsaid that this letter grants the Acadians the same privileges as British subjects. The letter says so expressly. Now our adversaries admit that the Acadians on taking the oath became British subjects. As such, then they had a right to sell or abandon their property at any time and depart, carrying their personal property with them.

removing parish priests and substituting others. Thus Father Felix Pain, parish priest of the Mines, having incurred the displeasure of Governor Armstrong, a kind of maniac who finally committed suicide, that official took on himself to remove the priest from his parish and appoint in his place Father Isidore, a friar then under an interdict, and he would have maintained him in that post, had not the parishioners at the Mines revolted and expelled the intruder.

The Acadians were prevented from building new churches, or repairing the old. Churches were demolished, among others that at Pré Ronde, near Port Royal. Some governors even attempted to force upon the missionaries laws for the administration of the sacraments of the Church.* Thus, for example, Governor Mascarene wrote threatening letters to the Abbé Desenclaves, because he had refused absolution to some penitents who would not make restitution where they were bound to do so.

But what was more alarming than all the rest, and what made the Acadians as well as their priests believe that their faith was in danger, was the attempt made to proselytize among them, the rulers professing to believe that it was the only way to make them good subjects.† These vexatious acts excited distrust which French emissaries turned to advantage by inducing some of the Acadians to violate the promised neutrality. This led to interminable complaints about the oath, which increased in bitterness down to the catastrophe in 1755.

These difficulties, however, led to no serious results during the first thirty years of British rule, mainly from the impotence in which the Governors of Nova Scotia were left, hav-

---

* Acadian documents, notes, and traditions, collected by the Abbé Sasseville, curé of Sainte Foy.

† The Governors of Nova Scotia pursued this course, not only from their own inclinations, but also to comply with instructions from London. "You will . . . . endeavor to undeceive them concerning the exercise of their religion." Board of Trade to Governor Phillips, December 28, 1720, "Nova Scotia Archives," p. 58.

ing at their command only a handful of soldiers entrenched behind the feeble bulwarks of Port Royal.

This fort was really the only point of vantage held by England in the province. The governors with their petty garrison, completely isolated and confronted by a conquered people, who formed, as we have seen, the sole civilized population of the peninsula, had to resort to much conciliation to obtain obedience. They could not even have made their authority respected, if they had not had an honest, peaceful population to deal with. To this lack of power, and to no other sentiment, must be ascribed the tranquillity in which the Acadians were left; for their new masters, alienated from the Acadians by prejudices of race and religion, so violent in that day, felt more repugnance than sympathy for them. Thus left to themselves rather than governed, the Acadians lived under the paternal direction of their missionaries, to whom, as a rule, they appealed to settle any differences among them. When they had recourse to the foreign judges, it was the French law, alone known to the people, which the judges tried to apply as well as they could.*

The small number of the Acadians which made them no object of dread, was at first a cause of security; but in a few years they increased with prodigious rapidity, and that by the mere expansion of families, for all immigration ceased after their separation from France. Colonel Vetch, the second English governor at Port Royal, estimated their total number in 1714 at 2,500 souls; and he added:

" The French are with the Indians the only inhabitants of this country "; " and as they have intermarried with the Indians, by which and their being of one religion, they have a mighty influence upon them." " One hundred of the French who were born upon that continent, and are perfectly known in the woods, can

---

* " The judges (are) far away, and though very judicious, little versed in the ' Coutume de Paris,' which is followed here." Abbé Miniac to Mr. Jacrau, Director of the Seminary of Quebec, April 26, 1744, in the Archives of the Seminary of Quebec.

march upon snowshoes ; and understand the use of birch canoes, are of more value and service than five times their number of raw men, newly come from Europe. So their skill in the fishery, as well as the cultivation of the soil."*

In 1755 the total Acadian population scattered along the shores of the Bay of Fundy as far as Chipoudy, and at some other points of the peninsula, as well as on Isle Saint Jean, now Prince Edward's Island, amounted to at least sixteen or seventeen thousand, that is to say, it had doubled in about every sixteen years.† They were divided into six main parishes, Port Royal, the oldest and one of the most populous; Grand Pré, and Rivière aux Canards on the Bay of Mines; Pisiquid, now Windsor; Cobequid, now Truro, and Beaubassin, at the head of Chignecton Bay; without counting several important missions, such as Chipoudy, Peticoudiac, and Memramcook, on the western shore of the Bay of Fundy, and those on Isle St. Jean.

As to the life of the Acadians, here is a picture drawn by a Protestant, Moise de Les Derniers, who often sat by their firesides:

The Acadians are the most innocent and virtuous people whom I have ever known or heard tell of in any history. . . . . They live

---

* "Nova Scotia Archives," p. 6.

† On this point the Abbé de l'Isle Dieu remarked : " Before the English devastated the posts which we had possessed in the interior of the Peninsula or Nova Scotia, we had more than 15,000 inhabitants." Abbé de l'Isle Dieu, "Tableau Sommaire des Missionnaires . . . . à l'Acadie francaise et anglaise," in the Archives of the Seminary of Quebec. A memoir by the Abbé Le Loutre, preserved in the same archives, and evidently of 1746, gives the population of the Acadians in the Peninsula at 8,600 communions, equivalent to about 11,500 souls. According to another memoir there were in 1743, 9,150 communions, say 12,500 to 13,000 souls. " Description de l'Acadie, 1748," Archives de la Marine, Paris. This calculation did not include the Chipoudy settlement, then fifty years old, nor those on the coast at Peticoudiac, Memramcook and its vicinity, to Isle St. Jean, which would add 1,000 or 1,500 souls, and make the total about 14,000. If we add the natural increase from 1748 to 1753, we get a population of 16,000 or 17,000. Even this does not reach the estimate given by Moise de Les Derniers, an inhabitant of Nova Scotia, who was employed to carry out some of Governor Lawrence's orders at the time of the deportation of the Acadians. "It was the common opinion of my acquaintances," says he, "that they were in all 18,000 souls."

in a state of perfect equality, without distinction of rank in society. The title of "Messieurs" is not known among them. Ignorant of the luxuries and even of the conveniences of life, they are content with a simple mode of life, which they easily derive from the cultivation of their lands. Very little ambition or avarice was seen among them; they helped each other's wants with benevolent liberality; they required no interest for loans of money or other property. They were humane and hospitable to strangers, and very liberal to those who embraced their religion. They were very remarkable for the inviolable purity of their morals. I do not recollect a single case of illegitimate birth among them, even now. Their knowledge of agriculture was very limited, although they cultivated their dyked lands pretty well.

They were completely ignorant of the progress of arts and sciences. I knew but a single person among them who could read or write:* some of them could do so, but very imperfectly, and no one among them had learned any trade. Each farmer was his own architect, and each proprietor was a farmer. They lived almost entirely independent of other nations, except to procure salt and tools, as they employed very little iron for any other farming implements.

They raised and made their own clothing, which was uniform. They were fond of black and red with stripes down the leg, bunches of ribbon and long streamers.

Notwithstanding their negligence, their lack of means and scanty knowledge of agriculture, they laid up abundant stores of provisions and clothing, and had comfortable houses.

They were a strong, healthy people, capable of enduring great hardship, and generally lived to an advanced age, although no one employed a doctor. The men worked hard in planting and harvest time, and the season when the dykes were to be made or repaired, and on any occasion when work was pressing. They thus secured for half the year, at least, leisure which they spent in parties and merrymakings, of which they were very fond. But the women were more assiduous workers than the men, though they took a considerable part in their amusements. Although they were almost all entirely illiterate, it was rare to see any one remain silent long when in company, they never seemed at a loss for a subject of conversation. To conclude, they seemed always cheerful and light-hearted, and on every occasion were unanimous.

---

* This must be the Notary Le Beau immortalized by Longfellow.

If any disputes arose in their transactions, etc., they always submitted it to arbitration, and their last appeal was to the priest. Although I have seen cases of mutual recrimination on returning from these decisions, you seldom, if ever, discovered among them any thought of malice or vengeance. In fact they were perfectly accustomed to act candidly in all circumstances; and really, if there be a people who recall the Golden Age as described in history, it was the old-time Acadians.*

The rupture of the peace between France and England, the influence of which was immediately felt in America, was the signal for woes which necessarily resulted from the false position in which Acadia had been placed, and which led at last to the dispersion of its inhabitants. It was a prey for which the two parties, face to face, were constantly contending.

In 1744, Du Vivier, a French officer who had Acadian blood in his veins, set out from Louisbourg at the head of an expedition, and landed on Nova Scotia, where he hoped to see the people rise and join him. If he had succeeded, Port Royal (Annapolis), with its ramparts destitute of soldiers, and made of sand that was crumbling away on all sides, must have fallen into his hands, and with that fort, all Nova Scotia. But the Acadians, as a body, refused to take part in the struggle, and thus saved British power in the peninsula. There were some exceptions, but they were rare and due especially to the more fiery than prudent zeal of the Indian missionary then maintained by France in the peninsula. The Abbé La Loutre, who was not then the Vicar-General of Nova Scotia, as English historians pretend,† had learned either in person or by the reports of other missionaries, the attempts made to

---

* This account of the life of the Acadian people has not, to my knowledge, been cited by any historian. The Memoir from which I extract it was written by Moïse de Les Derniers, at the request of Dr. Andrew Brown, of Halifax. I owe a copy to the courtesy of Mr. F. B. Crofton, librarian of the Nova Scotia Legislature.

† The Abbé Le Loutre was not appointed Vicar-General till 1754, that is to say, only about a year before his return to France. According to the Abbé de l'Isle Dieu, he held the title only for French Acadia, that is, the party lying west of the Messagouetche. "Tableau sommaire . . . . de l'Acadie."

pervert the Acadians, and had been greatly alarmed by the danger to which their faith was exposed. He hoped to deliver them from this danger by joining Du Vivier's expedition with his Indians, as it had in his eyes every prospect of success in restoring Acadia to France. He committed the great fault of not succeeding.

That the missionaries had ground for fear, we shall soon see. That very year, 1744, Shirley, Governor of Massachusetts, proposed to expel part of the Acadians from their lands, and gave them to English settlers so as to mingle Protestants in the population; moreover, he proposed to give the coins of Judas to every Acadian who renounced Catholicity, and rewards to all who sent their children to English schools.*

The fidelity of the Acadians was not yet shaken. Mascarène, Governor of Nova Scotia, could not help avowing that the safety of his province was due to their neutrality and the attitude taken by their missionaries; he bore public testimony to it. These are his words: "The missionaries . . . . made their conduct appear to have been on this occasion far better than could have been expected from them." . . . . "To . . . . the French inhabitants refusing to take up arms against us, we owe our safety." †

---

* This was Shirley's project, according to Beamish Murdoch. "He proposes to intersperse Protestant settlements among the French in Nova Scotia, taking part of the marsh lands from them for the new settlers; . . . . he recommends . . . . granting small privileges and immunities for the encouragement of such as should come over to the Protestant communion and send their children to learn English." The Protestant historian who relates this cannot refrain from censuring Shirley's project: "This suggestion," he says, "of offering worldly advantages in exchange of profession, can hardly be commended *in our day.*" "History of Nova Scotia," ii., pp. 129–131. In all this history, no one is more to blame than unworthy France under Louis XV., which, after exacting everything from the Acadians, did nothing for them. The Satanic scheme proposed by Shirley involves a double iniquity worth noting: 1. Buying consciences for money. 2. The arbitrary seizure of the lands belonging to the Acadians (taking part of the marsh lands from them for the new settlers). It shows how little regard they had for the property rights of the Acadians, at the very moment when their fidelity merited praise from their own governor, and how they came to deprive them of everything and banish them, as soon as they had strength and an opportunity.

† Letter of Mascarène, Dec., 1744, "Nova Scotia Archives," pp. 147–8.

In 1746 another French expedition, commanded by de Ramesay, came from Quebec to co-operate with the fleet sent from France under the Duke d'Anville. It achieved a glorious victory at Grand Pré, but was not more successful in delivering Acadia than Du Vivier's expedition.*

The Abbé de Miniac, grand archdeacon and parish priest at Rivière aux Canards, was then Vicar-General of the Bishop of Quebec in Acadia. He was an aged man of tact and experience, whose words and example must have exercised influence over his associates and the people.†

Although he was as much alarmed as his fellow-priests at the position of the Acadians, he did not regard these French expeditions with the same eye that the Abbé Le Loutre did. On the contrary, he saw that they would lead to inextricable complications.

"I would regard it," he wrote to Quebec, "as the direst misfortune for these people (Acadians), if another expedition comes from Canada; then there would be no consideration for us. We see already that the government is strongly prejudiced. Our letters are unanswered, and several of the people are in irons. In this embarrassing situation we are racked by the greatest fear. . . . . We have no longer any mode of communicating, and can obtain intelligence only from the coast. See how we are closed in." ‡

The character of Vicar-General Miniac and the course he pursued in Acadia are distinctly indicated in these few lines. He was evidently a moderate man, who endeavored to diffuse his own spirit around him. Would to heaven that he could have infused it into the Abbé Le Loutre!

---

* The "New York Post-Boy," February 23, 1746-7, attests the affectionate disposition of the Acadians and their clergy to the English, at this juncture. (Editors.)

† Some writers confound Mr. de Miniac with Mr. Manach, an Indian missionary who came later.

‡ Abbé de Miniac to M. Valier, Superior of the Seminary of Quebec. Acadia, Sept. 23, 1745. Archives of the Seminary of Quebec.

The Abbé Joseph Louis Després Le Loutre was a Breton, born, probably, at Morlaix in Finistere. This at least may be inferred from two of his letters written from Morlaix, where the family property seems to have been. He had studied at the Seminary of the Foreign Missions at Paris, and it was as a priest of that congregation that he was sent to America in 1737. He was in the first instance to proceed to Acadia to replace the Abbé de Saint Poncy, missionary at Port Royal, who had been recalled to France; he was then to apply himself to the study of the Micmac language to be able to aid two of his associates, the Abbé de Saint Vincent and the Abbé Maillard, commissioned like himself to minister to the different tribes of that nation.

Several circumstances prevented his assuming the direction of the parish of Port Royal; and after learning the Micmac language under the guidance of the Abbé Maillard, he proceeded to the Indian missions of Acadia.

The following extracts from two letters of the Abbé Maillard to the Director of the Foreign Missions at Paris give some insight into the character of the Abbé Le Loutre and his missions:

I have just come back to Louisbourg in time to meet Mr. Le Loutre, who is setting out for Akadie with the intention of wintering with the Indians of that country, who have long hungered for the spiritual bread of the Word. God does all things well: he has given me a most pleasant winter from the happiness I enjoyed in having Mr. Le Loutre, and has furnished a good opportunity of learning while teaching my associate. All bids fair for the new missionary. He is now prepared to display his evangelical talent wherever he finds Micmacs; he does not yet speak correctly: but he has the key to the principal conjugations. Practice will give him assurance as a speaker; he is a perfect Micmac in church, as he knows, reads, and chants, all our prayers perfectly well, it is only in familiar conversation that he betrays himself; he is going to visit the parts where I was last summer, where there are many Indians, and more French. But the fixed point of his mission is Mouchkoudoubougouek, and the tide water of Chigabenakady river, where all the Micmacs gathered when I was there, and where they are soon to return on the strength of my promise to winter with them.*

I cannot express the diligence with which he studied the language all the time we were together (at Malégoueche, in Cape Breton); he was so persistent that I could not open any book but my Micmac manuscripts, to answer as far as my scanty knowledge permitted, the hosts of questions that he put me daily. I never could get from him more than two hours after supper to read alternately the Holy Scripture and Moral Theology. He can now, thank God, get along with the Indians, whom he instructs and confesses very well; he has too the tact of making them fear him, which will certainly help to reform the worst among them. God give him grace to persevere as he has begun, and he will feel rewarded for all the pains he has taken. His present mission is in the districts of Acadia, where there are large numbers of Indians who have long desired a missionary who understands them. His comfort will be, that he will have a flock more docile than mine. We now need a third for the Indians on Ile St. Jean, who are extremely depraved, because they hardly ever see a missionary. But he must be a person of character to act in concert with the missionaries at Acadia and Ile Royale. By this means, we should soon succeed in overcoming the indocility of the Micmac, and putting an end to his inconstancy.†

The peace of Aix-la-Chapelle, concluded in 1748 between France and England, has been called a truce to prepare for another war. It may be added, that on this side of the Atlantic this respite could scarcely be called a truce.

The question as to the frontiers of the rival colonies left unsettled, opened the way to aggressions which were made incessantly by both parties.

English authors not unjustly reproach the French authorities for employing means unworthy of civilized nations, by secretly inducing Indians to continue the war, after peace had been signed. The Marquis de la Jonquière, Governor of Canada from 1749 to 1752, allowed himself to be drawn into acts which are inexcusable.

---

* Letter of the Abbé Maillard, Louisbourg, September 29, 1738. Archives of the Seminary of Quebec.

† Letter of same, October 1, 1738.

But let us examine the conduct of his adversaries, and we find that it was no better. "It is notorious," Count Raymond, Commandant at Louisbourg, wrote to the Court of France, "that scarcely a month has passed since the last peace, in which the English have not sent armed cruisers along the coast of this colony.

"From the end of 1749, the time when the English in any considerable number repaired to Chebucto (Halifax) to settle there, the French have been unable to sail in safety along the coast, and even near Canseau Island . . . . on account of the frequent menaces made them. They have continued to overhaul vessels of all kinds, seize all they found on board, and even the crew, as they have done on several occasions." *

Count Raymond supported these accusations with an array of facts given in the fullest detail. He states among the rest that the English had captured that very year, 1749, three sloops with their crews in a port on Isle Royale, and did not release them till they had confiscated all their cargo of fish. In August and September of the same year they carried off two priests: the Abbé Girard, from Cobequid, whom they kept as a prisoner for three months at Halifax; and the Abbé de la Goudalie, parish priest at Grand Pré, whom they compelled to return to France.

They attacked and captured French vessels passing between Isle Royale and Isle Saint Jean, ill-treated the crew, seized the cargoes, often even the vessels, although in every case passports in due form were produced.

A more serious affair was the capture on the 16th of October, 1750, of a brigantine belonging to the French navy, the "Saint François," loaded with provisions, uniforms, and arms, for the French posts on St. John's River. Besides these violations of the peace at sea there were others equally grave on land. The pretext for this class, was, as I have just remarked, infringements of the frontier of Nova Scotia, which had been

---

* "Lettres et Memoires sur le Cap Breton," p. 235.

a matter of dispute since the treaty of Utrecht. When that treaty was concluded the unpardonable blunder was committed of not fixing the frontier definitively; and the door was thus open to ever reviving difficulties.

England and France had indeed, at last, appointed a commission to settle this question; but while the commission, which met at Paris, was prolonging its meetings without attaining any results, events in America were marching on, and the two parties face to face had reached a practical result, established by the force of fact. The little river Messagouetche, which empties into the Bay of Fundy, about midway on the Isthmus, was regarded *de facto*, if not *de jure*, as the frontier between the English and French possessions. In 1750, three years before the commissioners met, Fort Beauséjour had been built by the French on the right bank of the river, and Fort Lawrence on the left by the English, to uphold their respective positions.

We shall see how in these conditions the English respected the peace established in Europe between the two nations.

On the 15th of September, 1750, an English detachment fired on a party of French sent out to reconnoitre. The next year another detachment fired on French troops, and this time without any provocation.

In June, 1751, a detachment of about 300 English soldiers sallied by night from Fort Lawrence, crossed the Messagouetche, and attacked a French post stationed at Pont-à-Buot. On two other nights similar detachments crossed the same river and destroyed the dykes constructed by the French.

These acts of hostility, committed in violation of the peace, increased steadily in number and violence till the final rupture between France and England, which was not till 1756.

It must not be forgotten that prior to that date, the French envoy Jumonville had been killed on the western frontier by Washington, Fort Necessity had been taken, General Braddock had been defeated on the Monongahela; and in the East, Fort Beauséjour had been taken and the Acadians in

Nova Scotia deported. If this state of things was peace, what is war? Finally, that this illusory peace might end as it had begun, the first encounter of the French and English fleets off Newfoundland presents the same disregard of international rights that was shown on the mainland. And it was not France which presents it. Hocquart, the French commander of the "Alcide," coming within hailing distance of one of the English vessels, asked the commander whether he brought peace or war.

"Peace! Peace!" he shouted back.

While his words were still echoing in the ears of the French officers the "Alcide" was riddled by a cannonade of balls and grape-shot.

The Acadians had always lived in the fond hope that their province would be reconquered by France. The missionaries and the representatives of the Court of Versailles had always kept up this hope; but after the settlement of Halifax, when they saw the English strongly intrenched in the peninsula, they banished all illusion, and great numbers emigrated to the western shore of the Bay of Fundy, to Isle St. Jean, and even to Cape Breton. Unfortunately this emigration was hampered by two obstacles: first, the opposition of the English officers, who, to retain the Acadians, prevented them as far as they could from carrying away their personal property; in the second place, the indifference of the French government, which, while it encouraged the Acadians, took no proper steps to compensate them for their losses by aiding them to establish new homes. A part of these unfortunate people, after spending the last of their means, lost all courage and sunk into the greatest misery.

The Abbé Le Loutre was at the head of this emigration scheme, although he had been appointed at first to the Micmac missions in Nova Scotia. Regarded with hostility by the English after the part that he had taken in Du Vivier's expedition, he did not consider himself safe in his mission at Shubenacadie when Halifax was founded within thirty miles of him, and he retired to Beaubassin, and then to Beauséjour. He was a man of undoubted activity and perseverance, but destitute of the other qualities needed by the difficult mission assigned to him. His project in itself was excellent, and had he succeeded, he might have withdrawn the Acadians from the calamities that overtook them some years later. Unfortunately, the Abbé Le Loutre, led on by a blind patriotism, became the tool of the unworthy intrigues and schemes of some of the French officers, and thus compromised the Acadians more than he served them. It is true that it is hard to pronounce a fair judgment on this missionary on the testimony of his enemies, and even of the French officers of his time, who for the most part were imbued with Voltairean ideas, and as much prejudiced against the clergy as the Protestants of that time were; but we know enough from official dispatches to say that he disregarded the duties of his profession and committed acts which cannot be justified.

Many of the imputations brought against him are doubtless unfounded, at least are not proved; but by his whole conduct he has deserved to have his memory assailed.

When the English began to fortify the left bank of the Messagouetche by building Fort Lawrence, the Abbé Le Loutre wished to make all round a desert by inducing or compelling the people at Beaubassin to emigrate. As many of these ill-starred people hesitated or refused to abandon their property, he set his Indians on them, who compelled them to flee by setting fire to their houses. The enemies of the Abbé Le Loutre pretend that he applied the torch to the church himself. The least that can be said, is, that by his violences he suggested what he was capable of.

The first mistake on the part of the Abbé Le Loutre was to place himself at the disposal of the French government, from which he received considerable sums, not only to build barracks in order to settle the Acadian emigrants on the French part of the isthmus; but also to strengthen the friendship of the Indians, and keep alive their hostility to the English.

One of the gravest accusations brought against him is that, in the name of the French government, he paid the Indians for English scalps.* The intendant at Louisbourg, Mr. Prévost, wrote to the Minister on the 16th of August, 1753: " The Indians took eighteen English scalps a month ago, and Mr. Le Loutre was obliged to pay them 1,800 livres Acadian money, for which I reimbursed him."

This transaction appears all the more reprehensible, because, although war existed in fact in a more or less active form, it had not been officially declared between the two crowns. English authors, speaking of this occurrence, represent it in a still more odious light by pretending that it was done when perfect peace existed. We all know by what has been said already, what that assertion is worth. Those same authors undoubtedly did not reflect on the consequences that would follow. Would they be as ready to admit that the Acadians were carried off in time of peace? Yet, it is certain, that at that date war had not been declared between France and England.

Moreover, they show themselves unjust toward the Abbé Le Loutre in not stating with the culpable acts ascribed to him those worthy of praise, which won the gratitude of his very enemies, when both cases rest on the same authority. Prévost, the intendant, relates in a letter to the Minister, dated October 15, 1750, that thirty-seven English prisoners had been taken by the Acadian Indians, seventeen of them soldiers and six women, and brought to Port Toulouse, in Cape Breton. " It was Mr. Le Loutre," he adds, " who rescued them from the hands of the Indians and promised 8,155

---

* Rewards for scalps were the general rule. In 1750 Governor Cornwallis issued a proclamation at Halifax, offering £50 for Indian prisoners or scalps. (" New York Post Boy," July 13, 1750.) His proclamation of June 21, 1750, recites offers of £10 sterling for the head or scalp of an Indian, and offers £50. (Same, July 23, 1750.) In 1745 the General Court of Massachusetts offered £100 for any Indian killed, if scalp brought in; £105, if he was taken alive; females and children, if killed, £50; and £55, if taken alive. Supplement to " New York Post Boy," Sept. 23, 1745. (Editor.)

livres 7 sous as security, for which the Indians kept as hostages a lieutenant in the infantry and two subalterns." *

The anonymous author of the "Mémoires sur le Canada," who furnishes or sustains several of the charges brought against the Abbé Le Loutre, seems to have been the personal enemy of that missionary. At least one cannot help thinking so, when we see how vindictively he pursues him, interpreting against him not only what he did, but even what he thought; while he lavishes praises on the most shameless officials, Bigot, the intendant, for example, whom he describes as a man "full of good faith and probity." † Moreover, hatred of the Catholic clergy is everywhere apparent in these Mémoires, which are deeply imbued with the spirit of the eighteenth century. It will be admitted that such a source is, at least, suspicious.

Another anonymous writer says that the Abbé Le Loutre's "conduct would have been deemed imprudent even in a sergeant of grenadiers. He had incited the Micmacs and Souriquois to take English scalps, and went at their head with a crucifix. Several young Acadians allied to these Indians followed the Abbé Le Loutre, and notwithstanding all the representations of the older men, the whole colony was declared to be in rebellion. . . . . Their priests, it was said, collected arms, and made arsenals of the churches. If this was true," the same author adds judiciously, "the priests ought to have been punished; they deserved it, and the Acadians were innocent." ‡

On his side Moise de Les Derniers relates that he had heard it said that the Abbé Le Loutre had declared from the pulpit that the English nation was "the enemy of God and the friend of the devil, and that Christ had been crucified in England." The Abbé Le Loutre having thus excited public

---

* "Collection de Documents sur la Nouvelle France," iii., p. 456.

† Ib., p. 40.

‡ Duc de Nivernois, on the Dispersion of the Acadians. Dec. 2, 1762. "Archives des Affaires Etrangères," Paris.

opinion against him, it is not surprising that such things were ascribed to him. An English officer, well known in the two camps, Captain Howe, having been drawn into an ambuscade and killed by the Indians, it was said to have been done at the instigation of the Abbé Le Loutre.

Edward Cornwallis, Governor of Nova Scotia, offered a hundred pounds for his head; and he wrote to Mgr. de Pontbriand, Bishop of Quebec, a letter full of threats, in which he asked him, whether it was he who had sent the Abbé Le Loutre as a missionary to the Micmacs, and whether it was for their good that he excited these wretches to wreak their cruelty on those who had shown them every kindness.*

---

* If we may credit an eye-witness, a friend and spy of the English, the famous Pichon, the goodness vaunted by Governor Cornwallis had been displayed too late to gain much credence among the Indians. The settlers of Halifax had from their arrival provoked the Indians. "About the beginning of 1750," says this author, who cites approvingly Count de Raymond's words, " the English on reaching Chibucto, spread the report that they were going to exterminate the Indians. Their actions showed the design, for they sent out detachments in all directions to pursue them. The Indians taking alarm, determined to declare war openly on men whom they had never ceased to regard as enemies." . . . .
"How many acts of inhumanity," adds Count de Raymond, "would have been committed by that naturally vindictive nation, if the missionaries had not exerted all their power to restrain them? It is notorious that the Indians believed everything lawful against their enemies. Hence it cost infinite pain and effort to repress the license which they deemed most lawful, as they regarded it as a retaliation; and how many English lives their charitable zeal saved! These same missionaries can show in writing the lessons of mercy and humanity to be exercised in time of war, which they inculcated in their Indians. They even embodied it in a catechism which they taught the children, and which has already produced good effect." These were the labors of missionaries to civilize the Indians, and where are the civilizing efforts of the English? The authors who make so much of the Abbé Le Loutre's conduct, take good care not to study his patient labors. They are still more careful not to consider the atrocious actions worthy of savages, committed by their people in peace as well as in war, like those of which the Commandant at Louisbourg reminded the Indians. "Toward the close of July, 1749, at a time when the suspension of hostilities between the two countries was not yet known in New France, the Indians had captured some Englishmen of Newfoundland, but when these prisoners informed them that a suspension of arms had been signed at Aix-la-Chapelle the year before, the Indians believed them on their word, ... treated them as brothers, untied them, and took them to their cabins to entertain them; but in return for this good treatment, these treacherous guests during the night butchered twenty-five Indian men and women." "Toward the close of December,

The Bishop of Quebec wrote to the Abbé Le Loutre to reproach him for his conduct: " You have at last fallen into the very trouble which I had foreseen and which I predicted long ago. The refugees could not escape falling into misery sooner or later, and accusing you of having caused their misfortunes. . . . . The Court deemed it necessary to facilitate their leaving their lands, but that does not fall within the scope of our profession. It was my opinion that we ought to say nothing, either to oppose the carrying out of the project, or to persuade them to it. I reminded you long ago, that a priest ought not to meddle in temporal affairs, and that if he did, he would always raise up enemies and produce discontent among the people.

" Have you the right," the bishop continued, " to refuse the sacraments (to those who wished to return to their lands), to threaten them with being deprived of the services of a priest, and that the Indians would treat them as enemies ? I conscientiously wish that they would leave the lands which they possess under the English flag ; but is it clearly proved that they cannot in conscience go back there, when there is no danger of perversion ?" *

When Beauséjour capitulated the Abbé Le Loutre escaped in disguise and made his way to Quebec, where he embarked for Europe on a merchant vessel. The ship was captured at sea, and he was carried to England and then to the Island of Jersey, where he was confined for eight years as prisoner in Elizabeth's castle.

A memoir written in 1764 informs us that after his return to France he lived on the revenues of his patrimony, which was a large property, and on a pension of 800 livres, as-

---

1744, Ganon, commanding an English detachment, found two cabins of Micmac Indians (near Port Royal), in which there were five women and three children, two of the women with child ; but though they were all objects to awaken humanity, the English not only plundered and burned the two cabins, but massacred the five women and three children. The pregnant women were even found cut open." " Lettres et Memoires sur le Cap Breton," pp. 132, 135.

* Mgr. de Pontbriand to the Abbé Le Loutre, " Nova Scotia Archives," p. 240.

signed to him by the King on the Bishopric of Lavaur.*
According to the same "Mémoire" the Abbé Le Loutre
"paid out of his own means and funds entrusted to him, the
ransom of English prisoners whom he rescued from tortures
prepared by the Indians. After spending twenty years of
his life among the savages scattered in the woods, and the
French families dotted along the coast and in our forts . . . .
he saw the King, pleased with his services, reward him by
bounties, and what is more flattering, by his confidence ; he
saw the English pay on his word the ransoms he had advanced
to save their prisoners, and during the eight years' imprisonment they considered a just punishment of his patriotic zeal,
he received many marks of esteem at their hands."

Moreover, we know by a passage in the Lettres Edifiantes
that the Abbé Le Loutre took an active part in establishing
in France the Acadians who took refuge there.

I have alluded to the partiality of some historians. Another wrong which they commit, is to use the faults of the
Abbé Le Loutre, to accuse the other Acadian missionaries
and cover them all with the same reprobation. It is certain
that these missionaries, who were all French, kept alive in the
Acadians love for their mother country and the hope of being
one day reconquered. Was this a great crime ?—when it
was not distinctly settled whether the Acadians were English
subjects or not, as it is now pretended that it was.

The oath of fidelity which they had been allowed to take,
which qualified them as French Neutrals, and left them, as it
were, midway between the two parties, leaves the matter
open to grave doubt. On this point there is a very curious
memoir, worth reading, written about 1762, by the Abbé de
l'Isle Dieu, Vicar-General of the Bishop of Quebec. It is,
moreover, certain, that taking the frontier as claimed by
France, embracing more than half the peninsula, the greatest
part of the Acadian population was on French soil.†

---

* "Mémoire des Missions Etrangères," Archives of the Seminary of Quebec.
† Consult on this question of frontier the fine work with maps, recently issued

Had England desired to detach the Acadians from France, they ought to have given them missionaries who were not French (either Swiss or Belgian), as they might have done under the treaty of Utrecht.*

As Catholic priests and spiritual guides of the Acadians, the missionaries were obliged to watch that they did not lose their faith. Now they saw the unremitting efforts made to deprive them of it and allure them to Protestantism. They protested as in duty bound; they denounced these attempts, and thereby necessarily excited the distrust of their parishioners against their masters.

But whose fault was it? They were fatally placed between two evils, to betray their duty, or be regarded as traitors. They preferred to do their duty. This has been alleged as a crime. It is only a greater merit on their part.

I will cite only one example to show how full of prejudice and party spirit are some of the judgments passed on these missionaries. The Abbé Maillard is one of those assailed, and he was particularly exposed, having had charge of the Micmac missions before Le Loutre, whose instructor he was in the Indian language, and then having the care of the Micmacs on Cape Breton, while the Abbé Le Loutre had that of the Nova Scotia Micmacs. If the Abbé Maillard had re-

---

by Justin Winsor, Librarian of Harvard College, "Narrative and Critical History of America." The pretensions on both sides were exorbitant. While France conceded only a sterile strip along the eastern coast of Nova Scotia, England insisted not only on the whole peninsula, but on all that now forms New Brunswick and the gulf shores as far as Rimouski. The confusion in men's minds caused by this disagreement between the two powers can be easily imagined. The Acadians and their missionaries naturally took French ground. This was enough to draw out recrimination and put them in the position of rebels. England felt so uncertain whether the Acadians were British subjects, that all who were brought into her ports after the dispersion (and their number amounted to about 1,500 according to de la Rochette) were treated as prisoners of war and received rations, that is to say, were recognized as French subjects. It was only in the English colonies that the authorities refused to recognize or treat them as such.

* Government seems to have entertained this idea for a time, but did not follow it up. It was held surer to draw the Acadians gradually to Protestantism.

turned to Europe after the dispersion of the Acadians, we should know no more of him than of his fellow missionaries, of whom we lose trace amid the clergy of France; but he never left the district around the Gulf of St. Lawrence, and he spent his last years at Halifax, amid those who had been his bitterest enemies. He won them all by his eminent qualities and his virtues. He made his enemies his admirers and friends. At his death, the highest civil and military officers in Halifax, the Governor and his Council, followed his funeral cortège.

This is the testimony of those who were most hostile to him before they knew him.*

After this dissertation, which may seem useless to some, but which is not devoid of importance to those who follow closely the historic movement in the country, it is necessary to return to events, before summing up the situation in a few words.

Before Halifax was founded the effective power of the Governor of Nova Scotia did not extend further than the cannon of Port Royal could reach. These Governors had under their control really only the inhabitants of that parish. After them the nearest were the people in the Bassin des Mines, but there were twenty leagues of mountain and forest between them.

The other parishes, still more inaccessible, were strung along to the head of the Bay of Fundy. Up to this time not a single English colonist had settled in the province. The Acadians were therefore the real masters of Acadia, and able to impose conditions if they consented to remain.

As the Treaty of Utrecht guaranteed the free exercise of the Catholic religion, there could be no question of imposing on them the Test Oath, which involved an act of apostasy; a particular formula of oath had to be adopted. The Acadians had insisted and obtained as an express condition that they should not be required to bear arms against the French or

---

* " Nova Scotia Archives," p. 184.

Indians. It was only after they had taken the oath with this condition that the Governors wished to retract it.

The Acadians, relying on their good faith, insisted with a constancy and obstinacy that does them honor, but which finally entailed the dispersion of the whole colony. One of the reasons of their resistance was the fear that the English would ultimately exact of them an oath contrary to their faith. The attempts made to pervert them prove that their fears were not groundless.

Edward Cornwallis, the founder of Halifax, and his successors in the government of Nova Scotia, employed every means, persuasion and threats, to wring from the Acadians an unreserved oath.

We must recollect what England's penal laws against Catholics were at that date, and under what a yoke the Irish were crushed, to understand the consequences entailed by such an oath. Were not the missionaries to the Acadians, as guardians of their faith, justified in expressing their fears on this point? Could they, in conscience, forbear showing their flocks the danger, when they beheld the incessant attempts made to allure them to Protestantism? This proselytizing had become so active that it was the topic of a special memorial sent to France.*

To put an end to all these vexations and also to yield to the invitations given them to settle in Canada, the Acadians in 1750 sent a petition to Governor Cornwallis, asking his authorization to leave the province.

It was the only reasonable course left them, as on the one hand they did not wish to take any other oath to the English government, and on the other hand, oaths more and more compromising were required of them.

At this point began the critical state of the Acadian question, which closed in the catastrophe so well known to all.

---

* "Etat présent des missions de l'Acadie. Efforts impuissants des gouverneurs Anglais pour détruire la religion Catholique dans l'Acadie." The test oath was not abolished in Nova Scotia till 1827. It was Haliburton, elected by the Acadians of Clare County (Baie Sainte Marie), who effected its repeal. The fine picture which he drew of the Acadians and their missionary, the Abbé Sigogne, in the speech he made on the occasion, is well worthy of perusal.

HOW FATHER HARDING'S DEED OF ST. MARY'S CHURCH PROPERTY CAME TO BE RECORDED BY BISHOP EGAN.

STATEMENTS in one of the violent Hogan pamphlets of Matthew Carey have misled many. He was most violent, as an Episcopalian noticed at the time, when he assumed to be calm and unbiased. The existence of a deed to Father Harding was controverted by him, but the deed had been put on record in 1811. The following letter of Bishop Egan to Archbishop Carroll, and the deed, tell the story:

I.

PHILADELPHIA, *Feb.* 19, 1811.

MOST REV. SIR:

In several conversations I had with Bishop Neale in Baltimore and afterwards in Georgetown respecting the Church of St. Mary's, he always seemed positive in his assertions, that the said Church belonged to Mr. Hardin, and that if on my arrival at Philadelphia I would examine the papers of the Presbytery more minutely, I would find that he was right in what he said. Accordingly, on my return home, I did examine the papers more diligently, and found a deed in which the lot of ground on which the Church of St. Mary's stood, with the free liberty of ingress and egress, belongs solely to Mr. Harding and his heirs. The only witness now living to this deed is Mr. Thos. Fitzsimons, him I consulted on this occasion, as I knew I could do so with safety. I also left the deed with him to have it recorded. He told me he wou'd let me know after he had consulted the office whether Mr. Harding had made any conveyance of this property to the congregation of St. Mary's or not. I just now received from him the following note : "The recorder's office has been examined, and it is found that on the 30th of Sept., 1766, Mr. Hardin conveyed to Adam Cake the lot between 4th and 5th streets, except that part on which the Church stands, etc. You may therefore rest satisfyed that the Church, with some distance to the west and so bound on 4th street, with free egress, etc., remains on Mr. Harding's heirs." So far Mr. Fitzsimons.

Now, as agent to Mr. Francis Neale, I think it my duty to inform him of this deed, and have his instructions how I am to proceed in this business. But as it is a very delicate subject and will, I have no doubt, when once known, excite very great commotion throughout the whole congregation, I would wish, before I write to him, to have the Archbishop's advice. I hope, therefore, most Rev. Sir, you will have the goodness to communicate your instructions to me on this subject. This affair occupied me so much for some days that I had no time to consider the Archbishop's inquiries respecting the attack made in one of our papers against the Pastoral Letter ordaining prayers for his Holiness. I can now assure him that it has made no impression as far as I can discover; that it was by mere accident I heard of it, and that it was considered adviseable here to pass it by unnoticed.

I remain, Most Rev. Sir, with the highest veneration, your most obliged and humble serv^t and B^r. in Christ,

✢ Mich'^{L} F., Bish^p of Philada.

II.

This Indenture, Made the twenty-third day of May, in the year of our Lord one thousand seven hundred and sixty-three, Between Daniel Swan of the City of Philadelphia, in the Province of Pennsylvania, coachmaker; Thomas Malaby, of the said city, Rigger; John Cottringer, of the said city, taylor; William Hussey, of the said city, Taylor; and James White of the said city, merchant of the one part, and the Reverend Robert Harding of the City of Philadelphia, Gent., of the other part, whereas Joseph Shippen of Germantown, in the County of Philadelphia, Gent., with Mary his wife, in and by a certain Indenture of bargain and sale bearing date the tenth day of May, one thousand seven hundred and fifty-nine, did, for the consideration therein mentioned, grant, bargain, sell, alien, enfeoff, release, and confirm unto James Reynolds, of the said county, mast-maker, and Brian O'Hara, of the said city, peruke-maker, a certain lot or parcel of ground situate on the West side of Fourth Street in the said City of Philadelphia, containing in breadth on Fourth Street aforesaid, sixty-three feet, and in depth three hundred and ninety-six feet as by the said Indenture of bargain and sale recorded at Philadelphia in Book H, vol. 11, &c., page 308, relation being thereunto had may more fully and at large appear, and whereas the said James Reynolds and Bryan O'Hara, by their Indenture of bargain and sale bearing date the second day of January following, did, for the consideration therein mentioned, grant, bargain, sell, alien, enfcoff, release, and confirm the said described lot or parcel of ground of sixty-three feet front by three hundred and ninety-six feet in rear or depth unto the said Daniel Swan, Thomas Malaby, John Cottringer, William Hussey, and James White, their heirs and assigns as in and by the said last recited Indenture likewise recorded in the Rolls office at Philadelphia, in Book 26, vol. 11, pa. 308, &c., may appear, now this Indenture witnesseth that the said Daniel Swan, Thomas Malaby, John Cottringer, William Hussey, and James White as well for and in consideration of the sum of *five shillings* to them in hand paid by the said Robert Harding, at or before the ensealing and delivery hereof, the receipt whereof is hereby acknowledged as for other good causes and considerations, them, the said Daniel Swan, Thomas Malaby, John Cottringer, William Hussey, and James White, thereunto especially moving have and either of them hath granted, bargained, sold, aliened, enfeoffed, released, and confirmed, and by these presents do, and either of them doth, grant, bargain, sell, alien, enfeoff, release, and confirm unto the said Robert Harding his heirs and assigns *a certain* lot or piece or portion of ground situate on the West side of Fourth Street aforesaid, containing in breadth at the distance of thirty feet from Fourth Street aforesaid fifty feet, and in rear or depth beginning at the said distance eighty feet for him, the said Robert Harding, to build and erect a Chapel thereon, it being part, portion or parcel of said first above described lot of sixty-three feet by three hundred and ninety-six feet, and bounded on all sides by the same, with the free and uninterrupted use of said vacancy and of ingress, egress, and regress, Together with all and singular the streets, ways, alleys, passages, waters, water courses, rights, liberties, privileges, hereditaments, and appurtenances whatsoever thereunto belonging or in any wise appertaining, and the reversions and remainders, rents, issues, and profits thereof, and also all the estate, right, title, interest, use, possession, property, claim, and demand whatsoever of them the said Daniel Swan, Thomas Malaby, John Cottringer, William Husey, and James White, either in law or in equity or otherwise howsoever of, into, or out of all and singular the premises To have and to hold the aforesaid lot, piece, or parcel of ground, hereditaments, and premises hereby granted, bargained, and sold, or mentioned and intended so to be, with the appurtenances unto the said Robert Harding, his heirs and assigns, to the only proper use and behoof of the said Robert Harding, his heirs and assigns forever, as fully, amply, and effectually to all intents and purposes as they, the said Daniel Swan, Thomas Malaby, John Cottringer, William Hussey, and James White can or may hold and enjoy the same by force or in virtue of the last recited Indenture, or otherwise howsoever, and the said Daniel Swan, Thomas Malaby, John Cottringer, William Hussey, and James White, do covenant for them and their heirs that they and their heirs, the aforesaid described lot or parcel of ground, hereditaments, and premises hereby granted or mentioned to be granted, with the appurtenances unto the said Robert Harding, his heirs and assigns against them the said Daniel Swan, Thomas Malaby, John Cottringer, William Hussey, and James White, and their heirs respectively, and against all and every other person and persons whatsoever lawfully claiming or to claim by, from, or under them or any or either of them shall and will warrant and forever defend by these presents. In witness whereof the said parties to these presents have interchangeably set their hands and seals hereunto dated the day and year first above mentioned, and written.

Sealed, and delivered in the presence of us. The above words for him the s⁴ Robert, to build and erect a Chapel thereon, being first interlined.
PATRICK FARRELL,
THOS. FITZSIMMONS,
BRYAN O'HARA,
THOS. LENNON.

DANIEL SWAN, [L. S.]
THOS. MALABY, [L. S.]
JOHN COTTRINGER, [L. S.]
WILLIAM HUSSEY, [L. S.]
JAMES WHITE, [L. S.]

Phila., ss.: On the 24th day of May, Anno Domini, 1763, before me, John Stamper, Esq., appeared Daniel Swan, Thomas Malaby, John Cottringer, William Hussey, and James White, parties to the above written Indenture of bargain and sale, and acknowledged the same to be their act and deed respectively, and desired that the same may be recorded as such. Witness my hand and seal the day and year aforesaid. JOHN STAMPER. [L. S.]

Recorded the 29th day of January, 1811.

STATE OF PENNSYLVANIA, } ss.
CITY AND COUNTY OF PHILADELPHIA,

I, Geo. G. Pierie, Recorder of Deeds, etc., in and for said City and County, do hereby certify that the above and foregoing is a true and correct copy of deed found of record in my office, in Deed Book I C, No. 12, page 348, etc. Witness my hand and seal of office, this 23d day of January, A.D. 1888.

[L. S.] J. S. M. GEO. G. PIERIE, *Recorder of Deeds*.

NOTES ON PARKMAN'S "CONSPIRACY OF PONTIAC."—(*Tenth edition*, 1882.)

By Oscar W. Collet.

"The historian is restricted to the meagre outline of recorded authority": *Consp. of Pontiac*, I., 230.

The following pages are the nearest approach convenience permitted to compliance with the request for a paper on Parkman's "Conspiracy of Pontiac."

I have not attempted to digest and arrange the matter in a connected essay, much less to review the Conspiracy as a whole; but limited myself to grouping my notes under general heads and sub-titles, and writing them out as comments on particular statements which appeared to call for criticism. If the paper lacks the unity of a general review, or the liveliness and interest of a sketch, it offers, at least, the compensation of being more serviceable to historic truth.

As far as I know, this is the first attempt to controvert or correct statements found in the "Conspiracy of Pontiac"; and I hope the discussion, if not exhaustive, may at least shed some light upon the points considered, lead to such further examination as will expose the facts as they are, and correct what I believe to be mistakes, or vindicate as true what seems to be false. I have tried to weigh words and be cautious in statement; and am not conscious of a bias, or other wish than to follow truth wherever it leads.

PONTIAC AT ST. LOUIS.

The last days of Pontiac, according to Parkman, were intimately associated with St. Louis. The chief visited the post in 1769, was honorably entertained, departed thence to

Cahokia, where he was killed. St. Ange, Commandant at St. Louis, recovered his body, and gave it a military burial near the fort of the village. Such, briefly set out, is the historian's account * given on the authority of Nicollet, P. L. Cerré, and, chiefly, Peter Chouteau.

As I propose to subject Parkman's statements and his authorities to a critical analysis, it will be more convenient to begin at the end, in order to start with what can be determined with certainty and sufficient accuracy of detail—the *manner*, and *place*, and *date* of Pontiac's death. The historian says he was assassinated in the forest near Cahokia, in April, 1769. Father Meurin's testimony definitely settles the three points: He writes from Tamarois, June 14, 1769: *Pontiak fut assassiné dans ce village en la seconde semaine après Pâques:* Pontiac was assassinated in this village in the second week after Easter. The *manner* of his death was by assassination; the *place*, within the village itself of Cahokia. I do not wish to be hypercritical in rendering the word *dans* a more inclusive term here, it seems to me, than our preposition *in;* but it does not appear to allow Parkman to say, "in the adjoining forest." The *time*, as Easter fell on March 26th, was between the 2d and 8th of April. It cannot be determined from Meurin's letter whether he was, or was not, personally present in the village when the crime was committed; but in either case the accuracy of his testimony would not be affected.

PETER CHOUTEAU.

Let us now go back to the witnesses, beginning with Peter Chouteau, and examine whether dates, age, alleged and established facts, will coalesce.

September 16, 1847, Chouteau wrote: . . . . " permit me, on this occasion, to say, that Mr. Laclède, with whom I was acquainted (*although very young*) was . . . . worthy of the honors now paid to his memory."† Mr. Chouteau was born in

---

* Consp., II., 308-11. † Primm, p. 25.

1758, Laclède died in 1778; and it is plain, that if he could speak of himself as *very young* when he knew his own father, with whom he had lived for twenty consecutive years, time had so ravaged his memory that it could no longer be trusted to report correctly a dominant fact of his life, a fact which, beginning with infancy, and ever present until early manhood, bound up with home and kindred, it may be supposed, of all the facts of his life would be the one most vividly and accurately remembered. Besides, this letter shows on its very face, what will be drawn out presently, that Mr. Chouteau's statements do not hang together; for if he was acquainted with Laclède only when he was *very young*, how could he testify as a fact of knowledge and judgment, that Laclède was worthy of the honors being paid to his memory.

But the weakening of contiunity of ideas, the uncertainty of memory, the substitution of vague and confused hearsays and imaginations for facts of personal experience manifested themselves long previous, when, in 1835, he testified in an important land suit, that the first he knew of St. Ange was at Vincennes; and that when the country was to be delivered to the British, St. Ange went to Fort Chartres and delivered it. St. Ange left Vincennes in the early part of 1764; and the five-and-a-half-year-old infant knew St. Ange at Vincennes, where the infant had never been! But even had the child been present in the Illinois, and seen with his childish eyes whatever there was to be seen, how far would that have gone toward giving him knowledge of persons and events to which he gravely testified in a court of justice as facts of personal experience?

Certainly, it is not a man's fault that increasing years waste his faculties, that he loses the power to discriminate between realities and dreams, that his memory substitutes imaginations for facts, and adheres in good faith to shadowy, confused forms of what he may have heard, as though things he had seen and knew; but testimony given in this condition of mind cannot be received ; for even if it does include some fact, or the semblance of fact, it is impossible to determine what the fact is.

So much on the general trustworthiness of the principal witness; let us go into details. Parkman, on the authority of Chouteau, tells us that side by side with Laclède in the founding of St. Louis, was Peter Chouteau. But this gentleman, Laclède's oldest child, and born in 1758, was not six years old when St. Louis was begun in 1764; and even at that, according to a deposition of his,* he did not arrive at the post until about six months after it was founded. This may pass for imagination No. 1.

At the date which I establish as the probable time of Pontiac's visit to St. Louis, if he was ever here, which I deny, the end of March, or the beginning of April, 1769, Peter Chouteau, born in October, 1758, was ten and a half years old, and his communications to Parkman were made in 1846,† seventy-seven years after the event. He told the historian he had often seen Pontiac.‡ If the genealogical and chronological data above given are collated with the movements of Pontiac it will be perceived that the statement from every point of view is a mistake. Pontiac spent the winter of 1766 in the forests of the north, and from this time until just previous to his death "records and traditions are silent concerning him."§ No one has imagined that the Chief was at St. Louis more than once ; Parkman rejects Chouteau's statement to Nicollet of the Indian having resided in the village, and it is not pretended that the child Chouteau was at Fort Chartres or Kaskaskia in 1764–5 when Pontiac was there. Even had he been, what would the observations of the little six-year-old be worth ? I cannot see how Chouteau could possibly have seen Pontiac at any time, and therefore put down the statement that he *had seen him often* as imagination No. 2.

* Ms. Comrs. Min., I., 282.   † Consp., II., 258.
‡ Consp., II., 258.   § Consp., II., 306–8.

Pontiac, soon after his arrival in the Illinois, March, 1769, says the historian, on the authority of his creole informant * repaired to St. Louis to visit his former acquaintance, St. Ange, then in command at that post. "After leaving the *fort*, Pontiac proceeded to the house of which young Pierre Chouteau was an inmate; and to the last days of his protracted life the latter could vividly recall the circumstances of the interview. The savage Chief was arrayed in the full uniform of a French officer, which had been presented to him . . . . by the Marquis of Montcalm toward the close of the French war, and which Pontiac never had the bad taste to wear except on occasions when he wished to appear with unusual dignity. St. Ange, *Chouteau and the other principal* inhabitants of the infant settlement, whom he visited in turn, all received him cordially, and did their best to entertain him and his attendant chiefs. He remained at St. Louis for two or three days, when, hearing that a large number of Indians were assembled at Cahokia," where a social gathering of some sort was in progress, he went over with a part of his followers, in spite of the risks to which he would expose himself, as St. Ange urged in the effort to dissuade him from going; and Chouteau never saw him again.

As the informant could not possibly know whether Pontiac's coming to St. Louis was *soon after* his arrival in the Illinois, or if he did come, his object, we may number these statements as imaginations 3 and 4.

The narrative analyzed and resolved into distinct propositions or statements, sets out *first*, that Pontiac was lodged in the "fort"; and *next*, that from the "fort" he proceeded to make visits to St. Ange and others. St. Ange lived in the Government House, which the historian designates a "storehouse," on the west side of Main Street; the Chouteau-Laclède residence was on the same side, on the square next north, about one hundred and fifty yards distant. Now, as

---

* Consp., II., 308.

there was no fort in St. Louis in 1769, or any building designated, known, or used as such, the Chief could not have gone into or out of "the fort": imagination No. 5.

Pontiac proceeded to the house of which Chouteau was an inmate, and had an interview with him; that is, with the ten-and-a-half-year-old boy: imagination No. 6.

This boy, who, in 1847, had so completely forgotten all about his father, Laclède, as to believe that he knew him only when he was "very young," in 1846 could still vividly recall a fact with its attending circumstances which occurred seventy-seven years previous, and all about (*a*) a uniform, and (*b*) by whom and when it was given to Pontiac, as well as (*c*) what had been the Chief's rule as to wearing it, though he had never seen him before. These three imaginations bring up the score to 9.

Chouteau, ten and a half years old, one of the principal inhabitants of the village, and entertains Pontiac. I add two to the list of imaginations, making 11.

Chouteau fixed upon 1768 as the date of Pontiac's death, the Nipissings as his tribe, and lastly that he was buried by St. Ange near his fort, which three with the others make 14 imaginations.

Some of the informations listed are impossibilities, some known to be errors, and not a single one is probable as a fact of personal experience.

I note an omission which struck me when first I read the story, has haunted my imagination as often as I thought of this strange narrative since, and which, I marvel, the historian did not remark: the absence of Laclède's name, of Laclède the most prominent inhabitant of the village, and to whose house, if we are to believe what we are told, Pontiac's first visit was made. In place of the founder of the post, we find a ten-and-a-half-year-old boy the centre of what was done and said. Had Mr. Chouteau so entirely forgotten his own father that the mention of his name by some one was necessary to recall his memory? It looks that way.

If Chouteau, who, according to Parkman, had often seen Pontiac and knew him well, could be depended upon to report anything trustworthily respecting him, one would suppose it must be the personal appearance of the Chief. The following is Chouteau's description in Nicollet :* "Pontiac is a remarkably well looking man; nice in his person, and full of taste in his dress, and in the arrangement of his exterior ornaments. His complexion is said to have approached that of the whites." But Parkman, notwithstanding the creole authority on whose value he insists later in his work, casts aside this fancy description and gives another quite different. "According to Canadian tradition," he says, "Pontiac was not above middle height, though his muscular figure was cast in a mould of remarkable symmetry and vigor. His complexion was *darker* than is usual with his race, and his features, though by no means regular, had a bold and stern expression. . . . . His ordinary attire was that of the primitive savage— a scanty cincture girt about his loins, and his long, black hair flowing loosely at his back."† I think it probable that the Chouteau-Nicollet description is pure romance, and that from 1765 to 1769, Pontiac was little more than a miserable sot.

If what I have said be taken together, I think it makes a cumulative improbability that forbids the acceptance of the Peter Chouteau testimony, or any part of it. Let me here guard myself sharply against the suspicion of charging, even by implication, the witness with intentional invention. I have no doubt he spoke innocently. But I am dealing with the facts of history and aiming to vindicate the truth. Chouteau's communications to Parkman, which he has incorporated into his history, appear to me, at best, but dim reminiscences of confused, indefinite hearsays of occurrences in the long ago, amplified and distorted by imagination, repeated in good faith; but seventy-seven years is an immense chasm to span

---

* Page 82. † Consp., I., 202.

with memory's bridge of confused hearsays; and in my judgment the structure was too frail to allow the car of truth to pass over to boyhood days and return in safety.

P. L. Cerré's testimony is hearsay. He knew nothing of Pontiac, and professed only to repeat what he supposed he had heard from his father, Gabriel by name, who died about forty years previous to Parkman's visit. Gabriel Cerré's account, whatever it may have been, was also hearsay. It is not pretended that he was in St. Louis in 1769, and he did not remove hither until about 1781. It is not claimed that Menard, the third witness, who lived at Kaskaskia, was here in 1769; and besides, it does not appear that he is responsible for any part of the story that the Ottawa Chief came to St. Louis.

A statement of Nicollet, as he expressly says, made on the authority of Peter Chouteau and Menard (that is this part of his narrative) is to the point in this discussion : " Pontiac's last residence," he says,* " was in St. Louis. One day he came to Mr. de St. Ange and told him that he was going to pay a visit to the Kaskaskia Indians. Mr. de St. Ange endeavored to dissuade him from it, reminding him of the little friendship that existed between him and the British. Pontiac's answer was: 'Captain, I am a man! I know how to fight. I have always fought openly. They will not murder me; and if any one attacks me as a brave man, I am his match.' He went off; was feasted ; got drunk ; and retired into the woods to sing his medicine songs." . . . . What relates to St. Louis must necessarily be from Chouteau. Here we are gravely told that Pontiac was a *resident* of St. Louis, a contradiction of the information communicated ten years later to Parkman, and which he wisely rejects. But what is more, the ten-and-a-half-year-old boy was so intimately mixed up with St. Ange and Pontiac that he knew all that passed between them, and was able to repeat to Nicollet the very

---

* Page 81.

words of the Chief's reply when the Commandant endeavored to dissuade him from going over the river to Cahokia. To believe such testimony is to beguile one's self with dreams. Besides, whether Pontiac did or did not go into the Cahokia woods, is hearsay evidence.

I remark that repetition does not establish a fact. I seem to see in all that is said about Pontiac's appearance at St. Louis unmistakable marks of a common origin. Observe, the testimony from first to last is connected with a fort twice identified. Pontiac, whether resident or visitor, is lodged in the fort; he goes out of the fort to pay visits; he is buried with honors near the fort. Now a fort is a conspicuous object, continuing the same, and always before the eyes: in form, appearance, and purpose it differs from other structures; it is not only distinct in character, but the only work of its kind in a locality. How is it possible to mistake it, how possible to forget it? I hold that if such an object or physical fact as I have described is invented and intimately interwoven with a narrative, the entire texture of the narrative is destroyed. But so surely as the ink drips from the pen to form these lines there was not even the pretence of a fort at St. Louis in 1769.

If so transient an occurrence as the visit of an Indian chief to a village which in no way influenced the affections, the passions, or the personal interests of a single person, and was not connected with any other event in which the locality was concerned, is so intimately associated in the mind of him who narrates the visit as to be inseparable from a public, notorious, unchanging physical fact which had a well-known definite beginning in time, is it not evident that this physical fact must dominate and be the keynote to the narrative? I mean that the narrative, if it embodies some truth, and in so far forth only, must be founded upon some occurrence contemporaneous with such physical fact. I am not offering this as a possible explanation of a story of which I have never believed a word, but part of the argument I am drawing out.

The narrative of Pontiac's visit or residence in St. Louis, and everything connected with it, originated with Peter Chouteau.

It should be noted that Nicollet's history is founded upon the so-called Journal of Augustus Chouteau. Now, A. Chouteau's journal is silent as to Pontiac's visit, for Nicollet tells us where he got that part of his story which connects the Chief with this place, namely, from Peter Chouteau. Augustus Chouteau does not allude to Pontiac in any of his depositions, nor does Peter Chouteau, though he gave many. I have gone through, page by page, the volumes of the Commissioner's Minutes, and of Bates' Minutes, and though every event of our early history is on some side touched upon, I have no recollection of Pontiac's name being mentioned by a single one of the old witnesses whose testimony is recorded in those manuscript books. Had the Chief's visit been a reality, some of them must have known it, very many heard of it. I know of no tradition connecting Pontiac's name with the village. The report that he was buried near the old Spanish fort at 4th and Walnut, which was begun in 1780, and the only fort we ever had here, is of recent date, started after Nicollet's time, and I believe started from Peter Chouteau or P. L. Cerré. Primm could scarcely have had information of the supposed visit and burial, or, probably, he would have mentioned or alluded to the subject in his historical address: and although I have heard him time and again repeat old traditions and stories relating to early days in St. Louis, the name of Pontiac never fell from his lips. This omission is of some consequence; for whatever may be said of Primm's inaccuracies and exaggerations as a historian, my long personal acquaintance with him seems to justify the opinion that he had a copious fund of story, anecdote, and tradition of whatever had occurred in the old time. If my memory serves me well, there is no mention of Pontiac in St. Louis by Beck, Breckenridge, Bradbury, Darby, a gatherer of old stories; Hall, the Duke of Saxe-Weimar, Perkins, Peck, Perrin du Lac, Stoddard, or Schultze. Shepard repeats the Parkman story with embellishments, as well as the burial near the Spanish fort. Reynolds gives a sketch of Pontiac, says nothing of his coming to our village, and that he was buried at Cahokia.

This absence of mention is, of course, a negative argument: but had the occurrence been real, surely some memory of it would have survived and been brought out in one or another way; whereas, nothing is heard of it until Nicollet, a stranger, visits St. Louis, and an old man is found who was, and had been from the start, its sole depository, and who for the first time produces it before the public. Ten years later he repeats his story with modifications and contradictions to Parkman.

PONTIAC'S BURIAL.

St. Ange has left in this locality the deserved reputation of a prudent, cautious, and circumspect officer; he was so regarded by Aubry and Ulloa. I do not think he did or would have attempted what is imputed to him—send over into British territory for the body of Pontiac, on which he had no claim, and especially at a moment when jealousies were so very rife on the English side of the river, and mistrust of the French and of Franco-Spanish influence. I am decided in the opinion he would not have done so without asking permission of the British authority, which it is pretty certain would not have been granted. I can scarcely imagine that such a proceeding would have been thought of, or allowed, if St. Louis was, as Parkman states, but which I do not believe, a focus of intrigue with the Indians against English interests.*

Again, it would seem probable from the face of the account as presented by Parkman and Nicollet, that Pontiac was killed in the evening—if in the forest, some time would elapse before the discovery of the body, perhaps a day or more, and ere St. Ange could hear of the murder and be able to remove the corpse, decomposition would have set in, and the hogs or wild animals mangled it. The burial-at-the-fort story

---

* Consp., II., 307.

and assassination in the forest do not seem to harmonize. If the killing occurred in the village, as it did according to Meurin, the body would certainly not be allowed to remain there like the carcass of a beast, but at once put into the earth. In either case, it must be remembered that speedy burial was the universal custom—always on the day of death, if possible: frequently, when a person died in the morning his body was interred by mid-day; and if soon in the afternoon, the funeral was before nightfall. St. Ange, for instance, died early in the morning, and by twelve o'clock of the same day his corpse was in the cemetery; the five or six victims of the attack on St. Louis in 1780, slain, it would seem, about eleven o'clock A.M., received burial in the afternoon.

I think Reynolds' statement, who gathered his information at an early date on the spot, as to the place of Pontiac's burial, should not in this case be lightly put aside.

To sum up: it appears to me that the oral testimony directly given to the historian, and that filtered through Nicollet, on which Parkman has built up his pleasant story of Pontiac's visit to St. Louis, when winnowed, leaves no wheat. Of course, it was not impossible for the Chief to have come to St. Louis in 1769; but no proof that bears scrutiny has been produced in support of such visit, and therefore it is not to be accepted as a fact, for history should be an account of real, not imaginary or conjectural, events. As to Pontiac's visit and the details and circumstances connected with it, there is much that is beautiful and poetical, and it rounds off well the story of his life; but viewed as history it is simply a phantom gibbering in the outward form of truth.

If you ask: how can the story of Pontiac's visit be explained, how could it get into circulation, if it had no foundation? Men, in matters of this sort, do not invent out of nothing. I answer, that I have traced it to Chouteau, who communicated it to Nicollet and Parkman, and through them it has obtained currency. How it got among Chouteau's notions I know not. A story of the same class, connected with the attack on St. Louis in 1780, long maintained itself in public credulity. Col. Benton, writing before 1820, on the authority of old inhabitants who were present, puts it into print, to the effect, that George Rogers Clark brought over from the Illinois side a number of troops and aided the inhabitants in repulsing the savages, which savages, by the way, did not approach nearer than about a mile of the village, and which inhabitants made no defence whatever. The story has been repeated many times. American troops, it is said, were at Cahokia: the rest is an imagination.

The St. Ange-Sterling story is even a more pointed illustration of fiction intruding itself into our early history. It runs thus: In 1765, St. Ange surrendered Fort Chartres to Captain Sterling, and removed to St. Louis. Soon after the British captain died, and St. Ange returned to the fort, assumed command of the English troops and over the country, and continued until a second time relieved by a British officer. This incredible story has been repeated in many books, some by writers of note, even authentic documents pretended to be cited in its support, until I publicly exposed its absurdity and proved its falsehood; and notwithstanding, even to-day, the stale buttermilk is churned over for the twentieth time in "Billon's Annals of St. Louis"—a book, it is true, of no authority—and the reader gravely told there is no reason to doubt the old woman's tale. How it originated I know not.

I have discussed at some length the question of Pontiac's visit to St. Louis and his burial near the fort, not so much on account of its intrinsic importance, as because it touches our local history, which it is of interest to rid of errors and imaginations. Our land-claim books and court papers for the fifty years following the change of government contain not a little of the sort of testimony passed under review—old creole testimony; and it is not new to meet with witnesses deposing, with much circumstantiality of detail, to what they did not know. But I have not criticised in a cavilling spirit, or with the slightest wish to vindicate any opinion which did not embody the strict truth; and my conclusions are reached after deliberation with sincere desire to be right.

The opinion I hold is, that Pontiac never was in St. Louis: that probably he had become a drunkard in his last days: that he was killed in an Indian drinking frolic at Cahokia, and buried there.

SKETCH OF A SILVER CROSS

WHICH A YOUNG MAN FOUND A FEW YEARS AGO, BY SEEING THE TIP OF ONE ARM OR CROSSBEAM PROTRUDING ABOVE THE GROUND.

THE locality in which it was found is a prominent bluff of the Mississippi River, in Illinois, opposite the village of Montpelier, Muscatine County, Ia. The place was not the summit of the bluff, but somewhat on the declivity toward the adjacent river, in a sort of ravine, in a wild, weird place.

THE POSSESSOR.

The finder thought little of it, and sold it to Mr. G. W. Robinson, of Montpelier, Muscatine, Ia., who polished it as bright as a silver dollar, and is now the proud possessor. (I believe that for a good price he would part with it, but believe that he expects to receive something handsome.)

The whole piece is one unbroken silver plate, as thick as a silver quarter-dollar, bright and smooth, of almost the exact figures as herewith sketched; length, $9\frac{3}{4}$ inches; across, 8 inches; width of the cross-tree, $1\frac{1}{8}$ inches; on face and reverse sides engraved figures and lines are on the cross, and on the face the words are stamped in: MONTREAL, and P.A., and ·V·J. It is all plain, legible, nothing oxidized or rusted; the top and rounded ends show wear, and in the top end is a silver ring, for pendant, and the meeting ends of the wire band are soldered together.

REV. JOHN F. KEMPKER.

RIVERSIDE, Iowa, Jan. 11, 1888.

SOME LANCASTER CATHOLICS, AND OTHER HISTORICAL NOTES.

By S. M. Sener.

It is well known that a Colonial Monastery existed in Lancaster County known as the "Ephrata Community," but it is not generally known that among this peculiar "Society of the Solitary" (Protestant), there were some who had been Catholics and subsequently came back again to the "Faith of their Fathers," yet such appears to have been the case. A word about the Society here will not be amiss. In 1719 a great number of Dunkers, or First-Day Baptists, emigrated from Germany to this country and settled in Lancaster and Franklin Counties in Pennsylvania. Among them was one Conrad Beissel, who held that the first day of the week should not be observed as the Sabbath, but that it should be the seventh day. This led to a split in the denomination and Beissel and his followers then formed the "Society of the Solitary," in 1733. They adopted the garb of the Capuchin or White Friars, which was worn by both the brethren and sisters. Celibacy was urged upon all who entered the Society, and monastic names were given likewise. The Society located at Ephrata. The convent life of these people was rigid. Their cells or rooms in the cloister were but twenty inches wide, and five feet high. Their bed consisted of a bench and a billet of wood, and their fare was frugal. They became wealthy and owned a paper-mill, grist-mill, and also established a printing-office, and from here were issued those extremely rare German volumes known as the Ephrata imprints. The old hand-press used by them is in possession of the Pennsylvania Historical Society. The Society began to decline and passed out of existence about 1800. The buildings used as the cloisters are still standing, but are fast falling into decay. Begging the reader's pardon for this sketch of the Society, I will now proceed to narrate the life history of the *Catholic* member. In Schwarzenau, Germany, lived a family of father, mother, and four sons, named Eckerline. The father (Gabriel) died, and the widow and four sons came to Pennsylvania in 1725. They had been Catholics,* but in Germany joined the Dunkers.

Israel, the second son, joined the Solitary in 1728, and the others, Samuel, Emanuel, and Gabriel, in 1730. In 1740, Israel, known as Br. Onesimus, was elected Prior. He endeavored to enhance the value of the property by building a second cloister and named it Zion. A difficulty occurred through the proposed length of this building, and over an innovation in the shape of a bell which he ordered from Europe for the building. This bell is to-day in possession of Grace Lutheran Church, Lancaster, and inscribed on its rim is the following: "Auspicio Viri Venerandi Onesimi Societatis Ephratensis Præpositi." It was placed there by my grand-uncle, Gottlieb Sener, he being a Lutheran (myself being a convert since 1874), in 1854, when it was sold by the parties who now own the property. On account of this trouble the Eckerlines and some few other brothers were expelled from the cloister in 1745, and began to wander around. In New York City they were taken for Jesuits from Louisiana or Mexico, on account of their habit, and were imprisoned, but subsequently were released. Finally, Israel, Gabriel, and Samuel settled near Fort Duquesne. They made fast friends with the Delaware Indians. In 1757 the Mohawks made a raid on the hermitage which had been erected by the Eckerlines, and plundered it, after which they burned it down. Israel, who was writing at the time, was surprised and bound along with Gabriel. The others escaped, and one of their number, named Schilling, brought the news to Ephrata. Israel and Gabriel

---

* Rupp's "Hist. of Lancaster County," p. 222.

were taken to Montreal, in Canada, and were placed in the Jesuit residence there. From Montreal they were taken to Quebec and suffered terrible hardships during the winter. Then they were carried as prisoners of war to France, where they died, and before his death Israel (according to the "Chronicon Ephratense," page 200) had "a great love for the Roman Catholic Church, and received the tonsure and was named BON CHRÉTIEN." For most of the facts in reference to the Eckerlines, I am indebted to the "Chronicon Ephratense," a very rare volume printed in the German language by the Society at Ephrata in 1786, and which was compiled by Brothers Lamech and Agrippa. Chapter xxix. of the Chronicle is almost entirely devoted to the eventful narrative about the Eckerlines. Dr. Oswald Seidensticker, of Philadelphia, has written a volume on Ephrata, also in the German language, and it contains much valuable information in regard to them.

In Finotti's "Bibliographia Catholica Americana," mention is made (page 27) of a book entitled "Anti-Christian and Anti-Social Conspiracy," printed at Lancaster in 1812, by Joseph Ehrenfried. Ehrenfried was born of Roman Catholic parentage, in Mayence, Hesse Darmstadt, Germany, on December 25, 1783. He was educated for the priesthood, but was never ordained. At nineteen years of age he came to this country, and arrived in Lancaster County some time in 1802. He commenced his career as a school teacher in 1803, in the "Grove School-House," in East Donegal township, Lancaster County. Later he came to Lancaster and became translator in Albright's German printing-office, and in 1808, along with William Hamilton, established the "Volksfreund," which was sold by them in 1817 to John Baer, by whose sons the paper is still issued.

During Governor Ritner's administration he was State printer. He helped to establish German papers in Harrisburg and Allentown. From 1845 to 1860 he was deputy register of Lancaster County. He was married in 1809 to

Mrs. Ann Smith (*née* Hubley), a descendant of Bernard Hubley,* and they lived to celebrate their golden wedding. He died March 6, 1862, and is interred in Woodward Hill Cemetery. In 1810 he printed a German edition of "Thomas à Kempis," a copy of which I have in my possession and which is not mentioned in Finotti.

An unfortunate matter in connection with Mr. Ehrenfried was, that in 1816, through the influence exerted upon him by Prof. Frederick Damish, a Saxon music-teacher, he became a receiver of the doctrines of the New Jerusalem Church and an apostate to our religion. A number of his descendants are living to-day in Lancaster, and, strange to relate, are Catholics, having become converts about ten or twelve years ago. I have been materially aided in the search for information in regard to Mr. Ehrenfried by S. S. Rathvon, Ph.D., who is reader of the New Church in Lancaster.

In the July number of the MAGAZINE, page 312, Rev. James Nash, in his sketch of St. Malachy's Mission at Doe Run, Chester County, Pa., mentions a Rev. M. Malone as having attended that mission in 1846, and says that he belonged to Lancaster. Father Malone was a nephew of Michael Malone, who died a few years ago, after handsomely endowing St. Mary's Orphan Asylum here. Father Malone was born in Killeen, Queen's County, Ireland, September 29, 1815. He studied in the Seminary of Mountrath, Kildare Diocese, and completed his studies at St. Charles Borromeo Seminary in Philadelphia. During the riots of 1844 in that city, he escaped injury by jumping from a second-story window of that institution one night clad in his night garments. He was ordained on the Feast of Corpus Christi in 1846, by Bishop Kenrick, and was appointed to West Chester, where he remained for two years, then going to Minersville, where he died on April 16, 1877, aged 62 years. He was buried at Minersville, on April 19, Bishop Shanahan officiating, on ac-

---

* See "U. S. C. HIST. MAG.," Vol. I., page 50.

count of the illness of Archbishop Wood. An extended account of his funeral obsequies may be found in the "Catholic Standard" for April 28, 1877. His brother, Mortimer Malone resides in Lancaster.

The "Lancaster Free Press" of September 29, 1823, records the death of Rev. John Joseph Holland, at St. Mary's Church, and of him says the following: "Pastor of the Catholic church of this city, by whose death his congregation is bereaved of an able and faithful instructor and society in general of a valuable member."

Father Molyneux is mentioned as having been at Lancaster in the list of attendant clergymen contained in the early register of St. Mary's Church. The fact is established in the "Memorial to the Earl of Halifax, by the people of Maryland," in which it is stated that Father Molyneux was at Lancaster in 1744, before the treaty was held there in June and July, between the Commissioners of Pennsylvania and Maryland and the Indians.*

In reference to Father Fitzsimmons, who was at Lancaster in 1804, I have ascertained that he came here from Canada and was sent away from here through an unfortunate fight instigated by the High Dutch party under John Risdel, and was sent to Father Gallitzin at Loretto, at the latter's request. Several letters between Father Gallitzin and Bishop Carroll show this clearly.†

As to Father Pellentz having been at Lancaster, a manuscript of Bishop Bruté, of Vincennes, states that he was the founder of the Conewago and Lancaster Missions.‡

Recently I was shown a small catechism of 48 pages, of which 40 were catechetical, and the balance devoted to hymns and the manner of service at Mass, which was printed in Lancaster in 1831. The following is the title of the book, and I offer it as a contribution toward Catholic Bibliography:

---

* Shea's "Cath. Church in Colonial Days," pp. 401 and 408.
† Brownson's "Life of Gallitzin," pp. 174–5–6.
‡ DeCourcy's "Cath. Church in U. S.," edition of 1879, p 121.

A | CATECHISM : | or short abridgment of | CHRISTIAN DOCTRINE | newly revised, for the use of | THE CATHOLIC CHURCH, | in the United States of America, | to which is added, | A SHORT DAILY EXERCISE, | with several hymns. | *Published with the approbation of the* | MOST REV. ARCHBISHOP MARECHAL. | Printed by | H. W. VILLEE, | North-Queen street, Lancaster. | 1831. |

The volume is bound in a peculiarly mottled paper, and I have never seen or heard of another copy, and it is probably unique.

THE ORIGIN OF THE MISSION TO THE FLATHEAD INDIANS.

By Edmond Mallet.

I.

FROM time immemorial the Flathead tribe of the Salish nation of Indians has inhabited the Bitter Root valley in the Rocky Mountains. Its early history is enveloped in the obscurity of past ages.

The first white men who saw these Indians were the Chevalier La Vérendrye and his party of Canadian explorers, who discovered the Rocky Mountains in January, 1743, whilst searching for the great River of the West, by which they hoped to penetrate to the Pacific Ocean. The Indians were then on their winter hunt for buffaloes on the eastern slope of the mountains, evidently between the headwaters of the Missouri River and its tributary, the Yellowstone. The fall of Canada and of the Illinois country into the power of England, and the cession of Louisiana by Napoleon I. to the American Republic, arrested the onward march of the intrepid Canadian and French pioneers toward the setting sun: it had been reserved to noble representatives of the young American Republic to make alliances of friendship with the tribes of the innermost recesses of the Rocky Mountains, and to follow the course of the great Columbia River to the confines of the Western Sea.

Pending the negotiations which resulted in the transfer by France of the Northwest to the United States, under the title of the Louisiana purchase, President Jefferson organized an exploring expedition "to trace the Missouri to its source, to cross the Highlands, and follow the best water-communication which offered itself from thence to the Pacific Ocean."* Cap-

---

* Letter of Thomas Jefferson to Paul Allen, August 18, 1813, in Lewis and Clark, " History of the Expedition," etc., Phila., 1814; I., xl.

tain Meriwether Lewis was given command of the expedition, with First Lieutenant William Clark as his associate. Fourteen soldiers of the United States Army, nine young men from Kentucky, and two Canadian voyageurs, all of whom were enlisted for this special service, composed the body of the expeditionary party. Later it was increased to thirty-two persons, including five Canadian hunters, guides, and interpreters, an Indian woman (the wife of one of the interpreters), her young child and a Negro servant belonging to Lieutenant Clark. The expedition left the Mississippi, above St. Louis, Mo., on May 14, 1804, and after wintering at the Mandan villages, on the Upper Missouri—sixty-six years after La Vérendrye visited this Indian tribe at the same place—reached a village of Shoshones, or Snake Indians, in the Rocky Mountains, on August 13, 1805.

Having left the headwaters of the Jefferson Fork of the Missouri and obtained horses at the Shoshone village, located on the headwaters of the Salmon, a tributary of the Snake, or Lewis River, which flows into the Columbia, the expedition moved in a northwesterly direction to cross the Bitter Root Mountains. On September 4th, they found a party of 430 Flatheads encamped on the Bitter Root River, a tributary of the Flathead. This stream is now known as the St. Mary's River, it having been so named by Father Peter John De Smet, S.J., the Apostle of the Flatheads. As the journals kept by the Lewis and Clark Expedition contain the first detailed account ever written as to these Indians, I shall take the liberty of presenting a few extracts from the one which was first given to the public in book form. Sergeant Patrick Gass—who, by the way, was a Catholic, and who lived long enough to be known as the last survivor of the expedition *—

---

* Patrick Gass was of Irish parentage, and was born June 12, 1771, at Falling Springs, Cumberland County, near the present city of Chambersburg, Franklin Co., Pa. When a young man, he worked as a carpenter, and built a house for James Buchanan, the father of President Buchanan, who he always called "Little Jimmy." He saw Gen. Washington in 1794 at Carlisle. In 1803 he was a soldier, stationed at Kaskaskia, and responded to the call for volunteers for the

in his journal thus mentions the first view the expeditionary corps had of the Flatheads:

Wednesday, 4th. . . . . We kept down the valley about 5 miles, and came to the Tussapa band of the Flathead nation of Indians, or a part of them. We found them encamped on the creek, and we encamped with them.

Thursday, 5th. This was a fine morning with a great white frost. The Indian dogs are so hungry and ravenous, that they eat 4 or 5 pair of mockasons last night. We remained here all day, and recruited our horses to 40 and 3 colts; and made 4 or 5 of this nation chiefs. They are a very friendly people; have plenty of robes and skins for covering, and a large stock of horses, some of them very good; but they have nothing to eat, but berries, roots, and such articles of food. This band is on its way over to the Missouri or Yellowstone river to hunt buffaloes. They are the whitest Indians I ever saw.

. . . .

Monday, 9th. . . . . At 2 o'clock we again went forward, and crossed over the Flathead river, about 100 yards wide, and which we called Clark's river.

. . . .

Tuesday, 10th. . . . . At night our hunters came in, and had killed 5 deer. With one of the hunters, 3 of the Flathead Indians came to our camp. They informed us that the rest of their band was on the Columbia river, about 5 or 6 days' journey distant, with pack horses; that two of the Snake nation had stolen some of their horses, and that they were in pursuit of them. We gave them some presents, and one stayed to go over the mountains with us; the other two continued their pursuit.*

Lewis and Clark Expedition to Oregon. After the death of Sergeant Floyd, who was buried at Floyd's Bluff, Iowa, he was promoted sergeant, and was instructed to keep a journal of the expedition, which journal he prepared for the press with the assistance of an Irish schoolmaster named David McKeehan, the year after his return from the Pacific Coast. In 1859 his biography was published by the editor of a country newspaper in a volume entitled "The Life and Times of Patrick Gass, now sole survivor of the Overland Expedition to the Pacific, under Lewis and Clark, in 1804-5-6; also a soldier in the War with Great Britain, from 1812 to 1815, and a participant in the Battle of Lundy's Lane," etc., by J. G. Jacobs. Portrait, 12mo, 280 pp. Wellsburg, Vu.: 1859.

* Gass, "A Journal of the Voyages and Travels of a Corps of Discovery," Pittsburgh, 1807, pp. 132-34.

The above observations certainly refer to the tribe now known as the Flatheads; but Sergeant Gass in subsequent pages of his journal, speaks of other bands of Indians under the general appellation of "Flatheads," who were really Nez Percés, Umatillas, Walla Wallas, etc., belonging to a different nation.

The only other observations which Sergeant Gass makes concerning the "Flatheads"—and these appear to apply more particularly to the Nez Percés and other tribes of the Upper Columbia, with whom he confounds them throughout his journal,—is the following—he makes a comparison on the return trip, of the conduct of the women of the Lower Columbia, with the conduct of those of the Rocky Mountain region:

. . . . To the honor of the Flatheads who live on the west side of the Rocky Mountains and extend some distance down the Columbia, we must mention them as exceptions, as they do not exhibit those loose feelings of carnal desire, nor appear addicted to the common customs of prostitution: and they are the only nation on the whole route where anything like chastity is regarded.*

The account of the Indians given in Captain Lewis's journal which was published several years after the volume from which I have quoted, is more detailed, and therefore more satisfactory; but want of time and space will not allow me to make citations. He distinguishes between the Flatheads and their neighbors, the Nez Percés, but calls the Flathead tribe the "Ootlashoots," and their nation, whose correct name is Salish (and which is composed of the Flathead, the Pend d'Oreille, the Cœur d'Alêne, the Chaudiére or Colville, the Spokane, and the Pisquouse tribes), "Tushepaws." †

---

* Gass, "A Journal," pp. 189, 190.

† The Lewis and Clark corps did not see the Flatheads on the return journey over the Rocky Mountains in 1806. They, however, learned that they were called "Shalees," a band of the Tushepaws, by the Nez Percés, or Pierced Noses. They were shown an old road much beaten by the frequent visits of the Ootlashoots, from the valley of Clark's river to the fishery on the Salmon river, and later they observed a road which led to "a fine extensive valley on Clark's river, where the Shalees or Ootlashoots occasionally reside." Lewis and Clark, "History of the Expedition," ii., pp. 324, 329.

The next accounts of the Flatheads are given in the histories of the expedition fitted out by John Jacob Astor to establish the Pacific Fur Company at the mouth of the Columbia, in 1811-13.* Gabriel Franchère, the first to publish a narrative of these expeditions,—there were two, one by sea from New York, and another overland from St. Louis,—having been mostly employed on the Lower Columbia, does not mention the Flatheads. Indeed Ross Cox, "the little Irishman," as he was called by his companions, is the only one who gives authentic additional information concerning the interesting tribe whose history I am examining.

The Northwest Company, which was waging a disastrous opposition to the Honourable Hudson's Bay Company in the Canadian Northwest, on learning of the departure of the Astor overland expedition, determined to oppose also the Pacific Fur Company. Scarcely had the expedition by sea arrived at the mouth of the Columbia, and founded Astoria, when a party of Northwesters appeared beyond the Rocky Mountains and founded a post named Fort Spokane, on the Upper Columbia. From this point the Northwest Company sent adventurous agents to establish posts in the very midst of the various tribes: among those established was one in the midst of the Flatheads, by a clerk of the company named Finan McDonald. The Pacific Fur Company, to oppose McDonald, immediately sent two of its clerks—Russell Farnham and Ross Cox—with a party of twelve men, mostly Canadians, to the same place. Farnham's post was established on November 10, 1812, and was abandoned in May, 1813. Cox thus speaks of his visit to the Flatheads on this occasion :

On the 10th we came to a small village of the Flathead nation chiefly consisting of old men, women, and children. We were

---

* Franchère, "Relation," Montreal, 1820; the same, Eng., "Narrative," N. Y., 1854; Cox, "Adventures on the Columbia," N. Y., 1832; Irving, "Astoria," Phila., 1836; Ross, "Adventures of the First Settlers on the Oregon," Lond., 1849. For a biography and portrait of the Catholic traveller, Gabriel Franchère, see Tassé, "Les Canadiens de l'Ouest," Montreal, 1878; also the "Catholic Family Annual " for 1887.

quite charmed with their frank and hospitable reception and their superiority in cleanliness over any of the tribes we had hitherto seen. Their lodges were conical, but very spacious, and were formed by a number of buffalo and moose skins thrown over long poles in such a manner as to keep them quite dry. The fire was placed in the centre, and the ground all round it was covered with mats and clean skins free from the vermin we felt so annoying at the lower parts of the Columbia. They had a quantity of dried buffalo, of which we purchased a good deal; and as they gave us to understand that the great body of their tribe were in the mountains, hunting, we determined to stop here, and accordingly set about constructing a log house. . . . .

While the house was being built, many of the tribe arrived, from whom we purchased a number of beaver skins. Their hunt had been rather unsuccessful, and attended with disastrous results; for they informed us that after killing buffalo sufficient for the winter, they were surprised by their old enemies, the Blackfeet Indians (whose lands lie on the east side of the Rocky Mountains), who killed several of their warriors and took many prisoners. They appeared much dejected at their misfortunes, and one of the chiefs seemed deeply to lament the loss of his wife, who had been captured with some other women, by the enemy. Part of the tribe pitched their tents some distance above us at the Northwest establishment. They were passionately fond of tobacco, and while they remained with us never ceased smoking. Having bought all their skins, and given them credit for some articles until the spring, the greater part of them set off to make their winter's hunt which their recent misfortunes had protracted to a very late period. When the house was finished, I got a good canoe built of cedar planks, in which I embarked with six men, and taking leave of Farnham on the 18th of December, descended the Flathead river on my return to Spokane.*

The War of 1812 proved disastrous to the Pacific Fur Company. On October 16, 1813, the company having been dissolved, its establishments, with the stock on hand, were transferred to the rival association. Cox now joined the victorious Northwest Company, and was a second time sent to the Flatheads, where he remained from December 24, 1813, to April 4, 1814. He devotes a whole chapter of his book to

---

* Cox, "Adventures," pp. 102, 103.

his observations among the Flatheads during the winter. Whilst he again shows that these Indians possessed many good natural qualities, he also demonstrates, notably by suggestions of hideous and revolting treatment of female prisoners captured from their traditional enemies, the Blackfeet, that they were at that time, like all savages, a barbarous, and —would I were not compelled to say it—a brutal people. Happily for them and for the name of humanity, there were already in their midst and at the posts which they frequented, men whom the successors of Laval had marked with the sign of the Cross, and who, like Saint John the Baptist, the patron of their nation, were as a voice in the wilderness crying, "Make straight the way of the Lord."

II.

The French Canadians were the pioneers of Christianity and of civilization in the Great West. In the Oregon country they were the first, with their brethren, the Christian Iroquois and Nippissings, to impress their religion upon the benighted Columbian tribes, and also the first to establish permanent agricultural colonies in their midst. They were in every expedition of discovery, in every commercial enterprise. Of the Astor party which went to Oregon on the ship "Tonquin," they numbered eighteen out of thirty-three persons, and of the overland party under Hunt, forty out of sixty. They were greatly in the majority in every party of the Northwest Company, and the same is true of the Hudson's Bay Company after it had absorbed its rival organization, in 1821. At this period, and up to the time of the great American emigration, the French was the language of the country among the whites, and the Chinook jargon, which the Canadians formed, was the language used with the Indians. They married the native women, and their solicitude for the religious and moral welfare of their wives and children prompted them to petition for missionaries of their faith. The Oregon Mission, founded by the saintly Archbishop Blanchet, had its origin in these petitions; it was also the influence of their respect for religion which produced the Flathead Mission of the Rocky Mountains. In their isolation and miseries in the great Fur Land, they never entirely forgot the Christian teaching of their pious mothers, who prayed and wept for them on the banks of the Saint Lawrence during their long years of absence. The votive offerings in the old church of Ste. Anne on the head of the island of Montreal, the crosses at the foot of dangerous rapids on the Ottawa, the Winnipeg, the Saskatchewan, the Athabaska, and the Columbia, which missionaries and travellers observed in their voyages through the continent, show that some, at least, of these intrepid hunters, traders, and canoemen remained true to the noble traditions of their race.

That the Canadians carried their religion with them into the wilderness will best appear by a few extracts drawn from the early histories of travel in the Indian country. I give them not only to illustrate the influence of the Canadians in that country, but also to delineate the manners and customs of those days in the broad expanse beyond the Rocky Mountains.

Franchère, when returning overland to Canada from Astoria, in 1814, lost two of his companions, named Olivier Roy, *dit* Lapensée, and André Belanger, who were drowned in the Athabaska by the wreck of a canoe in one of the rapids. He thus describes the obsequies of one of them:

Toward evening, in ascending the river . . . . we found the body of Lapensée. We interred it as decently as we could, and planted at his grave a cross, on which I inscribed, with the point of my knife, his name and the manner and date of his death. . . . . The rapid and the point of land where the accident I have described took place, will bear and bears already probably the name of Lapensée.*

---

* Franchère, "Narrative," p. 306.

Cox thus describes the burial, in the same year, of one of his companions named Jean-Baptiste Lamoureux, who was killed on the Columbia in an attack by the Indians on a party of the Northwest Company:

> We put ashore at a low sandy point covered with willows and cotton-wood, for the purpose of breakfasting and interring the body of L'Amoureux. The men were immediately set to work to dig a grave, into which were lowered the remains of the unfortunate Canadian. A few short prayers were said in French, and after the earth was thrown in, to a level with the surface, it was covered over with dry sand in such a manner as to keep the natives in ignorance of the occurrence.*

Captain Bonneville, of the United States Army, engaged in a commercial enterprise, visited the Upper Columbia in 1832, and he recorded the fact in his journal that before missionaries of any denomination had visited the country, the Indians had made progress in Christian observances. These facts have been transmitted to us by Washington Irving:

> Fort Wallah Wallah is surrounded by the tribe of the same name, as well as by the Skynes, and the Nez Percés, who bring to it the furs and peltries collected in their hunting expeditions. The Wallah Wallahs are a degenerate, worn-out tribe. The Nez Percés are the most numerous and tractable of the three tribes just mentioned. Mr. Pembrune† informed Captain Bonneville that he had been at some pains to introduce the Christian religion in the Roman Catholic form, among them, where it had evidently taken root, but had become altered and modified to suit their peculiar habits of thought, and motives of action, retaining, however, the principal points of faith, and its entire precepts of morality. The same gentleman had given them a code of laws, to which they conformed with scrupulous fidelity. Polygamy, which once prevailed among them to a great extent, was now rarely indulged. All the crimes denounced by the Christian faith, met with severe punishment among them.
>
> There certainly appeared (continues Irving) to be a peculiar

---

* Cox, "Adventures," p. 162.

† Pierre Chrysologue Pambrun. For a biography of him, see Tassé, "Les Canadiens de l'Ouest," ii., pp. 299-320.

susceptibility of moral and religious improvement among this tribe, and they would seem to be one of the very, very few, that have benefited in morals and manners, by an intercourse with white men. The parties which visited them about twenty years previously, in the expedition fitted out by Mr. Astor, complained of their selfishness, their extortion, and their thievish propensities. The very reverse of those qualities prevailed among them during the prolonged sojourn of Captain Bonneville.*

Mr. Townsend, a naturalist, who accompanied the trading party with which Rev. Jason Lee, the leader of the first Methodist missionary party to the Columbia, travelled, relates the circumstances of a Canadian's death, and the ceremonies observed in his burial at the traders' rendezvous on Green River, north of Great Salt Lake, Utah:

In the evening, a fatal accident happened to a Canadian belonging to Mr. McKay's party. He was running his horse in company with another, when the animals were met in full career by a third rider, and horses and men were thrown with great force to the ground. The Canadian was taken up completely senseless, and brought to Mr. McKay's lodge, where we were all taking supper. I perceived at once that there was little chance of his life being saved. He had received an injury of the head, which had evidently caused concussion of the brain. He was bled copiously, and various local remedies were applied, but without success; the poor man died early next morning.

He was about forty years of age, healthy, active, and shrewd, and very much valued by Mr. McKay as a leader in his absence, and as an interpreter among the Indians of the Columbia.

At noon the body was interred. It was wrapped in a piece of coarse linen, over which was sewed a buffalo robe. The spot selected was about a hundred yards south of the fort, and the funeral was attended by the greater part of the men of both camps. Mr. Lee officiated in performing the ordinary church ceremony, after which a hymn for the repose of the soul of the departed was sung by the Canadiáns present. The grave is surrounded by a neat palisade of willows, with a black cross erected at the head, on which is carved the name "Casseau."†

---

* Irving, "Adventures of Captain Bonneville," N. Y., 1860, p. 300.

† Townsend, "Narrative of a Journey across the Rocky Mountains," Amer. Ed., 1839, p. 92.

Rev. Samuel Parker, a Presbyterian minister, who visited the Rocky Mountains in 1835 to '36, under the direction of the American Board of Commissioners for Foreign Missions, relates a sad occurrence which corroborates the testimony of Capt. Bonneville, and illustrates the Christian simplicity of the Indians. I forbear giving expression to the feeling of indignation, mingled with sadness, which the account of the writer's manifest lack of Christian feeling inspires:

.... The night of our arrival [in the Nez Percés' country], a little girl, of about six or seven years of age, died. The morning of the twelfth they buried her. Everything relating to the ceremony was conducted with great propriety. The grave was dug only about two feet deep. They have no spades, and a sharpened stick was used to loosen the earth, and this was removed with the hands; and with their hands they fill up the grave after the body is deposited in it. A mat is laid on the grave, then the body wrapped in its blanket with the child's drinking cup and spoon, made of horn; then a mat of rushes is spread over the whole, and filled up, as above described. In this instance they had prepared a cross to set up at the grave, most probably having been told to do so by some Iroquois Indians, a few of whom, not in the capacity of teachers, but as trappers in the employ of the fur companies I saw west of the mountains. One grave in the same village had a cross standing over it, which was the only relic of the kind I saw, together with this just named, during my travels in the country. But as I viewed a cross of wood made by men's hands of no avail to benefit either the dead or the living, and far more likely to operate as a salvo to a guilty conscience, or a stepping-stone to idolatry, than to be understood in its spiritual sense to refer to a crucifixion of our sins, I took this, which the Indians had prepared, and broke it to pieces. I then told them we place a stone at the head and foot of the grave, only to mark the place; and without a murmur they cheerfully acquiesced and adopted our custom.*

Rev. Mr. Spalding, another Presbyterian minister, when travelling to the Nez Percés' country in 1836, to select the site of his station, was witness of an edifying scene, an account

---

* Parker, "Journal of an Exploring Tour," 1838, pp. 275, 276.

of which he recorded in his journal, and afterward repeated to his society in Boston. I reproduce it:

> October 10, 1836. Marched about fifty-two miles and camped on a considerable stream running into Lewis river. Were greatly affected at night at witnessing the Nez Percés at prayer. They were assembled in a circle, on their knees, with an old man, to all appearance very earnest in prayer. I learned through the interpreter something of the prayer. It appeared to be the Lord's prayer, with perhaps some additions. I inquired of myself, Is it not possible that some of these poor benighted heathen are even now numbered in the sheep-fold of Christ? and while waiting the dilatory motions of the Christian church, may have been led by an unseen hand to the Lamb of God.*

Rev. Mr. Demers, Mgr. Blanchet's associate, who visited Fort Okanagan in 1840, in a report to his superiors, eulogizes a worthy Canadian whom he found in that place. After describing the post, he says:

> .... The population there is, however, yearning for God's word. I had the pleasure of meeting there a zealous Christian of the name of Robillard, who had taught the Indians their prayers. This unexpected help saved me much labor in this mission.†

Fr. De Smet, who visited the Flat Bows,—evidently the band since called Kootenais, of the Pend d'Oreilles tribe,—for the first time in 1845, pays a tribute of praise to another devoted Catholic instructor. He says:

> .... Since my arrival among the Indians, the feast of the glorious Assumption of the Blessed Virgin Mary has ever been to me a day of great consolation. I had time to prepare for the celebration of this solemn festival. Thanks be to the instructions and counsels of a brave Canadian, Mr. Berland, who for a long time has resided among them in the quality of trader, I found the little tribe of Arcs-a-plats docile, and in the best disposition to embrace the faith. They had already been instructed in the principal mysteries of religion. They sang canticles in French and Indian

---

* "Missionary Herald," 1837, xxxiii., p. 427.

† "Rapport sur les Missions du diocese de Québec," iii., p. 48.

tongues. They number about ninety families. I celebrated the first mass ever offered in their land; after which ten adults already advanced in age, and ninety children received baptism. . . . . They ardently desire to be taught agriculture, the advantages of which I have explained, and promised to procure the necessary seed and implements of husbandry.*

It is thus seen that humble Catholic Canadians and Iroquois had instructed the poor Indians of the Upper Columbia in the elementary principles of Christianity before the advent of missionaries of any denomination into their country, and inspired them with an ardent desire to receive among them those who, being specially sent, could teach them with the plenitude of Apostolic authority.

III.

In the autumn of the year 1831, four Indians from the Upper Columbia country arrived in the city of St. Louis, presumably with one of the fur-trading parties from the Rocky Mountains. The old French town of Saint Louis had at that time a population of about 6,000 inhabitants, and was the principal frontier city of the West. The appearance of strange Indians on the streets at that place, in those days, was of such common occurrence that our Columbians attracted no special attention, and it was only a long time afterward that they became an object of interest. It would require many ponderous volumes to reproduce all the fanciful stories that have since been written about them, and the purpose of their visit to the Mississippi Valley.

The first published statement of the Indians' visit is contained in a letter from Rt. Rev. Joseph Rosati, Bishop of Saint Louis, to the editor of the "Annales de l'Association de la Propagation de la Foi," dated December 31, 1831. This account, published within a few months after the occurrence

---

* De Smet, "Oregon Missions and Travels in the Rocky Mountains," 1847, p. 120.

to which it relates, is entitled to the greatest weight in establishing the facts in the case. I give a literal translation of so much of the letter as bears upon the subject:

> Some three months ago, four Indians who live at the other side of the Rocky Mountains, near the Columbia River, arrived in Saint Louis. After visiting General Clarke, who in his celebrated travels had seen the nation to which they belong and had been well received by them, they came to see our church, and appeared to be exceedingly well pleased with it. Unfortunately, there was no one who understood their language. Some time afterward two of them fell dangerously ill. I was then absent from Saint Louis. Two of our priests visited them, and the poor Indians seemed delighted with their visit. They made signs of the cross and other signs which appeared to have some relation to Baptism. This sacrament was administered to them; they gave expression of their satisfaction. A little cross was presented to them; they took it with eagerness, kissed it repeatedly, and it could be taken from them only after their death. It was truly distressing that they could not be spoken to. Their remains were carried to the church for the funeral, which was conducted with all the Catholic ceremonies. The other two attended and acted with great propriety. They have returned to their country.
>
> We have since learned from a Canadian, who has crossed the country which they inhabit, that they belong to the nation of "Têtes-Plates" (Flat-Heads), which, as with another called the "Pied-Noirs" (Black-Feet), have received some notions of the Catholic religion from two Indians who had been to Canada, and who had related what they had seen, giving a striking description of the beautiful ceremonies of the Catholic worship, and telling them that it was also the religion of the whites; they have retained what they could of it and they have learned to make the sign of the cross and to pray. These nations have not yet been corrupted by intercourse with others; their manners and customs are simple, and they are very numerous. We have conceived the liveliest desire not to let pass such a good occasion. Mr. Condamine has offered himself to go to them next spring with another. In the meantime we shall obtain information on what we have been told and on the means of travel.* . . . .

---

* "Annales de L'Association de la Propagation de la Foi," Lyon, 1832, v., pp. 592, 600. Compare with "Annals de la Propagation de la Foi," 1840, xii., p.

The register of burials of the Cathedral at Saint Louis shows that one of the Indians, Narcissus Keepeellelé, or Pipe Bard of the Nez Percés tribe of the Chopoweek nation, called Flatheads, aged about forty-four years, who came from the Columbia River beyond the Rocky Mountains, was buried in the Catholic cemetery on October 31, 1831, Rev. Edmond Saulnier officiating; and that the other, Paul, "Indian of the nation of Flatheads," was buried in the same cemetery on November 17, 1831, Rev. Benedict Roux officiating.*

From the authorities cited, the following facts are estab-

275; the same, Eng., "Annals of the Propagation of the Faith," Lond., 1839-40, I., p. 377; Verhaegen, in "The Indian Missions under the care of the Missouri Province of the Society of Jesus," Phila., 1841, p. 7; De Smet, in the same, p. 25; De Smet, "Letters and Sketches, with a Narrative of a Year's residence among the Indian Tribes of the Rocky Mountains," Phila., 1843, pp. 16, 91, 173; De Smet, "Origin, Progress, and Prospects of the Catholic Mission to the Rocky Mountains," Phila., 1843, p. 2; Shea, "History of the Catholic Missions among the Indian Tribes of the United States," New York, 1855, pp. 458, 467; Blanchet, "Historical Notes and Reminiscences of Early Times in Oregon," Portland, 1883, pp. 29, 30; Van Rensselaer, "Sketch of the Catholic Church in Montana," in "American Catholic Quarterly Review," 1887, xll., p. 428.

Fr. Grassi, of the Rocky Mountain Missions, in a lecture delivered a few years ago before the Cercle Catholique of Quebec, gave an entirely new version of the circumstances which induced the Flatheads to send to Saint Louis for Catholic missionaries. As the newspaper account of this lecture, which I have before me, may not be entirely reliable, I think it prudent not to state his argument.

* Le trente et un d'octobre mil huit cent trente et un, Je sousigné
Narcisse al inhumé dans le Cimitière de cette Paroisse le corps de Keepéellelé
Keepéellelé
Sauvage ou Pipe Bard du Né Percé de la tribe de Chopoweek Nation appel-
tête platte lée tete plate agé d'environs q'uarante quatre aus administré du St.
Baptême venant de la rivière Columbia au dela des Rocky Mountains.
EDM. SAULNIER,
Pr.

Le dix sept de Novembre mil huit cent trente et un, Je, sousigné
Paul al inhume dans le Cimitière de cette Paroisse le corps de Paul
Sauvage
de la nation sauvage de la Nation des têtes plattes Venant de la rivière Columbia
des têtes au dela des Rocky Mountains, administré du St. Baptême et de l'ex-
plattes trême onction.
ROUX,
Pr.

I am indebted to Very Rev. H. Van der Sanden, Chancellor of the Archdiocese of Saint Louis, for an official copy of the above certificates from the Registry of Sepultures kept in the cathedral.

lished: (1) that the visit of the Indians was in 1831; (2) that one of them at least was a Chupunnish or Nez Percés; and, (3), that if the original purpose of these Indians' visit was to obtain missionaries, they were missionaries of the Catholic Faith—about whom they had heard through the Canadians and Iroquois—that they desired.

Rev. Matthew Condamine, who offered his services to evangelize these Indians, was at that time a member of Bishop Rosati's household at the Cathedral, and had special charge of a mission at "Vide Poche," since known as Carondelet, and now a suburb of Saint Louis. He was never to see the Rocky Mountains: it was reserved for another to carry the Catholic Faith to the Upper Columbia.

Nearly two years after the departure of the two companions of the Indians whose mortal remains were deposited in the Catholic cemetery at Saint Louis, a sensational account of the visit of the Flatheads, furnished to Mr. G. P. Disosway by Mr. William Walker, the exploring agent of the Wyandottes, appeared in the columns of the "Christian Advocate and Journal" of New York, the principal organ of the Methodist Episcopal Church. The substance of the account was that a deputation of Flathead chiefs, who had been sent by the council of their nation, had come to Saint Louis from the Columbia River to inquire concerning the true God, about whom they had heard from an adventurer, who was providentially present at one of their idolatrous feasts, and who told them that their mode of worshipping the Great Spirit was displeasing to Him, and that the white men away toward the rising sun had a Book that taught them how to worship God acceptably. General Clark explained the Christian doctrine to them, but alas! they did not all live to bear home the tidings. Change of climate and mode of life produced diseases, and two of them finished their pilgrimage at Saint Louis. The other two, it was understood, had reached their homes in safety.*

---

* Holdich, "Life of Wilbur Fisk, D.D.," 1856, p. 276. Compare with Lee and

On reading this article, Willbur Fisk, D.D., President of the Wesleyan University in Connecticut, sent forth a ringing appeal for missionaries to answer to the Macedonian cry of the Flatheads. The excitement produced by this appeal, and its echo through the press and pulpit, became phenomenal. In a short time the contributions to the missionary societies were more than doubled, and at last their managers were obliged to assign the care of the proposed Flathead mission to the branch societies in Connecticut, to prevent the subject from absorbing the whole of the missionary efforts of the people of that denomination.

In the year 1834, Rev. Jason Lee, of Stanstead, Canada, with his nephew, Rev. Daniel Lee, and three laymen, started from Saint Louis to found a mission under the auspices of the American Methodist Episcopal Church, among the Flatheads; but instead of stopping in the Rocky Mountain region, the party proceeded down the Columbia and established their mission in the midst of the French Canadian colony on the Willamette. The reason for this departure from the original plan is related by the historians of the mission and is interesting in this connection :

> In treating of the occasion in which the Oregon mission originated, it was shown that the supposed claim of the Flathead Indians on the first missionary efforts made in the country, were unfounded; and subsequent inquiries had furnished reasons to the missionaries that could not justify even the attempt to commence their mission among them. 1. The means of subsistence in a region so remote and so difficult of access, were, to say the least, very doubtful. It is not a small matter to transport all necessary implements and tools to build houses and raise our provisions, six hundred miles. 2. The smallness of their number.

Frost, "Ten Years in Oregon," 1844, pp. 110-12; Hines, "Oregon : its History," 1851, p. 9; Catlin, "Illustrations of the manners, customs, and conditions of the N. A. Indians," 10th ed., Lond., 1866, ii., pp. 108, 109; Gray, "History of Oregon," 1870, p. 106; Spalding, "Early labors of the missionaries of the A. B. C. F. M. in Oregon," (Senate Ex. Doc. No. 37, 41st Cong., 3d Sess.,) 1871, p. 8; Eells, "History of Indian Missions on the Pacific Coast," 1882, p. 18; Barrows, "Oregon," 1884, pp. 103-13; Bancroft, "History of Oregon," 1886, pp. 54, 55.

Their perpetual wars with the Blackfeet Indians had prevented their increase; and they were, for their safety, confederated with the Nez Percés. 3. Their vicinity to the Blackfeet, as well the white man's enemy as theirs, and who would fall upon the abettors of their foes with signal revenge. 4. A larger field of usefulness was contemplated as the object of the mission than the benefiting of a single tribe. The wants of the whole country, present and prospective, so far as they could be, were taken into account, and the hope of meeting these wants, in the progress of their work, led to the choice of the Walamet location, as a starting point, a place to stand on, and the centre of a wide circle of benevolent action.*

In the year 1835, Rev. Samuel Parker, as missionary, and Marcus Whitman, M.D., as physician, were sent to the Oregon country to examine into the condition of the Indians with the view of establishing missions under the auspices of the American Board of Commissioners for Foreign Missions. The Flatheads, hearing that missionaries were crossing the Laramie plains, Insula, one of the most influential chiefs, with a party, started to meet them en route, but having been attacked by a war party of Crows, they missed them. They, however, overtook them at the rendezvous on Green River, where a number of other Indians were gathered. Rev. Mr. Parker and Dr. Whitman assembled the Flathead and Nez Percés chiefs, and laid the object of their appointment before them. Having received encouragement, especially from the Nez Percés, the envoys held a conference, and it was determined that Rev. Mr. Parker should continue his tour of exploration, whilst Dr. Whitman should return to the States to recommend the sending of missionaries immediately.†

Late in the same year Ignace La Mousse, called "le Vieux Ignace," an Iroquois, from the Caughnawaga mission at Sault Saint Louis, near Montreal, who had settled with the Flatheads eighteen years before, started for Canada with his two sons

---

* Lee and Frost, "Ten Years in Oregon," p. 127.

† "Missionary Herald," 1836, xxxii., p. 71 ; Parker, "Journal of an Exploring Tour," pp. 77, 78.

to have them baptized, but having learned that there were priests at Saint Louis of Missouri * he changed his course toward the banks of the Mississippi. The two boys, one of them aged only ten years, were instructed and baptized by the Jesuit Fathers at their college and received the Christian names of Charles and Francis Xavier. After going to confession, and receiving a promise from Bishop Rosati that, according to his request, missionaries would be sent to his people as soon as possible, Ignace and his sons returned to their home at the headwaters of the Flathead river.†

In 1836 the American Board of Commissioners for Foreign Missions sent a party, consisting of Rev. H. H. Spalding, missionary, and Dr. Whitman, physician and catechist, with their wives as assistant missionaries, and Mr. W. H. Gray, as mechanic, to establish a mission among the Nez Percés and Flatheads. The Nez Percés kept their engagement, made with Dr. Whitman the preceding year, to meet them en route to conduct them to their country, but the Flatheads appear to have changed their minds, for they did not meet them; at least no mention is made of them by the missionary party in

---

* After a careful examination of all the authorities, Catholic, Protestant, and Secularist, cited in this study, and of numerous n..tes, based on the testimony of old Flathead and Nez Percés Indians, reputed wise men among their people, in my possession, I am disposed to conclude that the Indians who visited Saint Louis in 1831 were not Flatheads of the Salish nation, but were Nez Percés of the Sahaptin nation ; and that their visit was induced by worldly considerations rather than by a desire to inquire or learn of God or Religion.

† " Annales de la Propagation de la Foi," 1836, ix., p. 103 ; the same, 1840, xii., p. 275. Bishop Rosati's statement that the Iroquois father was killed by the Sioux on his return to the Rocky Mountains is erroneous ; it was on another journey to Saint Louis that he was killed, as will appear in subsequent pages of this study.

All the Catholic writers who have heretofore written on the visit of " le Vieux Ignace " to Saint Louis, give the year 1834 as the date. A letter of Fr. Theodore de Theux, mentioned in the September, 1836, number of the " Annales " gives the date as the eve of the feast of St. Francis Xavier preceding, and the following transcript from the Baptismal Record kept in the Saint Louis University, kindly furnished me by Very Rev. H. Moeller, S.J., its president, establishes 1835 as the correct date. Unfortunately the original record is not signed :

"1835 2 Decembris Carolus & Franciscus Xavierius filii legitimi Ignatii Patris Indiani ex Tribis vulgo Flatheads solemniter baptizati fueruut."

their reports of their travels in the Indian country. The missionaries were much tempted to go to Puget Sound, among the real Flatheads, to establish their mission, but they finally established themselves on the Upper Columbia,—Rev. Mr. Spalding and wife, among the Nez Percés, at Lapwai ; and Dr. Whitman and wife, among the Cayuses, also of the Sahaptin nation, at Waiilatpu.

The story of the Flatheads having induced the missionary movement to the Oregon country, the Presbyterian missionaries of the Upper Columbia were desirous of taking this tribe under their care, and they accordingly sent Mr. Gray back to the States, in 1837, for assistants to enable him to found a station amongst them.* Instead of taking the usual southerly route, he followed that leading through the Bitter Root valley, in order that he might visit the Flatheads in their own country. The Indians appear to have given him no encouragement, for three of them, with another Indian of a neighboring tribe, under the leadership of " le Vieux Ignace," the Iroquois, started with him and his party for Saint Louis, according to Gray himself, " to urge their claims for teachers to come among them." † This, without tergiversation, means " to renew their petitions for Catholic missionaries." But the valiant Iroquois and his Indian companions never reached their destination, as they were all killed by the Sioux on the Platte River! ‡ "Thus perished," says a judicious writer,

---

* Bancroft, " Hist. of Oregon," i., p. 137.
† Gray, " Hist. of Oregon," p. 173.
‡ Gray's account of the killing of the Flathead party which travelled with him, is as follows : " The party reached Ash Hollow, where they were attacked by about three hundred Sioux warriors, and after fighting for three hours killed some fifteen of them, when the Sioux, by means of a French trader then among them, obtained a parley with Gray and his traveling companions—two young men who had started to go to the States with him. While the Frenchman was in conversation with Gray, the treacherous Sioux made a rush upon the three Flatheads, one Snake and one Iroquois Indian belonging to the party, and killed them. The Frenchman then turned to Gray and told him and his companions they were prisoners. . . . ."—Gray, " Hist. of Oregon," p. 173.
The Flathead tradition on the massacre of their brethren is as follows: " Three Flatheads, a Nez Percés and an Iroquois Indian, whose son, named

referring to Old Ignatius, "he who might justly be called the Apostle of the Flatheads, and through them of many of the Indian tribes of the Rocky Mountains."*

In the following year Very Rev. Francis Norbertus Blanchet, Vicar-General to the Bishop of Quebec, with Rev. Modestus Demers, his associate, crossed the Rocky Mountains through the Athabaska Pass, and descended the Columbia River to Fort Vancouver, where they established the first Catholic mission in the Oregon country. When passing Fort Colville, on November 6, 1838, a large number of Colvilles, Pend d'Oreilles, Spokanes, and Pisquouse, of the Salish nation, of which the Flatheads are the principal tribe, flocked to see the "French Chiefs," of whose coming they had been advised by an express which had come to the Fort a week before. The Abbé Blanchet assembled the Indians several times during his stay of three days at the Fort, instructing them in the elements of religion and confirming them in their good dispositions. At Fort Walla Walla the Cayuse and Walla Walla tribes also assembled to see the Catholic missionaries. The sacrifice of the mass was offered up in their presence, after which the Indians made a formal call on the Abbé Blanchet.

Strange as it may seem, in the summer of 1839 the Flat-

François La Mousee, is still living in the Bitter Root valley, among the Flatheads, started again for St. Louis, but by a misunderstanding they were all killed by the Sioux not far from Fort Laramie. When the delegation reached Fort Laramie, a Protestant minister—so the report runs—whom they met there, joined them. They met with a scouting party of Sioux, who inquiring from the white man, the minister, what tribe the Indians belonged to, and hearing from him that they were Snake Indians, they determined to kill them. The minister thinking that the Sioux were at enmity with the Flat-Heads, and friendly with the Snake Indians, or he himself having been mistaken about them, was the cause of their death. The Iroquois being dressed like a white man, the Sioux told him to get out of the way, that they would not kill him. The brave Iroquois answered that he would not abandon his friends, and if they would not let his companions go free, he was willing to share their fate and die with them. They were thus all killed."—"Historical Notes on Saint Mary's Mission in the Bitter Root Valley," MS., pp. 2-4.

* Van Rensselaer, "Sketch of the Catholic Church in Montana," in "Amer. Cath. Qr. Rev.," xii., p. 494.

heads had not heard of the arrival of the Canadian missionaries, who, it is true, had passed a considerable distance to the north and west of their country. Constant in their devotion to the Christian principles received from their fathers, and persevering in their purpose to obtain missionaries of their faith for their adopted country, two other Iroquois, named Pierre and "le Jeune Ignace," determined to undertake the dangerous journey to Saint Louis, to prevail upon the bishop, if possible to send the missionaries promised to their chief, who had nobly laid down his life for the Faith and for his compatriots. The devotion of the Indians touched the paternal heart of the good bishop, and he gave them a positive promise that a missionary would visit them in the following spring. In a letter to the Father-General of the Society of Jesus in Rome, dated October 20, 1839, Bishop Rosati relates the facts connected with the visit of the Indians, and of his determination to establish a mission in their country. After reviewing the several efforts made by the Flatheads, or rather the Iroquois, to obtain missionaries, he concludes:

Finally, a third deputation has arrived at Saint Louis, after a long journey of three months. It is composed of two Christian Iroquois: these Indians, who know how to speak French, have edified us by their truly exemplary conduct and interested us by their conversation. The Fathers of the College have heard their confessions, and to-day they approached the holy Table at my Mass, in the cathedral church. I afterward administered the sacrament of Confirmation to them, and in an address which preceded and followed the ceremony, I rejoiced with them in their happiness and gave them hopes of soon having a priest.

They will depart to-morrow: one of them will carry the good news promptly to the Flat-Heads; the other will spend the winter at the mouth of Bear river, and in the Spring he will continue his journey with the missionary whom we will send them. Of the twenty-four Iroquois who formerly emigrated from Canada, only four are still living. Not only have they planted the Faith in those wild countries, but they have besides defended it against the encroachments of the Protestant ministers. When these pretended missionaries presented themselves among them, our good

Catholics refused to receive them: "These are not the priests about whom we have spoken to you," they would say to the Flatheads, "these are not the long, black-robed priests who have no wives, who say Mass, who carry the crucifix with them!" For the love of God, my Very Reverend Father, do not abandon these souls!*

IV.

In the year 1835, the Second Provincial Council of Baltimore confided the Indian missions of the country to the Society of Jesus, and the Fathers of the Province of Missouri at once prepared to establish missions among the tribes west of the Mississippi. After making a tour to the Atlantic cities to obtain funds for the purpose, Rev. Charles Felix Van Quickenborne, S.J., superior, started westward from Saint Louis, and founded a mission among the Kickapoos, near the present Fort Leavenworth, in Kansas. This was in 1836, and in his travels the missionary found at the confluence of the Kansas and Missouri Rivers, twelve families who had recently come from the Rocky Mountains with the intention of settling near the missions, in order that they might have their marriages blessed by the Church, and find faculties for saving their souls. Three of the men were Canadians, and they informed Fr. Van Quickenborne that the Flatheads had been instructed by a Canadian doctor, and that they observed many Christian usages, such as the sanctification of the Lord's Day, abstinence, and the fasts prescribed by the Church, and they desired a priest to instruct them in religion. With these Indians, they said, were a large number of Catholic Algonquins and Iroquois, who had come from Canada; they had married Flathead women, and they now wished to have their marriages blessed and their children baptized. The good missionary, relating these facts to another Father of his Order, in Europe, referred to the annual trips of a steam-vessel from

---

* "Annales de la Prop.," xii., pp. 275-77.

Saint Louis to the headwaters of the Missouri, and added that he regarded it a duty to send some one to encourage the Indians in their commendable desires, until something more could be done for them. "I most willingly offer to go myself on this holy expedition," he said with generous enthusiasm.*

At about this time another worthy son of Loyola, then a young priest, whose name is now a household word, synonymous with virtue and charity, in the city of Philadelphia, offered his services to carry the standard of the Cross to the faithful Iroquois and the devoted Flatheads in the Rocky Mountains. I knew him; he was my friend; and I utter his name with reverence—Felix Joseph Barbelin,—" Father " Barbelin, as we all affectionately called him.

Like the Rev. Mr. Condamine, and the Rev. Fr. Van Quickenborne, who in their charity ardently desired to carry the Gospel to the Flatheads, Father Barbelin was never to see these Indians in their mountain home. In a letter to his brother in France, written in the year 1864, Father Barbelin, recurring to events of by-gone days, said, in his characteristic French way of expressing himself:

"Twenty-seven or twenty-eight years ago I offered myself for the Indians of the Rocky Mountains, but our Rev. Father Provincial told me that he had other Indians, and he sent me to Philadelphia to help Fr. Ryder, who had charge of St. Joseph's." † Fortunate Indians of Philadelphia, to have had such a missionary!

In the year 1837 Rev. Peter John De Smet, S.J., who five years before had withdrawn from the American mission to return to his house in French Flanders, on account of ill-health, returned to the United States, and in the following year he established a mission among the Pottawatomies, then located on the Missouri River, near the present city of Omaha.

---

* " Annales de la Prop.," x., pp. 144, 145.

† Donnelly, " A Memoir of Father Felix Joseph Barbelin, S.J.," Phila., 1886, p. 359.

He was preparing to advance his missionary work farther west, into the country of the Sioux, when the Iroquois, Pierre and "le Jeune Ignace," appeared in Saint Louis to again press the claims of the Flatheads for missionaries. The bishop, unable to longer delay complying with their petition, after consulting with the vice-provincial of the Society of Jesus, appointed Fr. De Smet to visit the Flathead country to ascertain the true condition of affairs in that region, and to lay the foundations for a mission, if in his judgment such an enterprise could be undertaken with any degree of success.

It had been designed by the superior of the Jesuits to send two Fathers on the tour of exploration to the Rocky Mountains, but so poor was the diocese of Saint Louis and the Missouri Province of the Society of Jesus at that time, that the necessary amount of $1,000 for an outfit could not be secured, even through the medium of a loan. It was accordingly determined to send Fr. De Smet without a companion.*

Fr. De Smet undertook his tour of exploration in the spring, starting from Saint Louis on April 5th, and from Westport, near Kansas City, on April 30, 1840. Here he joined the annual expedition of the American Fur Company to the rendezvous on Green River, which arrived at that place on June 30th. An escort of Flathead warriors was there awaiting him. On Sunday, July 5th, the day before his departure for the Flathead camp, Fr. De Smet celebrated the holy sacrifice of the mass *sub dio*, on an altar placed on an elevation in the prairie, around which boughs and garlands of wild flowers had been planted in the form of a large semicircle. The missionary addressed the motley crowd of attendants in French and English, and also spoke to the Flatheads and Snakes through interpreters. The Canadians sang a portion of the mass in Latin, and canticles in French, whilst the Indians chanted hymns in their native tongues; and for a long time afterward the place where the edifying ceremony was held,

---

* "Indian Missions," p. 8.

was known as "La prairie de la Messe."* On the following day Fr. De Smet bade adieu to his companions of the plains, and with his Indian escort, and a dozen Canadian hunters, who followed him to have an opportunity of going to their religious duties, started northward through the mountains in the direction of the headwaters of the Henry's Fork of the Snake or Lewis River. After journeying eight days through mountain defiles and rugged valleys infested by bands of warlike Blackfeet and Crows, the party arrived safely in the camp of the Flatheads and Pend d'Oreilles, in the beautiful valley called Pierre's Hole, situated north of the group of peaks known as the Trois Tétons.

"Immediately the whole village was in commotion," related Fr. De Smet to his friend Fr. Barbelin, in a letter describing his reception; "men, women, and children all came to meet me and shake hands, and I was conducted in triumph to the lodge of the great chief Tjolizhitzay (the Big-face). He has the appearance of an old patriarch. Surrounded by the principal chiefs of the two tribes, and the most renowned warriors, he thus addressed me: 'This day Kyleeyou (the Great Spirit) has accomplished our wishes, and our hearts are swelled with joy. Our desire to be instructed was so great, that three times had we deputed our people to the Great Blackgown in St. Louis, to obtain a father. Now, Father, speak, and we will comply with all you will tell us. Show us the road we have to follow, to come to the place where the Great Spirit resides.' Then he resigned his authority to me; but I replied that he mistook the object of my coming among them; that I had no other object in view but their spiritual welfare, that with respect to temporal affairs, they should remain as they were, till circumstances should allow them to settle in a permanent spot. Afterwards we deliberated on the hours proper for their spiritual exercises and instructions. One of

---

* De Smet, Letter to Fr. Barbelin, in "Indian Missions," p. 23; also in his 'Letters and Sketches," p. 15.

the chiefs brought me a bell, with which I might give the signal.

"The same evening about 2,000 persons were assembled before my lodge to recite night prayers in common. I told them the result of my conference with the chiefs; of the plan of instructions which I intended to pursue; and with what disposition they ought to assist at them, etc. Night prayers having been said, a solemn canticle of praise of their own composition, was sung by these children of the mountains, to the Author of their being. It would be impossible for me to describe the emotions I felt at this moment. I wept for joy, and admired the marvellous ways of that kind Providence, who, in His infinite mercy, had deigned to depute me to this poor people, to announce to them the glad tidings of salvation." *

Two months were spent by Fr. De Smet in the camp, living like the Indians, on the products of the chase. During this time he prepared six hundred persons for baptism and instructed two thousand. After describing the every day life of the Indians during his stay, he exclaims: "Who would not think that this could only be found in a well-ordered religious community, and yet it is among Indians in the defiles and valleys of the Rocky Mountains!"

On the eve of the new year, Fr. De Smet was back at the University of Saint Louis, having returned through the Blackfeet, Crow, and Sioux country, instead of by the more southern route.

Immediately after his return a special appeal was made for the necessary funds to establish a permanent mission in the Flathead country, and through the exertions of zealous Fathers of the Society of Jesus, among whom Fr. Barbelin was conspicuous, a sufficient amount was realized to send a well-appointed missionary party. It consisted of Fr. De Smet; Fr. Nicholas Point, a Breton; Fr. Gregory Mengarini, a

---

* De Smet, Letter to Fr. Barbelin, in "Indian Missions," pp. 24, 25.

Roman; Bro. Joseph Specht, an Alsacian; and Bro. Charles Huet and Bro. William Claessens, Belgians, all members of the Society of Jesus. They left Saint Louis by steamer on April 30, 1841, and after seven days' journey on the bosom of the Missouri, arrived at Westport, where they remained until May 10th, awaiting the formation of a party of emigrants which was to travel overland to California. All preparations having been made, the caravan took up its march across the country to the Platte River, whose banks were followed for more than two months.

The Flatheads had promised Fr. De Smet to send a delegation to meet him at the foot of the Wind River Mountains on July 1st, but it was not until after the middle of the month that the caravan reached the height of lands between the Sweet Water and Green Rivers,—the first a tributary of the Platte, which flows eastward into the Missouri, and the latter a tributary of the Colorado of the West, which flows southward into the Gulf of California. The caravan crossed the divide at the South Pass, and John Gray, a noted mountain-man, was sent to a hunters' camp, some distance away, to inform the Indian and Metis hunters of the arrival of the missionaries. The camp of ten lodges was already on the march toward Green River, when Fr. De Smet sent a second messenger to the hunters to request Gabriel Prud'homme, a Canadian Metis, who had been adopted by the Flatheads, and Charles La Mousse, the eldest of the two Iroquois youths who were baptized in Saint Louis, to meet the Fathers before reaching the rendezvous. On the following day the caravan arrived at Green River and soon afterward the hunters also arrived. Here it was learned that the Indian escort had waited for the Fathers until July 16th, when it had been compelled to go on a hunt, their provisions having become completely exhausted.

The missionaries had a wagon and four carts with them, but their horses were so jaded that it was necessary to procure new ones before undertaking the journey through the mountainous region separating them from the Jefferson Fork of the Missouri, where the Flatheads were encamped. It was accordingly determined that Gabriel and another horseman should go to the place where the Flatheads were hunting, four hundred miles away, for fresh horses, whilst François Saxa dit Lamousse would accompany Fr. De Smet to Fort Hall, a post of the Hudson's Bay Company, situated on the Snake or Lewis River, to purchase supplies for the journey.

After travelling several days through the Bear River valley and the plains watered by the Portneuf, Fr. De Smet arrived at Fort Hall on the 15th or 16th of August. At about the time that the caravan reached the fort, Gabriel arrived with a small delegation of Flatheads, under an old chief named Wistelpo, with horses to conduct the missionary party to the Indian camp. On August 19th, leave was taken of the emigrants, and the missionaries wended their way up the Snake River and across the mountains to a large plain, through which passes the Beaver Head River, one of the sources of the Missouri in the Rocky Mountains. Here, on August 30th, they were met by a larger delegation of Flatheads, under chief Ensyla,* who came to escort them to the camp on the Beaver Head, the tribe being on the march toward the plains, on the eastern slope of the mountains, on their summer hunt for buffaloes. Great was the joy of the Fathers and of the Indians at being at last united. After a few days spent in happy intercourse, the missionaries, with an escort of a few lodges of Flatheads, started for the Rocky Mountains, whilst the Indians, promising to join the Fathers in the autumn, at one of two places agreed upon for the mission in the Bitter Root valley, went on their hunt in the plains between the Yellowstone and the Missouri.†

---

* This evidently is the Flathead chief heretofore mentioned as "Insula," in connection with Rev. Mr. Parker's conference with the Indians at the rendezvous on Green River in 1835, as related on page 72 of this paper.

† "Historical Notes on Saint Mary's Mission in the Bitter Root Valley," MS., pp. 8, 9.

Fr. De Smet with his party now ascended the slope of the mountains, recrossed the divide through Deer Lodge Pass, and descended into the prairie below. They now followed Hell Gate River,—to which the Fathers gave the name of St. Ignatius,—and on September 24th they arrived at the stream upon whose banks they were to found their first mission. This was the Bitter Root River,—a tributary of the Flathead or Clark River, which flows in a northwesterly direction until it falls into the great Columbia of Oregon. Several days were spent in following the stream toward its source, until the place designated by the Indians was reached. Here, on October 3, 1841, the feast of the Holy Rosary, Fr. De Smet, with his heroic band of missionaries, in the presence of a few Canadians, Iroquois, and Flatheads, planted a cross on the river bank, and after chanting the "Vexilla regis," took solemn possession of the surrounding country in the name of the Christian religion, and laid the foundation of the first Catholic Church in Montana and in the Upper Columbia country. To the river, the highest peak overlooking the valley and the mission, was given the name of Saint Mary.* Thus, ten years after the visit of the four Columbian Indians to Saint Louis, of Missouri, was established the Flathead mission of the Rocky Mountains.

V.

Nearly fifty years have passed since Fr. De Smet and his noble band of Jesuit missionaries planted the standard of the Christian religion in the wilderness under the protection of Mary, the Mother of Christ. What wondrous changes have taken place in the intervening time! From that one lonely mission have sprung a dozen others, not only among the several tribes of the Salish nation, but also among the fierce

---

* De Smet, "Origin, Progress, and Prospects of the Catholic Mission," p. 5; "Historical Notes on St. Mary's Mission," MS., p. 10.

Blackfeet and Crows, the traditional enemies of the Flatheads! Then, the place is no longer a boundless waste, for the iron-horse now passes with lightning speed through the Bitter Root valley, stopping at intervals to receive passengers at the station of De Smet. But the great Black-Robe is no longer there! his mortal remains sleep on the banks of the Mississippi, and his monument, as Evangelizer and Pacificator of the Indians, stands in his native city in far-off Belgium—all has changed, save the fame of the Founder of the Mission, which proclaims him the Apostle of the Rocky Mountains.

SIR JOHN JAMES OF CRISHALL, ESSEX, BART.

THE BENEFACTOR OF THE PENNSYLVANIA MISSIONS.

BY JOHN GILMARY SHEA.

It is a curious fact that an English gentleman who stands pre-eminent as the founder of a fund for the support of missions in this country, and whose benefactions continued for a century, has been comparatively unknown. The fund bore his name, but of him personally, little has been recorded. In the last century the Rev. Patrick Smyth published an absurd story in regard to it, and in our time strange theories have been set up.

While writing "The Catholic Church in Colonial Days," researches left me in doubt whether the benefactor of Catholics in Pennsylvania was Sir John James, of Heston, or his namesake and contemporary of Crishall. Investigations not then completed produce the conviction that he was Sir John James of Crishall, Essex: and it is purposed gathering here such facts in regard to him and the fund as may aid further studies.

A family from Holland bearing the name of Hacstrecht, from a place of that name in the Low Countries, settled in England about the reign of Henry VIII., and in time adopted the name of James. John James of this family acquired the manor of Christhallbury, in the County of Essex, and erected Christhall Hall. He was knighted by Charles II. on the 14th of May, 1665. His arms were argent, a chevron sable between three fers de moulin, transverse of the second.* He

---

* Burke gives the arms of the Baronet as : Quarterly, first and fourth argent, two bars crenelle or counter embattled gules ; second and third argent, three fer de molins barways, sa.

left the estate to his nephew, James Cane, of London, who assumed the name of James, and was created a baronet on the 28th of June, 1680. He died on the 19th of May, 1736, and was succeeded by his son, Sir John James, Bart., who was born, apparently, about 1694.*

Sir John, by reading the life of Saint Francis Xavier, probably in Dryden's elegant translation, began to form a higher idea of the Catholic religion. The Rt. Rev. Bishop Challoner converted him to the Catholic faith, and Sir John, by a secret trust in his will, as was then the custom, gave four thousand pounds to the Vicar-Apostolic of London, to be held as a fund, directing that of the income, £40 were to be applied toward maintaining " two Priests for London to assist the poor," and the rest for missioners in Pennsylvania. Sir John James of Chrishall, who died Sept. 28, 1741, at the age of 47,† is apparently the convert of Bishop Challoner, and establisher of the fund, who is said to have died Sept. 28, 1742, the discrepancy being of a single figure.

Sir John James of Crishall died unmarried, and was buried at Crishall. He left his estate by will to charitable uses, but the next heir, Haestricht James, after a long litigation, had the bequests set aside as contrary to the statute of George II., and obtained the estate.‡

As any bequest for Catholic purposes would have been void, it would be necessary to make the bequest to some person absolutely. In this case it was in all probability made to Richard Challoner, and accordingly, as a personal bequest, was legal. The lawsuits would necessarily cause delay. This seems to harmonize with the facts in relation to the fund.

---

* Philip Morant, "The History and Antiquities of the County of Essex," London, 1768, il., pp. 603, 604. Townsend, "Catalogue of Knights from 1660 to 1760," London, 1833, p. 38.

† "Gentleman's Magazine," London, 1741, p. 554. "Sep. 28. Sir John James, Bart., aged 47."

‡ Burke, " A Genealogical and Heraldic History of the Extinct and Dormant Baronetcies," etc., London, 1844, p. 280.

The first payment of income noted in Bishop Challoner's Ledger was made by the Executors to him from Michaelmas, 1748, and the principal was paid to him in February, 1751.

The whole £4,000 was at first invested by the Bishop in East India 3½ per cents., but half of it was soon sold out and invested at Paris in the French India Company's stock.*

After deducting the fixed amount set apart for the London poor, the residue was forwarded in Colonial times to the Superior of the Jesuit mission in Maryland, who divided it between the missions of St. Mary's at Philadelphia, St. Paul's at Cushenhopen, St. John Nepomucene at Lancaster, and St. John Francis Regis at Conewago. The first allusion to it is in a letter of Father Henry Neale from Philadelphia in 1746. The amount sent to America was at first £100.

In 1765 each of the four Pennsylvania missions received £20 from the income of the fund, and this continued till the beginning of the French Revolution, when the part of the fund invested in French securities decreased so much in value that it was sold and the amount reinvested in English securities, the loss by the operation being about one-third of the Pennsylvania portion. In consequence, the Pennsylvania income, which till 1792 had been £80, became in 1793 only £59.10s.8d.†

---

* Letter of W. A. Canon Johnson. Bishop Challoner's Ledger brings the account down to 1780.

† Memorandum in handwriting of Father George Hunter, 1765; Memorandum in handwriting of Bishop Carroll, 1795. Bishop Douglass wrote to Bishop Carroll, Feb. 5, 1793 : "You are doubtless sensible that a great part of our property was vested in the French funds. When things began to be violent in that country, it was judged most advisable to sell out as much of that property as could be sold, and place it in some more secure hands. Accordingly, amongst the rest, we sold those actions from which near two-thirds of Sir John James', or what we call the German funds derived their support. But the market price of actions was then reduced so low, the English Funds had increased in value in the same proportion as the French funds were depressed ; and the price of exchange for bills of remittance of money to England was so very considerably against us, that by one way or another the produce of those actions which in the year 1785 and 1786 produced about £70 per annum, being now placed in one of our stocks (4 p. cents.), produce only £48.10.8 p^r annum, which, with £51 p. an. in the same hands it was in before, makes £99.10.8, the whole pro-

It subsequently declined to £55, and for a long time never exceeded it.*

The Rev. Patrick Smyth, an Irish clergyman who had been for a time in the United States, published a pamphlet in Dublin in 1788, in which he gives this queer account of Sir John James' fund:

About fifty or sixty years ago an English gentleman of the name of James, a Protestant of the Church of England, had an occasion to visit Philadelphia. Charmed with the admirable discipline and regularity which was then established in that beautiful city, he lamented the deplorable state of religion among its inhabitants. As a good Protestant he regretted that the Pennsylvanians rejected, in effect, the necessity of baptism. His ardent desire for their conversion did not cool on the extensive bosom of the Atlantic. Upon his arrival in England their sad infatuation engrossed his thoughts and wrung his heart with anguish.

He spoke incessantly of his poor mistaken friends. He did more. He chose twelve Protestant clergymen, whom he engaged at a certain salary, to instruct his much esteemed acquaintances in the New World. He entered into articles with them, and tied them down to that strict degree of temperance still observable in the Confederated States. The dishes were specified, and the quantity of wine and other liquors mentioned with the utmost scrupulosity.

The preliminary articles being thus ratified, Mr. James, after having sold the greatest part of his property in England, embarked with his apostles for the capital of Quakerism. His breast glowed with ecstasy at the thoughts of his approaching success. That fashionable indifference for all religion which is affected by every deistical coxcomb, was then little known in the world, nor was the abused name of universal benevolence perverted to the worst purposes of infidelity. . . . . The honest Quakers received their visitors with unaffected tokens of cordiality. They expressed their acknowledgments to their old friend for his zeal and

---

duce of Sir John James' establishment. And as he ordered that in the first place £40 per annum should be paid to persons for services in London, you see there will remain only £259.10.18 p^r an. to be remitted to you for Pennsylvania."

* Campbell, "Life and Times of Archbishop Carroll," "U. S. Cath. Mag.," iv., p. 255.

heard his reverend associates enforce the grand object of their mission. But they heard them unmoved. Whether it was owing to the want of perseverance in the ministers, or to a levity of behavior in some of them, they made little or no impression on the meek disciples of Penn. Perhaps, too, the frugality of Mr. James' table and the necessary abstemiousness which became irksome to English appetites, contributed to render this extraordinary project abortive. Be this as it may, the twelve missionaries, like the Israelites of old, sighed for the flesh-pots of Egypt, and in a few months after their first landing re-embarked for Europe, leaving their patron on the banks of the Delaware to vent his disappointment to the waves.

In this dejected state of mind he met a German with whom he had formerly some mercantile dealings. He complained to him of the desertion of his missionaries. The blunt German replied that it was not at all surprising if attention were paid to the many inconveniences the gentlemen had to encounter; that English divines, accustomed, perhaps, to luxury, could but ill brook the scanty provisions afforded at a Quaker's ordinary; that the Germans, his countrymen, were not so much in the habit of faring sumptuously every day; that if the administration of the sacrament of baptism to the good Quakers was all he sought for, the priests of his own religion (for the German was a Catholic) held it also essential for salvation; that, moreover, the Jesuits were fitted by their peculiar education to accommodate themselves to the manners of any moral people, and that if they were effectually encouraged in Pennsylvania, he would pledge himself they should attend to their functions with assiduity and perseverance.

Foreign as this purpose may have been to Mr. James' original plan, he cheerfully acceded to it. He advanced a small salary to enable four German Jesuits to preach in Pennsylvania, and signed articles binding himself, his heirs, etc., forever to pay the same annually out of his estate in England. I could only learn that this good man shortly after returned to Europe, and that his foundation, through the wise management of the Jesuits in England, is considerably increased.*

In the reply which the Very Rev. John Carroll, afterward

---

* Smyth, "The Present State of the Catholic Missions conducted by the Ex-Jesuits in North America," Dublin, 1788.

Bishop and Archbishop of Baltimore, prepared to Smyth's virulent pamphlet, he says:

> The relation of Mr. James' foundation is likewise discordant from the fact. From Mr. Smyth's account one would imagine that Mr. James was a Protestant, and lived in America when he solicited for German Jesuits; the fact was otherwise. He then was a Catholic in England, and had become a Catholic by meeting accidentally with the life of St. Francis Xavier, and afterwards by conversing with the late excellent Dr. Challoner. It is unnecessary to follow him thro' all his mistakes on this subject.*

That so extraordinary an event as the arrival of an English gentleman with twelve Anglican clergyman on a mission to convert the Quakers, should have escaped the notice of all historical scholars, is impossible. That is a pure romance.

That Sir John James entered into any arrangement with the Jesuits in England or paid salaries, must be also relegated to the domain of fable. Mr. Foley, in his exhaustive search of the records of the English province, found no note of any relation between Sir John James and the order, and a special examination made for me at Stonyhurst came to a similar result.

Converted by Bishop Challoner, Sir John left the fund to him for two objects: the first, absolute; the second, the Pennsylvania mission, contingent. The fund never at any time passed into the hands of the Jesuits. And of German Jesuits in Pennsylvania prior to 1741 there is no trace.

What the exact terms of the trust were in regard to the Pennsylvania mission is not known: but it was, apparently, to the purport that it was to be applied to the mission at Lancaster and others in Pennsylvania; for it has always been regarded as attaching to Lancaster, and when in our time (1886) Lancaster became part of the diocese of Harrisburg, the Sir John James fund inured to the benefit of that diocese.

---

* Carroll's Reply to Smyth.

The whole establishment of the fund, therefore, seems to point to some missionary work among the Germans at Lancaster prior to 1741, the year in which Sir John James died, for the fund was known also as "The German Fund."

In 1874 the income of the fund applicable to Pennsylvania had risen again to the old figure of £80 a year. In July, with the approval of Bishop Wood, of Philadelphia, the capital was sold in London; and (together with all unpaid interest) the proceeds of the sale were paid to Bishop Wood, to be invested by him for the purposes of the founder of the fund. Now the Pennsylvania portion of the Sir John James bequest is in the hands of the Bishop of Harrisburg.

CATHOLIC AND ANTI-CATHOLIC ITEMS FROM NEW YORK PAPERS, 1765—1778.

EXTRACT OF A LETTER FROM FORT CUMBERLAND, IN NOVA SCOTIA, AUGUST 26, 1765.

"BOSTON, September 12.—There has been a commotion among the Indians, chiefly about this place, where there has been the St. John's River, and some from Pasmaquady and Mickmakas, from about the middle of July to this time. There has been canoes here, and at Bay Vert, to the number of 40 or fifty at once; they say they had the promise of a French priest to be at Pigto this summer, to which place many of them went; part of the St. John's tribe that came up the Bay of Fundy, remained here, and sent three men to Pigto for intelligence; they appeared somewhat discontented, but behaved as civilly as Indians can be expected to do; they have alarmed the inhabitants by their assembling, in such a manner, that they left their homes, and got under cover of the garrison, but were no otherways damaged. We have sent from this place to Pigto, where the Indians were all peaceable and quiet, and no French priest there; so every person has returned to their respective habitations."—(" Supplement Extraordinary N. Y. Gazette or Weekly Post Boy," September 19, 1765, No. 1185.)

"QUEBEC, July 3.—Saturday the 28th ult., at 11 o'clock P.M., arrived in this city from London, on board the 'Commerce,' Capt. Johnson, Mr. Briand, Bishop of Quebec, for the Roman Catholics, who manifested on this Occasion all their Affection for what concerns their Religion. On the Day following, at 5 o'clock in the morning, the Bells of all their Churches announced his Arrival to the whole City, which gave such general Satisfaction to the Canadians, that many

of them were seen to shed Tears thro' Joy. It was really affecting to see them congratulate each other wherever they met, and to hear them incessantly say one to another, ' It is then true that we have a Bishop; God hath taken pity of us:' And to see them afterwards run in Crowds to the Parish Church to see this Bishop, whom they look upon as the Support of their Religion, and as a Pledge of the King's paternal Goodness to them. In Fact, at the same Time that they publicly bless the Lord for having given them a Bishop, they loudly proclaim their Gratitude to his Majesty for having attended to their Requests: It is likely that this Favour conferred on the Canadians by the King, will effectually attach them to the British Government. It is also very pleasing to them, to have received on this Occasion the Congratulations of several Persons of Note of our Nation, who indeed seem to partake of their Joy. And we doubt not, but that the Canadians, who appear to be very susceptible of Gratitude, will by those Means become more firmly united to us."
—(" N. Y. Gazette or Weekly Post Boy," July 31, 1766, No. 1230.)

" LONDON, September 28.—Private letters from North-America inform, that some Spanish Jesuits had found means to make their escape from Mexico, to a neighboring English colony, with near two millions in money and jewels."—(" Supplement N. Y. Journal or General Advertiser," January 7, 1768, No. 1305.)

" LONDON, November 14.—They write from Quebec, that several Spanish Jesuits from South America had lately arrived there, said to be very rich in money and Jewels, where they proposed to shelter themselves from the further persecutions of fortune, by taking the Oaths to his Britannick Majesty."
—(" N. Y. Journal or General Advertiser," January 21, 1768, No. 1307.)

EXTRACT FROM A WHIP FOR THE "AMERICAN WHIG," BY TIMOTHY TICKLE, ESQ.

No. VIII.

" To answer the same pious Purpose, of casting an Odium upon the Church, she is represented by the 'American Whig' as being inclined to Popery; because Mr. Houdin was admitted to officiate as a Clergyman, without Re-ordination. Mr. Houdin, it is true, was born and educated in the Popish Religion, and ordained by a Popish Bishop in France, he left Canada, and came to New-York, where after some Time, he openly in the Face of the Congregation in Trinity Church, in this City, renounced and abjured the Errors of Popery, and was admitted to officiate in the Church without Re-ordination."—(" N. Y. Gazette and Weekly Mercury," May 23, 1768, No. 864.)

" PHILADELPHIA, December 19.—Last Tuesday died in this City, the Rev. F. Luke O'Reiley, of St. Croix. He was a Gentleman of an amiable Character, who came to the Continent some Time ago for the Benefit of his Health; but (being too far gone) his Disorder was too powerful to be removed by the most skilful Physicians who attended him."—(" N. Y. Gazette and Weekly Mercury," December 26, 1768, No. 895.)

" WEST-CHESTER, July 23.—A Large Watch, made by Davis, in the Village,* pretty much of the complexion of that worn by our good Proctor: 'twas put into the hands of an anti-catholic about three years ago, named P. M——r, who it seems broke into gaol; the messenger who carried it him, no better. The time when Mr. Heron refused to return no more than 3 coppers change out of a 16s. 3d. bill for repairs, is forgot by the poor catholic owner, who has lost the said Village-made watch. Now the point is to See if a body could Hear of her.

" ☞ Tell Mr. Rivington there was a tree struck with thunder† here yesterday: and two cows, the property of

---

* Dublin.   † Lightning rather.

John Oakley, struck dead about 200 yards from the tree which was a very large one, and is burned down."—(" Rivington's N. Y. Gazette," July 28, 1774, No. 67.)

"LONDON, September 9.—We are assured, from very respectable authority, that General Carlton is gone over to his government of Quebec, with positive orders to embody THIRTY THOUSAND Roman Catholic Canadians immediately as a militia.

"The militia of Canada, by the laws of that country, now fully established by the Quebec Act, are under the same military law as regular troops. General Carlton is universally allowed to be the most skilful officer in the British service.

"With so formidable a Popish army, commanded by so able a General in the service of the Crown, in a profound peace, and entirely without the control of Parliament; is it not high time for Protestants of all denominations in these kingdoms, to take some effectual measures for the security of their civil and religious liberties?

"Is it not expressly contrary to law, for a Popish army to be inlisted in the service of the Crown of Great Britain?"— (" N. Y. Journal or General Advertiser," November 3, 1774, No. 1661.")

"TO THE BR—ISH MINISTRY ON THE QUEBEC BILL.

"WHAT ye have gain'd of late let others tell,
Who know the country, and your motives well;
What ye have lost all see. With all your arts
Ye've lost unnumber'd honest English hearts,
Of value more than all these Popish parts."

"EMIGRANTS.

"THREE things we seek abroad, flying or fled
From hence—Religion, liberty and bread,
Grant us, oh heav'n! a favourable wind,
Papists and pensioners may stay behind."

"ON THE BISHOP'S VOTING FOR THE QUEBEC BILL.

"A WISH.

"When shall we see again religion's power,
Seven English Bishops going to the Tow'r!

"On the Quebec Bill, and other late measures,
THAT nation never can continue long,
Where bribes determine what is right or wrong;
Whose faith with change of place must go to wreck,
Here Protestants, but Papists at Quebec,
Where none must say, Sire taken by decoy,
Yourself and your's hast'ning to destroy!
All this is true, but say so, if you dare,
Truth does not pass for truth in ev'ry air."
—("N. Y. Journal or General Advertiser," November 3, 1774, No. 1661.)

EXTRACT OF A LETTER FROM QUEBEC, APRIL 27, 1775.

"NEW YORK, May 15.—The Governor's Commission from the King was read here on Monday the 24th Instant; he has very ample Powers, he choses all the Members of the Council himself; and can discharge them at Pleasure; can oblige what Number of his Majesty's Subjects in Canada he pleases to march against any Enemy or supposed Enemy when he shall think fit, can build Forts or do anything else with the People's Money and demolish them at Pleasure. In short he is possessed of absolute and despotic Power only with this Difference (if it is any) that the Majority of the Council (who hold their Seats as before mentioned) must approve of his measures. The Council consist of 23 Persons, 7 of them Roman Catholics."—("N. Y. Gazette and Weekly Mercury," May 15, 1775, No. 1231.)

EXTRACT OF A LETTER FROM MONTREAL DATED MAY 6, 1775.

"PHILADELPHIA, May 31.—In consequence of the collections for those who suffered by the fire in 1765, in this place, after the last distribution was made, there remained in the hands of the Committee in London about 90 l. sterling, with which they purchased a bust of his present Majesty, and sent it to this place, to be put up in some public part of the town, with a brass plate on the pedestal, setting forth his liberal donation to the people on that melancholy occasion. It was fixed up on the public parade some little time after its arrival here, by the common consent of the people; but by no authority whatever. In the night of the 30th of April and 1st of May, on which day the Quebec Bill took effect, some mischievous persons blacked the face of this bust, hung a chaplet round its neck, with a cross, pendant, and a label, Behold the Pope of Canada, or the fool of England. This conduct incensed many, and a proclamation was made by no authority, offering a reward to any one that would discover the perpetrators. . . . ."—("Supplement N. Y. Journal or General Advertiser," June 8, 1775, No. 1692.)

" Now SELLING AT BELL'S BOOK STORE, in Third-street,
" Philadelphia,
" A MANUAL OF CATHOLIC PRAYERS,
" AND OTHER
" CHRISTIAN DEVOTIONS,
" For the use of those ROMAN CATHOLICS who ardently aspire after salvation.

" N. B. At said Bell's may be had HOLY BIBLES for the pocket or the family, with the psalms of the Presbyterians."
—("Pa. Evening Post," December 28, 1778, No. 560.)

MEETINGS OF THE UNITED STATES CATHOLIC HISTORICAL SOCIETY.

A PUBLIC Meeting of the United States Catholic Historical Society was held at 20 West 27th Street, on Jan. 19, 1888.

Dr. Charles Carroll Lee was called to the chair; there were present the Recording Secretary, F. D. Hoyt; members of the Executive Council, Rev. R. L. Burtsell, D.D., Rev. James H. McGean, W. A. Sloane, John Gilmary Shea, and members Rev. Arthur Donnelly, and V. Rev. Charles A. Vissani. After the reading of the minutes of the last meeting and reports, a paper entitled "Pope-Day in America" was read by John Gilmary Shea.

At a meeting of the Society, held at 20 West 27th Street, on February 21:

Frederick R. Coudert, President, in the chair; F. D. Hoyt, Recording Secretary; Rev. R. L. Burtsell, D.D., James H. McGean, Charles Carroll Lee, M.D., John Gilmary Shea, W. A. Sloane, Very Rev. Charles A. Vissani, Rev. Arthur Donnelly, Joseph Thoron, Rev. Gabriel A. Healy, Thomas Addis Emmet, D.D., LL.D.; quorum of members.

After reading the minutes of the last meeting, a vote was taken on the proposed amendments to the Constitution, which were adopted.

The Librarian reported the following contributions to the Library:

From John Murphy & Co., Baltimore:

> The Foundation of Maryland. By Bradley T. Johnson.
> The Great Seal of Maryland. By Clayton C. Hall.
> Proceedings of the Maryland Historical Society on the 150th anniversary of the settlement of Baltimore.
> Sir George Calvert, Baron of Baltimore. By L. W. Wilhelm.
> Local Institutions of Virginia. By Edward Ingle.

From John G. Shea:
  The Latest Studies in Indian Reservations. By J. B. Harrison.
  Collections of the Wisconsin Historical Society. Vol. VII.
From the Society:
  The New England Historic-Genealogical Register for July and October.
From the Publishers:
  The Ave Maria for 1887.
From Hoffman Bros., Milwaukee:
  Catholic Directory for 1888.
From the Iowa Historical Society:
  Annals for 1887.

The election of officers for the year 1888 was then held, and the following were elected:

Honorary President, Most Rev. M. A. CORRIGAN; President, FREDERIC R. COUDERT; Vice-President, CHARLES CARROLL LEE, M.D.; Recording Secretary, FRANCIS D. HOYT; Corresponding Secretary, MARC F. VALLETTE, LL.D.; Librarian, JOHN G. SHEA, LL.D.; Treasurer, PATRICK FARRELLY. Trustees: Rev. R. L. BURTSELL, D.D., WILLIAM LUMMIS, CHARLES W. SLOANE, Rev. JAMES H. MCGEAN, R. DUNCAN HARRIS, J. FAIRFAX McLAUGHLIN, CHARLES G. HERBERMANN, LL.D. Councillors, Rev. JAMES J. DOUGHERTY, V. Rev. CHARLES A. VISSANI, O.S.F., JOHN A. MOONEY, JAMES S. COLEMAN, JOHN D. KEILY, JOSEPH J. MARRIN.

The paper of the evening, "The Acadians before their Dispersion," by Rev. H. R. Casgrain, of Quebec, was read by Dr. Charles Carroll Lee.

The following gentlemen were duly elected members of the Society:

CHARLES V. FORNES, 458 Broadway, New York; Rev. PATRICK HENNESSY, St. Patrick's Church, Jersey City, N. J.

NOTES.

WHEN WAS ST. GENEVIEVE FOUNDED?—In F. A. Rozier's pamphlet notice of St. Genevieve, 1735 is given as the birth year of the village, which Mr. Shea, in his history of the American Catholic Church, adopts, in the absence of other authority, no one, it would seem, having thought it worth while to investigate the question. I asked Genl. Rozier why he fixed upon that date? and he made answer: "They say so." That is, it rests upon a floating tradition. The tradition is not to be followed, as I propose to show.

St. Genevieve, it may be well to remark, after Arkansas Post, the oldest settlement on the west bank of the Mississippi, is situated not far from Fort Chartres and Kaskaskia. A hamlet on the bottom land, two or three miles below the present town, grew into a village of some importance. It was ruined by the flood of 1785, which rose to the eaves of some of the houses, and in part washed away. Most of the inhabitants removed to the bluff beyond the reach of a similar accident, and began a new settlement; but as some clung to their old dwellings, and reoccupied them after the subsidence of the waters, the spot was called the "old village," and retained the name for many years. It is used to-day by way of distinction. Of course it is the "old village," which no longer exists, of which there is question in this investigation.

Pittman writes: "The first settlers of this village (St. Genevieve) removed about twenty-eight years ago from Cascasquias." As by "ago," the author appears to mean previous to 1769-70, his data would fix 1741-2 as the date of the removal: but "about" may be stretched to allow us to say 1745. Pittman was an English officer, who came to the Illinois not long before the date of his book; and on the point in question spoke from hearsay.

Father Vivier, a Jesuit Missioner stationed in the Illinois country, writing from there in 1750 (Let. Ed., vii., p. 100), uses these words: "There are in this part of Louisiana five French villages." The names of these villages are well known, and will be given presently. He describes the Saline just below the site of St. Genevieve, speaks of the lead mines back of it, but neither by direct statement, nor by allusion, allows us to presume the existence of the sixth village. One may fairly assume from this writer's account, that St. Genevieve had not yet a place on the face of the earth.

Bossu, a French officer, who came up to Fort Chartres from New Orleans with Macarty, writing from the Illinois, May, 1753, says (i., p. 109): "The five villages of the French (in the Illinois) are Kaskaskia, Fort Chartres, St. Philip, Cahokia, and Prairie du Rocher: there is now a sixth, called St. Genevieve." By "the five villages" he means those well known since many years, and called "French" to distinguish them from the Indian towns in their vicinity; and the words *il y en a maintenant* un sixième appelé *Sainte Geneviève*, I think evidently imply a settlement of very recent date, thus confirming Vivier's excluding testimony.

Lastly, we find it stated ("Carayon Ban." p. 14): "Since fifteen years there was established at a league distance from Kaskaskia, on the opposite shore of the Mississippi, a new village under the name of St. Genevieve"; and as the authority quoted is dated 1764, it fixes 1749 as the year of the beginning of the settlement. Still, I think that what the document says, fairly interpreted, would allow a margin of from 1748 to 1752 for the commencement of the hamlet. The Carayon Relation is from the pen of one of the Illinois Jesuits who had personal knowledge of the matters about which he was writing.

I know of no other authorities.

It is assumed that they to whom this argument is addressed know that the west bank of the Mississippi was as much a part of the District of the Illinois as the east.

The testimony of the last three witnesses, to my mind, overrides Pittman's. They concur in fixing the date of the beginning of St. Genevieve at about 1750. According to the canon of historic proof we should hold this to be the true date until it can be shown to be wrong.

OSCAR W. COLLET.

ST. LOUIS, 1888.

REV. R. MOLYNEUX'S MEMOIR OF REV. FERDINAND FARMER.—
"A biographical memoir of this distinguished missionary (Fr. Farmer), written by Father Molyneux, has been sent to Father Termanini at Viterbo" (Abp. Carroll to Rev. C. Plowden). "Termanini was a personal friend of Abp. Carroll, and the Bibliotheca Soc. Jesu says of him, 'that after the suppression he wrote the lives of eminent Jesuits, but dying before the publication of his work, it was given for preservation to Clarissimo Josepho Mariæ Sozzi.' No one seems ever to have heard of this gentleman, and accordingly I fear that, like many other books which neither time, nor favor, nor money can replace, this too is lost forever."—Letter of Father Meredith, S.J., April 13, 1843.

EARLY PRIESTS AT ALBANY.—Feb. 22, 1807, Rev. Mr. Hurley. Nov. 11, 1808, Rev. James Burke (or Bushe), pastor of the Catholic Church at Albany, died there. Jan., 1813, Rev. Paul McQuaid, at Albany. He was ordained in Canada, Sept. 23, 1808; was at St. John's, N. B., in 1816; in Newfoundland in 1818; at Boston in 1821.

PRIESTS AT FREDERICK, MD.—NOTES FROM BISHOP BRUTÉ.—
"In conversation with Sister Joanna Smith, formerly of Frederick, about 60 years old, (says Mr. Bruté in a manuscript dated January 6, 1833,) the pastors of Frederick, within her memory, were, before her birth, some coming from Georgetown, Father Leonard Neale (a different person from the Abp.)

"1st. 1744, Father Frambach.

"2d. 178-, Father Cerfoumont—retired to Conewago.

"3d. 179-, Rev'd Mr. Ryan—moved to Hagerstown in 18—, died in Emmittsburg, in 1817 or '18.

"4th. Rev'd Mr. Dubois. in 1794.

"Sister Joanna remembers that Father Frambach could not yet safely attend the Catholics scattered through Virginia, but was sometimes hotly pursued by the Protestants. Once they surrounded, during the night, the house in which he slept. He escaped, reached the stable, and fled on his horse, they following in sight until he arrived at the Ferry of the Potomac, and got safely to the Maryland shore. Since he dared not sleep in houses, he always slept by his horse in the stable, whenever travelling in Virginia for his ministry.

"Sister Joanna often heard her parents speak of the times of persecution before the Revolution. Her mother was an O'Neale, who said that in St. Mary's County they had yet hiding holes in the walls, where the priest used to secrete himself if pursued.

"Mrs. Brooke (Aunt Chloe) has thus added to and corrected Sister Joanna's statement: 'Before Father Frambach, there was a Rev'd Mr. Smith from Ireland, who remained but one year, seemed too worldly, was removed by Arch. Carroll, and returned to Ireland, where he wrote a pamphlet against the Clergy of this country, for which he was censured by his Bishop. A copy of the pamphlet reached Abp. Carroll.

"'Rev'd Mr. Cerfoumont did not live in Fred'k, but attended it from Conewago, once a month.

"'(Fred'k attended from Conewago, 46 miles, as late as 1790 or 92.)'"

AN EARLY PRIEST AT PRINCETON, N. J.—Died at Princeton, New Jersey, February 12, 1807, Rev. Anthony Schmidt, a respectable Catholic Priest, formerly a curate at Guadaloupe, aged 75 years.—"N. Y. Spectator," Feb. 25, 1807.

REV. RAPHAEL FITZPATRICK.—Died, at Philadelphia, suddenly, on Wednesday (May 25) evening last, the Rev. Rapheal Fitzpatrick, one of the clergymen of the Roman Catholic Church in that city. —"New York Spectator," June 1, 1803.

ANECDOTE OF PRINCE GALLITZIN, BY RT. REV. MICHAEL O'CONNOR.—"Rev. Mr. Rafferty was here a few days ago. He told me amongst other things that he heard from Mr. G. himself, that he received at one time a pressing invitation from the late William, King of Holland, with whom he had been well acquainted in his youth, to go spend the remainder of his days with him. The attachment of the old man, however, to his Allegheny mission would not allow him to think of exchanging it for the Court. His attachment to his people was once curiously illustrated. The late Matthew Carey, of Philadelphia, once asked him how he could get on without society, on the top of the mountains. He was quite indignant at the implied insult offered his people, and he begged leave to assure the gentleman that he had the best kind of society there."—Letter, Pittsburgh, Feb. 15, 1856.

REMINISCENCES OF REV. JOHN SHANAHAN.—" Bishop Connolly made one visitation of his diocese in the year 1822: when he visited St. Mary's, in Albany, Rev. Richard Bulger being then the pastor, and where he received Mr. Keating Rawson, of Lansingburg, into the Church, and Miss Eldridge, of the same place; visited also St. John's Church, of Utica, and enjoyed the hospitality of John C. Devereux, and thence to Rome where he was cordially received by the respected proprietor of that town, viz., Dominic Lynch, Esq. In 1819, through the exertions, etc., of DeWitt Clinton, the Erie Canal began to be made; and this was the first cause of encouragement to Irish Emigrants to New York. Consequently we find the Catholics increase along the line of that commercial route. The first church in Bishop Connolly's time, that was built, was St. John's, in Utica, and attended by Rev'd John Farnan: the second was St. John's in Paterson, by Rev'd Richard Bulger, and about the same time the Church in Carthage, on the Black River, was raised, the congregation of which were chiefly, if not all, Canadian French Catholics. Simultaneously with the Church in Utica, was erected St. Patrick's Church, in Rochester, then a small village. This last-mentioned Church was erected by the zeal of Rev'd Patrick Kelly, who visited many stations all along the Canal, east to Auburn, and west to Buffalo. The said Rev'd P. Kelly is now on the mission in Michigan. The last Church built under the auspices of Bishop Connolly, was St. James' on Jay Street, Brooklyn, Long Island, and where, on a temporary altar of a few boards clumsily laid together, your humble servant celebrated his first mass, about the 20th or 22d of September, 1823. In the next place it must be understood that in those days every priest had appointed catechism classes before divine service on Sundays, and had Rosary Societies not only in each church, but also in most of the Stations attached to them. Then the congregations were small, but they were zealous and faithful."—Letter, March 28, 1856.

A HEME CATECHISM.—Father Geronimo de Zarate Salmeron is one of the early writers of this country in the Indian languages. He composed a Catechism entitled " La Doctrina cristiana con todas las demas cosas importantes al ministerio," in the language of the Hemes of New Mexico.—(Dedication of his "Relaciones de todas las cosas.")

QUERIES.

WHAT COLLEGE DID THE HOLY MAN OF TOURS ATTEND?—In his boyhood, Leon P. Duprat. subsequently known as "the Holy Man of Tours," came to the United States from Martinique, and entered a college. Can any reader tell what and where the institution was?
NEW ORLEANS.   D. C.

DR. O'FALLON'S COLONIES.—Dr. O'Fallon, agent of the Yazoo Co., about the beginning of this century, undertook to plant a colony in the West. Did he succeed in this attempt?
BALTIMORE.   M. A. S.

N. DAME DE GUIAUDET.—A very handsome cross was found on the Watkins farm near Scipioville, Cayuga Co., N. Y., on the site of a Huron Cayuga village occupied in 1677, and is now in the possession of Gen. John S. Clark. Each arm of the cross ends in a fleur-de-lis. On one side is the figure of our Lord, on the other that of the Blessed Virgin holding the Divine Child. On the transverse bar is

    N D A   M E
    D E G V   I A V D

           E T

The letters are below the figure of Our Lady. Can any reader tell where the shrine of Notre Dame de Guiaudet was?

NOTICES OF RECENT PUBLICATIONS.

ECCLESIASTICAL HISTORY OF NEWFOUNDLAND. By the Very Reverend M. F. HOWLEY, D.D., Prefect-Apostolic of St. George's. West Newfoundland. Doyle & Whittle, Boston, 1888. 8vo, pp. 426. Maps and illustrations.

Certainly a remarkable work, patient in research, judicious in treatment, graceful in style, and produced in elegant and attractive form. Terra Nova, the first land sighted by Cabot, the first where a priest of English speech offered the holy sacrifice, the unnamed Bristol priest who sailed with Cabot—Newfoundland became in time the scene of Sir George Calvert's first independent essay at colonization, and the spot where he first endeavored to show the world an example of Catholic and Protestant living side by side with equal rights and equal privileges. Then came French settlements with priests; the final triumph of England, a few Catholics, persecution, courageous struggle under unchristian and inhuman laws, till peace dawned at last, and the Church acquiring liberty grew with the multiplied energy of long-repressed vitality. Dr. Howley had a noble theme, and he has treated it admirably.

Our accomplished author gives briefly the settlement of Greenland by the Northmen and their Vinland voyages, but judiciously abstains from attempting to fix any spot in Newfoundland as certainly visited by the Catholic priests of Scandinavian race.

Although England and France both made attempts to settle Newfoundland, we have no certain information of the presence of any minister of religion till Sir George Calvert obtained his separate patent. Then three secular priests, educated at Douay, "Seminary Priests" as the term was then, came over, and a Protestant clergyman, Rev. Mr. Stourton, for Calvert, in his broad and noble love of religion and morality, wished his Protestant settlers to enjoy the services of a minister of their own faith. We owe to the bigotry of this man some knowledge which might otherwise have been lost. There are indications, too, of a Carmelite mission.

When the French gained a foothold on Newfoundland they must have had priests at the principal stations, to judge by their system elsewhere; but the indications are few and vague. Even Bishop Laval, in a long report on his Vicariate, makes no mention of Newfoundland, although he alludes to Sir George Calvert and gives the names of two of the secular priests who accompanied him. Yet, about 1663 the priest at Placentia was murdered, and the artist priest, the Abbé Paumiés, who had sailed from France at Whitsuntide in that year with Bishop Laval, but on a different vessel, finding the people at Placentia without a priest, remained there till the next year.

In 1689 Bishop St. Vallier, to whom the people at Placentia appealed, promised to send them some Recollect Fathers, and authorized these Franciscan Fathers to establish a convent there, as they did, Father Joseph Denis being one of the first, and a few years after the Bishop made the Superior his Vicar-General.

France yielded up all claim to Newfoundland in 1713, and the Catholic service, though tolerated for a time at Placentia and St. John's, soon disappeared with the French settlers, who gradually withdrew.

Meanwhile Irish Catholics had come in under the English flag, but they must long have been without a priest. In 1755 a house was burned by the authorities because Mass had been said in it, and an attempt was made to arrest the priest. A true Catholic, named Keating, was fined £50 for allowing Mass to be said in his fishing-room; his fishing-room was set on fire, and he was expelled. Other cases of government arson are recorded. Year by year the terrible oppression of Catholics continued, and to this day tradition corroborates the records of floggings, house-burnings and levelings, expulsions and robberies.

It was not till England was humbled by the peace of 1783 that she relented. The next year saw a quasi toleration permitted in Newfoundland. Two Augustinian priests, the Rev. Messrs. Kean and Londregan, could breathe freely. Other priests came. In 1784 the Sovereign Pontiff made Father James Louis O'Donel Prefect-Apostolic. Though the spirit of persecution had not altogether departed, religion gained; Father O'Donel was consecrated Bishop of Thyatira and Vicar-Apostolic in 1796.

All this in detail the Very Rev. Dr. Howley describes graphically, and brings the consoling narrative of progress down through the administrations of Bishops Lambert, Scallan, Fleming, and Mullock. His work gives portraits of the two last-named Bishops, and many interesting views of places connected with the Catholic history of the island.

A HISTORY OF THE RISE AND PROGRESS OF CATHOLICISM IN WALLINGFORD, from the exiled Acadians of 1756 to the dedication of the Church of the Most Holy Trinity in 1887. By JOHN G. PHELAN. 8vo, 40 pp., frontispiece.

This sketch, dedicated to the Rev. Hugh Mallon, is a very interesting contribution to local church history, written in a true antiquarian spirit, but not in the style of a Dryasdust. He pictures the stern old system of Connecticut, the advent of a few of the wronged and robbed Catholic exiles, the Acadians, in 1756, whom the Selectmen were empowered to bind out "with the other town's poor," Catholics who had been happy, prosperous, and peaceful in their pleasant homes and farms on the Bay of Fundy, till in hatred of their religion they were as Popish Recusants stripped of all they had. He shows the decline of Congregationalism, and the growth of the Church of England. Then the Revolution, and Lauzun's legion quartered at Lebanon, and other French troops at Hartford, which claims that the first Mass was said there by the Abbé Robin, a fact as to which that priest himself is silent. Our author finds Dr. William Hart, a native of Ireland, educated at Rheims, who died in Wallingford in 1799, apparently a Catholic. In 1813 Mass was said by Rev. Dr. Cheverus in New Haven, then came other priests and a bishop, and on the 22d of December, 1847, the first Mass in Wallingford was offered by Rev. Mr. McGarisk at the house of James Hanlon, and Mr. Phelan tells us that he knows five who attended it. Then the progress was rapid, and he sketches well the history till the completion of the noble church which now attests the zeal of the Catholics of Wallingford.

THE IOWA HISTORICAL RECORD, published quarterly by the State Historical Society at Iowa City. July, 1887. Iowa City. 1887.

This interesting quarterly gives in the present number a sketch and portrait of Gen. James Wilson; the Locating of a Government Road from Nebraska to Virginia City; Sketches of Unitarianism and Methodism in that State; an article on Geography and Early American History; a list of Donations to the Society, which speaks well for the interest in its work; recent Deaths and Notes.

THE CHURCH IN NORTHERN OHIO, AND IN THE DIOCESE OF CLEVELAND, from 1817 to September, 1887. By Rev. GEO. F. HOUCK, Chancellor of the Diocese of Cleveland. Benziger Brothers, New York, 1887. 8vo, pp. 266.

The Rev. Mr. Houck has patiently for years past been collecting data for the history of each parish and institution in the diocese to which he belongs, making his Chancery really and truly a repository of information as to the past and present condition of the bishopric. His contributions to the "Universe," extending over several years, give the history of the churches, but enjoyed only a local circulation. The present volume takes a different plan, and will find a wider circle of readers; its attractive form is but an index of the excellent literary work.

After a sketch of the first efforts of the Church in Northern Ohio, the author takes up the pioneer work of the Dominican Fathers, beginning with Father Edward Fenwick's visit' in 1817; then the labors of the Redemptorists, and of the Sanguinists, a community which in this country began its unassuming ministry in Ohio. This is followed by notices of the first secular priests, of whom a comparatively large number became bishops. Sketches of the early churches, religious communities follow, with brief notices of Bishop Edward Fenwick and Archbishop Purcell.

Having thus prepared the way, the reverend author begins the History of the Diocese of Cleveland from the consecration of Bishop Amadeus Rappe in 1847 to 1887, including the administration of the first Bishop, that of Very Rev. Edward Hannin, sede vacante, 1870-72; and of Right Rev. Richard Gilmour from 1872. Sketches of the lives of the Bishops are followed by brief notices of 328 priests who have ministered in that portion of Ohio. Tables of the priests in the diocese September 1, 1887, giving time and place of birth, date of ordination, and place and date of present appointment; tables of the churches and stations in 1847, with similar tables for 1887; as well as of religious and charitable institutions, attest the patient industry of the author, and afford for all time a groundwork of comparison.

Catholic Progress in Northern Ohio and the Diocese of Cleveland, 1817-87, with a chronology, comes next, followed by a note on Bishop Edmund Burke, and Catholic Miscellanea, containing extracts from Catholic newspapers, 1827-56, bearing on the history of the Church in the diocese.

Every page attests careful, persistent, and accurate research, and the whole work presents for Cleveland data such as no other diocese possesses in an accessible form.

When we look at the report of the actual condition of the Diocese of Cleveland, which embraces the part settled by fanatical emigrants from New England, it is hard to believe that the first priest to officiate in Cleveland was the Dominican Father Martin, whom so many of our readers will remember in New York.

Our readers must not suppose that the volume is simply a volume of statistics. The historical sketches, from that of Bishop Fenwick to that of Bishop Gilmour, are charmingly written. Each and all had difficulties from within and from without; had trials that would unman the bravest. It is impossible to read the touching pages of Rev. Mr. Houck without being edified and moved. The portrait of the stalwart Bishop Gilmour is grandly given: essentially the man for the place and for the time: brave, outspoken, fearless, meeting public objections intelligently and clearly, he has made the enemies of the faith the stepping-stones to a position of general consideration and respect.

CHURCH AND STATE IN THE UNITED STATES; or, The American Idea of Religious Liberty and its Practical Effects. With official documents. By PHILIP SCHAFF, D.D., LL.D., Professor of Church History in the Union Theological Seminary at New York. New York and London: G. P. Putnam's Sons, 1888.

The subjects embraced in this treatise are so important that it is well to have them treated by a man of the ability of Dr. Schaff, who enters a comparatively untried field. He thinks and writes under strong bias, and shows it in introducing the School question and State grants, giving as facts what the same historical research which he shows elsewhere would convince him are fictions. The best and most interesting portion is the study of the religious element in the Constitution of the United States, and in the first Amendment, with the State action which led to its adoption. Yet the study is incomplete, in that it lacks the history of the religious question in the original Constitutions of the thirteen States and the debates of the conventions which adopted them. These give the clue to the spirit in which they received the Constitution of 1787, and which dictated the amendments they desired.

The Constitution itself touched on religion only in one place. In the third section of Article VI. it declares, "but no religious test shall ever be regarded as a qualification to any office or public trust under the United States." This clause was proposed by Charles Pinckney, of South Carolina, the only State which by its original Constitution had declared Protestantism to be the established Church. It was supported by Gouverneur Morris, of New York, who, in his own State Constitutional Convention, had fought the battle of religious freedom against John Jay. Roger Sherman thought the precaution unnecessary, but, on the final vote, North Carolina voted against it, and the Maryland delegation gave no vote; some adopting more liberal views, others clinging to the old persecuting spirit. Yet the clause was essentially necessary. For generations it had been required by England that all officials should take a fearful oath declaring any man worthy of hell-fire who interpreted literally the words of Christ on two important points. The oath or declaration had not been adopted spontaneously by any colony, and it was well that the new Federal government should have no power to require that or any similar test.

When the proposed Constitution went to the States for consideration, the Conventions of Massachusetts and North Carolina showed that some still desired the retention of the oath excluding Catholics, such as New York required for naturalization. In Massachusetts, however, the ministers in the Convention showed more liberality than some of the lay delegates, and the Constitution was accepted. North Carolina came to no decision and remained out of the Union.

Several of the States, however, demanded a Bill of Rights or an express guarantee of religious liberty. A clause introduced by Jefferson in the Virginia Declaration of Rights was substantially proposed as an amendment by Virginia, North Carolina, and Rhode

Island, and more briefly by New York, and was proposed in Pennsylvania. New Hampshire, instead of enunciating principles, proposed an amendment terse and distinctly limiting the power of Congress, "Congress shall make no laws touching religion or to infringe the rights of conscience."

In the first Congress Madison introduced nine amendments, one covering this point. Twelve amendments were subsequently submitted to the States, but as the first and second were rejected, the third, which thus became the first, was adopted in these words, and became part of the Constitution of the United States: "Congress shall make no law respecting an establishment of religion or prohibiting the free exercise thereof, or abridging the freedom of speech or of the press, or the right of the people peaceably to assemble and to petition the Government for a redress of grievances." The New Hampshire idea was thus virtually adopted, though not in words.

Dr. Schaff assigns the credit of the clause to the States which proposed such an amendment and to James Madison, but as most of the States merely adopted Jefferson's words, the idea seems to belong to him and the restrictive and positive form to New Hampshire.

It is somewhat strange that none of our historians have at all entered into the action of the States and the resultant amendments, and in this portion of his work Dr. Schaff has rendered essential service. He also discusses the limitation of religious liberty, as in the case of the Mormons and the attempt to introduce a religious amendment into the Constitution. He treats the relations of the States to the question of religions, but less fully; and in the military and naval service of the United States, Catholics have been punished for refusing to attend Protestant services, and, indirectly, have been ostracised.

As to the question of religious liberty in Europe, to which much of his space is devoted, it is not our place to enter.

ANNOUNCEMENT.

THE Rev. Thomas J. Shahan, D.D., of the Cathedral, Hartford, Conn., is preparing a History of the Catholic Church in the Diocese of Hartford. It will be divided into sections: 1. The biographies of the Bishops. 2. A general history of the Diocese. 3. An account of each parish and mission church. 4. Biographies of deceased priests and of clergymen who formerly labored in the Diocese. He solicits aid from all interested, who can, by documents or otherwise, contribute to the completeness of the proposed work.

UNITED STATES CATHOLIC HISTORICAL MAGAZINE.

HISTORY OF THE CATHOLIC CHURCH IN MONROE CITY AND COUNTY, MICH.

BY RT. REV. CAMILLUS P. MAES, D.D., BISHOP OF COVINGTON.

NOTE.—At the urgent request of my friend, Mr. John Gilmary Shea, I have consented to the publication of this first part of my sketch, written when Rector of St. John's Church, Monroe, ten years ago ; I bowed to his well-known discrimination in matters historical when he assured me of its interesting character, with the hope that a short vacation may, in the near future, enable me to finish this chapter of Northwestern history, which will speak better for the energy of the Catholics of Monroe in the last twenty-five years than the present narrative would warrant. C. P. M.

I.

THE city of Monroe, Mich., is situated on the banks of the shallow River Raisin, at some distance from its mouth, which opens through dredged channels, known as the United States Canal and the City Canal, in the swamp-edged Lake Erie.

The early settlement that gave rise to the quiet little City of Flowers, with its thickly-bowered streets, extended some three miles up the river, and was made in 1784, by French Canadian Catholics, who called their new home " La Rivière aux Raisins."

The banks of the river, known to the aborigines by the name of Numma Sepe (Sturgeon River), had years before been a favorite camping-ground for the children of the forest. The Ottawas had an encampment on the southern embankment, and the Indian huts on the northern side sheltered a branch of the gentle Pottawatomies, who, at that time, occupied the larger portion of the southern peninsula as their privileged hunting-grounds.

However, the name of "La Rivière aux Raisins" was no misnomer, nor was it of recent origin, as appears from the following description of the country written by the Franciscan Father Hennepin,[*] who sighted it first from the deck of the "Griffon," in the month of August, 1679:

"We here behold one of the finest perspective views in the world. The Strait [Detroit River] is a mile wide, ... the whole region along and between the two lakes [Erie and Huron] is beautifully situated and is very productive. The banks of the River are extensive prairies, and are set off with hillocks and crowned with wild grape vines, fruit-trees, and shrubbery." ....

The first account we have of the settlement of "La Rivière aux Raisins" is derived from a letter of Rev. Dufaux, resident priest of Assumption (now Sandwich, Canada), to the Right Rev. J. F. Hubert, Bishop of Quebec, whose ecclesiastical jurisdiction extended at that time over the whole Northwest. It is dated January 28, 1788, and is kept in the Archiepiscopal Archives of Quebec, Canada. .... "The River Raisin is being settled by people who are at a loss what to do. Thirty-

---

[*] Father Louis Hennepin (1640-1701) was a native of Ath, Hainaut, Belgium. He, and his two companions, Fathers Gabriel de la Ribourde and Zenobius Mambré, accompanied Lasalle on the first sailing vessel that ever navigated the waters of our western lakes, the "Griffon," with a crew of twenty-eight men. They set sail from a spot five miles above Niagara Falls, where the ship had been built, now known as Lasalle, New York State, on the 7th of August, 1769. They sighted the island at the head of Lake Erie on the 11th, and entered the next day the smaller lake above Detroit, which they named "Lac Ste. Claire," after the Saint whose feast is celebrated on August 12th in the Catholic Calendar.

two habitants have already built huts; several intend to join them in the spring. Over a hundred farms have been located in that part of the country, and I think that within a short time they will want a pastor. I intend to go down there this spring to select a piece of land for a graveyard; however, I will not bless it until a chapel or a residence, for the priest who will attend them, has been built. Shall the pastor of Assumption [Sandwich] or the one of St. Ann's [Detroit] take charge of that small mission? I desire to know your Lordship's wishes in that regard.—Poor John Drouillard, who was just establishing himself in the new settlement, died there. Those who brought his corpse to the Fort [Detroit] came very near perishing on the road. I celebrated a funeral service for him a few days ago. Happily that I had made him go to his Easter duty last fall, upon his return from Sandosqué [Sandusky, Ohio]." . . . .

The Bishop of Quebec must have assigned the new mission to the pastor of St. Ann's church, Detroit, for Rev. Peter Fréchette, of that place, came to the River Raisin settlement in 1788.

II.

The Catholic congregation, now known as St. Mary's, was organized on the 15th of October, 1788. On that day Father Fréchette called a meeting of all the "habitants" of the River Raisin settlement, for the purpose of selecting a convenient spot for the building of a church and pastoral residence.

The document from which we gather the following details is drawn up in legal form by "Portier Bénac, Ecuyer, Juge de Paix," and is signed by the following gentlemen, all residents of the place. Have signed with their own hand: Jacques Gagnier, Charles Réaume, Portier Bénac, Louis Gaillard, Joseph Bourdeaux, le Chevalier de Chabert, Joseph L'Enfant, père; Joseph L'Enfant, fils; Joseph Pouget, Cicot.

Have signed with a cross: Amable Belair, Jean Dubreuil,

Baptiste Tailland, Louis Le Duc, Joseph Le Duc, Louis Devaux, Benjamin Mavar, Gabriel Godefroy, Baptiste Drouyard, Dejeanne, Jean Louis Lajeunesse, Louis Susor, François Soudriet, Baptiste Couture, père; Pierre Tessier, Antoine Campeau, Joseph Mommini, Baptiste Couture, fils; Joseph Drouyard, François Thibault, François Gendron, Nicolas Drouyard, Baptiste Montbien, Joseph Bien, Baptiste Lapointe, Jacques Prudhomme, Jean Baptiste Bissonnet, Joseph Bissonnet, Chrysostome St. Louis Villers, Pierre Foucero, Jean François Dussault, Basile Couzineau, Gabriel Bissonnet, Alexandre Fovel, Etienne Jacob, François Hanau, Amable Malloux, fils; Joseph Hyvon.

These gentlemen being assembled, unanimously selected the farm of Mr. Mommini, Sr., as the most central and convenient spot for the building of a church. They bought "un arpent et deux perches" from that gentleman for the sum of four hundred francs, and Joseph Hyvon donated "un demi arpent" for the same purpose. The chapel, the first church building ever erected in Monroe County, was built soon after on the aforesaid place, and was not taken down until 1842. The pastoral residence was built next to it, and its crumbling remains are still to be seen on the North River road, some two miles west of the present St. Mary's church.

The following gentlemen were Syndics of the congregation previous to the year 1794: Louis Lajoie, père; Louis Couzineau, père; Jean Baptiste Couture, père; Louis Susor, père; Etienne Roubidoux, Jacques Gagnier.

The Navarre family, not mentioned among the first signers, and now so numerous in this county, must have settled at the River Raisin shortly after 1784, for the first church trustees on the list are: Charles Réaume and François Navarre. Their successors in office were: Joseph Jobin and Joseph Pouget, elected in 1794.

Father Fréchette attended the congregation until 1794, when a priest was appointed by the Bishop of Quebec to reside permanently at the River Raisin. Rev. Dufaux, of

Assumption, writes as follows, November 7, 1794: "I am delighted to hear that the people of the River Raisin have a pastor, a priest of well-known merit. They were sadly in need of one. My opinion is that he will suit the congregation of the River Raisin very well, but I doubt whether the River Raisin will suit him." *

This priest was Rev. Edmund Burke, probably a native of Ireland. Born in 1753, Father Burke landed in Quebec May 16, 1787. He was successively appointed pastor of St. Peter and St. Lawrence, Isle d'Orleans, in 1791; two years later missionary priest at Halifax, Nova Scotia; and in 1794 Vicar-General of Upper Canada and missionary priest at the River Raisin.†

Shortly after his arrival, Father Burke called a meeting of the members of his congregation, and the following document ‡ explains its object and result:

"DONATION OF A FARM BY MR. IRACQUE.—ELECTION OF A PATRON SAINT.

"On the sixteenth of November of the year one thousand seven hundred and ninety-four, after due convocation of the 'habitans de la Rivière aux Raisins,' they have unanimously selected Saint Anthony of Padua as patron of the church. On this occasion Mr. Joseph Iracque made a donation to the church of a farm of ' trois arpents § moins une perche et demie ' broad, and of 'quatre vingts arpents' deep, bounded Northeasterly by the farm of Joseph Bellaire and Southwesterly by the farm of the said donor Joseph Iracque, which donation the acting trustee, Joseph Jobin, and the two other trustees,

---

* MS. Letter in Archiep. Archives, Quebec.
† Cfr. "Répertoire général du Clergé Canadien, etc.," par l'Abbé C. Tanguay, Quebec, 1868.
‡ MS. in the archives of St. Mary's church, Monroe, Mich.
§ One arpent was equal to 144 square rods.

Jacques Prudhomme and Antoine Campeau, have accepted in the name of the congregation, with the consent of all the 'habitans' present.

      (Signed), "Jo. HIBACQUE.

"Witnesses: JEAN BAPTISTE LaSELLE,
    "A^{TE.} RIVARD,
    "JACQUES GAGNIER,
    "J. PORTIER BÉNAC, Justice of the Peace,
    "CHARLES RÉAUME,
    "JOSEPH BARILLE.
         his
      "JOSEPH + JOBIN
         mark.
         his
     "JACQUES + PRUDHOMME
         mark.
         his
      "ANTOINE + CAMPEAU
         mark.

"I have read the above act, and I approve it this sixteenth day of November, one thousand seven hundred and ninety-four.
      (Signed), "EDMUND BURKE,
    "Vicar-General of Upper Canada."

Mr. Martin Nadeau was elected trustee on the 4th of January, 1795, and Mr. John Dussault January 6, 1796. We translate the first of these acts from the registers of St. Mary's church, calling the attention of the historian to the fact that River Raisin was at one time in the "County of Kent," the extensive limits of which have been narrowed down to the present county of the same name in Canada.

    "ELECTION OF A 'MARGUILLIER.'

"In the year of our Lord 1795, January 4th, after due convocation of the 'notables habitans' of this parish of St.

Anthony on the River Raisin in the county of Kent from the altar during the parochial mass, they have elected Martin Nadeau, Trustee, by a plurality of votes cast in conformity with the laws of Church and State.

(Signed), "FRANÇOIS NAVARRE, JACQUES GAGNIER,
"FRANÇOIS DELŒUIL, LOUIS GAILLARD,
"JEAN BAP^{TE} LaSELLE, JOSEPH BARILLE,
"EDMUND BURKE, V. G."

Father Burke worked hard for the welfare of his flock; but unaccustomed to the ways and manners of the French Canadians, he soon offended them by his plain talk about their duties toward church and priest. He left the River Raisin in 1795,[*] and spent some months at St. Ann's, Detroit, and Assumption, Sandwich. He then went back to the River Raisin, where we find him legalizing the election of John Dussault as trustee, on January 6, 1796, to leave it again soon after. He remained a few months longer in the two above-mentioned congregations, and finally left for Quebec on the 4th of July, 1796.[†] He was appointed missionary priest of Niagara in 1797.

The Holy See nominated him July 4, 1817, Bishop of Sion, "in partibus infidelium," and first Vicar-Apostolic of Nova Scotia. Consecrated in the Cathedral of Quebec July 5, 1818, by Monsgr. Joseph Octave Plessis (11th Bishop, and later (1819) 1st Archbishop) of Quebec, Right Rev. Edmund Burke died at Halifax, his Episcopal residence, December 1, 1820, at the age of sixty-seven years.

III.

Father Fréchette left Detroit the same year, 1796, in consequence of the cession of the whole Northwestern Territory to

---

[*] MS. letter of Rev. Fréchette, October 23, 1795, to the Bishop of Quebec. MS. anonymous letter, May 17, 1795, to the same.—Archiep. Archives of Quebec.

[†] "Répertoire général, etc." Sup. Cit.

the United States of America, and returned to Quebec. The Bishop immediately appointed him pastor of Belœil and St. Hilaire, where he died January 3, 1816, at the age of sixty-four years.*

The Church of Michigan now became a portion of the Diocese of Right Rev. John Carroll, first Bishop of Baltimore, Md., whose jurisdiction extended at that time over the whole of the United States.†

Bishop Carroll sent Rev. Michael Levadoux to the residence of Detroit, Mich. Territory, with the title of Vicar-General and pastor of St. Ann's church, in the summer of 1796. This reverend gentleman, a Sulpitian, arrived in Baltimore in 1791. In the fall of 1792 he was sent, with Father Gabriel Richard, as missionary priest to Kaskaskias and Prairie du Roche,‡ whence he was transferred in 1796 to Detroit. He, for the first time, visited the River Raisin, which the Americans now very generally styled Frenchtown, on the 31st of August, 1796.

The proceedings of that day are set forth in the following document, translated from the Registers of old St. Mary's:

"In the year 1796, August 31st, Rev. Michael Levadoux, Vicar-General of the Right Rev. Bishop of Baltimore and of the United States, having called together the parishioners of St. Anthony's at the River Raisin, has propounded to them the following questions: 1st. If they desired to have among them a minister of their faith who would procure them all the spiritual help which the Holy Church grants to her children? 2d. What were the measures which they would take to support him in a suitable manner?

"They agreed: 1st. To pay in the hands of three syndics, to be nominated for that purpose, one twenty-fifth part of all

---

* "Réportoire général, etc." Sup. Cit.

† He became also temporary administrator of Louisiana in 1802, upon the transfer of its Bishop, Luis Peñalver y Cardenas, to the See of Guatemala.

‡ Cfr. "The Life of Bp. Flaget," by Right Rev. M. J. Spalding, p. 82. "The Catholic Church in the U. S.," by DeCourcy, p. 66.

that they would harvest on their farm, and every individual one cord of wood, to be delivered at the pastoral residence. The three syndics to be responsible for the payment, and to be authorized to prosecute delinquents by law. 2dly. To pay the aforesaid dime this very year, whether the priest arrive or not, to defray the necessary expenses of the church; the balance to constitute a church fund.

"Three syndics were then appointed: for the lower side of the River Raisin and Sandy Creek, Mr. Antoine Campeau, acting trustee, unanimously; for the upper side of the River Raisin, Mr. Jean Dussault; for Otter Creek, Mr. Pierre Fourerault. These gentlemen have then and there accepted the office.

"3dly. It has been resolved to distribute 'blessed bread,'* as a sign of union every Sunday, the bread to be offered by every family in turn, and on holidays of obligation by those who volunteer to give it on such day without prejudice of their turn.

"Have signed † with their own hand, Antoine Rivard, père; Antoine Rivard, fils; Jacques Navarre, Isidore Navarre, Jean Baptiste Laselle, Joseph Pouget, Antoine Robert, Pierre Baron, Hyacinthe Bernard *dit* LaJoie, François Delœuil, Jes. Hiraque, Portier Bénac, Pierre Belair, Prosper Thibault, Louis Gailiard, Joseph Bourdeaux, J. B. L'Ile Ronde, Louis Guy, B^{te} Couture, fils.

"Have signed with a mark: Mr. Antoine Campeau, Jean

---

*In the early Church the faithful used to offer at the Offertory of the Mass the bread and wine necessary for the sacrifice. What was not needed for the actual sacrifice was removed after the oblation to God had been made by the officiating priest, and that blessed bread was afterward distributed to the ministers of the altar or to the poor. After that custom had been abolished the Catholics of France continued to offer ornamented loaves of bread, which were deposited near the altar, and after the Offertory cut to pieces and distributed among the faithful present. This was called 'le pain bini,' and is referred to here.

The practice of taking up the collection at the Offertory is a remnant of that early custom.

†The general reader will excuse this lengthy nomenclature which is of very great interest to the descendants of the 'anciens habitans' in Monroe County. So many new families have arrived since 1788, that this census is hardly a repetition of the former one.

Dusseau, Pierre Fourerault, Joseph Jobin, Alexis Soleau, Etienne Jacob, Louis Susor, fils; Pierre Desmars, Ignace Thuault, père; François Barbau, Jean Baptiste Conture, père; Joseph Carrier, Jean Baptiste Montbrilla, Etienne Roubidoux, Joseph Bissonnette, Louis Bernard, Nicolas Drouyard, Jean Baptiste Dubreuil, Isidore Robert, Jean Marie Navarre, Jean Mommini, Etienne Laviolette, Antoine Nadau, Michel Bourdon, Jean Jacob, Joseph L'Enfant, père; Louis L'Enfant, Joseph L'Enfant, fils; Dominique Drouyard, Jean Belair, Joseph Réaume, François Soudriette, Louis Couture, François Léonard, Joseph Chatellerault, Louis Roubidoux, Charles Lajoie, Pierre Cloutier, Pierre Constant, Alexis Labbadie, Etienne Laviolette, Jacques Martin, Charles Prouhe, Louis Couzineau, Jacques Prudhomme, Baptiste Ro, Jean Lapointe, Chrysostome Villers, Louis Bourdeaux, fils; Charles Roubidoux, Réné Cloutier, Zacharie Cloutier, Antoine Beauregard, Jean Baptiste Poujet, Jacques Jacob, fils; Benjamin Navin, Pierre Soleau, père; Baptiste Susor, fils; François Bérard, Joseph Robert, Baptiste Réaume, fils; Joseph Ménard, François Menard, Vincent Maheu, André Poufard, Louis Bourdeaux, Pierre Beauchamp, Baptiste Jérôme, Baptiste Riopel, Paschal Bissonnette, Joseph Hyvon, Pierre Tessier, Alexander Oualet, Jacques Gagnier, Louis Mommini, Baptiste Mommini, Baptiste Drouyard, Louis Bodin, Colet Bonhomme."

On the 11th of January, 1797, Messrs. Joseph Maynard and Chrysostome Villers were elected trustees for 1798 and 1799, respectively.

Very Rev. M. Levadoux attended the congregation regularly, and ordered the income of the church in such a manner that about two years after his arrival, the people felt able to support a priest of their own, and toward the end of June, 1798, the Vicar-General appointed Rev. John Dilhet pastor of St. Anthony's of the River Raisin.

Father Levadoux remained pastor of St. Ann's, Detroit, until 1802, when he left for France. He was Superior of the Seminary of St. Flour, France, when Bishop-elect Flaget, of

Bardstown, Ky., visited Europe in 1809–10, and helped the Prelate much in securing a band of zealous missionary recruits, among them the Rev. S. Bruté, afterward first Bishop of Vincennes, Indiana.*

IV.

Father Dilhet was introduced to his new charge on July 1, 1798, by the Vicar-General. Both said Mass in the chapel; and at a meeting held after the services, the people pledged themselves to pay four per cent. of all manner of grain they harvested, for the support of their priest.

Like all the sturdy old pioneers of those days, Jean Dilhet was a Sulpitian. Trained at that school of self-denial and of strict discipline which saint-like Olier founded, and the no less respected and equally earnest Emery directed in those times of terror, Rev. Dilhet went immediately to work to put his congregation on a good footing.

On the very day of his arrival, he has a resolution passed which stamps him at once as a true priest of God. His yearning heart misses the presence of his Eucharistic Jesus; and the available funds, about 100 "écus," are applied toward building a suitable Tabernacle, and purchasing a ciborium and chalice for the worthy celebration of the holy Sacrifice of the Mass, and the becoming custody of the sacred species.

His first care was to know his parish thoroughly; he describes it as follows:

"The parish of St. Anthony, on the River Raisin, embraces the settlements on the River Raisin, those on Otter Creek and Sandy Creek, those on the Miamy † and Portage Rivers,‡ those on Huron Creek South,§ those at the little Lake Sanduské, at

---

* Cfr. Life of Bishop Flaget, *sup. cit.*, p. 64.

† Now the Maumee River, emptying into Lake Erie at Toledo, Lucas County, Ohio.

‡ Portage River emptying into Lake Erie at Port Clinton, Ottawa County, Ohio.

§ "La Rivière aux Hurons Sud," now Huron Creek, wending its way to Lake Erie through Monroeville, Huron Co., and Huron, Erie Co., Ohio.

the little and at the great Sanduské Village,* at the Glaise,†
at Fort Wayne or Miami,‡ at the Huron River North, at the
Huron Village,§ at the Grosse Roche,|| at Mont Wagon,¶ at
St. Joseph's,** etc.

"In a word, it extends North to the 'Rivière aux Ecorces,'
South to the Illinois, Kaokias, and Post Vincennes,†† East to
Lake Erie, and West it has no limits.

"This parish has within its limits people who belong to
different civilized nations and many savage tribes. The
former, citizens of the United States, are either French,
Canadian, American, English, Irish, or Scotch. The Indians
are: Hurons, Ouatouais, Ouatomis, Santeux, Chouanons,
Wolves, Foxes, etc.

"Among these, many have been baptized, especially those
born of parents belonging to civilized nations; most of the
Huron tribe have also been baptized. But all are not Catholics. By baptism they belong to the church; but by Creed
they belong to different heterodox sects; v. g., the Anglican,
Presbyterian, Quaker. Owing to the fact that there is no
minister of their denomination in this part of the country, the
majority live in the most complete religious indifference. The
few who claim to hold on to some kind of principles, profess
tolerantism or deism, rarely incredulity, impiety, or atheism.

"The 'Hurons,' many of whom have received baptism and

---

* Sandusky Bay and Sandusky, Ohio.

† Likely the French name of the Creek near Clay Junction, Wood County, Ohio.

‡ Fort Wayne, Indiana.

§ Both on the limits of Monroe and Wayne Co., Mich. The latter is now called Rockwood

|| Probably Flat Rock, Monroe Co.

¶ Signifying: Wagon Mountain. Is not the modern "Monguagon" town in Wayne Co. a corruption of the early French name?

** On St. Joseph's River, near Lake Michigan, at that time there was not a single inland settlement between Monroe on the eastern and St. Joseph's on the western shore of Michigan.

†† Now Vincennes, Indiana.

have been brought up in the Catholic faith by ancient Jesuit missionaries, are divided in three classes: Some, even among the Chiefs, would like to have missionaries and practice the Catholic religion; others, especially the youth, are indifferent; a third class have even been prejudiced against the Catholic missionaries by the false teachings of the Anglicans.

"The other Indian nations are less favorably disposed towards the Gospel. The 'Pououotomis,' 'Ouatouais,' and 'Chouanons' have preserved, from their intercourse with the old missionaries, some idea of baptism, and a great respect for the priest, whom they call 'Father'; but their being addicted to the most enervating and unwholesome liquors is the great, perhaps, indeed, the insurmountable obstacle to the spread of the Gospel among them. Trade with the civilized nations has made them lose all love for work and for the hunt, especially since they receive presents. They have no more the same frankness, the same love of country; but they still tenaciously cling to their superstitions; and, though they believe in the existence of the Master of Life, they worship him not. In life and death they exclusively invoke the 'manitous' of the second rank, agreeably to the exhortations and practices of their jugglers and magicians, whom they look upon with awe as their medicine-men."

V.

Father Dilhet's next care was to place his parish on a permanent footing, and to secure undisputable possession of the lands bought by his people or donated to them. He carefully inquired into the mode of conveyance of the farms belonging to the church, and having found them defective, he immediately took the necessary steps to remedy the evil. The three contracts were found to be drawn up and registered according to law, but two of the former owners had gained possession by a viva voce transfer of the Indians' title. Messrs. Joseph Hyvon and Louis Mommini were instructed to legalize their claim by having a deed in fee-simple signed before witnesses by the Indian grantors. Joseph Ménard-*dit*-Montour, the trustee in charge, was likewise instructed to secure legal quit-claim deeds from the Indians, and have them registered.

These instruments were accepted and approved at the regular meeting of the parish, October 14, 1798, and handed to Etienne Dubois for registration.

Before the advent of Father Dilhet, the Hiracque farm had been sold by the trustees to Amable Bellair, without the authorization of ecclesiastical authority. A petition was consequently drawn up, praying for the necessary permission, and presented to Very Rev. Vicar-General Levadoux. He pronounced the reasons for the sale sufficient and lawful, and ratified the contract. The price paid by Amable Bellair was thirty "poutes"* in wheat, five of which he paid that year (1798), giving his note for the remainder, twenty-five poures, to be paid in wheat.

The trustee system being at that time in vogue, Rev. Dilhet took the necessary steps for the legal administration of the church property, and gives binding force to the parish transactions, subject to the approbation of ecclesiastical authority.

The mode of administration of the temporalities of the Catholic Church would be one of the most interesting studies, alike for the historian and the statesman. The Catholic Church is essentially democratic in the true sense of a word, the daily abuse of which has almost obliterated its true meaning in the minds of our contemporaries. When reading over these Rules and Regulations for the administration of the temporal affairs of the parish of St. Anthony, written eighty years ago, and scrupulously adhered to by both priest and people at a time when Michigan was yet an unreclaimed wilderness, one cannot but wonder at the impudent language of ignorant men who wildly expatiate on the tyranny of the Church of Rome,

---

* A poute was equal to $2.50. The value of the old Canadian monetary system was as follows: 12 deniers—1 sol; 20 sols—1 livre; 15 livres—1 poute. Six French livres were equivalent to one dollar of our American money.

and the servitude in which she kept her children, till the dawn of an overboasted civilization forced her to let go her hold on the uneducated masses of her slaves. In the Northwestern woods and swamps fifty years before the progress of the nineteenth century dared penetrate the recesses of the Wolverine wilds, a well-regulated community lived under the paternal sway of a Catholic priest. The people had their general and particular assemblies, their trustees and officers; they freely discussed all topics of general utility to the community, and knowingly adopted such measures as in their own judgment were best calculated to promote the public good. Their pastor was more of a guide and a father than a superior; and the simplicity of their faith, which made them render to the minister of God the filial veneration and obedience due to his supernatural character, contributed more than all modern inroads of infidelity and deification of self, to render them happy and prosperous.

We are not going to lay before our readers the lengthy laws and regulations which governed this congregation, the second oldest in the State. The curious inquirer can gain a general idea of them by reading the Fifth Article of the " Rules for the Administration of the Church," printed in the Old Ritual of Quebec, which were also unanimously adopted by the general assembly of the people of St. Anthony's congregation at the River Raisin, September 16, 1798.

Owing to circumstances not under the control of the Church, the title of church property is vested in the Bishop of the Diocese, but the people still have their church committee, whose office is, in many respects, similar to that of the trustees of old.

VI.

The zealous pastor next turned his attention to the beautifying of the church premises and of the ornamentation of the church itself. A fence inclosing three "arpents" around the church and pastoral residence is constructed; a new row of pews is built in the church ("du coté du Lutrin") on the side of the singing-desk; "flying benches"* are ordered for the accommodation of the growing number of parishioners, and to swell the church receipts; a collection is ordered in the parish for the adorning of the altar, and the proceeds of the Sunday collections are set aside for buying yearly some piece of silverware for the more becoming celebration of the Holy Sacrifice. The amount of those collections during the year 1798 was twelve dollars.

Father Dilhet also urged the people to build a new fence around the cemetery, and to take steps to select and buy a new graveyard as soon as possible, the one in use being very low and wet. A large cross was erected outside the church as a station for the Sunday processions, and the pastor encouraged the erection of similar wooden crosses along the main roads in the parish, a pious practice of Catholic lands which he did not succeed in introducing. Two contribution-boxes, one for the poor, the other for the souls in purgatory, were put up in the church, to foster the spirit of temporal and spiritual charity in the hearts of the people.

A resolution passed May 19, 1799, to make a canopy for the Blessed Sacrament and providing for the necessary preparations for the procession of Corpus Christi, proves that the beautiful custom which still prevails in the City of Flowers, of all the Catholics of the three congregations yearly coming together to do honor to the God of the Eucharist, is of no recent date.

The people, however, did not always answer to the generous expectations of their zealous pastor. The church was a miserable shanty, and Father Dilhet was anxious to have a new one built. Mr. Jobin was charged to get plans and specification of cost for a new church from Detroit. But the project dragged on for many years until the poor priest was obliged to leave for want of support.

---

* "Bancs volants," likely to be used in the aisles, so called because they could be moved and used wherever required.

Most of the Canadian settlers were very poor. For years they had been visited in the distant missions of the Northwest by Jesuits and other missionaries of religious orders, who, sustained by voluntary contributions from France, never asked any compensation for their services. These Fathers even distributed freely among them medals, beads, prayer-books, etc., without charge. As a natural consequence the Canadians were not accustomed to contribute to the support of their pastors, and but too often neglected that divine precept so flagrantly that the poor priest had to leave or starve.

Father Dilhet requested them to build a barn to store the wheat they had to bring in payment for their dues. The meeting agreed to it in December, 1798, but in April, 1799, they decided that the priest could put up a partition in the largest room of the pastoral residence, which they also used as a meeting hall, and store it there. Even that was not yet done in the following June, and there had, as yet, been no need for it, as they had brought little or no grain. The garden enclosed around the pastoral residence was rented out to another party for the benefit of the church. The roof of his house leaking badly, the priest got the Sieur Baron, "couvreur"—roofer—to repair it. At the next meeting they found fault with the work done, and the trustee in charge was obliged to give his note for the amount paid, that note to be held against him until the return of Baron, when the repairs would be done according to the directions of the committee appointed by the parish. This was done in May, 1799.

The acting trustee, Mr. Joseph Montour, went out of office December 31, 1798, at which time he had on hand "359 livres 9 sols" of the church funds, for which he gave his note. Mr. Jacques Martin was elected in his place January 6, 1799, and Mr. Chrysostome Villers entered upon the duties of acting trustee.*

---

* There were three trustees, each of whom became acting trustee the last year of his term of three years.

VII.

The great ambition of Father Dilhet was to build a new church less unworthy than the one in use, of the majesty of the God who dwelt therein, and sufficiently large to accommodate the fast increasing Catholic population. He had not been one year in the parish when he brought this subject so dear to his heart to the notice of his parishioners, who hailed the idea with delight, and began to freely discuss the matter.

At the meeting of July 21, 1799, a resolution was passed, "to take up a collection for the new church in the parish of St. Anthony and in those of the Fort on both sides of the River" (viz.: St. Ann's, Detroit, and Assumption, Sandwich). Messrs. Joseph L'Enfant and Louis Roubidoux were appointed to take the subscriptions, and in order that all might contribute their mite, the pastor proposed that the less rich should contribute within one or two years the sum of five "poutes" ($12.50), to be paid in regular instalments of money, provisions, or labor. The new church was to be 60 ft. long, 40 wide, with a height of ceiling of 20 ft.; and in addition for vestry-room or sacristy of 24 x 12 feet. Mr. Jobin was appointed superintendent of the work, and Mr. Etienne Dubois, secretary, and both were promised a remuneration for their time.

In September Mr. Antoine Nadeau put in a bid for putting up the frame and covering it in for 200 poutes ($500), but entered into a contract with the trustees on September 29th to do the job at $2.50 a day and board, the parish to pay the hands he employed. Mr. Jobin was to receive $2.00 a day when actually employed in superintending the work, and Etienne Dubois "six livres" ($1.00) when collecting. The stone for the foundation was to be taken out of the River Raisin by the parishioners, who were also to furnish the timber. Messrs. Jobin and Nadeau pledged their farms for the faithful performance of the work. Only seventy-six poutes had been subscribed for the new church before the end of the year!

In the meantime, Father Dilhet did all in his power to render the services of the church attractive, and to keep good order during the celebration of the Mass. Pierre Tessier was appointed warden (bedeau), at a salary of $25 a year; Mr. Etienne Dubois got a few groats for his services as a singer, and Mr. Villers was appointed doorkeeper and usher, when he stepped out of office as a trustee. Before the election of a new one took place on the 29th of December, the pastor reminded his people of the qualities required in the one to be chosen for so important an office; he should be a good practical Catholic, have paid his dues, and subscribed toward the building of the new church. Mr. Isidore Navarro was elected by an almost unanimous vote, and Pierre Joleau entered upon his duties of acting trustee on the 1st of January, 1800.

Father Dilhet had more than reason enough to insist on the last two conditions; the subscription for the new church made no headway, and what was still worse, many did not pay their dues. Things came to such a pass, that in order to bring the parents to a sense of their duty, not to let their priest starve, he refused to baptize the children of those who could easily fulfil that command of the church and neglected it.

For a time they left the priest severely alone, neglecting the customary meetings, paying nothing, and seemingly abandoning the idea of building a new church. But when they saw that the priest was in earnest (this state of affairs had lasted from March to December, 1800), they finally entreated him to call a meeting of the congregation at the pastoral residence. Accordingly, on the 14th of December, 1800, Father Dilhet convoked the people after high Mass, and inquired of them the object of the meeting.

They stated how sorely they were grieved at the sight of so many children, of parents who obstinately refuse to pay their dues, deprived of the Sacrament of Baptism. They recognize the priest's right to act as he has done, but beg of him to use other means to enforce the payment of dues. Father Dilhet congratulated them on this act of faith in the necessity of the sacrament of regeneration, consents to their request, and inquires whether the trustees, who, by their acceptance of the office, shouldered the obligation of seeing the priest supported, will collect the dues, the larger part of which have as yet never been paid. These gentlemen show great reluctance; they dislike to force payment, and suggest that the pastor act in their stead and refuse to admit delinquents to their Easter duty.

One gentleman finally realizes the meanness of the whole proceeding: François Navarre, justice of the peace and captain of militia, rises. He himself had allowed some expressions to drop from his lips, which, the pastor remarked, might make a very bad impression on the people. He now appeals to the honor and self-respect of his fellow-parishioners; he reminds them that they pledged themselves to pay four per cent. of all their grain as dues, and entreats them to fulfil their obligations.

After a short exhortation of the pastor, urging them never to condemn him without a hearing, and to state their grievances to him instead of slandering him among themselves, the meeting adjourned until December 28th. The pastor again called their attention to the ruinous condition of the house and the necessity of building a church. The parishioners then elected Mr. Etienne Dubois trustee; and Mr. Jacques Martin entered upon the year's active duties of that office January 1, 1801.

The first meeting of that year, Jan. 6th, was characterized by the same unfeeling and sordid spirit which had made Father Dilhet's life an uninterrupted martyrdom of body, intellect, will, and feeling. His every act was found fault with in order to cover up the people's contemptible neglect of duty. Had he not said Mass without notifying the trustees? Had he not buried children without the authorization of the same? —Surely he had done so; what of it? What right had they to interfere?

But when the church question came up for discussion, most

of the men had disappeared, and it was not until the 23d of March following that the pastor could get them together again. At that meeting the size of the prospective building was changed to 36 x 60; dissatisfaction being expressed with the work done, Messrs. François Navarre and J. B. Laselle were appointed to examine the work and the accounts of Mr. Jobin, whilst the first named and Joseph Menard were elected Syndics to resume the subscription for the new church.

A sign of the times.—Mr. Louis Valade died during the year 1800, and left his personal effects to the church to have Masses said for his soul. Trustee Jobin went to Detroit, and asked of the Judge of Probate for authorization to sell the property and to use the sum realized from it according to the testator's intentions. Religious convictions were not yet looked upon as a sign of insanity or a sufficient proof of undue influence to set aside a will. The instrument was probated; and at his next visit to Detroit Mr. Jobin was empowered to carry out the provisions of the will.

VIII.

The 18th day of June, 1801, was a red-letter day for the poor Canadians of the River Raisin. The first Bishop who ever set foot on Michigan soil came from Detroit, to administer the Holy Sacrament of Confirmation to the members of St. Anthony's parish and neighboring settlements. Rev. Dilhet records that solemn occasion in the following words:

"On the 18th of June, 1801, Mgr. Peter Denant, Catholic Bishop of Quebec, arrived towards 3 P.M. at the River Raisin, and disembarked in front of J. B. Réaume's house, where Mr. J. Dilhet, pastor of the parish, received him without any solemnity, the Bishop having refused the offer of being received in due form. He was introduced into the said house by the Pastor, and entered it with Mr. Michael Levadoux, Vicar-General of the Bishop of Baltimore, Mr. Marchand, pastor of the Assumption of Detroit [now Sandwich], and Mr. Payet, his secretary. Mr. Hubert Lacroix welcomed the Bishop in the name of all the parishioners, after which the many people present fell on their knees to receive the Bishop's blessing. Having entered the carriages which were in readiness for the party, they started for the church, escorted by nearly fifty men on horseback, and by a great crowd on foot. Along the road people left their houses to ask His Lordship's blessing. After a light collation, the Bishop entered the church to give solemn benediction, before the bestowal of which Mr. Levadoux preached, announced that the Right Rev. Bishop of Baltimore, John Carroll, had requested the Bishop of Quebec to administer Confirmation in the parish, and gave out the order of services for the following days.

" The next day being Sunday, the Bishop of Quebec, after a discourse on Confirmation, administered that sacrament to those who presented themselves at the communion railing. He did the same the two next days."

One hundred and ninety persons were confirmed on that occasion, among them an Indian woman named Marie Matchibicin.

Father Dilhet profited by the religious excitement which that uncommon event had produced at the River Raisin, to encourage his people to new exertions in behalf of the new church. He offered to donate half of his perquisites for three years, if the dues paid in reached four hundred or more " minots " of wheat, and urged the syndics, Navarre and Jobin, to have the ready squared timbers lying at Otter Creek brought to the church grounds without delay.

But new difficulties arose. The timber in Otter Creek was accidentally burned during the autumn of 1801 ; many parishioners thought that the superintendent, Jobin, was paid too much for his services ; and the latter insisted on squaring up accounts and withdrawing. His accounts were approved,* and the parish was found to owe him 419 livres, which the syndic

---

* Each man was allowed 1½ lbs. of meat a day.

François Navarre promised to pay as soon as money came in his hands. The people wanted to work out their subscriptions on the church, buying their own victuals, and so sparing expenses; but as usual, each one waited for every other one, and in June of the next year, not a thing had been done to further the enterprise.

In the meantime the remaining timber was rotting in the shanty; the trustees proposed to sell it, buy Mr. Chanest's house (adjoining the church lot) for a presbytery, and change the presbytery in use into a church. But the pastor was getting sick of all that talk, and determined to make a bold strike —a last noble effort to build a church—failing which he would leave the field.

On the 27th of June, 1802, Father Dilhet invited the whole congregation, men and women, boys and girls, to remain in church after Mass. Having donned his surplice and said a fervent prayer at the foot of the altar, he ascends it and begins an impassioned appeal to their faith and generosity. He reminds them of the urgent necessity of building a temple to the true God, of the engagements entered into at their first meeting called by order of the Bishop of Quebec by Rev. Father Fréchette, and at subsequent meetings at which he himself presided. He recalls to their minds the subscriptions which they promised to pay, the neglect which all had been guilty of, and the failure of all their plans, because no one had faith enough in the enterprise to give his bond for the faithful performance of the work. Shall they therefore give up all hope? No! He will take the responsibility upon himself; his zeal for God's glory and his affection for all his parishioners ask no less a sacrifice, and he is ready for it. All he asks of them is to subscribe what they can; he will consider as paid for his own support all arrears of dues paid toward the construction of the church, and if necessary he will sell all he has, his flour, his stock, his furniture, ay, his linen, to help along so noble a work!

A few men walked up to the table in the sanctuary to subscribe a few bushels of wheat, some pounds of lard, a barrel of flour, or a day's work. And that was the end of it! Not another meeting did they attend.

Father Dilhet now gave in. He wrote to the syndic François Navarre, asking what was being done, but received no answer. He therefore sent his resignation to the Bishop of Baltimore, expressing the hope that a new priest might succeed better, and quietly performed his usual priestly functions, awaiting the wished-for intelligence of his removal.

IX.

François Soudriet, père, had succeeded Pierre Tessier as warden (bedeau), and assumed his robe of office in September, 1801. The following year the singer Dubois left the River Raisin, and Alexis Loranger* succeeded him in that office for the consideration of £15, £4 more being allowed him for keeping the church accounts.

Joseph Robert was elected trustee December 27, 1801, and Isidore Navarre entered upon the duties of acting trustee January 1, 1802.

The difficulties about the church building, for which the pastor held François Navarre, the latter's brother, mainly responsible, had created considerable animosity and bad feeling; and when a meeting was called February 27, 1803, in which the pastor announced his determination to leave the parish, Isidore Navarre refused to render account of his year's administration. After many urgent requests to do so, he finally consented, but insisted on selecting his own men to examine his accounts, and named his own brother François, and Joseph Robert. In vain did the pastor object to such a one-sided arrangement; the people endorsed the faction and the meeting broke up.

Only twelve to fifteen men answered the next call for a meeting June 16, 1803, and when the people accused

---

* He writes his name "Lauronger" up to 1820.

the pastor of preventing them from electing trustees, he answered that he would continue to do so until they saw fit to bring those officers to account for their administration of the temporalities of the church to the pastor and congregation. Mr. Jobin promised to induce Mr. Isidore Navarre to comply with that duty, and Rev. Dilhet called a general meeting three days later, at which they elected Messrs. Ignace Duval,* père, and Robert Navarre, fils, as trustees. Mr. Joseph Robert had become acting trustee for 1803; Mr. Etienne Dubois, elected to the office in 1801, having left River Raisin, he took upon himself to inform Robert Navarre of his election; Mr. Duval being present, accepted.

Determined to put everything in order before he left, Father Dilhet called another meeting of the parish after High Mass of Assumption Day, August 15, 1804. There being no immediate hope of building a church, he then sold the squared timber in the shanties to Messrs. Jacques Laselle and François Navarre for $200, allowing Mr. Laselle to pay to Mr. Jobin the sum due him, with the understanding that if the church building were resumed these gentlemen would return timbers of equal dimensions, or pay $100 each if the new church were to be built of stone.

Father Dilhet received his recall to France in the beginning of the year 1804, and assembled the people on January 15th. He there read the letter of Bishop Carroll asking the people to make up a sufficient cum of money to defray the expenses of the journey of another priest to Michigan, if they desired to enjoy sacerdotal ministrations. Mr. Ignace Duval, acting trustee for that year, was entrusted with the duty of collecting it.

The next month Rev. Dilhet succeeded in getting together twelve men to elect new trustees; Robert Navarre had refused the position tendered him in 1803. Two new trustees were therefore elected, Mr. François Navarre, who refused the

---

* The Duvals were called Thuott-dit-Duval; it was also written "Thuyot" and "Tuyot." The nickname Duval prevailed in the course of time.

position, and Mr. Antoine Beauregard dit LaJoie,* who, being present, accepted the trust. The pastor also succeeded in his effort to bring the two ex-trustees to render accounts, March 13, 1804, and a few days later he left the River Raisin by way of Detroit.

Here he was informed that before returning to France he was ordered on a missionary tour north to Michillimackinac, and as soon as navigation opened he sped on his mission.

He was back at the River Raisin in September, and the people having made no provision to defray the traveling expenses of a new priest, he read from the altar the following document:

"Rev. John Dilhet, priest of Detroit and missionary apostolic, on his return from his mission to Michillimackinac, by order of Mgr. John Carroll, Bishop of the United States, makes known that he will henceforth reside no longer at the River Raisin, but in Detroit. He will, however, come from time to time on a missionary tour to the River Raisin as often as the needs of the mission or the wishes of the people require it. During his absence new-born children will be privately baptized; people shall assist at public prayers every Sunday and holyday of obligation, and come to Detroit to fetch him on sick calls; Mr. Alexis Loranger, singer and catechist, shall regularly say the prayers in church and teach catechism on Sundays and holydays; will record the burials celebrated in the absence of the missionary priest, to whom he shall deliver a copy of the same at his next visit to the River Raisin, and will publish the bans of marriage only after receipt of an order from the priest signed by himself, the certificate of said publications, and of the impediments known to him countersigned by him to be sent to Detroit." †

At his next visit to the River Raisin in December, he remained over a week, and called a meeting of the habitans

---

* The first name prevailed, but was changed to Bernard.
† Baptismal Register of St. Mary's church.

January 6, 1805. Mr. Joseph Jobin was elected syndic to superintend the construction of a new presbytery, and the change of the old one into a church.

Rev. Dilhet paid his last visit to the parish of St. Anthony in May, 1805. Mr. François Navarre came forward and announced his willingness to serve his term of trusteeship to which he had been elected the year previous, and Joseph Jobin was associated with him; Mr. Beauregard serving his term of acting trustee during the year 1805. The priest urged the people again to provide the necessary means to bring a new priest, as he was on the eve of his departure for France, and having settled his accounts, signed a petition for a new priest, and given up the keys June 3, 1805, he left the River Raisin, where he had done so much unappreciated hard work.

X.

With the retirement of Rev. Jean Dilhet, St. Anthony's of the River Raisin became a missionary station of Very Rev. Gabriel Richard, of St. Ann's, Detroit. He visited it for the first time October 6, 1805, when he stayed a week.

He presided at the annual meeting for the election of a trustee February 2, 1906, when Hubert Lacroix was elected, François Navarre being trustee in charge for that year.

The energetic Sulpitian also tried his hand at shaming the congregation into building a new church; it was resolved at the assembly of October 12th of that year, that each man and young man should haul one load of stone and two loads of wood to the kiln to burn lime; but that was the end of it, and Father Richard, who would stand no nonsense of that kind, carefully avoided calling meetings thereafter.

Joseph Jobin entered upon the active duties of the trusteeship January 1, 1807, and François Laselle was elected at the annual meeting of January 25th.

No election was held in 1808 and 1809, and Messrs. Hubert Lacroix and François Laselle succeeded one another agreeably to their order of election. The latter continued acting trustee during the early part of 1810, when a meeting was called February 14th, at which the parishioners endorsed his continuance in office until the end of the year, and elected Mr. Isidore Robert for 1811, and Joseph Bissonnett for 1812. Jacques Laselle was appointed syndic to settle all old accounts due to the church.

Mr. Joseph Bourdeau was elected trustee for 1813, at a meeting on January 13, 1811, and the presbytery was ordered repaired and rented to swell the income of the church. It was rented to Charles Millet.

In the meantime Father Richard had been coming three or four times a year, patiently hoping that the people would do something for his support, and defray his traveling expenses. It was slow work, however, and he came to the conclusion that he had to ask it of them. Like everything else, he did it in a practical way. On the 15th day of January, 1811, three of the most influential members of the congregation, Messrs. François Navarre, Joseph Robert, and Joseph Bourdeau, gave to the Rev. Gabriel Richard their bond in the sum of $200 to be paid in grain before Easter of that year for his services during the year 1811, the Rev. Gentleman obliging himself to come four times a year for from one to two weeks to attend to the spiritual wants of the people at the River Raisin.

That meant business, and the acting trustee, Joseph Robert, caught the spirit of the energetic priest. He called a meeting of the old and new trustees at the house of François Laselle the 24th of the same month, ascertained the extent of the indebtedness of each to the church, and made them give their personal note for the amount.

Joseph Bissonnett became acting trustee January 1, 1812; Jean Baptiste Laselle was elected for 1814, the 9th of the same month; and on the 16th of February Jacques Laselle and Martin Nadeau endorsed the $200 bond, Father Richard's annuity for 1812. Mr. Bissonnett resumed the position of acting trustee March 23, 1813, when Joseph Bourdeau, trustee in charge during that year, died.

Father Richard's second visit during the year 1812 ended May 27th, and in consequence of the war with Great Britain, declared June 12, 1812, did not call again until peace was restored. Baptisms for that period are recorded in the Detroit registers, and Father Richard writes: "The pew rent has not been collected during 1813 because the 'habitans' were dispersed owing to the war. Most of them have spent the year in Detroit."

Jean Baptiste Laselle had assumed the office of trustee January 1, 1814, and was re-elected for 1815, at the annual meeting held February 12th of that same year. Mr. Pierre Fournier was elected for 1816; and Mr. Medard Labadie for 1817.

Father Richard visited the River Raisin for the first time after the war, February 14, 1815. In June of that same year a meeting was called at which the following resolutions were passed:

"Resolved, 1st, to prepare for the building of a stone church in 1816.

"2d, Whereas two places are proposed for its erection, viz., the ground where the presbytery now stands, and the farm of Doctor Joseph Dazet,* to which Jacques Laselle offers to add a strip west of it of two arpents wide by 120 deep; and

"Whereas, Doctor Dazet asks $1,000 to be paid by the first of next September, and Jacques Laselle $500 to be paid within two years;

"Resolved, that a subscription paper be circulated, upon which all those who are in favor of the second location shall sign or cause to be written their name and the sum they intend to contribute.

"Resolved, that François Navarre, François Laselle, and Isidore Navarre shall contract with Doctor J. Dazet if the subscription succeed.

---

* The Doctor was a Frenchman, who lived on the lot now occupied by Mr. Ilgenfritz in the 4th Ward. He left Monroe about 1830, and died in Detroit.

"Resolved, that the subscriptions shall not be binding unless it reaches the sum of $1,000."

Only about $500 was subscribed, and the project of removal was therefore abandoned.

XI.

The people of the River Raisin, or Frenchtown, as the Canadian settlement began to be called, had suffered much during the Anglo-American war. Many of the men had shouldered the musket, their families had temporarily removed to Detroit, and when peace left them free to return they found their farms devastated and buildings ruined by English and Indians. They were without provisions, and so poverty-stricken that they had not wherewith to buy seed grain. The Government came generously to their assistance, mainly through the exertions of Rev. Father Richard.

At a meeting held December 17, 1815, of which the priest was chairman, and François Laselle secretary, the following resolutions were passed by acclamation:

"The habitans de la Rivière aux Raisins in meeting assembled,

"Resolve: that they are deeply affected by a just sentiment of gratitude towards the Government of the United States for the generous assistance which the said Government has tendered them after the misfortunes caused by the late war;

"Resolve: that they gladly concur in any resolution which has been or will be agreed upon by the habitans of Detroit and of the neighborhood to testify of their respectful gratitude to the President of the United States for the solicitude that the Government has shown towards the citizens of the Territory of Michigan in the distribution of provisions and of seed grains."

At the same meeting, Robert Navarre was elected acting trustee for the year 1818.

The 28th of the same month the old and new trustees had a

business meeting to ascertain the financial situation of the parish. The safe was opened, and it was found to contain:

1. Notes of different parties to the amount of . £4,914 19 6
2. In silver money $7 75 . . . . 46 10 0
3. In "gringlettes" 0 37½ 2 5 0
4. In small bills 12 16½ 73 0 0

£5,036 14 6

Which at six livres tournois to the dollar, amounts to $839.45.

The Right Rev. B. J. Flaget, Bishop of Bardstown, to whose jurisdiction Michigan had been transferred in 1810, having set out on a protracted journey to the more distant stations of his extensive diocese in 1814, Father Richard was in hopes that he would also visit Michigan, because of the difficulties that had sprung up among the Catholics of Detroit,* and towards the end of 1815 he ordered a collection taken up to defray the travelling expenses of the prelate. But Bishop Flaget returned from Missouri to Kentucky in 1816, and at the meeting of May 19, 1816, of the habitans of River Raisin, Rev. Father Richard had the following resolutions passed:

"Resolved: that the amount of the subscription made April 24th and following days, to defray the travelling expenses of the Right Rev. Bishop, shall be used to bring to this parish a resident priest.

"Resolved: that the acting trustee shall solicit new subscriptions to this fund to make up a reasonable sum, say about three hundred dollars.

"Resolved: that if that sum is not made up, the trustee shall call upon those parties, whose notes are held by the church, to make payments on account to make up the deficit."

A business meeting of the trustees was held on the 26th of the same month, at which the pastor received:

---

* "Life of Bp. Flaget," p. 182.

May 26.—Payment of bills on account $80 81¼
    Money from the offer-box 7 18½
May 27.—Subscription money in bank notes . . 47 43¼
   " 66 muskrats, at 2 sh. . . . 16 50
   Part of the collection " de l'enfant Jesus " * 35 50

 Father Richard advanced the balance, and sent the same year $300 by Colonel Gratiot, who was going to Washington, the sum to be handed to the Archbishop of Baltimore to pay the travelling expenses of a priest to be sent to the River Raisin.

 March 2, 1817, Antoine Lafontaine was elected trustee, to act as such in 1819 ; Medard Labadie having succeeded Pierre Fournier as acting trustee in the beginning of the year. At Father Richard's first visit in 1818, Jacques Navarre was elected trustee at a meeting of February 15th.

 Bishop Du Bourg, of St. Louis, having offered to the Bishop of Bardstown the services of four of his priests for the missions of Indiana and Michigan until the latter could be able to make permanent arrangements for the attendance of these districts, the Rev. Messrs. Bertrand and Janvier were appointed for Detroit, April 25, 1818.†

XII.

 The difficulties among the Catholics of the Northeast coast, in the vicinity of Detroit, had now become so serious that an open schism was threatened, and on the 24th of February, 1817, Bishop Flaget had issued a pastoral letter, strongly denouncing the course adopted by the disaffected faction, and interdicting their church. The intelligence of this sad condition of affairs gave the Bishop much concern, and hastened his departure for Michigan.

---

* That collection called of the Infant Jesus was made every Sunday for the altar ; it was to be used to bring a priest here, or for the purchase of ornaments.
† Cfr. "Life of Bp. Flaget," by Right Rev. M. J. Spalding, p. 177.

On the 15th of May, 1818, he left St. Thomas Seminary, Ky., on his way thither. He was accompanied by the Rev. MM. Bertrand and Janvier, and two young men going to Detroit, named Godfroy and Knaggs. The party performed the entire journey on horseback. Having said Mass at Urbana on the 24th of May, the party was much perplexed on account of their ignorance of the remaining route, which lay through a thinly settled country. Fortunately a young officer named Gwynn was going to Detroit, and he kindly offered his services as guide. On the 28th they arrived at the Rapids of the Miami of the Lakes, and found two towns springing up on opposite sides of the river.

"Their next station was the River Raisin, where they remained three days, till the last of the month. The Bishop found the church and altar at this place in so wretched a condition, that he could not say Mass; he, however, preached on the 31st, and enjoined a public penance on a man who had married out of the church. He has this entry in his journal:

"Took tea with Mr. Anderson,* a member of Congress, and a Presbyterian in religion. I found in his face the imprint of piety; nothing could be more edifying and religious than the conversation of this excellent man. I should be much surprised if he and all his family do not become Catholics." †

The Bishop reached Detroit June 1st, and sailed thence with Rev. Bertrand, on his way to Montreal and Quebec, the 17th of the same month. He left Rev. Janvier in Detroit, as assistant priest to Father Richard.

Rev. Janvier visited the River Raisin for the first time in the beginning of September, 1818; the first baptism recorded by him, being dated September 7th.‡

Bishop Flaget reached Detroit from the north, October 11,

---

* Corner of Elmwood Avenue and Anderson Street.

† "Life of Bishop Flaget," p. 185.

‡ Bishop Spalding says that Right Rev. Flaget took Rev. Janvier along with him to Sault St. Mary's from Detroit, on his return from Canada, September 2d. This entry of the record contradicts that statement.

1818, being ill with the fever. He gave confirmation there on the 1st of November to over 200 persons, and "being somewhat recovered on the 17th, he started for the River Raisin, where he devoted nearly six weeks to arduous missionary duties. He then gave a course of instruction to the children preparing for first communion, and held conferences for the instruction of the people. Finding that abuses and scandals had crept into this and several of the other congregations, he thought it expedient to exercise the rigor of ecclesiastical discipline against some who had given public scandal. Thus he publicly excommunicated a man who had married out of the church, and caused two females—sisters—who had been unfortunate, to do public penance. They were called to the altar railing, where, kneeling, they humbly confessed their fault, and implored pardon for the public scandal they had given, and bowing down, kissed the floor. The Bishop hereupon gave them a fatherly and fervid exhortation; and 'the ceremony made many weep.'

"He returned to Detroit on the 30th of December, ... and remained in that city throughout the entire winter and spring." *

He administered, on the 5th of December, 1818, the same sacrament to the first Irish child baptized at the River Raisin, Mary Jane, daughter of Patrick O'Rorke and of Mary Lynch, who signed the baptismal register with James McManus; and on the 28th the two children of the said McManus and of Honora O'Rorke. (One of the retinue of the Bishop was Rev. W. S. Jones, who baptized a son of Judge Laurent Durocher.) Father Janvier also helped the Bishop, hearing confession and administering the sacraments.

On the 14th of April, 1819, the Right Rev. Bishop, accompanied by Father Bertrand, "revisited the River Raisin, where he gave a retreat, which was followed by the conversion of some great sinners. He here administered confirmation,

---

* Cfr. "Life of Bishop Flaget," pp. 196–7.

and made arrangements for the erection of a new church. In May he returned to Detroit and prepared for his journey homeward"* to Kentucky.

The arrangements for the erection of a new church mentioned in the above extract proved as abortive as the preceding ones. The people had a meeting December 26, 1819, and elected the following syndics for the purpose: Messrs. François Nuvarre, Gabriel Godfroy, Pierre Fournier, Joseph Bissonnet, Robert Navarre, Jean Baptiste Cicott, and Medard Labadie. The zealous Bishop confirmed them in their charge the same day, and urged them to make immediate arrangements with the pastor of St. Ann's, Detroit, to build a new St. Anthony's church of stone. In March, 1820, the people confirmed the gentlemen named and their right to go to work, but forbade them to levy a tax for the purpose without the authorization of a future general assembly of the people, thus killing the whole thing in the bud.

Rev. Janvier remained with Father Richard during the years 1819 and 1820, and attended the mission at the River Raisin during that time.

Mr. Joseph Duval had been elected trustee January 3, 1819; Mr. J. B. Cicott, February 20, 1820; Mr. Martin Nadeau was elected January 7, 1821.

In May, 1821, a resolution was passed to haul sand during the month of June, in order to heighten the cemetery ground at least four feet, and enable them to bury above the old corpses.

The Sunday-school lacking in interest and failing to draw many children, a full board of directors was appointed to reorganize it. The following is a literal translation of the resolution: "This thirty-first day of the month of May, 1820, the notable habitans of the parish of St. Anthony, on the River Raisin, in meeting assembled to organize a Sunday-school, resolve: to teach reading, writing, oral recitation of the cate-

---

* Cfr. "Life of Bishop Flaget," p. 198.

chism and of the Holy Gospels, and other useful and moral subjects. Messrs. John B. Cicott, Gabriel Godfroy, and François Navarre are unanimously elected to form a permanent board to direct the establishment and working of the said Sunday-school. They shall mature a plan and constitution for the administration of said establishment, and appoint persons to instruct the children. They are empowered to take all necessary measures to make the school a success.

"These gentlemen have appointed principal of the school and master of French, Mr. Alexis Loranger, who will begin the school next Sunday, June 3, 1821, in the pastoral residence.

(Signed,) "FRANÇOIS NAVARRE,
"J. B. CICOTT, Jr.,
"GABRIEL RICHARD, priest,
Pastor of St. Ann's, Detroit."

XIII.

Rev. Anthony Ganiltz was the third resident pastor of St. Anthony's church. He had been on the mission in Kentucky, but belonged, at this time, to the diocese of Cincinnati. He passed through Fort Wayne, Indiana, where he baptized four persons, April 22, 1822, and arrived at the River Raisin the following week.

The following is a translation of the act of installation:

"This twenty-eighth day of the month of April A.D. 1822, Mr. Anthony Ganiltz, priest, has taken possession of the church of St. Anthony of the River Raisin, of which he has been nominated pastor by Monseigneur Edward Dominick Fenwick, Bishop of Cincinnati, and administrator of the Michigan and Northwestern Territories, in the presence of the inhabitants assembled to assist at the holy mysteries, in the presence of Mr. G. Richard, Vicar-General, and of Mr. Vincent Badin, assistant priest of St. Ann's parish, Detroit, who have signed the present act.

"GABRIEL RICHARD, p^{tre} Curé of St. Anne, du Detroit, Vic.-G.
"FRANÇOIS VINCENT BADIN, prétre."

In the May assembly Father Ganiltz asked that a small kitchen addition be built to the presbytery, and that a cord of wood for kitchen be brought to him by every family, pursuant to resolution of December 28, 1800.* They promised to think over the kitchen matter; as to the bringing of wood, many called the right of the priest in question; they finally agreed to do so, provided the priest did not sell any of it, and that the people had the right to come before and after services to warm themselves at that wood fire!

Father Ganiltz could not stand such niggardly disrespect and starving process. He left the River Raisin July 17, 1822. He leaves his opinion of the place on record: "To-day being the 17th day of July, 1822, I, Anthony Ganiltz, who had been nominated pastor of this parish, happily got rid of it, after having suffered hunger, thirst, sorrow, and abandonment for three or four months, and every kind of misery. 'In exitu Israel de Œgypto. Hœc est dies quam fecit Dominus. Farewell, poor church and still poorer presbytery; may I never lay eyes on you again!"

"P. S.—I have not the courage to copy the other baptisms, but I here leave a record of them. My successor, who will perhaps have his stomach better filled (le ventre mieux garni), can copy them if he sees fit. 'Habitavi cum habitantibus Cedar, multum incola fuit anima mea.' Poor Kentucky! Why did I leave thee?"

Some other clergyman who fared no better in after years, paraphrased this remarkable rubricated entry, as follows: "Poor Ganiltz, you have suffered; so have I! 'In hac terra plagarum.'"

Joseph Loranger was nominated trustee in May, 1822, and Gabriel Godfroy Feb. 9, 1823. In April of that year the trustees bought the right and title of Vincent Soleau, being an undivided part of the late Peter Soleau, his father, for $250.

---

* He explained that he was so poor, owing to the expenses of his journey, that he did not have a dollar wherewith to buy a stick of wood.

Father Richard, of Detroit, attended the mission after the departure of Rev. Ganiltz, until October 10, 1824, on which day he introduced in the pastoral charge of St. Anthony's of the River Raisin, Rev. Jean Bellamy, a priest of the Diocese of Rennes, France.

Father Bellamy immediately called upon the people to keep their pledges of former years, and to build a decent church. In the assembly of December 5, 1824, they resolved: 1st. To build a brick church with stone foundations, 60 x 87, and 30 feet high; 2d. To build it on the farm opposite the Monroe bridge.

Etienne Thuotte dit Duval was elected trustee to assume charge within two years, and François Robert to be his successor, January 2, 1825.

At a subsequent meeting of the people, Feb. 20, 1825, the resolutions were altered as follows: 1st. To build a church opposite the city of Monroe; 2d. To build it 42 x 80, and 30 feet high. Messrs. Hubert Lacroix, Gabriel Godfroy, François Navarre, and Laurent Durocher were appointed to tax the people pro rata.

However, some people objected that the farm selected for the purpose of building the church, opposite the city of Monroe (where St. Mary's now stands), was too expensive a piece of property. But Father Bellamy, in no way discouraged, spoke as follows, from the pulpit, Sunday, September 4, 1825:

"My brethren, I offer you the following means to decide where the new church shall be built: next week, I will call on all the parishioners with two lists; one for subscriptions for the farm opposite Monroe; the other for the old place where the wooden chapel stands. Both the subscription lists shall be binding, and the larger sum will decide of the church site. If those in favor of the farm below subscribe the larger sum, the church will be built below, and the sums offered for the church up the river will be paid towards that site. Likewise, if those in favor of the church up the river subscribe the larger sum, the chapel will be built there, and the sums offered for the church below will be considered subscribed towards the building up the river. If possible, I will publicly announce the result of the subscriptions next Sunday, and the church site will be known. The names of the subscribers and the amount subscribed will be kept in the registers for ever. After the church is built, those who have contributed most towards it will have the right to select their pew, paying, however, the sum agreed upon for each seat by a commission appointed for that purpose. From the day of saying the first Mass in the new church, a reasonable sum shall be charged as entrance fee, for a period of ten years, to all new-comers, who not being in the parish had no opportunity of contributing towards the erection of God's house.

"Those who will have subscribed the larger sum towards building either up or down the river, will yet have the privilege of locating the church on the farm offered by Miss Angelique Campeau, if that site suits them better. But no matter what place is chosen, Rev. Gabriel Richard reserves to himself the right to designate the ultimate site of the church.

"Subscriptions will be received in days' work, wood for the limekiln, wheat, lime, cattle, and money. But the stone and building lumber are excepted, because furnished independently of the subscription."

"All this has been unanimously accepted. The subscription made according to announcement, has possibly decided the church site. The subscriptions for the old place where the wooden chapel stands amount to $1,859, and the subscriptions for the farm opposite Monroe amount to $736. God be praised! J. BELLAMY, Pastor."

The pastor communicated the result to Rev. Father Richard, who sent the following letter :

"DETROIT, November 24, 1825.

"To all the Gentlemen, residents of the parish of St. Anthony on the River Raisin, Otter Creek, and the Bay Miamy.

"DEAREST BRETHREN: The zeal which you have lately

evinced, by the subscriptions which you have made to construct the church of St. Anthony of the River Raisin, has filled our heart with joy. We hope that church will be built in the course of the year 1826. We have not the least doubt that the zeal and the agreeable manners of your pastor have largely contributed to that success; we hope that you will neglect nothing to keep so worthy a pastor. In order to help him to execute the plans he has made to establish schools, we admonish you that those who shall neglect to pay their dues, at the rate of four per cent. of all grains agreeably to custom, shall have no right to his services, and that we order him by the present letter to refuse all the helps of his ministry to those who being Catholics shall not have satisfied to that duty before the fortnight of Easter of each year. However, as we do not wish to punish the children for the faults of the parents, we allow him to confer private baptism only to infants, and to visit and shrive the sick, making the latter fulfill that obligation of paying dues in so far as they are able. We also order that those who do not till the land, shall pay to their pastor a reasonable sum by yearly subscription, regulated according to the revenue which they obtain from their industry.

"The present letter shall be read at the parochial Mass by the Rev. Pastor of St. Anthony's, and copied by him in the Register of the Assembly Acts of the parish of St. Anthony.

"Witness our hand. Signed at Detroit, Nov. 24, 1825.

"GABRIEL RICHARD, Vic.-General of the
Rt. Rev. Bishop of Cincinnati."

But Father Bellamy succeeded no better than his predecessors. For two years he struggled on, and finally gave up the fight; the last act signed by him is dated Aug. 13, 1827. He left the River Raisin, and the spiritual care devolved again upon Rev. Richard.

CHRISTOPHER DAVENPORT — THE BROTHER OF NEW HAVEN'S FOUNDER A FRANCISCAN FRIAR.

By Rev. T. J. Shahan, D.D.

Two hundred and fifty years ago, in April, 1638, the city of New Haven, in Connecticut, was founded by a number of English colonists, who were dissatisfied with the restraints put upon their religious freedom at home, and sought in the new world a spot where they might follow in peace the dictates of conscience. This occasion was recently commemorated at New Haven with a great deal of display and enthusiasm.

The leader of this band of emigrants was the Rev. John Davenport, a bold and masterful spirit, who guided the counsels and fashioned the legislation of the colony for many years. He has been called the founder of New Haven, and in the commemorative ceremonies of the two hundred and fiftieth anniversary of the city the place of honor was justly assigned him.

It will be news, no doubt, to many that the brother of John Davenport, the Puritan, was a Catholic priest, a Franciscan friar, and one of the foremost characters of English history during the turbulent period of the seventeenth century.

The materials for the following sketch of this truly great man are drawn chiefly from Wood's "Athenæ Oxonienses"; Nicéron's "Mémoirs pour Servir à l'Histoire des Hommes Illustres"; Oliver's "Collections illustrating the history of the Catholic Religion," etc., London, 1857, pp. 550–1; Gillow's "Bibliographical Dictionary of English Catholics"; Canon Flanagan's 'History of the Catholic Church in England";

Neal's "History of the Puritans," and Hanbury's "History of the Independents."

Though he never touched our shores, yet an unusual interest cannot but attach to the Catholic brother of so strong an opponent of the Catholic Church as was the younger Davenport.

Born at Coventry, in Warwickshire, in the year 1591, he passed his boyhood in the quiet retirement of that ancient city. In 1613, together with his brother John, he went up to Oxford and entered at Merton College, where, in spite of certain disagreements with the warden, Sir Henry Savil, he remained two years, while John left and went to Magdalen Hall in the same university.

It was a time full of momentous changes. Earl Somerset had ceased to be the favorite of James I.; Sir Edward Coke, the great lawyer, had fallen from his high estate; the Calvinistic churches were torn by the errors of Arminius and the articles of the Synod of Dort; Tyrone and Tyrconnell had fled from Ireland with a remnant of faithful henchmen, and such as had not died of grief, were subsisting in Rome on the charity of the Popes. The anti-Catholic feeling under the theological monarch ran high in England. Sigebert Buckley, the last of the dispossessed Benedictines of Westminster Abbey, and its true heir, had died in prison in 1610 at the age of ninety-three, after forty years of incarceration. In the same year the brothers entered Oxford, Roger Cadwallador, a priest, was executed at Leominster in presence of two great fires, one to burn his heart and bowels, the other to boil his head and quarters. The previous year Father William Scott, a Benedictine, was executed for the faith, as another, Father John Roberts, had been three years before (1610).

Christopher Davenport and John Davenport, on entering the ancient halls of Oxford, were therefore able to understand the advantages likely to accrue from adhering to the established order of things, and the discomforts which any other course would entail upon them. John went up to London to become a minister of the Church of England, later a Puritan, or rather an Independent, and finally the founder of a modern theocracy in the then virgin wilderness of the Connecticut. Christopher in the meantime had fallen in with a Roman Catholic priest (with several, according to Nicéron) in the neighborhood of Oxford, one of that noble band of missionaries of whom it has been said that "no eye ever saw them enter the kingdom, and no county was without them." With this priest, probably a professor of Douai College, he went in 1615 to that famous seat of learning.

This school, founded by Cardinal Allen, an Englishman of eminence, and issued from an old Catholic family of Lancashire, had been since 1568 the principal feeder of the English Catholic Mission, and held that honor until the Reign of Terror. Here Christopher Davenport remained for a short while in doubt as to what state of life he should embrace. Several English Franciscans who had completed their noviceship in various convents on the Continent were about this period trying to form themselves into a provincial body. With these Davenport finally determined to unite, and with this object in view he entered the novitiate of the Flemish Franciscans at Ypres, October 7, 1617. After completion of his religious profession, he returned to Douai, and was incorporated October 18, 1618, among his English brethren.

The new college of St. Bonaventure was then building for them, and here he made another course of study, and rose to the dignity of lector of theology in that school. Leaving Douai a second time, he went to a Spanish university (Salamanca, his contemporaries think, but not improbably Valladolid), where, according to the words of his biographer, Wood, he "made great progress in the study of the supreme faculty" (theology). Doubtless he was induced to this by the representations of the Spanish priests in Douai (then a part of Spanish Flanders), who desired to see so noble a genius profit by the teachings of the greatest Continental university of its day. On finishing his studies in this Spanish university he returned to Douai, where he occupied for a time the post of superior and professor of theology, and finally received from the faculty of his order the degree of Doctor of Divinity.

But the mission of Christopher Davenport was not in Spain, nor among the thoughtful schoolmen of old Douai. In the year 1625 Henrietta Maria of France, daughter of Henry IV., was married with marvellous pomp before the great portal of Notre Dame de Paris to Charles I. of England. She stipulated for the free exercise of her religion, and brought over in her train many priests and chaplains to carry out its services, at least within the court. Among these came Christopher Davenport, now known as Father Francis a Sancta Clara, though he went also at times under the aliases of Francis Coventry and Francis Hunt. After ten years of close study and extensive travels he landed again on English soil, in the prime of life, in vigorous health, and filled with the enthusiasm of the ancient faith of the Land of Mary. He was destined never again to leave England, save for short intervals during the reigns of Charles I. and of Cromwell when flight became expedient. "Here," says his English biographer, "Christopher Davenport did great service for the Roman Catholic cause, by gaining disciples, raising money among the English Catholics to carry on public matters beyond the seas, in writing of books for the advancement of his religion and order, by his perpetual and unwearied motion day and night to administer among the brethren, and by tendering his services to consult and help warping Protestants, etc." When Laud, the Archbishop of Canterbury, was accused by the Puritan Prynne, one of the chief heads of complaint was, "that for the advancement of Popery and superstition in the realm the same Archbishop had wittingly and willingly received, harbored and relieved divers Popish priests and Jesuits, namely one called Sancta Clara alias Davenport, a dangerous person, and Franciscan friar who hath written a Popish and superstitious book called ' God, Nature, Grace,' etc."

Laud's friends replied that he had received Davenport only as a favorite of the Queen, a person of great parts and of very engaging manners, while Laud himself denied having used him as an instrument to bring about the union of the Church of England with the Mother Church of Rome.

The leading idea of Christopher Davenport's life was the reconciliation of England and Rome. While he directed the affairs of the English province of the Franciscans (some thirty members in 1625), and ministered to the scattered Catholics in secret hiding-places, his busy mind was planning one of the most difficult feats of diplomacy.

The sum of his ideas and designs is to be found in an Appendix to the work, "Deus, Natura, Gratia, etc.," entitled "A Paraphrastic Exposition of the Articles of the Anglican Confession, etc." (republished in London, 1864). This work met with great opposition not only from Protestants, but from some Catholics who thought that out of excessive desire for England's conversion, he was conceding too much. In Spain it was placed on the Index. An effort was even made to have it placed on the Roman Index, but it failed, and 200 years later it is said to have served Cardinal Newman as a basis for the famous Tract 90.* In this work the Franciscans mitigated to some extent the Protestant Articles, exposing them in their most favorable light, hoping to smooth the way for the return to England of the Bishop of Chalcedon, or for the admission of some other bishop. In the House of Commons (1640) a member referred to it in the following terms: "True it is that for the union of Christendom all the blood in the House were of no loss or price, though I value it at a very high rate. But let us agree with them of Rome in all points, and differ with them in one (Supremacy of the Pope) and agreement in all else is to no purpose. But if we agree to

---

* Deus, Natura, Gratia, sive Tractatus de prædestinatione de meritis et peccatorum remissione, seu justificatione, et denique de sanctorum invocatione, ubi ad trutinum fidei Catholicæ examinatus Confessio Anglicana, etc. Lugduni, 1634, 8vo.

that, then we are sworn at the threshold, and forsworn when we come into the House. And now as the hinge and gin do answer one another, so those of Rome answer those amongst us, one called St. Clare, though he hath another name, undertakes to bring all our articles of religion enacted in this House into an agreement with Popery, etc." ("Calendar of State Papers, Domestic, 1640," p. 38). He wrote many other works—on predestination, on the Immaculate Conception, on the hierarchy of the Church, on disputed points of metaphysics and theological controversy. His facile pen was never idle and produced at frequent intervals many memorable works. They were usually printed, on account of the persecutions, in small octavo for handy use and to be carried about with ease.

He republished all his own works at Douai in 1661, in two folio volumes, at an expense of £220—having no patrons to defray the cost. Among his English works we know the following:

"Enchiridion of the Faith, Being a Dialogue Concerning the Christian Religion."

"A Clear Vindication of the Catholics From a Foul Aspersion to-wit: That They Have and do Promote a Bloody Design, etc."

"Explanation of the Roman Catholic Belief."

The latter work he presented to Oliver Cromwell and several other members of the famous Parliament of 1656.

In a letter dated London, November 18, 1635, to Father Luke Wadding, at Rome, he gives a view of the domestic opposition to his famous book. The letter is as follows:

FRANCIS A SANCTA CLARA TO LUKE WADDING, GUARDIAN OF ST. ISIDORE, GENERAL CHRONOLOGIST OF THE HOLY ORDER OF ST. FRANCIS, CONSULTER OF THE INQUISITION.

VERY REVEREND FATHER:

I did see a letter of yours to our Vicar of Douai, the contents whereof giveth me matter of obligation to your paternity, for your charitable offices concerning my book so much ventilated in your parts as here by our aemulos. God forgive them. You have heard that the chief of all the ancient orders in England did send to Rome their approbation of it in a joint letter, and that the testimonies of the good effected in better disposing the minds of our countrymen to terms of re-union with the Church, which is the aim of all endeavours. Notwithstanding this, there is one Fray Ludovicus a Scta Maria, a man known to your paternity and whom for his seditious and afterwards luxurious and lascivious life, to avoid a greater scandal to our holy order, we were obliged to expel from our province, first by consent of our *intermedium capitulum*, and after our provincial chapter, he then suing to be incorporated to us. Hereupon that we might more easily get him out of England, we permitted him to get letters commendatory from many persons of quality here to gain a better color for his sending hence. Hence he being exasperated against me, whom he conceives his enemy for his wicked life, at his coming to Paris, he dealt by false calumnies to draw the guardian Doles to deal with the Sorbonne to censure the book which they refused, and as we hear is gone to Rome to do what his malice can direct him. Our Provincial wrote to our General to detain him in those parts, for if (he) shall return there is great danger that he will *redire ad vomitum*, yet we doubt whether our General hath received the letters. You will, ... if you can, know the truth, for our Provincial would write again, if he knew that they were not received. There is also another occasion which happily presenteth itself which inviteth me to write to yr paternity. The bearer hereof is sent from our Queen to his Holiness and is to remain there as ledger. You know we have one Saint Gregorio Pansano (Panzani) of the Oratory, who resideth here, from his Holiness, thus, as we hope, there will be a beginning of correspondence. He goeth *in recto* from the Queen, but, etc., the agent of the Benedictines called Father Wilfrid and Senior (Signor) Georgius Conalus are designed from here to be his assistants in this good business. If yr paternity will seriously annect yr advice in occurrences it will be exceedingly well accepted here, and if you please by letter to signify to me yr willingness in it, I shall acquaint such here with it as shall authorize you as the others are. I desire much that no other order should surpass our holy order in acts of true Christian fidelity or zeal to our country, and therefore do desire that your well-deserved acquaintance and experience there may also appear in this common business. You may enclose a letter at any time in this agent's packet *to me*, and

I shall return you an answer by him again. Thus with desire to be remembered to Fa. Anthony Punch, etc., I rest begging your holy prayers. There is no news here, only all things are in great quiet.

R. Fa. your paternity's humble brother,

FR. A. S. CLARA.

("Calendar of State Papers, Domestic, 1635," p. 488).

He published at St. Omer, in 1618, "The Chronicles of the Franciscan Order," a translation from the Portuguese. The manuscript is yet kept in the convent of Our Lady of Dolors, at Taunton, in Somersetshire. He also wrote a book on its ancient standing in the Kingdom of England, besides a handbook for the guidance of religious, works of devotion, and numberless little pamphlets, etc., long since lost to our knowledge.

Adroit, patient, of polished manners, and invincible in dispute because of his long practice in the schools, he made many converts, and it would not be too bold to attribute a number of the most notable conquests of the Church in the seventeenth century to the man whom all recognized as unsurpassed for learning, culture, affability, and experience. During his lifetime Goodman, Bishop of Gloucester, entered the Church, Sir George Calvert, Lord Baltimore and founder of Maryland, became a Catholic, as did Sir Toby Matthews, at once a Catholic, a priest, and a Jesuit without the knowledge of the government and without sacrifice of his principles. Other eminent converts of that day were John Sergeant, secretary to the Bishop of Durham, and Sir William Davenant, poet-laureate. Christopher Davenport was three times chosen provincial of the English Franciscans, (in 1637, 1650, and 1665,) "being accounted," says his literary biographer, "the greatest and chiefest pillar of his order and the onliest person to be consulted on the affairs thereof." "He was equally esteemed," says Niceron, "by Catholics and Protestants for his ability, his knowledge and his fine qualities." He labored for more than fifty years with a prudent zeal for the spread of the Catholic faith, both by word of mouth and by his many writings. His attachment to his order is evident from the very name he bore, Francis a Sancta Clara, being a reminder of its two great and saintly founders. More learned, more experienced, more severely tried than his brother, he seems to have surpassed him in breadth of character, in controlling noble souls to good ends, in suavity and gentleness of spirit, in moderation, and in that cheerful, vivacious, and engaging exterior which his contemporaries so highly praise. He was held in great esteem by Charles I. for his conciliatory disposition, and it is no small proof of his attractiveness, learning, and influence that he reconciled with the Church Anne, Duchess of York, daughter of Edward Hyde, Lord Clarendon, and was the confessor and intimate friend of the converted Bishop of Gloucester, whom he attended on his death-bed.

He died early in the morning of the 31st of May, 1680, at the venerable age of eighty-nine, at Somerset house, near London, and was buried in St. John's Church of the Savoy hospital in the Strand. During life he had often expressed a desire to lie in death with his brethren in old St. Ebbe's, Oxford. That church adjoined the Franciscan school in the days when the children of St. Bonaventura and Scotus were mighty wranglers in the academic confines, and in it are deposited the bones of many of the Grey friars. His old friend, perhaps his *Socius*, Friar John Day of Holy Cross parish, Oxford, was buried there also. But he had not his wish, and his remains lie buried in the heart of busy London, a more fitting resting-place for the tireless worker. In the Capitular Register of the Province it is said that he accomplished three Jubilees,—of religion, of the priesthood, and of the mission. To the end he was a loving and considerate father, a watchful shepherd, and faithful laborer on the English mission during a space of fifty-seven years.

He lived ten years after John Davenport, having seen the latter quit for Boston 'the republic his wisdom had planned, his foresight protected, and his energy advanced. He died on the eve of the English revolution, having lived to see the

Fathers of his province begin to labor in America, and after having seen the failure of the theocratic principle in New Haven, and the absorption of his brother's colony by the shrewder and more democratic settlement of Connecticut (Hartford), while the last shreds of the Pequot lands were slipping from the grasp of the unhappy tribe, and the fierce old Sachem Uncas was drawing near to the end of his tragic life.

Together these brothers went down into the arena of life, but the same lot fell not to both. The one, wearied and sick with Old World strife, abandoned early the scenes of discord and embitterment to find peace and freedom in the wilderness; the other, from the early dawn of his life to its late close, stuck to "the laboring oar" in a period of storm and ceaseless change and agitation. While John and his associates dickered with the Indians for Montowese, or visited in secret the trembling regicides, or from the brows of their rocky warders looked in unshackled freedom and with swelling bosoms on the shining expanse of waters, Christopher with his Franciscans bent themselves to the superhuman task of reconciling the schismatic and heretical island to the old Mother Church. The one was among the parents of a new generation, of those who builded better than they knew, whose planting prospered where that of others, under better circumstances of time and climate, failed, while the other was of that spirited and fearless few whose courage rises as the fray grows hopeless, and whose self-sacrifice is the noblest testimony to the sincerity of their belief and the truth of their doctrines.

"I sing the hymn of the conquered, who fell in the battle of Life—
The hymn of the wounded, the beaten, who died overwhelmed in the strife,
Not the jubilant song of the victors, for whom the resounding acclaim
Of nations was lifted in chorus, whose brows wore the chaplet of fame—

But the hymn of the low and the humble, the weary, the broken
  in heart,
Who strove and who failed, acting bravely a silent and desperate
  part;
Whose youth bore no flower in its branches, whose hopes burned
  in ashes away,
From whose hands slipped the prize they had grasped, who stood
  at the dying of day
With the work of their life all around them, unpitied, unheeded,
  alone,
With death swooping down o'er their failure, and all but their
  faith overthrown."

COLUMBUS AND THE MEN OF PALOS.

BY JOHN GILMARY SHEA.

THE little Spanish town of Palos, which receives scanty mention in the pages of the historian, the geographer, or the traveller, owes a temporary lustre to the great voyage of Christopher Columbus, which revealed to Europe a new world. In the history of that illustrious and unfortunate discoverer it assumes a prominence that raises it from obscurity.

Palos and its people deserve the credit of having previously opened for the explorer the way to a successful consideration of his project at the Court of Ferdinand and Isabella; and when Columbus came vested with authority from the Catholic sovereigns, Palos has the additional credit of having afforded him the men and the means, without which it would have been impossible for him to make the experimental voyage.

Nay more, there are strong indications that in the experiences of the men of Palos, he had read more of the mysteries of the great ocean than he had gleaned from the Imago Mundi or from Solinus and the other works over which he had pored; and that he there added to the store of indications which he had gathered as evidences of a continent within sailing distance westward.

Palos was at that time a busy port, with a long street of Santa Maria la Rabida leading to a rocky pine-clad promontory crowned with a Franciscan convent, from whose roof and dome a panorama of land and ocean met the eye, stretching away northward beyond the frontier of Portugal.

The town had its men of means, owners of vessels that plied on the ocean and the Mediterranean, traders in peace, and when the tocsin of war sounded, ready to cope with Moslem or Portuguese or Frenchman.

It lived and prospered by the sea, and its inhabitants looked to the ocean for their gain and prosperity. Naturally everything relating to navigation was a matter of study, and as naturally the convent of Santa Maria la Rabida felt the influence.

As such houses were generally in those times, this convent not only afforded religious guidance and comfort to the people, but was at once the hostelry, hospital, and school for the town near it, and we may well suppose that there was always in the community of gray-robed religious, some friar versed in the learning most required by the people of a seaport town, cosmography, astronomy, and navigation.

No picture is more vividly impressed on our minds from childhood than that of Christopher Columbus, knocking at the portal of this convent of Santa Maria la Rabida in 1485, to ask shelter for himself and his son Diego. But to those who have studied his life, it is an unsettled question how or why he came to this spot. He had just left the Court of Portugal after his long and fruitless efforts to induce the king to send him out on a voyage of discovery, and after advantage had been taken of his statements, by sending out a surreptitious expedition.

Having determined to lay his plans before the Spanish Court, which was then at Cordova, Columbus was on his way to that city, but the convent of La Rabida was not on his direct route.

The port of Palos and the reputation of its pilots and captains could not have been unknown to Columbus. Pedro Correa, who had married a sister of his late wife, lived hard by at Huelva; and if this gentleman was not also known as Muliar, Columbus had another kinsman of that name in this immediate vicinity.

He had therefore friends in this part of the peninsula, but he was destined to find in this modest and secluded convent near Palos, some of the most influential friends he ever had, disinterested men, ready to support his theory as to a voyage westward and to aid him at court to secure its fulfilment.

From the convent of La Rabida you now look down on vineyards and stretches of sand, on the river Tinto and on the Odiel. The little hamlet of Palos, with its few laborers and vineyard men, is hidden from the sight. The little city of mariners and merchants has vanished. There is no semblance of a seaport, and the thriving city which the monarchs of Spain in the fifteenth century could order to furnish and equip caravels for a long voyage, does not in the nineteenth century possess even a fishing-smack. The ruins of a lighthouse alone suggest that ships once frequented its waters.

In the days of Columbus it had all the bustle of a seaport town, and adventurous mariners trod its streets who could recount voyages on all known seas.

When the wayfarer at the convent in 1485 began to talk to his friar hosts of his project of sailing westward till he reached Asia, he found more ready listeners than he had met at the Court of Portugal. To the Franciscan friars of La Rabida there was nothing very startling or impracticable in the theories and projects of Columbus. Two of the religious took especial interest in him. Father Antonio de Marchena was an "astrologer," as a student of astronomy was then styled. To him the theory of Columbus presented no scientific difficulties; and as to the practical test, there was a witness in Palos who declared it feasible.

Such a voyage out into the ocean had already been attempted, and clear-headed mariners in Palos believed it could be made successfully. Had not Martin Alonzo Pinzon, the wealthiest ship-owner in the town below, talked in the same strain, and had he not brought from Rome accounts of a Mapa Mundi and of books in the Pontifical Library, that told of land beyond the ocean? Had not Pedro de Velasco, a citizen of Palos, discovered the Island of Flores? Had not Pedro Vasquez de la Frontera, whose roof-tree they could see, sailed westward in the Portuguese service till the ship's course was impeded by vegetable growth, which seemed so impenetrable that the commander lost heart and turned back, though Vasquez sturdily maintained that he must soon have reached land, had he but persevered?

The friars, accustomed to hear such accounts, found no difficulty therefore in looking with favor on the plans and projects of their enthusiastic guest, who wished to devote the wealth he might acquire to rescuing the holy land from the hands of the unbeliever. The science of Marchena supported the views of Columbus, and the heart of Father Juan Perez was won by the religious fervor of the Italian navigator. Though living in this retired cloister, he was not unknown at court. Queen Isabella had been his penitent, and had confidence in his judgment. Catching the Crusader enthusiasm with which Columbus exposed his projects, the two friars resolved to use their influence at court in his favor.

We can hardly suppose that a question of navigation and the sea was decided in their minds at once; or that it was not canvassed and examined by the aid of the experienced mariners of Palos. They could scarcely have ventured to present the project to the consideration of the court, without being able to declare that it had been considered and deemed feasible by the judgment of the practical seamanship of the port from which they came.

It seems almost impossible to believe that the projected voyage of exploration was not submitted to Martin Alonzo Pinzon, the most influential man in the place, to Velasco, one who had already revealed some secrets of the great ocean, and to Pedro Vasquez de la Frontera, who had already attempted what Columbus proposed. The voyage of this navigator under an Infante of Portugal, inspired perhaps by the very propositions of Columbus to that court, has been strangely overlooked. Yet the evidence of it exists in the documents of a lawsuit between the heirs of Pinzon and those of Columbus, which were examined by Navarrete, by Irving, and others, but of which a complete analysis has only recently been given by Captain Duro. The fact of his voyage is mentioned in the testimony of Alonzo Velez Allid, the Alcalde of Palos, who says he sailed till embarrassed by the *yerbas* in the sea, evidently the Sargasso Sea, which is covered for hundreds of miles with a mass of the curious berry-bearing sea-weed, in which peculiar fishes dwell and build their nests. The same statement is made by another citizen of Palos, Fernando Valiente, and another witness refers to a conversation between Columbus and Pinzon in the very house of this discoverer of the Sargasso Sea.

Las Casas, who generally follows Ferdinand's narrative, mentions both the reasons alleged in his time for the visit of Columbus to Palos; that given by Ferdinand, that he was on his way to the Spanish Court at Cordova, and turned aside to Palos to leave his son with Correa; and that maintained by others, that he wished to question the experienced navigators of Palos, and gather what further proofs or indications they had met with of the existence of a continent beyond the Atlantic. Las Casas leaves it to his readers to decide, and with the light of the testimony, we cannot believe that Columbus, ever on the alert to seek out evidence of his theory, would refrain from questioning men at this place, especially one who had belonged to a recent Portuguese expedition. The piety of Father Juan Perez, and the learning of the guardian of the convent, Father Antonio de Marchena, as we know, aided Columbus in his final appeal to the Sovereigns of Castile and Aragon.

Columbus reached Palos utterly without means, as is generally admitted, and we have now evidence not only that he formed an acquaintance with Pinzon before he left the place, but also received sixty ducats of gold from that generous man to enable him to reach Cordova.

It seems, therefore, that the good friars and sturdy mariners of Palos gave Columbus hospitality, encouragement, information, and substantial aid. To it he owed the favor he received at court, and the ultimate success, when after the fall of Granada, Isabel the Catholic resolved to undertake the proposed discovery.

That Columbus selected Palos as the port where the expedition was to be fitted out, could have been prompted only by his remembrance of its welcome. But it so happened that the people of Palos were in the position of culprits. For some things done and committed by them, as the royal document says, "in our disservice," they were condemned by the Royal Council to serve their Majesties for twelve months with two caravels, equipped at their own cost and expense, whenever and wherever ordered, under heavy penalties.

Columbus had been ordered to sail with three caravels. Palos was thus called upon to furnish two of them. The order was read to the Alcaldes of the place, at a church still standing in Moquer, the Church of St. George, in presence of Columbus and Father Perez; and the magistrates bowed in submission, professing their willingness to obey.

But the accomplishment of the royal command was not so easy. The owners of vessels, alarmed at the prospect of a voyage of unknown length and destination, sent their caravels away in every direction to prevent their being seized.

The Queen finally dispatched an officer, Juan de Peñasola, to enforce her orders. After meeting protests and delays, Peñasola seized the "Pinta," belonging to Gomez Rascon and Cristobal Quintero, of Palos, but it was found impossible to fit her for the intended voyage.

One vessel Columbus was to charter and fit out with the means placed at his disposal; with less difficulty he secured as this vessel, a caravel known as the "Mariagalante," or "Santa Maria," built in Galicia, in Northern Spain, and hence often referred to as "La Gallega," the Galician vessel.

But without the other two caravels he could not proceed. At this point Martin Alonzo Pinzon came forward. He had already befriended Columbus; his influence alone could solve the present difficulties. There was some understanding between him and Columbus, by which he not only furnished the third caravel, the "Niña," or "Santa Clara," but equipped the "Pinta," gave his own personal services to the enterprise, and summoned his brothers, kinsmen, and retainers to man the vessels. They promptly rallied around a man who was a terror to the Portuguese, of known determination and valor.

What the orders of the Court, and the sentence of the Council, and the presence of a royal officer could not effect was achieved almost instantly by the word of Martin Alonzo Pinzon—so great was his influence at Palos—an influence the family enjoys to some extent even now in those parts.

What was the agreement or understanding between Columbus and Pinzon? It was not committed to writing, and in the legal proceedings instituted by Pinzon's son, it is not made very clear. Las Casas, recognizing the fact that the fitting out of the expedition depended on securing the co-operation of Pinzon, says: "We must undoubtedly believe that he must have promised him something, because no man moves except for his own interest and utility"; and he concludes by declaring that it is very probable and near the truth, according to all that he could ascertain, that Martin Alonzo Pinzon alone, or with his brothers, furnished for the expedition a sum equal to that which Columbus had received from the Queen.

Without any distinct bargain he would thus be a partner, and we may well believe that Columbus promised Pinzon, as one witness declares, "half of all interest in the honor and profit," or as another declared he heard, "that he would share with him as with a brother."

Columbus fitted out the "Mariagalante," engaging such men as he could find, and his crew was a motley one, made up of men from all parts, not all Spaniards even, for an Englishman and an Irishman figure on the list, with Portuguese and men from various parts of Spain, but not a single man from Palos. They were evidently not a crew on whom much dependence could be placed.

But the caravel "Pinta," with Martin Alonzo Pinzon as captain, and his brother Francis as master; and the caravel "Niña," with Vicente Yañez Pinzon as captain, had crews almost to a man from Palos or the neighboring town of Moquer, kinsmen or adherents of the Pinzons, men who had sailed and fought many a time under their command, and were ready to follow them literally to the ends of the earth.

The "Pinta" had, indeed, on board its discontented owners, who endeavored to cripple her, so that Columbus might be forced to abandon all idea of retaining her in his service, but after he refitted her in the Canary Islands all trace of this feeling disappears. From that time these vessels seem to have been more easily and contentedly handled than the "Mariagalante."

Accordingly, when on the 16th of September they reached the yerbas, or sargasso, the men of Palos, who had heard of its existence, showed no alarm, but on board the vessel of Columbus himself the crew showed great discontent, " mi gente andaban muy estimulados." As some say, they became mutinous, and according to Hernan Perez Mateos, a witness in the lawsuit, Pinzon offered to go with some of his crew and compel submission.

The signs of land increased. Birds known never to be far from land were recognized; pieces of wood and cane cut by human hands were seen floating.

As the sun was sinking on the 25th of September Martin Alonzo saw what he took to be land in the southwest, and his cry: Land! Land! was followed by his hailing Columbus and claiming the honor. Men climbed the masts of the "Pinta," as others did those of the "Niña"; all agreed that it was really land. During the night the vessels ran southwestwardly, and in the morning no land was in sight. Columbus and Pinzon had been studying a map, apparently Toscanelli's, and Columbus, believing the nearest land to be Japan, thought that they had not sailed far enough, and preferred to make the mainland of Asia.

Yet there is every reason to suppose that Pinzon actually saw land, and was not deceived, as Columbus maintained, by a bank of cloud. So experienced a seaman would not be likely to make so grave a mistake, and Las Casas, who was too strongly attached to Columbus to be unjust to him, says distinctly: "Till night all continued to affirm that it was really land, and I certainly believe that it was so, because following the route they had constantly taken, all the islands which the admiral afterwards discovered on his second voyage were then in that direction—southwest."

Two weeks longer the vessels sailed on, making, however, less than four hundred miles, and then on the 11th of October, Rodrigo Bermudez, of Triana, a sailor on Pinzon's vessel, the "Pinta," which was in advance of the others, discovered land beyond all dispute. Las Casas in his Journal of the first voyage gives this credit fully to Pinzon's sailor; but the honor and the petty reward were claimed by Columbus, on the ground that at night he had seen a light moving in the darkness.

Up to this time the allusions to Pinzon in the diary show no feeling. Columbus indeed nowhere bestows any praise on his subordinates, and we, of course, look for none in regard to the services of Pinzon. But from the discovery of land which secured to Columbus his titles of Admiral of the Indies and Viceroy there is a marked change. A breach had taken place between the admiral and the stout captain of Palos. We have too scanty information to decide whether the fault lay in the arrogance of Columbus in the first flush of his new-won honors, or in the jealousy of Pinzon. The latter left us no account or statement of his voyage; but Columbus, in the diary of this expedition, speaks of the great evil that Pinzon had said and done, and in another place, alluding to him, declares that he "will not suffer the acts of bad men, of little virtue, who presume to do their own will with little respect, against a man who had conferred that honor on them."

Pinzon probably felt that his all-important services in fitting out the expedition entitled him to some consideration at the hands of his commander.* He may have felt, too, that

---

* "Eso merezco yo por haber os puesto en la honra en que estais."—Testimony of Francisco Medel, as to Pinzon's reply to Columbus.

his own claim to have first discovered land, and the still better established claim of one of his seamen, had been unjustly set aside.

Some time after, according to Las Casas, in November, or as others say, in October, he parted company with Columbus, unintentionally as he declared, mutinously as his commander maintained. It was not till the 10th of January, nearly two weeks after the grounding and loss of the "Mariagalante," that he rejoined the admiral, who was continuing his explorations in the "Niña."

They sailed for Europe in company, but in a storm the "Pinta" again parted company with the "Niña," and the caravels reached the peninsula at different points,—the "Niña" at Lisbon, the "Pinta" at Báyona in Galicia. Each then proceeded to Palos; Columbus in the "Niña," commanded by Vicente Yañez Pinzon, entered that harbor on the 15th of March, and later on the same day the "Pinta" also arrived, her commander broken in health and spirits.

The two Palos vessels thus returned in safety, after a voyage of nearly seven months, and their captains and crews long mourned as lost, were all restored to their homes and kindred. Not a single man of Palos was left in the fort on the Island of Santo Domingo, the garrison having been made up from the crew of the "Mariagalante."

Pinzon was conveyed from his house to the convent of La Rabida, where he sank rapidly in spite of the care of the friars, and when a messenger came from Queen Isabella to summon him to the court to make his report of the voyage, the staunch old captain of Palos had breathed his last, and his body was already doubtless committed to the earth in the little cemetery of Santa Maria de la Rabida.

During his stay at Palos Columbus was for at least a part of the time in the house of Martin Alonzo Pinzon and also at the convent. We can infer from this, at least, that a complete reconciliation took place. The friars, Father Juan Perez and Antonio de Marchena, friends of both, doubtless effected this restoration of friendly feelings between the two men, whom they respected.

From this time Pinzon and the men of Palos were consigned to oblivion. No reward, no honor, was paid to the men who had volunteered to carry out the expedition, when the powers at the command of Columbus had failed, and he was utterly without means to effect his project, but was on the point of disastrous defeat.

It was not till the Spanish monarchs finding themselves hampered by the powers granted to Columbus, when the discovery itself was doubtful, and the extent of the New World unknown, thought of the unrewarded services of Pinzon and his brothers. The grant of a coat of arms to their descendants, by the Emperor Charles V., acknowledged rather than paid the debt; and though the suit in behalf of the heirs of the Pinzons against the heirs of Columbus had the influence of Government, it brought nothing to the ancient family of mariners.

A city in the north of Spain, for its gallantry in repelling the French, was once honored by making every one of its inhabitants a nobleman; Palos, where so many from the discoverer of the Sargasso Sea had contributed to the discovery of a new world, which furnished unrewarded two of the vessels and their crews for the expedition of Columbus, received no honor; her commerce was allowed to dwindle away, till the city which gave many of the best pilots, like Alaminos, the man who threaded the bays and inlets of the American coast, vanished, and the mighty men of the sea are in our day represented by a deserted harbor and a few vine-dressers.

The port from which Columbus and the Pinzons sailed is one of the dead cities of Spain.

A movement for tardy reparation has been made by Captain Césareo Fernandez Duro, of the Spanish navy, an active member of the Royal Academy of History of Madrid, to whose close, careful, and judicious study of unpublished documents, we owe an exhaustive work on the alleged expedition of Governor Peñalosa from New Mexico towards the Mississippi in 1662, and more recently the first full analysis and extracts of the Pinzon-Colon lawsuit, which had hitherto been so uncritically used in researches as to the voyages of Columbus.

MAJOR GOSSELIN, U. S. A.

By Edmond Mallet.

Among the Canadians who played an important part in the Revolutionary war, Major Clement Gosselin was in his time one of the most distinguished.

Clement Gosselin was the son of Gabriel Gosselin and Genevieve Crépeau, and was born at Sainte Famille, on Isle Orleans, Province of Quebec, June 12, 1747. He seems to have belonged to a distinguished and influential family, which still numbers many members in the district of Quebec. In 1770 he married at Sainte Anne de la Pocatière, Marie Beuve Dionne, daughter of Germain Dionne and Marie Louise Bernier. According to an extract from the Register of Baptisms, Marriages, and Burials in the parish of St. Hyacinthe, on the Yamaska River, under date of May 12, 1791, now in my hands, it appears that he had previously married Charlotte Monilmete, then deceased. In 1791 he married Catherine Monty, who bore him a daughter named Marie Genevieve, who was baptized Sept. 20, 1804, by Rev. Mr. Bélaire, parish priest of St. Luc. This child is the only one that I have succeeded in tracing among his descendants.

When the Americans invaded Canada in 1775 with the view of wresting that colony from England, and enrolling its people in the revolutionary movement, which subsequently found its most sublime expression in the Declaration of Independence, a considerable number of Canadians threw off the yoke of their allegiance to the British crown and rallied to the American standard. Among those who offered their services to General Montgomery was Gosselin, who soon had an opportunity of showing his devotion to the American cause on the field of battle. This took place at the Rivière du Sud, when the Seigneur de Beaujeu, who was hastening to the relief of Quebec with a strong detachment of Canadians, was entirely routed by a squad of American soldiers and Canadian volunteers. Gosselin, taken prisoner in this action, was confined in Quebec till the spring of 1778, when he was released. He struck through the woods, and kept down the Connecticut River with one of his elder brothers, Louis Gosselin, and his father-in-law, Germain Dionne, and an Indian guide, and he joined Washington's army at White Plains, N. Y. Gosselin was commissioned captain of a company in Hazen's Canadian regiment, called "Congress' Own." He displayed great valor to his personal honor in the American cause to the close of the war. General Washington, hearing of his intrepid courage, as well as his devotion to the principles of the Revolution, confided several important secret commissions in Canada to him. In this capacity he traversed Canada in 1780, entering by the way of Lake Champlain and Richelieu River, and returning by way of the uninhabited woods of Maine.

At the battle of Yorktown General Lafayette commanded one of the Divisions of the American army, and in his general orders he praises the coolness and bravery displayed by Hazen's Canadian regiment during that heroic action. This little battalion of brave fellows was reduced to 250 men. During the action Captain Gosselin was severely wounded at the head of his company. When the army was disbanded in 1783, his intrepidity and distinguished services had won him the rank of major, and he was honorably dismissed.

I have been unable to find the discharge of Major Gosselin, but I had the good fortune to find that of one of his men, which I copy here on account of its historic value, which renders its precious.

The matter in Roman represents the printed portion of the document, the italics the words inserted with a pen:

By His Excellency | George Washington, Esq., | General and Commander in Chief of the Forces of the |
United States of America. |
These are to certify that the Bearer hereof *Sergeant Louis*

Marney of the United States of America—in *General Hazen's* Regiment, having faithfully served the United States *six years and Seven Months* and being inlisted for the War only, is hereby Discharged from the American Army—

Given at Head-Quarters the 30 June, 1783.

G? *Washington.*

By His Excellency's Command,

J. *Trumbull, Ind. Lp.*

Registered in the Books of the Regiment,

Benjamin Mooers, Adjutant.

The above *Lewis Marney Sergeant* has been honored with the Badge of Merit for *six* Years faithful service.

Moses Hazen |

Brig Gen'l.

[REVERSE.]

Headquarters, June 30, 1783.

The within Certificate shall not avail the Bearer as a Discharge, until the Ratification of the definite Treaty of Peace ; previous to which Time, and until Proclamation thereof shall be made, He is considered as being on Furlough.

George Washington.

After the war Major Gosselin, like hundreds of Canadian soldiers, received bounty certificates entitling them to certain lands in the vicinity of Lake Champlain. In 1789 he sold 1,000 acres in Champlain Town to James Rouse.

Sergeant Marney sold his land to Adjutant Benjamin Mooers the next year for $150.

In 1791 Major Gosselin married Marie Catherine Monty, daughter of Francis Monty, who had been an officer in Livingston's 1st Canadian regiment. The marriage took place Nov. 8th at Chazy, before James Murdock McPherson, Justice of the Peace, formerly lieutenant in Hazen's regiment. Although Congress appointed a Canadian chaplain, Rev. Francis Louis Chartier de Lotbinière, of the Order of Malta, for the Canadian troops, the chaplain does not appear to have followed the army, and the spiritual interests of our Canadians were sadly neglected. A very old priest named Francis Valley (François Vallée, if he was a Canadian), visited Hazen's regiment on the Hudson, before the disbandment of the troops, and administered the sacraments to some of the soldiers and their refugee families; but after they settled on their lands they were entirely deprived of the services of a priest.

As a good Canadian, Major Gosselin wished to have his marriage blessed by the Church, and accordingly proceeded to St. Hyacinthe the next spring. The Rev. J. B. Durouvray, formerly of Isle Orleans, made his marriage valid May 12, 1791, on presentation of a dispensation granted April 5th. He did not, however, remain in Canada, his previous acts exposing him in those days to be called rebel and spy. He returned to the valley of Lake Champlain, and died on March 9, 1816.

LE GARDEUR DE ST. PIERRE.

A FOOT-NOTE.

BY EDMOND MALLET.

["This commander is a knight of the military order of St. Louis, and named Le Gardeur de St. Pierre."—*Washington's Diary*.]

THIS was Jacques Le Gardeur, Esquire, Sieur de Saint Pierre, Knight of the Royal and Military Order of St. Louis, who belonged to the Repentigny branch of the noble family of Le Gardeur of Canada. The family is of Norman origin, and descended from Jean Le Gardeur, Sieur de Croysille, who was ennobled in 1510. Charlotte de Corday, widow of René Le Gardeur, Sieur de Tilly, of Thury-Harcourt, in Normandy, grandson of the Sieur de Croysille, came to New France in 1636 with her two sons, Pierre Le Gardeur, Sieur de Repentigny, and Charles Le Gardeur, Sieur de Tilly, and her daughter Marguerite, wife of Jacques Le Neuf de la Potherie, and settled near Quebec. Pierre Le Gardeur, and his wife Marie Favery, whom the Venerable Mother of the Incarnation and the Intendant Talon eulogized as a woman of extraordinary beauty of character, had three children born to them in France and three in Canada; and the youngest French child, Jean-Baptiste, who later inherited his father's titles, married Marguerite Nicollet, daughter of Jean Nicollet, who discovered Wisconsin in 1634. From this marriage issued Jean Paul Le Gardeur, the first Sieur de St. Pierre, who distinguished himself in the discoveries and explorations of the West, as well as in the wars between New France and New England.

Jacques Le Gardeur, second Sieur de St. Pierre, whom

Washington visited in the Ohio valley, was the youngest son of the above-named Jean Paul Le Gardeur, Sieur de St. Pierre, and of Josette Le Neuf de la Villière, his wife, and was born in 1701, at the seignory of Repentigny, situated near Montreal, which had been granted to Pierre Le Gardeur, Sieur de Repentigny, in 1647. At the age of fifteen he was already in the service of his country among the Indians. In 1732 he was ensign in the colonial troops, and in 1735 he was appointed commandant at Fort Beauharnois among the Sioux, on Lake Pepin, in Minnesota, which post he abandoned in 1737. In that year he was lieutenant, and commanded a company from Canada in the expedition against the Chickasaws, and erected a small fort on the Yazoo in Alabama. In 1745 he commanded scouting parties in the vicinity of Saratoga and Crown Point in New York. In the following year he conducted an expedition to Acadia. He was sent to command the post at Mackinaw in 1747, and restored order in the Upper Country, for which he was highly praised to the French Court by Governor La Gallisonière. In 1750 he was promoted to a captaincy, and placed in charge of a party to continue the explorations of La Vérendrye, the discoverer of the Rocky Mountains. He, however, failed to find the river of the West (the Columbia of Oregon), and personally penetrated west only as far as the Saskatchewan. He returned to Montreal in September, 1753, and was at once sent to the Ohio River department and its dependencies to relieve Marin, the commandant, who was dangerously ill at Fort Le Bœuf. In December of that year he received the visit of Major George Washington, whom he treated with marked courtesy. He was then indeed a veteran in the service of his country, but he was only fifty-two years of age. He was relieved by De Contrecœur just before the capture of Washington and his little army at Fort Necessity, and in the following year he commanded the corps of Indian allies in Baron Dieskau's ill-fated expedition, and was killed in the first engagement at the battle of Lake George, September 8,

1755. His relatives, De Repentigny and De Montesson, were severely wounded in the same battle; and long after the day of thanksgiving ordered to be celebrated in New England in honor of the victory at Lake George had passed away, his faithful Nippissings and Algonquins continued to take English and Iroquois scalps to avenge his untimely death.

Some of the younger members of the Le Gardeur family removed to France after the capitulation of Canada, and these distinguished themselves as generals in the French armies and as governors of provinces. One of them was commander of a ship in the fleet of De Grasse, which came to America to assist Washington in achieving the independence of the United States.

FATHER PETER MILET'S CAPTIVITY AMONG THE ONEIDA INDIANS, 1689-1694.

The Jesuit missionaries Father Isaac Jogues and Brother René Goupil were captured by the Iroquois and brought as prisoners to the Mohawk, to die by savage hands at Gandawagué, near the present Auriesville. Father Bressani and Father Poncet were subsequently taken by the same fierce tribe and cruelly tortured, but were finally saved. The next of the missionaries to fall into the hands of the Iroquois was Father Peter Milet, who in the following letter, written in 1691, gives an account of what befel him from the time when he was lured out of Fort Frontenac by the Indians.

He was sent from France to Canada in 1667, and soon after his arrival was assigned to the mission at Onondaga, and repaired to his field of duty with Father Stephen de Carheil, guided by the great chief Garakonthié. At Onondaga he continued the labors of Father Julian Garnier, and soon obtained the Indian name of Teharonhiagannra. In 1671 he succeeded Father Bruyas at Oneida, and established the sodality of the Holy Family to increase the piety and fervor of the Christian converts. Soenrese, a noted chief, became one of his flock and aided him greatly by his zeal. Meanwhile English influence was exerted to excite the Iroquois to war with the French, and de la Barre, governor of Canada, raised a force to invade the territory of the Five Nations. As the missionaries would no longer be safe in the cantons, they were all recalled, and in July, 1684, Father Milet reached the French camp on Lake Ontario, after having been nearly seventeen years among the Indians. He was sent subsequently to the fort erected by the French at Niagara, and remained there as chaplain till the post was abandoned in September, 1688.

The Marquis de Denonville was ordered by the king to send

some Iroquois prisoners to France to be put in the galleys. To obtain them, that governor not only resorted to stratagem, but employed the missionaries in his treacherous work in such a manner as to expose them to the greatest danger, and almost destroy the influence they had acquired in their long and painful ministry. As part of his plan, Denonville asked that Father Milet should be sent to Fort Frontenac, a p st near the present city of Kingston in Canada, to act as chaplain, instead of a Recollect Father, on the pretext that his great knowledge of the Indian languages and character would enable him to effect more good. He was there used, without any suspicion on his part, however, in entrapping some Indians, and the Iroquois, as we see by his letter, held him responsible.

In 1689, at the instigation of Leisler, the Five Nations of Iroquois raised the largest force they had ever put in the field, in order to attack Canada. They invested Fort Frontenac, and, as the letter tells, induced Father Milet and a surgeon to come from the fort to their camp to attend some sick people and made them prisoners.

The reader can follow in Father Milet's letter the narrative of what befel him.

Failing to capture Fort Frontenac, the Iroquois army descended the St. Lawrence, and made an unexpected attack on the village of Lachine, above Montreal, murdering most of the people and nearly destroying the place. The French retaliated by sending an expedition of Canadians and Indians which destroyed Schenectady. Then from New York and New England three expeditions as mentioned by Father Milet were sent to attack Canada by sea and land.

Amid all these stirring events the Jesuit missionary remained a prisoner at Oneida, although by his adoption as Otasseté, he became virtually one of the sachems of the nation. His influence was so great that the English used every exertion to put an end to his captivity, while the French were equally anxious to have him remain, so long as he was in no actual danger.

His history after the date of the letter will be seen in the appended documents.*

LETTER OF FATHER PETER MILET TO SOME MISSIONARIES IN CANADA.

ONNEIST, OCTAVE OF ST. PETER AND PAUL, 1691.

REVEREND FATHERS:

You will be, I am sure, very glad to learn the way in which the Iroquois and especially the Oneidas have preserved my life from my capture at Fort Frontenac to this time. It will, I believe, console you and good people will bless God. I will say but a word of the manner in which I was captured with Surgeon St. Amand, whom I took with me at the request of the Onondagas, in order to bleed some of their warriors, as they said, the better to deceive us. They had given us to understand that their people had gone to Montreal to make proposals for peace. The surgeon was taken to the cabin of the patients whom he was to attend, and I to that of the sachems and chiefs, who were assembled there to discuss various subjects, on which they said they wished to consult me, and have me pray for a pretended dying man, but really to make me a prisoner. I was asked whether the officers and soldiers did not go out. I answered: No, and that I was sent to learn what they desired of me and the others. "You must pay then for all," they told me, and at once two of the strongest fellows who had been selected to arrest me, sprang on me, seized me by the arms, took away my breviary and everything else I had about me. Every one addressed reproaches of one kind or another for having always been very much opposed to the Iroquois, but Chief Manchot of Oneida told me to fear nothing, that the Christians of Oneida whom I had baptized would preserve my life. I needed this support, because the English, it is said, had tried me and already burnt me in effigy. The said chief commended me to the warriors who were carrying me off, not to let me be stripped and take me in my clothes to their tribe; but as soon as he left me to join 300 Iroquois of all tribes who were leaving their ambuscade to endeavor to give me some companions in misfortune, and to surprise the fort, if they could, I was demanded, and at the

---

* For Father Milet, see the "Relations de la Nouvelle France," 1667 to 1672, those for 1673, and 1673-9; Charlevoix, "History of New France," iii.; "N. Y. Colonial Documents," iii., iv., ix.; "Collection de Manuscrits," i., ii., N. Y. Documentary History.

same time my girdle was taken off, another took my hat, a third took away my soutane, and a fourth my shirt. In fine others pulled off my stockings, and took away my shoes. They left me only my breeches, and even they were demanded by some men of importance, who said that they had dreamed, but my guard opposed these observers of bad dreams, and rescued me from the hands of those who wished to massacre me on the spot, and who incensed at the ill treatment they professed to have received from the French through my influence, had thrown me into the water and trampled me under foot.

The attempt of the Iroquois on Fort Frontenac having failed, because they did not succeed in capturing a Frenchman who contrived to get in and warn them of the ambuscade, I was untied from a sapling to which I had been bound, to await them on the banks of the lake, and I was put barehead into a canoe to take me in company with 3 or 400 Iroquois to an island two leagues below Fort Frontenac, where they awaited the main body of the Iroquois army of 1,400 men.

It was there that I was received with great shouts by the upper Iroquois,* who lined the whole shore to see me bound and brought as it were in triumph. Some rushed into the water to receive me as the canoe neared the shore, where they made me sing a song, as I did on the spot, and which they repeated and made me repeat several times for sport: Ongienda Kehasakchoua—I have been taken by my children. Ongienda Kehasakchoua—I have been taken by my children. To thank me for my song a Honnontouan (Seneca) struck me with his fist near my eye, leaving the mark of his nails, so that one would have thought it a stroke of a knife. After this I was taken to the cabins of the Oneidas, where they did not permit any other insult to be offered me, nor even let them compel me to sing again in the Iroquois style. Some individuals even sent for me and made me pray to God, and sing hymns of the Church, either alone or with other French prisoners, who were sometimes brought there, and who sang with me the *Veni Creator Spiritus*, etc.

Toward evening we dropped down eight leagues below the fort and spent two days there. It was at this place that a woman of Honnontouan (Seneca) whom I did not know, rendered me an important service, by giving me a kind of English cap, because I was bareheaded and often exposed to the rays of the sun, which had affected me greatly. This woman afterwards passing by this place made herself known to me. She is the mother of Andotien-

---

* Onondagas, Cayugas, and Senecas.

nons, a Christian at the Mountain.* God reward her for her charity which she rendered me so seasonably and with such a good grace.

From that place the army straggled to Otonniata,† where it remained three days. There a council of war was held. I was near passing the line and being immolated as a public victim. There were three Frenchmen prisoners with me, two whom Mr. de Valrenne had given to go with Onnonaragon to convey to Montreal the first information of the descent of the Iroquois, and who had fallen into the ambuscade laid for them two leagues from the fort, and the surgeon who was captured with me. The Onondagas who had taken up the war kettle at the instigation of the English had surrendered us to the four nations, and they had no one left to throw into that war kettle which was to rouse the courage of the warriors. The resolution was accordingly adopted to restore us to the disposition of the Onnontannes, so that they might themselves select the one best suited for their purpose, and the lot would probably have fallen on me, both because putting me to death would have been a mercy (? menace) of a war without peace, such as they seemed to desire, and because I was generally held up as a great Iroquois and English state criminal. One day at noon an Oneida chief came for me and took me bound as I was to the council of all the Iroquois nations assembled on a neighboring hill. I was placed beside the surgeon, whom I found in the posture of a prisoner of war as well as myself ; the two other prisoners were not there, because those who had the disposal of them were scattered hunting, and had taken them along. This is in my opinion what broke up the scheme, or what saved me that time from danger. "We are not all assembled," said a Goiogoen (Cayuga) sachem, and after looking at me for some time, he told me to pray to God. I asked him whether it was to prepare to die, and I was told No, and that I should only pray to God in my ordinary way. I accordingly rose and made a prayer in Iroquois, in order that all might understand it. I did not forget to pray in particular for all my hearers. When the prayer ended I was made to sit down on the ground : one of my arms was unbound, and I was soon after sent to the camp of the Oneidas. I had scarcely reached it before several of the leading men among them, came to express their joy that I had returned. They had been alarmed for me and told me,

---

* The Iroquois mission then on the Mountain near Montreal, and conducted by the priests of St. Sulpice, who subsequently removed it to the Lake of the Two Mountains, where it is still maintained.

† An island in the St. Lawrence.

that they had not taken part in the council held to put me into the hands of the Onondagas, that only the chief who had led me there, had done it of his own impulse, without consulting them, but that this should not occur again, and that I should be conducted to Onnei8t. In fact the next day they detached two chiefs with about 30 men to conduct me, while the army pursued its march towards Montreal.

On my journey I was pretty well treated in all the cabins of Oneida; they themselves prepared a mat for me, and if they had anything good to eat, they gave me my share among the first, but at night they never forgot to put the rope around my neck, feet, and hands, and around the body, for fear, they said, lest God should inspire me to escape, and they be deprived of the advantage and glory of conducting me to the nation, but I had no such thought, and preferred to die if God willed it, at Onnei8t, which was the place of my former mission rather than in any other place in the world. I was not loaded with anything during the march, except that towards the end of our journey. one of the two chiefs who had charge of me, gave me his bag, which was very light, to carry. At the last sleeping place. ten leagues from Onnei8t, I met a Christian woman named Mary, who in the name of her father and mother gave me a large rosary strung on tin, with a fine medal of the Holy Family. She told me to put it on my neck which I did. Happy meeting ! which filled my heart with consolation, and almost made the young braves who conducted me lose hope of being able to enjoy themselves seeing me burnt at their arrival. as it was the custom to do with the first prisoner brought in when they had determined on war; but they lost it almost entirely, when two leagues from the town we met another Christian woman of the first nobility at Onnei8t, who awaited me with her daughter, whom I had formerly baptized the same day as herself, and with her husband who was the second chief in whose charge I was, and who having left the army, on purpose to conduct me more safely had gone on two days ahead to notify his wife of my approach. They had all come there to meet me, with several little refreshments of that country, with which this Christian woman provided me abundantly and she asked me to whom of those who accompanied me, I wished to be given. Then she took the rope off my neck and unbound my arms. She gave me a white shirt and a blanket of fine stuff that belonged to her daughter. Would any one have believed that among savages there would be found such generous friendship and such deep gratitude for having received baptism as this ? It was the eve of St.

Lawrence's day and all the morning I had been preparing myself as well as I could for whatever might befal me, and to endure the fire, if need be, in imitation of that great Saint, but I confess that I could scarcely restrain my tears on beholding the charity and heart of these poor Indian Christians. Having recovered a little, I asked whether it was to adorn the victim and whether I was to die on my arrival. The good Christian woman told me that nothing had yet been settled, and the council of Oneida would decide in its own time.

A warrior had already lent me, at Otonniata, a little jacket, perfectly new, of which they did not wish to deprive me then, and the Christians having already given me new clothes, they made me continue my journey with the livery (totems) of the two most important families of Oneida, that of the Bear and that of the Tortoise.*

Messengers were at once sent to notify the sachems that I was near, in order that they should also come to meet me, and kindle a fire of awaiting within the town; they came, but they were not all in the same state of mind, as those of whom I have just spoken. One sachem, after saluting me in Indian fashion, three times tried to strike me in the face with his fist, but as my arms were free, I thrice parried the blow, almost without reflection, and when the Indian had desisted, they made me sit down near the sachems, and Chief Manchot, husband of the good Christian woman, who had chosen to conduct me thus far, harangued them and told them in the name of the other chiefs who followed the army, that I did not come as a prisoner, but as a missionary who returned to visit my flock; that it was their will that I should be taken to the council cabin and put at the disposal of the Agorianders,† or people who managed the affairs of the country, and not at the disposition of the soldiery or people, as he now placed me in their hands, and for himself he withdrew.

A sachem of the Bear family, a great friend of the English, then made a strong speech, declaring that I belonged to the side of the

---

* Each Iroquois tribe was divided into gentes or families, the Bear, Tortoise, and Wolf, being the chief with some smaller ones. A man could not take a wife from his own gens, but from one of the others, and his children belonged to the gens of their mother. The father's name and rank descended to his brother or to the children of his sister.

† The Agolanders were a noble class, possessing great influence. Cartier evidently found it dominant at Quebec.

Governor of Canada, who was overthrowing the Cabin,* and who had completely burned the towns of the Tsonnon8a (Senecas).† He said so much that I feared that the fire which was there, was kindled to burn me before I entered the town, as they sometimes do, but his speech at the close grew milder, and he said that as the chiefs had recommended that I should be taken to the Council Cabin, which is a privileged cabin, I must be taken there. This commission was entrusted to a man of the nation called Skannehok8ie, from the country of the Mohegans, and naturalized among the Iroquois.

I passed that bad country under the guidance of this protector, who carefully kept aloof several drunkards who wished to insult me and stop me on the way. I was astonished to see the number of people who appeared on all sides, and in this company I was made to enter the Council Cabin, which had become a Cabin of war by the intrigues of the English and other enemies of the Faith.

It was the cabin of our good Christian woman, for she received me there with great welcome, but it was soon afterwards necessary to conceal me, drunken men and women coming from all sides to assail us and utter a thousand insults against those who protected me, hurling stones against the cabin and threatening to overthrow everything and to set it on fire. "Since war," said they, "is begun, we must not be deprived of the first fruits that come to us." The good Christian woman, Gouentagrandi, told me that she suffered great distress, when war was sung in her cabin, rather than in some other, in order to be able to save my life more easily or to preserve that of the Governor of Canada or any other Frenchman of rank, if they had the misfortune to be taken prisoner, and in fact she has not only preserved me, but she has also preserved several other French, both in her cabin and in others, and it may be said that if any good has been done or is now done in this mission, it is to this good woman after God that the first praise is due.

On two other days after the fury of the drunkards had passed, my friends wished to have my case decided, and my fate settled, before matters became more exasperated, in case any Iroquois were killed at Montreal where they had gone in war. I was taken to the place where the chiefs of the two families, the Tortoise and the

---

* The five Iroquois nations in their symbolical language formed a cabin, the Mohawks holding the door and the Onondagas the fire. They called themselves as a nation Hotinonsionni (French notation) or Hodenosausee (English notation) meaning "They form a cabin."

† This alludes to Denonville's invasion of the Seneca territory.

Bear, had assembled to decide on my lot. Both concluded that they must wait for the return of the warriors and know more particularly their intentions and those of the Onondagas before coming to any determination; that meanwhile the town should be assigned as my prison, and that I might visit what cabins I chose. I remained in this state about three weeks, where I had nothing to suffer except from the drunkards, who were importunate and made various threats. In the visits which I made I was generally called *Genherontatie* (The dead or dying man who walks), and those who returned from Orange, a little English town, brought no tidings favorable to me. But if on one hand I had these little crosses to suffer, our good Susan and the other Christians, following her example, were a great source of consolation to me, for not to speak of the care they took of my temporal well-being, they brought me children to baptize, they sent the sick or afflicted to me to comfort, adults came to confession, and to give me an account of the state of their consciences since my departure. People came to me to pray to God, and for other spiritual necessities even in the little lurking places, where they hid me for fear of the drunkards. The mat was prepared for me on Sundays and holidays, and when we were disturbed in the cabins, the mat was taken into the fields to pray God there more apart and in greater peace.

What consoled me also greatly was two crosses which I found planted on the graves of two Christians who had died after I left this mission. I shall speak only of one for the present. I had a good Christian who made open profession of Christianity, and who laying aside all human respect, sang in the chapel when I formerly dwelt here in the capacity of missionary. He did not in my absence forget the esteem with which God had inspired him for his faith, but persevered constantly in his good practices, and having fallen from the top of a tree to the ground, crushing his whole body, he suffered his pains for thirty days that he survived his fall with great patience as the Christians assured me. He made them frequently come together to pray to God for him, especially as death approached, and he ordered that after his death a cross should be set up on his grave to show that he wished to die a Christian, and that he did not recognize as true kindred any but those who became Christians like him. It was the custom of these poor orphaned Christians to assemble and pray in this way for each other, especially in sickness and the various accidents that befell them. Even those who were not Christians imitated them, and made little banquets to bring them together and have their children baptized, and find through their prayers, some remedy either for body or mind; others sometimes expressed to me how much they had grieved for my absence, having no one with whom they could really console themselves, or who could heal their consciences, and who often found themselves shocked amid a perverse nation and in a strange disturbance of mind, when the enemies of the faith and of the French excited all to war. But let us come to the decision of my trial.

The Iroquois army which made the attack on (Lachine) having returned, it was found that three of this nation had remained there, among others a leading chief who got drunk and was killed in a cellar. He would not allow himself to be taken. This had irritated the Iroquois warriors, who not satisfied with the prisoners whom they had brought, demanded that I should be presented with the others, as being also a prisoner. Our Christians fearing that the warriors who love carnage and glory in killing men, might cut off one of my fingers or commit some other outrage on me, to open the way to my death, concealed me more carefully than ever, they made me sleep sometimes in one cabin, sometimes in another, and sometimes even in the fields, so that the warriors and drunkards could not find me. Above all others, my protectress combined prudence with her zeal to extricate me from the danger I was in. With this view she went to meet her relatives who were some of the most influential warriors in order to anticipate them. She told them how she had preserved me till that time, and that she was determined to continue to do so with all her might; that no ill treatment could be done to me that she would feel deeply herself, that she would not bring me forward till the sachems assembled to decide the fate of all the prisoners, and till I had been set at liberty. They replied that she had done well, and that so far as they cared she might adhere to her resolution.

At last the day came when our sentence was to be pronounced. We were four who ran a risk of being burned. We all appeared to be given or to be put in place of the Iroquois who had been killed by the French and then judged in a final tribunal. While they were examining our case I had time to hear the confessions of my comrades in misfortune and give them absolution. Two of them were burned: for my own part I could only commend myself to the Providence and the mercy of God. I was sent back to different Councils or from tribunal to tribunal, because, on the one hand, I passed among our Iroquois as a great criminal and great deceiver, who had caused their fellow-countrymen to be seized under pretext of a St. John's day festival, and on the other, I was protected by our Christians, some of whom were the most notable in the country, and they could not put me to death without afflicting them.

Many, however, thought that I would never get off; the rosary had already been taken off my neck and my face had been painted red and black as a victim to the demon of war and Iroquois wrath; but the family to which all had been already referred having assembled again, where the most important women were allowed to attend, a friendly act was done me by giving me instead of a chief who had died long before of disease, instead of for one of those who had been killed in the attack on the French at a place called La Chine above Montreal, or who had been arrested as prisoners at Fort Frontenac and transported to France, who were reckoned as numbered with the dead. This chief was named Otasseté, which is an ancient name of the first founders of the Iroquois republic.* The one named Gannasatiron, who by this donation became sole master of my life, used it very obligingly, he consulted only the warriors of his family and asked advice only from the two Christians who protected me most, and who of course concurred at once with him in the assurance of life which he gave me by these words: "Satonnheton szaksi—My elder brother, you are resurrected." At the same time he had two of the leading sachems summoned to report it to them: these sachems made fine speeches and congratulations exhorting me to uphold the interests of their nation more than I had yet done. Some days after a banquet was given to the notables of the town. [The friend ?] of Father de Lamberville, named Garakontié, brother of the chief of the Onondaga nation, and brother of the famous Garakontié who first bore that name, was invited to the ceremony, where a new name was given to me as an authentic mark that the Oneidas had adopted me and naturalized me as an Iroquois. My rosary had also been restored to me, and to crown my little happiness Gannasatiron fearing that I might feel hunger in his cabin, where there was not much corn, put me in that of my protectress, who is of the same family, where I had already remained for three weeks, and where I had been so well defended, and where all the important councils are held. It is there that we celebrate the holidays and Sundays, and where a mat has been prepared for me, and a little grotto which is dedicated to Our Dying Lord, X^{to} Morituro.†

---

* Otasseté was one of the hereditary sachems of the Oneida nation. The title descends in the female line, and Susanna's adoption of Milet apparently enabled her to bestow the name, which made him actually a sachem.

† Everything in this letter indicates that when he wrote he had received nothing from Canada, and of course without vestments and chalice, could not say mass.

The English were not pleased with the decision of the Oneidas in my favor: they at first reproached my main protectors Tegahoiatiron and his wife who had gone to trade with them, and had given them a little note which an Iroquois had made me write with charcoal, in the presence and at the request of my protectress to buy some goods for him which he ordered of an English friend of his. The English displeased at their sparing my life and wishing to use this opportunity for my ruin, at once mounted their horses to go promptly and report to all the Iroquois nations that I had written very bad things. The Christian woman who knew how reluctantly I had consented to write the note, because I clearly foresaw that ill-minded heretics would make trouble out of it, asked to see the note and recognizing : "Is this," she said, "the bad things that have been written to you ? It was I who made him write them there and I know that he mentions only such and such things in it. You must have a very badly formed mind to tell so many lies, to make all this long talk about a wretched note, of which I know the contents, and to slander in this way a poor unfortunate man." She shut their mouths that time and her husband added : "If you are at war with the French, fight them as much as you like, but do not bring false charges against a man who belongs to us, and whose business is very different from that of war."

This did not prevent the English from appealing from the decision of the Oneidas to the Iroquois of the Mohawk and Onondaga. These mounted men made several journeys about the matter, as well as for their great war project, but to no purpose. So far as I was concerned all their intrigues and their solicitations served only to teach them, that the Indians after having once given a person his life, it was not their custom to deprive him of it.

The English then having gained nothing by this journey, made other efforts to withdraw me from this place. One of their deputies came to me one day to compliment me in my little grotto in the name of the Commissary at Orange on the condition of my captivity, saying that he felt compassion for me, that he was making effectual plans to deliver me and have me sent back to Quebec; that he would give two Indians for me, &c. Thereupon I assured him that after the obligations I was under to the Oneidas I could not leave them. He interrupted his compliments to tell me that the English would not suffer me here: I replied that that was the affair of my brothers and of all the Oneidas, and that he must apply to them. He said he would do so. I was immediately summoned to attend the harangue of this envoy of the English general: he went out after me, and we entered the place of assembly, he by one door and I by another. The place where he was to speak was the cabin of my brother Gannasatiron. He began by saying that three English Governors were holding a council of war at Orange, but that the Governor of New York especially invited them to come and meet them and form a new alliance with them. The deputies of all the Irroquois nations proceeded to Orange where great rejoicings were made over the great success which their arms had recently had at the place named La Chine. He again exhorted them to war by various presents. He told them further that he gave up Fort Frontenac to them, and that they could easily become masters of it as the garrison was dying of hunger, but as the Irroquois army did not reach it till after the French had abandoned it, they had not the glory of having driven them out. Much provisions was still found there, which showed that famine had not driven them from that post, but rather the difficulty of revictualling when necessary, had induced the Governor of Canada to recal his soldiers.

Beside this the English had formed the project of three armies; the first was to go by the way of the river of the Irroquois (Sorel), the second by the way of Lake Saint Sacrement (Lake George) and the third by sea to besiege Quebec, where the three armies were to unite.

But this grand project did not succeed in the way they had flattered themselves: the two land armies were broken up by a special Providence of God. The small-pox stopped the first completely and also scattered the second in which there were 400 English who were compelled to march back by order of the Irroquois, who at least at that time might be said to be more masters of the English, than the English were of the Irroquois.

Of this second army nothing was left but a party which attacked the French at La Prairie de la Magdeleine. The Governor of New York put under arrest three or four of the principal English officers who had brought back their troops without having carried out the orders to wrest New France from us or sack it. From Quebec we learned of the wretched failure of their third army, and they did well to write to me about it and many other things, as but for this the English would have made the Irroquois believe them, by rehearsing their victories and prowess, but blessed be God that He has preserved Canada. May the danger they have escaped teach the people of the country wisdom in the future.

<blockquote>
Bella premunt hostilia,
Da robur, fer auxilium—
O Deus misericors.
</blockquote>

The Fish, that is the name of the Governor of Manath or New York, has earnestly exhorted the Irroquois not to listen to me, and especially to beware of my letters. His side must be weak indeed, if my pen can demolish it, but it must be that the Spirit of God is working, and I believe that it will be the sins of the English, rebels to their king, rather than my pen which will overthrow them. Here we see and hear of so many ill-devised plans emanating from the English, that the Irroquois seem much more reasonable than they are when they are not.

The Oneidas having adopted me for one called Otasseté, who in his lifetime was a member of the Council, and who was regarded from all antiquity as having been one of the mainstays of the nation, they oblige me sometimes to attend the Councils, if only to know what the matter is, to explain it to them, at least when they are important affairs that concern the country.

It annoys the English and those who uphold their interests to see me there, and they would much like to exclude me or deprive me of voting or being chosen to any position. The true Oneidas on the other hand and those who still support the cause of the Faith and their country, give me all the authority there that they can, and as the honor of God and the Church is often intermingled in public affairs of this kind, I am myself compelled to speak on many occasions which regard the service of God, because the Indians who depend on the English for their trade generally dare not say anything that can displease them, and I know hardly any one except our good Susanna Gouentagrandi who speaks to them boldly and who maintains thoroughly her rank of Agoianders for the faith and for the land of Oneida.

Gannasatiron, my brother, once spoke to them pretty boldly, for as they were always importunate and made several attempts to get me into their hands, sometimes with the sachems, and sometimes with him, because they always referred them to him, they asked him how it came that he alone was master of my person and not the sachems. "It is because I took him as my brother, and because I won him in war, and so far he belongs to me, as what you have in your house belongs to you. But to tell the truth I am no longer his master. He has become my elder brother and I have made the Christians his master, and as you will not find it easy to get much from them, I advise you to desist." Yet as they still pushed the matter, he said to the Commissary, K8iter (Schuyler), that he must give up all hope of carrying me off, and that he must say no more about it. The Commissary called me aside the next day, and told me through an interpreter, that up to this time he had done all he could to release me from captivity, but that I had not supported him, and that I had paid no regard to all his efforts, any more than I had to the obliging offers made to me by the Minister at Orange.*

I replied that I was much obliged to him and to the Minister for their offers, but that I should have been still more so, if the offers and compliments had been followed by any good result, but that they had been only words in the air, which did not harmonize and really contradicted each other, without my being able to see anything solid or even a single word in writing on which I could rely or by which any kind of satisfaction was made for all that they had unjustly made me lose at Onondaga, which was a place in some sort privileged and devoted to the discussion of affairs of peace, especially concerning the Iroquois nations, that moreover, no matter what tempting offers at Orange might be made to me, I could never resolve to leave the Oneidas, to whom I was under too great obligation, which I could never acknowledge except by sacrificing myself in imitation of Jesus Christ for their temporal and eternal welfare.

Thereupon we parted and since that time the English have left me in comparative quiet, although I know that while here I am a great thorn in their side, but if I could also serve them before God for their conversion and for the public repose, I would do so with all my heart and I would forget all the wrong they have done me.

From all the foregoing your Reverences may judge how much I need the help of heaven and the prayers of good people. To induce you more earnestly not to withhold them, I will say a word more of the zeal of my protectress.

The Mohawks who being very near the English are strongly attached to them tried to carry me off on pretext of wishing me to come on Christmas day to hear the confessions of some Christians who are among them, but our good Christian Gouentsgrandi who was not ignorant of their designs, told the messengers that any who were so anxious to pray to God and go to confession at Christmas could come themselves to Onnei8t, and that she saw through the trick of the English into whose hands they wished to deliver me.

Besides the wampum that the good woman has often given to speak in the councils, she has given several banquets to bring people together and to give greater solemnity to the festivals of Christ-

---

* Rev. Mr. Dellius.

mas, Epiphany, Easter, &c., to such an extent that in these banquets we have raised the standard of holy peace, and in case they do not wish to hear there of holy war, in the hope that Heaven will be on our side, and that those who obstinately refuse to hear the voice of God, who does not love the shedding of human blood, and who does not wish war unless it is holy, will sooner or later be punished, and on the other hand those who favor us will be rewarded. Yet we put all our little designs in the hands of God, and at the foot of the crucifix, seeking only the glory of His holy name, and the salvation with the quiet of the nations. I commend them once more to the holy sacrifices and prayers of your Reverences, of whom I am in heart and with respect,

  My Reverend Fathers,
    Your very humble and very obedient
      Servant in Our Lord,
        PETER MILET,
         of the Society of Jesus.

I would have much more to write, but time does not permit. This with God's help will be for another occasion.

CATHOLIC AND ANTI-CATHOLIC ITEMS FROM NEW YORK AND PENNSYLVANIA PAPERS, 1775—1782.

" LONDON, March, 1775.—The following address has been sent to Ireland for publication, and should be published in all the American papers:

"ADDRESS TO THE SOLDIERS.

" GENTLEMEN:

" You are about to embark for America, to compel your fellow subjects there to submit to POPERY and SLAVERY.

" It is the glory of the British soldier, that he is the defender, not the destroyer of the civil and religious rights of the people. The English soldiery are immortalized in history for their attachment to the religion and liberties of their country.

" When King James II. endeavored to introduce the Roman Catholic religion and arbitrary power in Great Britain, he had an army encamped on Hounslow Heath, to terrify the people. Seven Bishops were seized upon, and sent to the Tower. But they appealed to the laws of their country, and were set at liberty. When this news reached the camp, the shouts of joy were so great, that they re-echoed in the Royal Palace. This, however, did not quite convince the King, of the aversion of the soldiers to be instruments of oppression against their fellow subjects. He therefore made another trial. He ordered the guards to be drawn up, and the word was given, that those who did not choose to support the King's measures should ground their arms. When, behold, to his utter confusion, and their internal honor, the whole body grounded their arms.

" You, Gentlemen, will soon have an opportunity of shewing equal virtue. You will be called upon to imbrue your hands in the blood of your fellow subjects in America, because they will not submit to be slaves, and are alarmed at the establishment of Popery and arbitrary power in one half of their country.

"Whether you will draw those swords which have defended them against their ememies to butcher them into a resignation of their rights, which they hold as the sons of Englishmen, is in your breasts. That you will not stain the laurels you have gained from France, by dipping them in civil blood, is every good man's hope.

"Arts will no doubt be used to persuade you, that it is your duty to obey orders, and that you are sent upon the just and righteous errand of crushing rebellion. But your own hearts will tell you that the people may be so ill treated, as to make resistance necessary. You know that violence and injury offered from one man to another, has always some pretence of right and reason to justify it. So it is between the people and their rulers.

"Therefore, whatever hard names and accusations may be bestowed upon your fellow subjects in America, be assured that they have not deserved them; but are driven, by the most cruel treatment, into despair. In this despair they are compelled to defend their liberties, after having tried, in vain, every peaceable means of obtaining redress of their manifold grievances.

"'BEFORE GOD AND MAN THEY ARE RIGHT.'

"Your honour, then, Gentlemen, as soldiers, and your humanity as men, forbid you to be the instruments of forcing chains upon your injured and oppressed fellow subjects. Remember that your first obedience is due to God, and that whoever bids you shed innocent blood, bids you act contrary to his commandment, I am, Gentlemen, Yours, etc.,

"AN OLD SOLDIER."

—("N. Y. Gazette and Weekly Mercury," July 3, 1775, No. 1238.)

EXTRACT OF A LETTER FROM DUBLIN, DATED SEPTEMBER 9, 1775.

"PHILADELPHIA, January 3.—Lord Bute's plan is to humble the Americans. Three regiments of Roman Catholics are to be raised in Ireland to send to America, which has bred a great deal of disturbance. But it is hoped the Protestants will put a stop to it."

"FOR THE PENNSYLVANIA JOURNAL.

"SEASONABLE THOUGHTS.

"The Virtue of the British Court seems to have swallowed up all the virtue of the island of Great Britain. The common people are lost in a night of ignorance. They annex no ideas to Slavery but wooden shoes and soup meagre. Even the Roman Catholic Religion has now no terrors in it to Englishmen. . . . ."—("Pa. Journal and Weekly Advertiser," January 3, 1776, No. 1726.)

"PHILADELPHIA, January 24.—On Sunday last was interred in the Roman Catholic church-yard, in this city, the remains of Emanuel Holmes, painter and glazier, of the district of Southwark, a Portugese by birth, yet he loved liberty; for the defence of which he joined one of the companies of riflemen of this county, and constantly exercised with them. A foreigner, almost a stranger, without relations (except his wife and children), without dependants, extensive connections, or acquaintance; and, although esteemed an honest man, not eminent as a tradesman, yet his remains were attended to the church-yard, not only by the company in which he associated, but also by as great a number of other respectable citizens and people of his neighbourhood, as ever attended a funeral in that populous district: such is the respect shown to those who declare themselves willing to step forward in the defence of liberty, a respect which wealth cannot purchase, nor flattery bestow!" — ("Pa. Journal and Weekly Advertiser," January 24, 1776, No. 1729.)

"To Mr. Rivington,

"Sir:

"As your Gazette very often creeps out among the Rebels, in spite of all the care that is taken by their leaders to prevent the deluded multitude from knowing the truth, your inserting the following address in your paper may perhaps be of use to some of those unhappy people.

"To the Inhabitants of the once happy and flourishing Province of New York, by infatuation now called the independent state of New York, but which is more properly termed the state of Confusion. The Address of one of your late inhabitants in behalf of himself, and a number of your exiled countrymen.

"Know the truth, and the truth shall make you free.

"Dear Countrymen:

. . . .

"Consider the artifices used by those among you, who from the first had no other view than the aggrandizing themselves, by overturning our most excellent constitution, and persuaded you it was for the sake of that liberty, which you then knew not the want of. Let me seriously ask you, where is your liberty now? They also persuaded you it was to avoid taxation. But did you before now, know what taxes were? And, if their government should continue, is there not an insupportable load of taxes entailed on you and your posterity, not to third and fourth, but to the fourteenth generation. You were told that it was to avoid the establishing or countenancing of Popery; and that Popery was established in Canada (where it was only tolerated). And is not Popery now as much established by law in your state as any other religion? So that your Governor and all your rulers may be Papists, and you may have a Mass-House in every corner of your country (as some places already experience). Nay, have you not been taught to place your greatest hopes and confidence in that nation which is universally esteemed the greatest enemy both of religion and civil liberty? And how far it is in their power to give you any assistance, you may now judge from the success of the great fleet they sent you, which has almost exhausted you of provisions. . . . .

"We know that you were made to believe that, through the interposition of France, your King and your mother country (that country to which you owe so much) would be obliged to leave you to yourselves, and withdraw her fleets and armies. . . . .   A NEW YORK EXILE."
—[Rivington's] "Royal Gazette," January 6, 1779, No. 237.

"MR. RIVINGTON:

"The inclosed Song was transposed by a Refugee, and intended for the Loyalists out of the lines, whilst d'Estaing was in Georgia; the reason of your not having it at that time, was owing to its being mislaid. If you think proper to insert it in your paper, you'll oblige one of your constant readers, who begs leave to subscribe himself a

"JAN. 27, 1780.   LOYALIST.

"TUNE OF THE CUT-PURSE.

. . . . .

II.

"From France d'Estaing to America is come,
  And banditties of French will rob our estates;
These robbers are all protected by Rome,
  Consult but their annals, record but their dates.
      It's their politick's
      To burn Hereticks,
Or poison by water that's fetch'd from the Styx.
Let Frenchified Rebels, in vain then attempt
To bring our Church or our King to contempt;
  For no Rebel cut-purse shall e'er give us law,
  Should they prove as daring as Tyler or Straw.

III.

" The farces of Rome, with carrying her host,
  Are laugh'd at and jeer'd by the learned and wise;
  And all her thin tinsels apparently lost,
  Her stories of reliques and sanctified lies.
      Each ignorant Joke
      Believe, or you smoke,
  And if we are conquer'd we receive the Pope's yoke;
  But despising the councils of Adam or Lee,
  As Loyal Americans, we'll die or be free.
      For no Rebel cut-throat shall e'er give us law,
      Should they prove as daring as Tyler or Straw.

IV.

" Let curses most vile, and anathema's roar,
  Let half ruin'd France to the Pope tribute pay.
  Briton's thund'ring cannon shall guard safe our shore,
  Great George shall defend us, none else we'll obey ;
      Then France, join'd by Spain,
      May labour in vain,
  For soon shall th' Havana be ours again:
  The French then will scamper, and quit every State,
  And find themselves bubbl'd, when Morblieu! it's too late,
  For no Frenchman or Rebel imp of the law,
  In our old constitution can point out a flaw."
        —(" Royal Gazette," January 29, 1780, No. 348.)

"NEW YORK, August 2.—The French Admiral has taken possession of Rhode Island in the name of the King of France, and displayed the French colors, without the least deference to the flag of their ally, the revolted Americans; this affords disgust and mortification to the Rebels, evincing that their Roman Catholic friends intend to keep possession of all they seize on in North America."—(" Royal Gazette," August 2, 1780, No. 401.)

[Extract of] " AN ADDRESS TO THE PEOPLE OF THIS COUNTRY, BY AN AMERICAN LOYALIST.

... " People can still remember what were called privilege and freedom, in their happier period of political security. What is meant by those prostituted names now, they are obliged every day to feel. Military arrests, arbitrary imprisonments, a suppression of trials by jury, in cases where they are most essential; the infinite number of frauds practised upon the honest yeomanry, through the medium of an expiring currency, the unsupportable pressure of public taxes levied with no object in view, but unless it is to enslave the people; the introduction of foreign troops, and the toleration of the Roman Catholic religion, with many other incidents of the like stamp, all help to swell out the dark catalogue of grievances in New England."—(" Royal Gazette," October 7, 1780, No. 420.)

[Extract of] "TRANSLATION OF HIS MOST CHRISTIAN MAJESTY'S LETTER TO THE COUNT DE ROCHAMBEAU [on the success of the French arms.]

.... "I have written to the archbishops and bishops of my kingdom to cause te deum to be sung in the churches of their dioceses, and I address this letter to you to inform you, that I desire it may be likewise sung in the town or camp where you may be with the corps of troops, the command of which has been entrusted to you, and that you would give orders that the ceremony be performed with all the public rejoicings used in similar cases, in which I beg of God to keep you in his holy protection.

"Done at Versailles, the 28th of November, 1781.

" (Signed) LOUIS."
—(" Pa. Packet or General Advertiser," May 7, 1782, No. 881.)

SUMMARY ON THE CATHOLIC RELIGION IN THE ENGLISH COLONIES IN AMERICA.

[From the Italian in the Propaganda Archives. Communicated by Very Rev. Charles A. Vissani, O.S.F.]

I.

OF all the English colonies, the one which contains the most Catholics is the province of Canada, ceded to the British Crown by the treaty of Peace concluded at Paris, in the month of February, 1763. By this treaty were ceded the islands of Cape Breton, St. John, and the other islands in the Gulf of St. Lawrence.

The inhabitants of this vast province, of European origin, were then all Catholics, and besides these many zealous missionaries had converted a great number of the old savage inhabitants. And although some English Protestants have settled amongst them, for all that the mass of the people is Catholic. By the 4th article of the said treaty they are to enjoy the free exercise of the Catholic religion. And, in fact, it is known by letters recently come from those parts, that they not only freely profess the Catholic religion, but do it in the same public form they were wont to do under the French rule; but the Indian missions have suffered greatly from the calamities of war.

There is one Episcopal see at Quebec, capital of the province. Its jurisdiction is believed to extend over the neighboring provinces of Nova Scotia and Acadia, over which the French had pretensions. The last bishop died soon after the city of Quebec fell into the hands of the English. The jurisdiction is exercised by the Vicar-General Capitulars.

There was a seminary at Quebec under the direction of

secular priests of the famous congregation of St. Sulpice * at Paris, and they had another house also at Montreal, a city situated on the St. Lawrence River, more than a hundred miles above Quebec. It is believed that these two establishments are still maintained.

II.

In the provinces of Nova Scotia and Acadia there are few English settlements. The principal ones are Halifax and Annapolis, and the inhabitants of these places are Protestants; but in the rest of the country there are many inhabitants of French origin, who, before the late war, were called Neutral French; these are for the most part Catholics, and are attended by priests sent to them from Canada; but they do not enjoy the same liberty of exercising the Catholic religion openly.

III.

The great island of Newfoundland is comparatively deserted, although belonging to the English. It is not known whether there is any important establishment except the city of Placentia; nor is it known whether there are any Catholic inhabitants. For all that, a few years since, an Irish Augustinian religious received faculties from the Vicar-Apostolic of London to administer the sacraments, intending to go and reside on that island to assist many of his countrymen in their spiritual needs. These flock there every year to engage in the fisheries carried on in those parts.

IV.

Coming next to the rich and populous provinces which compose New England and New York, some few Catholics are scattered here and there, but they have no exercise of their religion, and no priest near them. And if we may

---

* A mistake. The Sulpitians were at Montreal, and Priests of the Foreign Missions at Quebec.

judge of the future by the present temper of the inhabitants, there is no likelihood of their permitting Catholic priests to be introduced, because they are chiefly rigid Presbyterians and other sectarians most hostile to the Catholic name.

V.

Among the former possessions of Great Britain on the American Continent the only colonies where priests are settled, are the two provinces of Maryland and Pennsylvania. In this last province the Catholic religion is formally tolerated by law. In Maryland the laws are hostile as in England, but for all that, they seldom think of enforcing them, and there is generally a kind of tacit toleration.

It is asserted that there may be about 16,000 Catholics in Maryland, about half communicants. They are attended by twelve missionaries of the Society of Jesus.

The number of Catholics in Pennsylvania is 6,000 or 7,000. They have a public church in Philadelphia, the capital city of the province. They are attended by four priests also Jesuits. These religious conduct themselves with great zeal and regularity of life.

There are also some Catholics in Virginia on the borders of Maryland; and in those parts of New Jersey which are on the confines of Pennsylvania, but they have no priests permanently residing among them; and are attended by the missionaries of the two provinces above-named.

It is not known that there are any Catholics in Carolina and Georgia, at all events there is no priest there.

VI.

Florida, a province ceded by Spain in the same treaty of Paris already mentioned, is almost deserted; but the few inhabitants remaining there are maintained in the free profession of the Catholic religion, in the same manner as the inhabitants of Canada.

VII.

Louisiana, or the province of Mississippi, which formerly belonged to the French, has been to a considerable extent ceded to the English by the same treaty, that is as far as the Mississippi River, which gives name to the province. And the same liberty is stipulated in favor of the Catholic inhabitants, who must be in considerable numbers; but what spiritual aid they have, the writer is entirely ignorant.

VIII.

In the islands the state of religion is much worse than on the continent. The Catholics there are almost all of Irish birth or origin, and are of ill-ordered life. To enter a little into detail:

In Jamaica there are some few Catholics. In these last times two priests attempted to settle there, but did not succeed in doing so. The inhabitants of that island are generally esteemed very regular livers.

In Barbaba there was lately an Augustinian religious who has since apostatized. The few Catholics there are now attended by the missionaries residing on the island of Montserrat. This, which is one of the smallest of the English islands, contains, however, the greatest number of Catholics, some 300 or 400; they are attended by three or four Irish missionaries; but they have no consideration or care for their negroes, who are very numerous.

In the island of Antigua there are also some Catholics of Irish origin, who were attended a few years ago by a Dominican Father of their nation, who being in London on some business, gave the Vicar-Apostolic a report not flattering to the morals of his countrymen there.

The island of St. Kitts also contains some Catholics, who call on the missionaries in the neighboring island of Montserrat for their spiritual needs.

IX.

But besides the islands above named, which have long been under the English sway, there is the island of Grenada, with the small island of Granadine, ceded to England by France at the same treaty of Paris; in which there is the usual stipulation for the free profession of the Catholic faith in behalf of the inhabitants. They were then all Catholics, but by the same treaty the three islands of St. Vincent, Dominica, and Tobago, which were previously called neutral, were ceded absolutely to Great Britain. The island of Tobago was deserted, but the two other islands have many Catholics of French origin; and although they have not the same assurance of religious liberty, we may hope from the present moderation of the English Government, that they will not be disturbed in its exercise.

X.

Among these different islands and provinces, there is certainly none which better deserve the attention of the Sacred Congregation, than Canada, both for its great extent, the great number of the faithful it contains, and the flourishing state in which the Catholic religion was when it came under the English sway. The death of the Bishop of Quebec was undoubtedly a great misfortune at that crisis. If the difficulties which have hitherto prevented the appointment of a successor to him continue, it would seem to be necessary that a Vicar-Apostolic should be sent there to maintain order, administer the sacrament of confirmation, and provide new pastors in place of those who have died, or are daily dying.

If a Vicar-Apostolic is sent there, it would be advisable to extend his jurisdiction over the neighboring provinces of Nova Scotia and Acadia, more especially as the Catholics who are there must be of French origin.

When the king of France founded the Bishopric of Quebec he united to the Mensa Episcopalis the two abbeys of Benevento (dioc. Lemovicen) of the Order of St. Anthony, and that of L'Etrée (dioc. Ebroicen) of the Cistercian Order, which together afforded an income of 12,000 French livres. But the present state of those abbeys is entirely unknown to the writer of the present notes.

XI.

The Vicars-Apostolic of London since the time of King James II. have always had authority over the English colonies and islands in America; but as it did not appear clearly on what foundation this custom was based, the Sacred Congregation de Propaganda Fide, in the month of January, 1757, obtained from Benedict XIV. of happy memory, a decree in favor of Mgr. Benjamin Petre, Bishop of Prusa, then Vicar-Apostolic of London, giving him for six years jurisdiction over all the American colonies and islands subject to the British sway, and after the death of that prelate, the same was confirmed March 31, 1759, for six years more to Mgr. Richard Challoner, Bishop of Debra, now Vicar-Apostolic of London.

The said Vicar-Apostolic is so far from any ambition or desire of increasing his jurisdiction in those parts, that he would with sensible pleasure behold the Sacred Congregation relieve him from a burthen, which already exceeds his strength, and to which he cannot give due attention. The great distance does not permit him to visit them in person. Hence he cannot have the necessary information to know and correct abuses; he cannot administer the sacrament of confirmation to the faithful there, who remain totally deprived of that spiritual aid; he cannot provide ecclesiastical ministers, partly for the same reason of distance, partly for want of means necessary to meet that expense.

If the Sacred Congregation, moved by these reasons, and others which will easily occur to the mind, should judge it more expedient to appoint a Vicar-Apostolic for the other

English colonies and islands, the city of Philadelphia in Pennsylvania seems the place best adapted for his residence, being a populous city, and a seaport, and consequently convenient for maintaining a free correspondence with the other provinces on the mainland, as well as with the islands. This further motive may be added, that there is no place in all the English dominions where the Catholic religion is exercised with greater freedom.*

ADVENTURES OF A JESUIT LAY BROTHER, WHO SET SAIL FOR MARYLAND IN 1657.

THE following letter from the archives of the English province will show what strange perils awaited the missionaries to this country in early days:

"VERY REVEREND FATHER:—

"Being on my way to Maryland by order of obedience to pass thence to the Indies, though I am unworthy of such a mission, and falling grievously sick there, permission was given me to transfer myself to Cadiz in Spain, and to Genoa, being well known and   if God had granted me such a grace, then when my health was restored to be bound on the first occasion to follow the journey of obedience. So having embarked on board a ship, 'Amborghes,' to go to Cadiz in Spain, I was, with the ship, taken by the Turks of Argel, so that I am a slave to their Pasha, who makes me carry a heavy chain to force me to get ransomed, saying that I am a gentleman. I have tried to obtain my ransom by legal means, for as I am

---

* This report was apparently made by the agent of the English bishops at Rome, and must be prior to Bishop Briand's appointment as Bishop of Quebec in 1766.

an Englishman they cannot make me a slave. Remaining thus in the miseries of the slavery, they have sent me here to Tunis to sell and keep me prisoner, as I am this day, saying that I am a priest, a Jew, or a French merchant; for as one of the English nation they cannot make me a slave, as there is peace betwixt my nation and that of Argel. Therefore I inform you of this, as I have been in the Society for from twenty-five to twenty-six years, and in it have always undertaken whatever holy obedience has commanded. I have always been in the colleges of Flanders. So, Very Rev. Father, I have recourse to your Reverence—not for a ransom, nor for any other thing, but only that your Paternity may procure for me proper prayers and all that belongs to a brother of the Society—for if I fail in that, my salvation will fail. I am ready to die in these people's hands, for the benefit of the Holy Faith, and to bear any labour, however intolerable,—but Father of my soul, if my conservation in the Society fails me, and I say it before the Lord God, I would die a thousand deaths in these troubles, only to shew forth the great glory of God's faith. Here I am in trouble and ready to die for God, that which fails me is my conservation in the Society. If that conservation does not fail me, whether I die or live in this slavery, I am contented. That which I most ask for is that I ask pardon of all those of the Society, and of all the world, and that God may pardon me that wherein I have offended Him. I have nothing more to ask of your Paternity, only your charity to preserve me in this most holy state. Rather would I die in the Society and be a slave, than be free with all the possessions of the world, and not be of the Society. My salvation is in the hands of his Paternity, and I have nothing further to say to him, than that I hope God may be served by me, in conforming with His most holy Will.

"From Tunis, in the Bagno of the Conception, 5th June, 1657. Your Paternity will do me the favour in sending me an answer; and to make it safer, to send it to the Father Vicar of the Mission in Tunis of the French nation.

" Your Paternity's most humble subject, and recognizing my obligation,

"THOMAS BRADFORD.

" Addressed to the
Very Rev. F. Prepositus, S. J., in Rome."

[June 5, 1657.]

He recovered his liberty, and died at Ghent, Nov. 1, 1668.

FURTHER NOTES ON POPE-DAY.
BY REV. T. J. SHAHAN, LL.D.

" IN town meeting, December 27, 1768, the inhabitants exhibited a commendable zeal to eradicate two distinct evils from their bounds. They first issued an edict against barberry bushes, imposing a fine of fifteen shillings, etc. . . . . The second denunciatious vote was directed against an evil of a different kind, and less doubtfully pernicious, though it was to be visited with only an equal penalty. This was the mock celebration of Pope-Day, which had been for some time annually celebrated on the 5th of November, the anniversary of the Gunpowder Plot. The edict was as follows :

"'Whereas the custom that has of late years prevailed in this town of carrying about the Pope in celebration of the 5th of November, has been attended with very bad consequences and pregnant mischief and much disorder, which, therefore, to prevent for the future,

"'Voted, That every person or persons that shall be any way concerned in making or carrying about the same, or shall knowingly suffer the same to be made on their possessions, shall forfeit fifteen shillings to the town treasury of New London, to be recovered by the Selectmen of said town, for the use aforesaid.'

" Descriptions of this obsolete custom may still be obtained from persons whose memories reach back to a participation in the ceremonies. The boys of the town, apprentices, sailors, and that portion of the inhabitants which comes under the denomination of the populace, were the actors. The effigies exhibited were two, one representing the Pope, the other the devil, each with a head of hollow pumpkin, cut to represent a frightful visage, with a candle inside to make it 'grin horribly a ghastly smile.' And the only difference between the two consisting in a paper crown upon the head of the Pope and a monstrous pair of horns to designate the other personage. These were fixed on a platform, and lifted high on the shoulders of a set of bearers, who, in the dusk of evening, with boisterous shouts and outcries, marched in procession through the principal streets, stopping at every considerable house to levy pennies and sixpences, or cakes and comfits, upon the occupant.

" When arrived opposite a door where they expected largesses the cavalcade halted, the shouts ceased, and a small bell was rung, while some one of the party mounted the doorstep and sung or recited the customary doggerel, of which the refrain was:

" ' Guy Fawkes and the 5th of November,
The Pope and the Gunpowder Plot
Shall never be forgot.'

" At the conclusion of the orgies the two images were thrown into a bonfire and consumed, while they danced around with tumultuous shouts.

" The ban of authority issued as above related in December, 1768, against this celebration had no effect.

" In defiance of the law Guy Fawkes and the Pope made their annual procession through the streets until the destruction of the town by the British, saving only two or three years, in which it was interrupted or greatly modified through an unwillingness to give an offence to our French allies, who were loyal subjects of the Pope. Washington, in one of his general orders, prohibited the army from making their usual demonstrations on this day, out of respect to the generous power that had come to our aid in the great contest, and the New London boys were too magnanimous in their patriotism not to follow such an example. After the Revolution Pope-Day, or, rather, Pope-Night, revived in all its details, and the restrictive acts of the town being entirely disregarded, Messrs. Shaw and Miller and other magistrates, determined to try what could be done by indirect measures. Judging that the most effectual method of destroying a custom so ancient and deep-rooted would be to supersede it with a new one, which, not being so firmly established in usage, might be assailed at any time, they suggested to the populace the substitution of Arnold for the Pope, and the 6th of September for the 5th of November. This was easily adopted, only the ditty now sung at the doors ran in this manner:

" ' Don't you remember the 6th of September,
When Arnold burnt the town;
He took the buildings one by one,
And burnt them to the ground.
And here you see the crooked sticks
For him to stand upon,
And when we take him down from them
We'll burn him to the ground,
We'll burn him to the ground.
Hark! my little bell goes chink, chink, chink!
Give me some money to buy me some drink,
We'll take him down and cut off his head,
And then we'll say the traitor is dead.
And burn him to the ground,
And burn him to the ground.'

"After a few annual jollifications in this form, the whole custom fell into desuetude" (Miss Calkins' "History of New London," cxxvii., p. 480).

In Deane and Willis' "Historical Notes on Portland" (Me.), under date of Nov. 5, 1770 (from the Journal of ——), is the entry: "Several Popes and devils to-night."

In Winsor's "Memorial History of Boston," i., p. 245, it is asserted that fear of conflagration was the reason which led to the repression of these processions.

LETTER OF RT. REV. JOHN CARROLL, D.D., TO
HON. SAM. DEXTER, ESQ., SECRETARY OF
WAR, ON THE INDIAN MISSIONS.

CITY OF WASHINGTON, Sept. 15th, 1800.

SIR:—After the termination of the last Indian war, the President, General Washington, recommended, in his speech to Congress, the adoption of such beneficent policy towards the Indians as would tend to their civilization, and teach them the advantages of the Christian religion. Some clergymen made a tender of their services to co-operate in this good work. The offer of the Rev. Mr. Rivet* was accepted, and he was directed to establish himself on the Wabash; and the President allotted to him a yearly allowance of $200, or $150, the writer of this not recollecting precisely the sum, whence he visits occasionally the neighboring Indians, and applies himself incessantly in fulfilling the objects of his appointment, and disposing them to maintain a friendly temper towards the United States. He is indefatigable in instructing them in the principles of Christianity, and not without success; which, however, would be much greater if the Traders could be restrained from spoiling the fruits of his labors by the introduction and sale of spirituous liquors. In the discharge of his useful occupations, Mr. Rivet has undergone much distress. The Indians afford nothing for his subsistence; on the contrary, he is often obliged to share the little he possesses with them, or lose his influence over them. This, and the non-payment of his annuity for more than two and twenty months, have reduced him to the greatest distress. Your predecessor directed the paymaster of the troops formerly sta-

---

* M. Jeanin had been for some time near the Illinois Indians, but soon left.
—C. I. W.

tioned at Vincennes, to account with Mr. Rivet for his yearly allowance in specie, paper payments operating as a very heavy reduction of his salary. The troops are now withdrawn from that post; he knows not to whom he is to apply for payment. If there be no agent of Government on the spot, I take the liberty of submitting to you whether it may not be advisable to have his annuity placed in the hands of some person, commissioned by him to receive it at the seat of government; and, should every other occasion of sending it fail, I will endeavor to discover, and, with your permission, make known to you some means by which he may be relieved from his present distress.

I am, with great esteem and respect, sir,
Your most obed't serv't,
✠ J. CARROLL.

WASHINGTON CITY, Sept. 15th, 1800.

FIRST DIOCESAN SYNOD OF BALTIMORE.
(From a contemporaneous manuscript.)

MR. CARROLL, Bishop of the United States, has ever faithfully discharged the engagements into which he entered with the Pope. He knew his duties and was truly disposed to fulfil them, but the Pope in his bull having recommended to him not only the establishment of a seminary but the Convocation of a diocesan Synod, from the second year of his episcopacy he was occupied in this business, or rather was occupied in it from the first, and he was unable to surmount the numerous difficulties which beset him until October, 1791. It was, then, to wit, on the 27th of October, 1791, that he dispatched his letters of Convocation through the whole extent of his diocese, appointing the city of Baltimore for this Synod, setting the 7th of November as the first day of the session, and inviting, without exception, every priest in his diocese who had the charge of souls. Conformably with his desire and Convocation, on the day above mentioned, there assembled at the Episcopal mansion:

Messieurs James Pellentz, a German Jesuit, and Vicar-General of the Bishop for the whole diocese.

James Frambach, also Vicar-General.

Robert Molineux, Vicar-General for the Southern States, a Jesuit.

Francis Antony, Vicar-General for the Northern States.

Francis Charles Nagot, Superior of the Seminary of St. Sulpice, of Baltimore; John Ashton, Jesuit, Curate of Baltimore; Henry Pile, Jesuit; Leonard Neale, Jesuit; Charles Sewell, Jesuit; Sylvester Bourmann; William Elling, a German; James Vonhuffel, a Hollander; Robert Plunchett, a German; Stanislas Cerfoumont, a Fleming; Francis Beeston, an English Jesuit; Lawrence Graesel, Joseph Edom, Louis Cahier de Lavau, Canon of Tours; Jean Tessier, Director of the Seminary; John Thayer, an American, from Boston.

Being all assembled and dressed in their surplices, the Bishop in his rochet, amice, cincture, stole, and white cope, holding his beautiful mitre and crosier in his hand, they went in procession to the Cathedral church of St. Peter, in which all matters had been prepared and arranged conformably with the Roman Pontifical. The Bishop then pronounced an eloquent discourse suitable to the occasion, after which they all together made the declaration of Faith. Messrs. Leonard Neale and William Elling were named Promoters, Mr. Francis Beeston, Secretary. This session lasted till three o'clock P.M.

In the second session they enacted Statutes on Baptism, its Conditional Repetition; the Register, and a Faithful Record of Acts; Adult Baptisms.

NOTES.

SILVER CHALICE FOUND IN PENNSYLVANIA.—"About the year 1804 a small silver chalice or ciborium was exhumed at Waterford, near the remains of the fort (French Fort Le Bœuf). This a certain pious Catholic, a Mrs. Van Kirk, is said to have possessed herself of to preserve it from desecration, and took with her when she subsequently migrated to some locality further down the river."—Letter of Bishop Young, of Erie, August 6, 1855.

EARLY NOTICE OF CATHOLICS AT BOSTON.—Villebon, the French Commandant on the St. John's River, in 1698, asked to have an Irish priest stationed there to afford religious aid to the Catholics at Boston.   B.

MARYLAND CATHOLICS DURING THE REVOLUTION.—"No wonder the Catholics of Maryland were found foremost in the ranks, no wonder that they were all, or nearly all, Whigs, and a Catholic Tory a rare character."—Speech of Hon. Mr. Kennedy in the Legislature of Maryland in 1826, "U. S. Cath. Miscellany," Sept. 2, 1826.

MADAME MONTOUR AND HER FAMILY.—In the "Catholic Church in Colonial Days," p. 401, mention is made of Madame Montour. In his Appendix to the annotated edition of William Marshe's "Journal of Indian Treaty at Lancaster," in 1744, Dr. Eyle states that Madame Montour was the daughter of M. Montour, who emigrated to Canada in 1665 ("Col. Hist. of N. Y.," Vol. V., p. 65). He had one son and two daughters, namely:

1, John; 2, Madame Montour (of noted celebrity); 3, a daughter, who married into the Miamis.

Madame Montour had children: 1, Margaret (French Margaret); 2, a daughter (?); 3, Andrew; 4, Lewis.

French Margaret had children: 1, Esther, known as Queen Esther; 2, Catharine ("Col. Rec.," Vol. VIII., p. 500); 3, Nicholas; 4, a son killed in Creek Indian campaign of 1753; 5, Molly ("Col. Rec.," Vol. VIII., p. 500).

Andrew Montour had: 1, John; 2, Nicholas; 3, Mary Magdalene, alias Peggy, who was baptized in Philadelphia by a Catholic priest in early youth, but subsequently became a Moravian, and married a man named Hands.

Lewis was killed in the French and Indian War.

Esther died at head of Cayuga Lake, about 1800. In the Wyoming Massacre of 1778 she was a perfect demon.

Catharine married an Indian named —— (English name Houston), (see "Penna. Archives," 1st Series, Vol. III., p. 558), had five or six children, as stated by Conrad Weisér. The following are only known of: 1, Roland; 2, John; 3, Belle. Roland was killed in 1781 in a skirmish (see Gilbert's "Narrative"). John Montour, according to General Clark, of Auburn, N. Y., died at Big Tree in 1830; and both Roland and John were educated at Elizabeth, N. J.

John Harris in a letter of 1758 says, "Madame Montour is dead." S. M. S.

THE OLD BELL OF THE KASKASKIA CHURCH.—Some years ago, with a member of the St. Louis press, I made an accurate description of the old bell on the Church of the Immaculate Conception at Kaskaskia. As it may interest your readers I send it.

Yours truly, O. W. COLLET.

Pour l'église des Illinois
Par les soins du Sr. Doutreleau
L. B. H. Normand à la Rochele
1741.

—all in relief. On one side three groups of fleur-de-lis in relief: on the other a cross, standing on a double pedestal, top and arms terminating, each, in a fleur-de-lis group, all in relief. Cross and pedestal much ornamented in relief. Casting is rough—ornaments on cross run together. Some of the letters of the inscription scarcely legible, and apart from the context could not be read with certainty.

A hole in the top where the casting was imperfect.

Weight, about 650 pounds—estimate.

Height, about 28 inches—eye measurement.

Remark.—Assuming 1741 as the date of the casting, it could scarcely have reached the Illinois before 1743.

QUERIES.

REV. FRANCIS VALLEY.—A very aged priest of this name is said to have been at Fishkill and Highland, N. Y., about 1783, and to have married John Mary Chartier to Sarah, daughter of Sergeant

Robineau, of Le Bert's Co., Hazen's Canadian regiment, in that year. Father Farmer visited Fishkill October 4, 1781, October 31 to November 4, 1783, to attend the Canadians and Acadians there, and may have been known as Francis Valley, but no such marriage is recorded in his Register. Can any one throw any light on the subject ? M. E.

PRIESTS IN VIRGINIA IN 1678.—Among accusations made against the Ven. Father de la Colombière was this one : "That M. la Colombière sends secretly priests into Virginia, amongst others MacCarty, an Irish priest, who was carried by La Colombière's servant, and by his order to M. Le Choquenna, who lives at the Savoy; and also La Colombière told me, 'That he deserved to go thither.'" The charge was made by Oliviér du Fiquet, an informer, and may be utterly unfounded; and Virginia used in a very vague way. Is there any trace of an Irish priest named MacCarty in any part of this country at that time ? J. D. S.

NOTICES OF RECENT PUBLICATIONS.

THE IOWA HISTORICAL RECORD, published quarterly by the State Historical Society at Iowa City. April, 1888.

This number contains a sketch and portrait of Leonard Whitney; Iowa and the Draft; the address of Hon. John H. Gear before the Old Settlers' Association; and what will especially interest our readers, "Catholicity in Shelby County, Iowa," by the careful writer, Rev. John F. Kempker.

LIFE, JOURNALS, AND CORRESPONDENCE OF REV. MANASSEH CUTLER, LL.D. By his grandchildren, WILLIAM PARKER CUTLER and JULIA PERKINS CUTLER. Robert Clarke & Co., Cincinnati, 1888. 2 vols., 8vo.

These volumes are not only an important addition to our historical literature, but a work that will be read with pleasure and interest even by those not given to antiquarian studies. Dr. Cutler was an active, far-seeing man, who was brought into contact with the leaders of our Revolutionary period, and at a later period was instrumental in encouraging the settlement of our Western country. He undoubtedly had a great part in obtaining the passage of the famous Ordinance of 1787, and appears prominently in the affairs of the

Ohio Company, and the attempted French settlement at Gallipolis. Active in mind and body, science, politics, medicine, and diplomacy were but so many openings for his energy. The "Life, Journals, and Correspondence" are extremely well edited, Dr. Cutler's Diary giving a vivid picture of his time and of the men with whom he came in contact. It is certainly a work of far greater attractiveness than most of our biographical works, and will long retain a charm for the general reader, while the historical student will resort to it for many clues which he cannot find elsewhere. It is published in the creditable style that characterizes all the works issued by Robert Clarke & Co.

BIOGRAPHY OF LIEUT.-COL JULIUS P. GARESCHÉ, Assistant Adjutant-General, U. S. Army. By his Son. Lippincott Co., Philadelphia. 8vo, 505 pp., portrait.

This beautiful volume, a tribute of Louis Garesché to his father, was printed for private circulation among the family and friends. It is thus relieved from criticism, were any just, and enters into details precious to those who knew and appreciated Col. Garesché.

Of a family which on his father's side had long been Huguenot, he had in his Catholic mother, Mimika Baudry, one to fill his heart with sincere and earnest devotion to the true faith. Julius was born near Havana, Cuba, April 26, 1821, and after a course at Georgetown College entered the Military Academy at West Point, issuing thence in time a second lieutenant. His classmates at the Academy bear testimony to his noble qualities, though few could appreciate the trials to which a young Catholic is subjected there and in the lower grades of the army. His early career, his service during the Mexican war, his post duty on the frontier, all were animated by the purest, most exalted, and most practical religious principles. An arrest on frivolous grounds, with privation of rank for months, but no trial, though he demanded it as of right, was a severe test, but he bore it with equanimity. He rose gradually in his profession, and was regarded as an officer of superior ability, thoroughly master of the science of war. His military writings all show how deeply he studied all bearing on his profession. The life of an officer on our frontier posts has little to arouse enthusiasm, or stimulate serious study; but Garesché looked to the future. Wherever stationed he was a high-minded, practical, active Catholic, taking part in all work to extend the influence of religion, prominent in societies, by example and by word bringing the feeble and fainthearted into the line of duty. He wrote well, as his contributions to

"Brownson's Review" and other periodicals show. He served during the Mexican war, but was not in any of the great battles. When the Civil war began he was Assistant Adjutant-General of the army. Promotions were flying around him, but he declined the commission of Brigadier-General. He asked only to be placed on the staff of Gen. George H. Thomas, but in 1862 was placed under Gen. Rosecrans, becoming his Chief of Staff. He had a presentiment that he would die suddenly, and fell as a Catholic hero at the battle of Stone River, December 31, 1862.

The present Life, alas! will reach but few. Let us express the hope that a smaller, handier volume on this chivalrous gentleman will yet appear, to be read by every Catholic boy in the land. No nobler example of the American Catholic in his whole career can be presented; whether in his loved home, among his fellow Catholics at the altar or in church work, or guided by faith in all the duties of his state of life, or finally in a noble death in the discharge of duty to his country, Julius Garesché is a model.

ANNOUNCEMENT.

A Life of the illustrious Bishop S. G. Bruté, of Vincennes, by the Abbé Charles Bruté de Remur, has recently appeared. (Vie de Mgr. Bruté de Rémur, 1er Evêque de Vincennes, Rennes, Plihon et Hervé, 1887.) It is somewhat remarkable that the author seems not to have known the Memoirs of Bp. Bruté, by Archbishop Bayley, or the funeral oration on him. He bases his work on Lady Herbert's abridgment, Mme. Barberey's "Life of Mrs. Seton," but draws also from the "Life of John Mary de Lamennias," and the Archives of Saint Sulpice.

The Marlboro (Md.) "Gazette" of July 18, 1888, contains a paper read at a meeting of the Washington Irving Literary Society by I. S. Wilcox, Esq., editor of the "Gazette." The Society met at the house of Judge William B. Hill, and the paper, interesting in itself, is doubly so to Catholics for its notes on Catholic local history, and for the curious fact that it was written in the very house where Archbishop Carroll was born. "The old house in which he was born," says Mr. Wilson, "is still standing, and these lines have been written within its walls." A water-color sketch was made several years ago of the venerable building by the artist, W. Seymour, for Mr. John G. Shea, who engraves it in his Life of the Archbishop.

UNITED STATES CATHOLIC HISTORICAL MAGAZINE.

A MEMOIR OF THE LIFE AND LABORS OF THE RIGHT REV. AMADEUS RAPPE, D.D., FIRST BISHOP OF CLEVELAND.

BY THE REV. G. F. HOUCK.

[Read before the United States Catholic Historical Society, Dec. 5, 1888.]

In this memoir it will be the aim of the writer to portray, in simple but truthful colors, the life and character of a model ecclesiastic—a priest and bishop—who for nearly fifty years labored unselfishly and unsparingly for God and His Church. He was a man that deserved well of those to whose spiritual and temporal interests he devoted himself as a father and friend. Though no Augustine or Thomas Aquinas in learning, he accomplished far more for religion than many whose talents and erudition gave them name and fame. He was one of the pioneer priests of Northern Ohio, and the first bishop of the present flourishing diocese of Cleveland—the Right Reverend Louis Amadeus Rappe.

He was born February 2, 1801, at Audrehem, a village near Ardres (District of St. Omer), Department of Pas-de-Calais, France. His parents, Eloi Rappe and Marie Antoinette Rappe *née* Noël, belonged to the peasantry, and were highly esteemed for their probity, industry, and Christian virtues. They had a family of ten children, five sons and five daughters. The subject of this memoir was the youngest of the sons. Of his four brothers, three were killed in the Napoleonic wars, the fourth died unmarried. Destined by his father to the life of a farmer, Louis Amadeus received but an elementary education, such as the village school afforded. Trained by his parents to habits of order and industry, he soon acquired a practical knowledge of husbandry, and thus became very useful to his father in the management of the farm. He took delight in his avocation; was passionately fond of horses, a liking which he retained all his life. He was also fond of youthful sports and athletic games. Sparkling with wit and cheerfulness, he was a general favorite with the young people of his native village. His career seemed well marked out, and his family and friends did not doubt his vocation—that of a farmer.

But God was there, with His secret and admirable designs! One evening, toward the end of the year 1819, when Amadeus was in his nineteenth year, and the family were gathered around the domestic hearth, the father expressed a regret that not one of his sons had a vocation to the priesthood. He said he had always hoped to see one of them at the altar, this wish having been the dream of his life, but that now it was not to be realized. Amadeus, struck by this remark, answered: " Well, father, if you wish it I will become a priest." It need hardly be said that this answer was not taken by the family in a serious light. A general laughter ensued, so diametrically opposed to that sacred calling were his well-known tastes. On the following morning he went to his father, saying: " Father, the remark which I made to you last evening is serious. It occupied my thoughts all night; I have seriously reflected upon it, and wish to be a priest."

The sentiment thus made known to the father and to the mother, consent was readily granted, but not without doubt and fear lest their son might not persevere. They were all the more apprehensive of his firmness and perseverance, as one of his older brothers began the course of studies for the sacred ministry, but failed to reach the altar.

Soon the necessary preparations for the departure of young Amadeus were made. He went to Furnes, a small village about six miles from Boulogne, to the pastoral residence of one of his relatives, the Rev. Mr. Noël, who was parish priest of the place. Our young aspirant to the sacred ministry took his first Latin lessons from this venerable priest, under whose wise direction he seriously reflected on his vocation, which, as he acknowledged, was put to a severe test for the first few months. October, 1820, he entered the college at Boulogne, then under the direction of the celebrated Abbe Haffreingue. As he was taller and older than his fellow-students he was given charge of one of the study-rooms, an office both delicate and at times difficult, but filled by him with kindness and prudence. Even at this epoch in his life he showed a keen sense of duty and a firm will. One of his relatives having seen him during a vacation full of mirth and glee, the life of the circles in which he moved, noticed that at college he was serious and sedate, and so told him. Amadeus replied: "When vacation is over I shut up all my mirth in a box, to be opened only the next vacation." As he was of a most cheerful disposition, it must have cost him no little effort to do so.

In 1821 he received tonsure at the hands of Cardinal de la Tour d'Auvergne Lauragais, Bishop of Arras. Having completed the collegiate course of studies in 1826, he went to the diocesan seminary at Arras, receiving Minor orders on December 22d of the following year. May 21, 1828, he was ordained sub-deacon, and on December 20th of the same year, deacon. The same prelate who gave him tonsure also ordained him to the priesthood on March 14, 1829.* The parish of Wismes, a small village near Fauquembergues, district of St.

---

* The facts in connection with Bishop Rappe's home, college, and seminary life were furnished the writer July, 1888, by a gentleman intimately acquainted with the lamented prelate, his cousin—Dr. De Wulf, now residing in Paris.

Omer, was his first appointment. There he remained till 1834, meanwhile also attending a neighboring mission church. The chaplaincy of the Ursuline Convent at Boulogne-sur-Mer having become vacant, and the Sisters knowing the sterling worth, indomitable zeal, and great prudence of Father Rappe, were desirous of having him appointed their chaplain and spiritual director. Mother Ursula, the superioress of the community, petitioned his Bishop to this effect, and her request was granted. Father Rappe remained chaplain to the Ursulines of Boulogne from January, 1834, till May, 1840. During this time he read, with intense interest, the "Annals of the Propagation of the Faith," which excited in him an ardent desire to devote himself to the American mission. In 1839 Bishop Purcell, of Cincinnati, passed through London on his way from America to Europe, and whilst in that city he was requested by the parents of three young English ladies to take them under his protection as far as the Ursuline Convent at Boulogne. There he met the zealous chaplain of the community and future missionary, Father Rappe, to whom he made known the spiritual destitution of his large diocese. Rev. Amadeus Rappe then offered to go with him to America. This he did, however, with great diffidence, owing to his age, thirty-nine, which he felt would be no small hindrance in adapting himself to the life of a missionary in a strange land. Another great obstacle for him was the fact that he was unacquainted with the English language. But he would allow none of these obstacles to hinder him from entering upon the toilsome and self-sacrificing life of a missionary. After receiving the necessary permission from his Ordinary to leave his diocese, he bade farewell to his charge, which deeply regretted to lose him who was to them a wise counsellor and prudent director.

The following extract from a letter written by the present superioress of the Ursuline Convent at Boulogne-sur-Mer, under date of September 20, 1888, describes Father Rappe's career as chaplain and spiritual director of said convent: "I can say that during the six years we were blessed with Father Rappe as chaplain, our convent prospered in every way. Nuns and pupils placed in him entire confidence, and he proved to all a safe and prudent director, as well as a kind and devoted father. Many were the young Protestant pupils * who, drawn by his zealous and interesting instructions and encouraged by his prudent and pious advice, entered the true fold of Christ. When his departure was known in the school, there was a general outbreak of sorrow and distress, and the day he left the convent, during his farewell discourse after Mass, tears flowed from all eyes and ill-suppressed sobs were heard all over the chapel. Nuns and pupils knew and felt they were losing a saintly guide and director, a loving father and friend."

He set sail for America, September, 1840, arriving at Cincinnati the following month. He was immediately sent by Bishop Purcell to Chillicothe in order to learn English. Mr. Marshall Anderson, a convert and most estimable gentleman, was his teacher. But Father Rappe found it very difficult to master even the rudiments of the language; in a few months, however, he was able to speak it sufficiently well to make himself understood, though his pronunciation was, and always remained, defective. About 1840 the present flourishing city of Toledo was founded. Catholics there were very few in number and had neither church nor priest; Tiffin was the nearest place whence sick-calls were attended. The Miami and Erie Canal was being built about that time, and there came quite a large influx of Catholic laborers who settled along the line of the canal and the Maumee River. There was much sickness then, the dread Maumee fever undermining the strongest constitution, and hurrying many of its victims to an early grave. To this uncultivated and uninviting field of labor Father Rappe was sent about six months after

---

* One of these pupils was the venerable Mother M. Austin, now, and since 1850, a member of the Ursuline Convent, Cleveland.

his arrival at Cincinnati. His "parish limits" extended from Toledo to the Indiana State line and as far south as Allen County. From the summer of 1841 till the spring of 1846 his labors, privations, and difficulties of all kinds were indeed trying; he never lost courage, but full of missionary zeal and self-sacrifice he labored faithfully among his people.

Before going to his mission, Bishop Purcell, well knowing the spiritual and social condition of the difficult charge he assigned to Father Rappe, suggested to him that for the sake of example to his people, it would be well were he to take the total-abstinence pledge. Father Rappe, a native of sunny France, where wine is the drink of all classes without being abused, thought this a very strange suggestion. He laughed heartily at the idea that he, always temperate in the use of wine, should now be asked to be a total abstainer. In fact he had never heard of such a practice as total abstinence from drink; much less that it was a requisite qualification for a missionary. The suggestion seemed to him absurd. He left Cincinnati for his field of labor, thinking that he was the victim of a practical joke, or of a cranky American notion. He arrived at his destination, on the banks of the Maumee; like Julius Cæsar, he came and saw, but unlike him, he was conquered. For the first time in his life he saw the grim and frightful visage of intemperance, the woeful condition of its victims. This sight so filled him with a horror of intemperance that he fought it then and during the remainder of his life by word and example. Then and there he complied with Bishop Purcell's well-meant suggestion, and took the pledge of total abstinence for life. He kept it faithfully in sickness and in health, till death. He preached and practiced total abstinence and on every possible occasion impressed his views regarding it on all who came in contact with him. He was a relentless foe of saloons, and their keepers he "tabooed." Though he aroused their hatred because he curtailed and at times ruined their liquor traffic, thousands bless his memory for the energetic measures he took in rescuing them from a drunkard's grave.* For five years, 1841-46, Father Rappe was alone in this section of the State, but his work grew beyond his strength. Hence Bishop Purcell sent him a co-laborer in the person of Father Louis de Goesbriand, present Bishop of Burlington, Vermont, who arrived at Toledo in January, 1846. At that time Toledo and the surrounding country, even as far west as the State line, were full of malaria of the most malignant type. Bishop de Goesbriand, in his reminiscences of Bishop Rappe's missionary life, says: "At certain seasons it was impossible to meet a healthy-looking person, and frequently entire families were sick and unable to help one another. Apart from the terrible malarial fever we were occasionally visited by such epidemics as erysipelas, and toward the end of 1847 we saw ship-fever-stricken emigrants landing on the docks, to die among strangers a few hours after arrival." After the Miami and Erie Canal was finished many of the laborers left with their families to seek homes in a more healthy climate. As the majority of them were Catholics Father Rappe's missions were greatly weakened. Very few Catholic families remained between Toledo and Defiance. Mass was said, however, each Sunday in Toledo and frequently at Maumee City, and on week days at Providence, Defiance, Poplar Ridge, and occasionally at Fremont and La Prairie. The roads were often almost impassable, but Father Rappe and his faithful companion found neither bad roads nor the inclemency of the weather a sufficient obstacle to prevent them from visiting each of their scattered missions at the time appointed. In his intercourse with his people, Father Rappe was most affable, and he knew well how to win their respect and confidence. He was acquainted with every family, and knew every member of each family. He had a special gift to teach catechism, and would spend weeks in a settlement preparing a few children for the reception of the sacraments. During this time of preparation he would instruct

---

* "How Bishop Rappe became a teetotaler." Catholic Universe, Nov. 22, 1888.

the children for hours each day, and always managed to rivet their attention. He was ever watchful of the spiritual welfare of the adult portion of his flock, urging them to frequent confession and a regular attendance at Mass.

To assist him in instructing the children at Toledo he secured several Sisters of Notre Dame from Cincinnati. They were of the band of *Religieuses* that had come with him from Namur, Belgium, in 1840, and established a branch of their community in Cincinnati. He secured a house, near the present site of St. Francis de Sales' church, Toledo, which was fitted up as a convent and select school for the little band of Sisters that shared with him the trials and hardships of missionary life. They remained at Toledo from 1846 to 1848, when owing to lack of support they were recalled to Cincinnati.

Bishop Purcell finding the labor of properly attending to his vast diocese, comprising the State of Ohio, too much for him, petitioned the Holy See for a division of his jurisdiction. Cleveland was considered as the most fit city in the northern part of the State for an Episcopal See and hence was so designated. Father Rappe, the zealous Missionary of the Maumee, was chosen as the first bishop of this new diocese. Although the Papal Bulls to this effect were issued April 23, 1847, they did not reach Cincinnati till the following August. The fact of their arrival was published in the "Catholic Telegraph," September 2, 1847, as follows :

"The Bulls for the consecration of Rt. Rev. Mr. Rappe for the new See of Cleveland have arrived. We very sincerely congratulate the clergy and congregations in the northern part of Ohio on this appointment; if zeal for the glory of God, and utter disregard of self, a blameless life, and fervent piety can qualify a man for the episcopacy, we know no one more likely to see his hopes realized than the Bishop-elect of Cleveland. This is his character amongst those who know him."

Father Rappe was consecrated at Cincinnati, October 10,

1847, by Bishop Purcell, assisted by Bishop Whelan, of Wheeling, Virginia. Two days after his consecration, and just before starting for Cleveland, he published his first pastoral letter, which is given here in full. It portrays clearly the apostolic zeal and devotedness to the cause of God on the part of Bishop Rappe.

AMADEUS.

BY THE GRACE OF GOD AND APPOINTMENT OF THE APOSTOLIC SEE BISHOP OF CLEVELAND.

To the Clergy and Laity of the Diocese of Cleveland:
Grace Unto You, and Peace from God our Father, and from the Lord Jesus Christ:

VENERABLE BRETHREN OF THE CLERGY AND BELOVED BRETHREN OF THE LAITY!

Overwhelmed by the labors and solicitude which his extensive diocese required, and full of zeal for the welfare of the flock which he has governed with unsurpassed wisdom and success, the Rt. Rev. John Baptist, Bishop of Cincinnati, humbly supplicated the late Provincial Council to establish another episcopal see in the northern part of the State of Ohio. This request was granted, and the city of Cleveland has been chosen to be the see of the new diocese. The Roman Court has approved and sanctioned these proceedings, and His Holiness, Pius IX., at the request of the Council, has elevated me to the Episcopacy. Had I consulted my fears I would have immediately declined accepting a station so encompassed with difficulties, but yielding to the voice of authority, and thereby made strong by the favor of the Almighty, I consented to forego my weakness and inability, to rely solely on Him who can strengthen the weak, and prepare them for the labor. "Go, and teach all nations: behold I am with you all days until the consummation of the world." That divine mission given by Jesus Christ to His Apostles, has been confided to me by their successors and the Apostolic See. Invested with this sacred power, and comforted by the grace of the episcopal office, I feel encouraged to work for the glory of our common Master and the welfare of our immortal souls.

It is indeed consoling, venerable brethren of the clergy, that in discharging the functions of a ministry so sublime and perilous, I will be seconded by your devotion, your talents, your virtues, and your experience. For several years I have fought in your ranks, shared your toils, admired your zeal, and witnessed with joy the success that crowned your efforts. It was then one of my greatest pleasures, whilst associated with you in the ministry, to call you friends, and now, placed at your head, as the first sentinel of the camp of Israel, I desire more than ever to be regarded as your friend and father, rather than your superior. My happiness will be henceforth to have part in your labors, to direct your efforts, to alleviate your cares, and to console your sorrows. Our number is small, but let us pray to the Lord to send more laborers into His vineyard, and whilst waiting with patience His answer to our supplications, let our union, our piety, our prudence and zeal make amends for the deficiency. In the daily morning meditations we will find a divine fire which illumines and vivifies; the reading of the Holy Scriptures will furnish us with arms against our enemies, and be our comfort in tribulation. The works of the Fathers and the acts of the Councils, but particularly of the Councils of Baltimore, which are so appropriate to the circumstances and wants of our mission, will be a pure source from which we can draw sound doctrine and wisdom to direct us in the various exigencies of our ministry.

Your spiritual necessities, beloved brethren of the laity, are not unknown to us; we wish to be intimately acquainted with your desires for the advancement of religion, and although we may be unable to provide resident pastors for every congregation, we will endeavor to console you in their absence by frequent visits, and by sending you, from time to time, faithful missionaries who will speak your language, and animate your piety.

We sigh for the day when we will be able to appear amongst you, to bless you, to instruct you, and to be edified by your devotion. Many a time have we been moved by the constancy of your faith and the beauty of your example. What a consolation for a pastor to be surrounded by a faithful flock, anxious to diffuse on all sides the sweetness of the doctrines of Jesus Christ. Those truly Catholic souls are His glory, and they give a powerful energy to His words. They are so many apostles before whose integrity and piety the demon of prejudice is passing away. The times are propitious! The eminent virtues of our prelates and clergy, their eloquence in the pulpit, their polemical works, so marked by ability and clearness, the numerous conversions, both at home and abroad, conversions in which the finger of God is so visible, since they cannot with reason be attributed to any worldly motive—all these circumstances directed by Divine Providence for the triumph of truth seem to have mitigated the violence of our dissenting brethren, and prepared the minds of the more learned portion of the community to examine and appreciate the divine excellence of our holy religion. It is for you, beloved brethren of the laity, to encourage this disposition to a sounder system. If the eloquence of an upright life does not convert our opponents, at least it silences the hostility of the unwise and imprudent. It is thus that we can most efficaciously contribute to the propagation of that faith which has conquered the world. Console, beloved brethren of the laity, and help your pastors by the sanctity of your lives. Have but one mind, no matter what may be your nation, your language, your position in society. You are all the children of the same Father, the members of Jesus Christ, destined for the same inheritance.

In order that you might preserve this sweet union of mind and heart, come often to the Sacred Table, to feed on the Bread of Life, to be strengthened by the God of charity. He will remind you that He loved you even to the shedding of His Blood, and therefore has the right to command that you love one another. Unite together every night in family worship, and the Lord will be amongst you. Observe punctually the Lord's day, and the laws of the Church and of the State, and educate your children in the fear and love of God. Do all in your power to provide for their instruction orthodox and pious teachers. We beseech you also, beloved brethren, by the mercy of Jesus Christ, to live soberly. Drunkenness, and the debaucheries which attend it, degrade man, disgrace the faith, and precipitate many into endless misfortunes.

As for us, venerable fellow-laborers, we will all endeavor to be the models of the faithful in conversation, in charity, in faith, in chastity. Our mission is a glorious one, and our reward will be equally glorious if we live according to our sublime vocation.

✠ AMADEUS,
Bishop of Cleveland.
Given at Cincinnati, October 12, 1847.

Within a week after his consecration Bishop Rappe took possession of his diocese, comprising all that portion of Ohio lying north of the southern limits of Columbiana, Stark, Wayne, Ashland, Richland, Crawford, Wyandot, Hancock, Allen, and Van Wert counties, and containing forty-two churches, attended by twenty-one priests. There was then but one church in Cleveland, St. Mary's on the "Flats," which served as his cathedral; and but one priest, the Rev. Maurice Howard. January, 1848, Father Howard was sent to Tiffin, and Father de Goesbriand was appointed his successor and Vicar-General. St. Mary's congregation was composed of English and German speaking Catholics, who had far outgrown their church when Bishop Rappe came to Cleveland. He succeeded in getting a German priest, by whom separate services were given to the German portion of the congregation, thus tiding over the necessity of building another church at that time. For several months the Bishop resided in a rented house, south of the Public Square; but in 1848 he bought a house on Bond Street, which he made his episcopal residence. To supply the wants of the growing Catholic population, a frame building, 30 x 60, was erected on Superior Street, a short distance east of Erie, near the site of the present cathedral, and next to the lots which Rev. Peter McLaughlin had bought in 1845 for church purposes. This frame building served several years as a "chapel of ease" for St. Mary's church, and as a parochial school, the first in the city. Folding-doors cut off the sanctuary during school hours. This little church was commenced and finished in December, 1848. It was used for the first time on Christmas of the same year, and hence was called the Church of the Nativity. Meanwhile Bishop Rappe had plans drawn and specifications made for a cathedral, to be erected at the northeast corner of Superior and Erie Streets. Mr. Keily, of Brooklyn, N. Y., was the architect. The corner-stone was laid on Sunday, October 29, 1848, Bishop Timon, of Buffalo, preaching on the occasion. The cathedral was consecrated November 7, 1852.

In 1849 the Bishop went to Europe for the purpose of securing priests for his diocese, and members of religious communities for schools and charitable institutions. On the feast of the Immaculate Conception that year he officiated at a solemn High Mass in the Ursuline Convent at Boulogne, where he had been chaplain. In the early part of 1850, the Bishop of Arras (native diocese of Mgr. Rappe) begged him to take his place partially for that year's episcopal visits in the diocese. Bishop Rappe, in consequence, visited a great number of the town and country parishes, preaching like a true missionary and administering the Sacrament of Confirmation. Everywhere he was received with respect, love, and real enthusiasm. He returned to Cleveland in August, 1850, bringing four priests, five seminarists, two Sisters of Charity; also four Ursuline nuns, and one postulant from the Ursuline Convent at Boulogne.* Two years previous he opened a seminary back of the episcopal residence on Bond Street with Father de Goesbriand as its first superior. Thither the seminarists, just arrived from France, were sent, some to complete their studies and one or two to be ordained shortly.

On his journey through France, in January, 1850, Bishop Rappe visited Lille. During his stay in that city he preached in many churches. His eloquence attracted large audiences, which were captivated with his brilliant pleadings for the missions of the "Infant Church" of America. Enthusiasm prevailed. Peter the Hermit was not more emphatical nor more successful. In young men's sodalities, in academies, or educational institutions, in fact everywhere, the missionary bishop was hailed, appreciated, respected, and admired. In the elegant drawing-rooms of French society or in the humble cottages of the peasantry, his dignified and kindly bearing was that of the cultivated gentleman, and of the kind, consoling pastor.

In one of the academies he then visited, a young pupil failed to return promptly after the Christmas holiday vacation, because she had forgotten the exact time set for the return of the pupils. As the badge which she had previously won and worn elicited on her part superior example, this mark of distinction was forfeited. The fact having been privately made known to the Bishop, his paternal heart was touched. The pupils being presented to him before the opening of the entertainment given by them in his honor, and the "decorated" pupils soliciting his presence thereat, he asked if all the latter were present. On learning that one of them was absent, he inquired the reason. This being given, he expressed his sympathies, and offered to plead in her behalf. At his

---

* The founders of the Ursuline Convent, Cleveland.

word the young recipient of the honors she had forfeited stepped forward, and at his hands received again the coveted badge, much to the delight of her generous companions.

During the Bishop's absence in Europe as above stated, Judge Cowles' mansion on Euclid Avenue was bought for the Ursuline Sisters. It is the present Mother-House of the Cleveland Ursulines. The Sisters took possession of their new home on their arrival in Cleveland, and almost immediately opened a select school and an academy. In 1851 the Ladies of the Sacred Heart of Mary established St. Mary's Orphan Asylum for girls. The first building used for the purpose was located on St. Clair Street, near Bond, Cleveland. Toward the end of 1853 the asylum was transferred to Harmon Street, its present location. During the latter year Bishop Rappe opened St. Vincent's Orphan Asylum for boys, on Monroe Street, Cleveland, and placed it in charge of the Sisters of Charity of St. Augustine, a community he had established. Thus the most pressing wants of the diocese were supplied. The Bishop now directed his attention to details of diocesan work, visiting every church and station at frequent intervals, giving missions, administering confirmation, and preaching. Though constantly at work, either at home in his cathedral or out in the diocese, he never showed signs of fatigue. Never satisfied with what he had already accomplished, he was always anxious to do still more for the glory of God and the good of religion. During the cholera of 1849, Bishop Rappe was frequently called upon in Cleveland to attend its victims. Dr. Storey, a prominent non-Catholic physician of Cleveland, had a cholera patient, a Catholic, the wife of a bigoted Englishman. Bishop Rappe was called to attend her. In spite of appeals, the husband refused the Bishop admittance to the bedside of the dying wife. Dr. Storey was in an adjoining room waiting till the Bishop had attended to the spiritual needs of the patient. Hearing words passing between the Bishop and the husband of the patient, and taking in the situation, he asked the Bishop to let him go to the patient's room first. He went in, took the husband by the nape of the neck and forcibly ejected him from the room, landing him on the sidewalk. Then, turning to the Bishop, the doctor said: " Bishop, go on with your work now; I'll attend to this fellow." Dr. Storey stood guard at the door till the Bishop had ministered the last sacraments to the dying woman.

The following incident, communicated to the writer by the Very Rev. Z. Druon, aptly illustrates Bishop Rappe's indomitable zeal and physical endurance in the performance of his manifold and arduous duties. "Among the many wonderful things done by Bishop Rappe, I remember the following, no doubt of frequent occurrence, which took place in 1851:

"One Saturday he left his house on Bond Street to go to St. Mary's, on the Flats, for the purpose of hearing confessions. He remained in the confessional till midnight without supper. The next morning at six o'clock he went again to hear confessions, said two masses, and preached twice. He did not go home for dinner, being satisfied with a little refreshment which was brought to him in the vestry. He sang vespers, preached in the Ursuline Convent and in St. Mary's Orphan Asylum, then went home for his supper, and preached again in the evening in St. Mary's. . . . . One Lent he went to St. Mary's *every* morning and never returned till noon, being engaged in preaching, catechising, and hearing confessions."

He was specially solicitous for Catholic schools, and where it was within the range of possibility, priests were obliged to establish such in their respective parishes. One of the prominent features in his long and laborious career, was his earnest work in behalf of higher Catholic education. As priest and bishop he fostered schools, academies, and colleges. It was he that gave the first impetus to the parochial system, now so flourishingly established in the diocese of Cleveland.

He also established institutions in which charity in various forms might be dispensed, and to this end introduced the following female religious communities into the diocese, besides those already mentioned, viz.: The Grey Nuns (*Sœur-Grises*) of Montreal, 1855; the Sisters of the Good Shepherd, 1869; and the Little Sisters of the Poor, 1870. He also welcomed the Franciscans to the diocese in 1867, giving them charge of St. Joseph's congregation, Cleveland, and two years later the Jesuits, to whom he entrusted St. Mary's congregation, Toledo.

Previous to 1865 Cleveland had no public hospital. As early as 1850 two French Sisters of Charity attempted to establish one on the West Side—then known as Ohio City. Their noble purpose failed of success for want of means, and so they returned to their native France the following year.

In 1863, during the Civil War, then at its height of bloody carnage, many sick and wounded soldiers were sent to Cleveland for medical treatment, but no provision had been made to receive and care for them. It was then that Cleveland realized the necessity of a hospital, which Bishop Rappe would long before have built had he had the means. He now saw a near realization of his long-cherished plan. He offered to build a hospital and provide efficient nurses, on condition the public would come to his assistance. This offer was gladly accepted, and two years later (1865) Charity Hospital, costing about $75,000, was opened to the public, and placed in charge of the Sisters of Charity. In every good work Bishop Rappe was in the front ranks, never shirking his part, never refusing his aid or countenance. Though perhaps meeting with disappointment, or receiving insult for his pains, he never halted, but courageously went on in his work.

In the founding of institutions of charity he never failed to call on the wealthy non-Catholics of Cleveland, and seldom, if ever, did they refuse desired assistance, many giving princely donations. Among them was Mr. W. J. Gordon, one of his intimate friends, who gave him the munificent sum of $10,000 for the erection of Charity Hospital.

It is related of Bishop Rappe that while he was collecting funds for the erection of this hospital, he called on a wealthy gentleman, Mr. A. S., for a donation. The first, and even the second appeal, met with a flat and rather discourteous refusal. But the good Bishop was not so easily vanquished. Mr. S. refused a third appeal with an unfriendly remark about the social condition of Catholics and about the Church. He also said that the proposed hospital would only be another "sectarian" institution, to the erection of which he would contribute nothing. The Bishop replied in his usual kind and suave manner, that he believed Mr. S. did not thoroughly understand the nature of the appeal; that he would call again in a week or two, when Mr. S. will have had time to consider the matter. Mr. S. replied that he was quite willing to give anything to the Bishop personally, but for the hospital nothing. The Bishop answered: "I do not ask for anything in my behalf; I ask it for God's work, for an institution that is to care for the sick regardless of creed or class distinction. It is for sweet charity I appeal to you." The result of this last appeal was that Mr. S. gave the Bishop a handsome donation for the hospital. Kindness and gentleness won!

A spirit of *nationalism*, un-Catholic and un-American in its nature, subversive of the best interests of religion, and the bane of any community composed of "divers tongues," was the beginning of a long and bitter opposition to Bishop Rappe. Though of French birth and tastes, and naturally full of love for his native land, he was thoroughly American in sentiment. He loved the land of his adoption as much as the land of his nativity. As priest and bishop he always endeavored to teach those under his charge to be true to their Church, and to the country whose Stars and Stripes protected them. As bishop he aimed to Americanize his people, and to this end urged the use of the English language in all the churches and schools of his diocese. In the administration of his diocese, he knew but one nationality—American. On this line he taught and fought, and for this he was opposed, sometimes publicly, more often privately.

This opposition, based on *nationalism*, grew into carping

and fault-finding with respect to Bishop Rappe's administrative acts. That he erred in these at times is quite possible. He would have been more than human had he not erred. But his errors had no lodging in his heart.

Ever and anon complaints were sent to Rome against him regarding his administration, but to the chagrin of his accusers he was sustained against them in nearly every instance. Charges against his administration of the diocese failing of their purpose, another mode of warfare was pursued. His character was next assailed!

Whilst he was at Rome attending the Vatican Council in 1869 and 1870, this assault was made. Charges based on *shadows*, were taken to Rome, and there urged against this "holy and apostolic old man," who had reached three-score and ten years of a blameless life.

Deeply wounded that in his declining years—forty of which he had spent in hard and unselfish labors as priest and bishop —he should be called upon to defend his reputation, he preferred rather to resign, which he did on his return from Rome to Cleveland, August 22, 1870. He thought it best to leave his mortally wounded innocence to God, who knew him guiltless of the charges made, and who would judge him and his accusers.

The time has not yet come to publish a more detailed account than the above of this sorrowful period of Bishop Rappe's life. That will be the task of his future biographer.

The Roman authorities were for a time deceived by the Bishop's accusers. In consequence they counselled his retirement, and accepted his resignation as Bishop of Cleveland. Soon Rome discovered the deception; the *amende honorable* was made, so far as it could be made under existing circumstances. Owing to the opposition to Bishop Rappe in the diocese of Cleveland, the Holy See did not think it wise to send him back, but offered him another diocese, as appears from the subjoined letter addressed to Bishop Gilmour by the Rt. Rev. Bishop de Goesbriand:

"BURLINGTON, VT., 21st December, 1884.
" *Rt. Rev. R. Gilmour, Bishop of Cleveland:*
" RT. REV., DEAR SIR :

"After consulting my records I find that Mgr. Roncetti, Ablegate of the Holy Father, arrived at Burlington, from Portland, in company of Father Ubaldo Ubaldi, Very Rev. Father Quinn and Rev. Father O'Farrell, of New York, on Saturday evening, July 24, 1875. The object of his visit was to see Rt. Rev. A. Rappe, whom he thought to be living in Burlington, but who was living at St. Albans with Father Druon.

"The Ablegate expressed himself disappointed in not meeting him. .I remember distinctly that after inquiring concerning Bishop Rappe, he opened in my presence, and read with much attention, a letter of Cardinal Franchi to himself, and said to me that he had been commanded to see Rt. Rev. A. Rappe, and authorized to offer him another diocese. The Ablegate left Burlington the next day and did not see Bishop Rappe. Whether or not he wrote to him I cannot tell, but it was certainly intended to speak to him of another see, for I remarked to Mgr. Roncetti, that the charge of a diocese would be too much for Bishop Rappe, who at that date must have been seventy-four years of age.

" What I have here written I am ready to swear to.
" ✠ LOUIS,
" Bishop of Burlington, Vt."

In this connection, the following is placed on record :

Cardinal Simeoni, Prefect of the Propaganda, in a letter sent to the Rt. Rev. Bishop Gilmour, May 8, 1885, referring to Bishop Rappe, says :

" . . . . *in illa miserrima conspiratione contra episcopum Clevelandensem, praedecessorem Amplitudinis Tuae, in qua ille sanctus et apostolicus senex falso . . . . accusabatur.*"*

---

* " . . . . In that most miserable conspiracy against the Bishop of Cleveland, your Lordship's predecessor, in which that holy and apostolic old man was falsely accused." . . . .

Dr. John Gilmary Shea in his recent work, "The Catholic Hierarchy in the United States," (page 206), referring to the resignation of Bishop Rappe, says:

"Bishop Rappe had built up the diocese and might have been expected in his declining years to enjoy a happy old age amid the clergy and people whom he had guided as a faithful pastor for twenty [twenty-three] years, but this was not to be. An ungrateful opposition sprung up, calumny assailed even the venerable bishop, who with a broken heart resigned his see on the 22d of August, 1870, and retired to the diocese of his good friend Bishop de Goesbriand, of Burlington."

In his "Lives of Deceased Bishops," Dr. Richard H. Clark says of Bishop Rappe: "While attending the [Vatican] council his reputation was assailed unjustly at Rome, by calumnies forwarded from the very diocese he had served so well. This movement was limited to a few. . . . . Rome, misled by calumnies, which it afterwards discovered and pronounced to be the fruits of a conspiracy, counselled his retirement. But he was never removed from his office as Bishop of Cleveland. On his return to Cleveland from Rome, he resigned his bishopric August 22, 1870. He had been Bishop of Cleveland, not only in name, but in deed, and left that title unsullied before God." * . . . . "Since his death I have seen the original letter, one from the Holy See, in which the means resorted to, to compel his retirement from his see, are spoken of as a 'miserable conspiracy,' the accusations against him are characterized as 'false,' (falso accusabatur), and in which Bishop Rappe is himself spoken of as 'that holy and apostolic old man,' (ille sanctus et apostolicus senex.)" †

At the Pontifical Requiem high mass for the deceased prelates of the Cincinnati province, celebrated in St. Peter's Cathedral, Cincinnati, March 7, 1882, at the time the IVth Provincial Council of Cincinnati was in session, Bishop Dwenger, of Fort Wayne, preached the sermon on the occasion. Referring to Bishop Rappe, he spoke as follows:

---

* Vol. 3, pp. 244, 245. † Vol. 3, pp. 248, 249.

" . . . . We remember to-day the first Bishop of Cleveland, Amadeus Rappe. Having known him from the days of my childhood, it is to-day a pleasant duty to do justice to his memory. He was elevated to the episcopal dignity, not so much on account of brilliant talent, as on account of piety and apostolic zeal. It was an edifying sight to see the hard-working apostolic Bishop visit every church of his wonderfully growing diocese every year, preaching, giving confirmation, hearing confessions; nothing was too hard for him; nothing could tire him. When I conducted missions and forty hours' devotions, I sometimes would feel a delicacy to urge the priests to go in the confessionals; but if the good Bishop was present I never hesitated to ask him to hear confessions, if I knew there was a crowd. Witness the wonderful growth of the diocese of Cleveland from the year 1847 to the time of his resignation. I do not deny that the saintly, apostolic Bishop, relying upon the advice and judgment of men whom he considered more learned than himself, did commit some error in the administration; but the austere, hard-working, apostolic man was innocent of the cruel accusations that were concocted against him, and saddened the last days of his life. I know how these accusations were concocted. I have spoken with the principal witness. I know he was innocent. Beautiful were the words the good Bishop used, when in 1870 he tendered his resignation to the Holy See. That for the good of his diocese he not only resigned his dignity, but also his good name; that for the sake of peace and harmony he desired no vindication." *

November 9, 1877, in the great basilica of Notre Dame, Montreal, the Rt. Rev. Louis de Goesbriand, Bishop of Burlington, Vt., preached the panegyric of his bosom friend and co-laborer on the Ohio mission—the saintly Bishop Rappe, who had died two months previous.

Referring to Mgr. Rappe's last sad days as Bishop of

---

* "Catholic Telegraph," March 9, 1882.

Cleveland, the panegyrist said: "Providence had blessed in a most superabundant manner the labors of the zealous missionary prelate. The same Providence now wished to sanctify him in the crucible of trials, afflictions, and adversities. In 1869, faithful to the voice of Pius the IX., he repaired to Rome, there to assist at the Vatican Council. During his long abode of eight months in the Eternal City his health greatly declined, he lost the sight of one eye and a similar affliction menaced the other. On his return from the Council a still greater trial awaited him. During his absence serious difficulties had arisen. The venerable Bishop understood that it was necessary to yield to the storm gathering on all sides; a younger hand could perhaps govern the diocese better than his. He imitated the example of several saintly bishops, and resigned his office of Bishop of Cleveland. Like unto his Master and model, his admirable zeal and self-sacrificing devotion were not appreciated. His labors, his toiling for God's honor, his unbounded charity and compassion for the flock that he loved more than his life—all was ill-requited; all was repaid by ingratitude."

Bishop Rappe left Cleveland for Burlington a few days after his resignation (August, 1870), and called on his old friend, Bishop de Goesbriand. "Bishop," said he, "I come to you an old man, to offer you my services in any capacity in which I can aid you." The offer was accepted, and he was assigned some missions in the neighborhood of St. Albans.

The same restless zeal and indefatigable earnestness which characterized him while doing God's work in Ohio as a missionary priest, and as the head of an extensive diocese, also shone brightly in him when he resigned his responsible office of Bishop and reassumed the *rôle* of a missionary in the diocese of his devoted friend and erstwhile Vicar-General, Bishop de Goesbriand. In Vermont, as of old and for nearly thirty years, his incentive motto was: *Da mihi animas!* Give me souls! These he sought in the highways and byways, in forests, towns, and cities on the mainland, and on the isles dotting Lake Champlain. He sought them in hovels and in mansions. No difficulty too much, no obstacle too great to prevent him from pursuing the stray sheep. He could easily have retired into private life, having years sufficient to justify him in doing so, and means enough to support him decently to the end of his days. But no! His zeal would not permit him to be idle. Making his home at the pastoral residence of his time-tried friend, the Very Rev. Z. Druon, V. G., in the city of St. Albans, Vt., he attended a number of missions and stations in the neighborhood, and throughout Northern Vermont, *e. g.*, Enosburg, Alburg, l'Isle de la Motte, Franklin and Richford. His first visit to l'Isle de la Motte, one of his missions, was made on a Saturday night. None of the people knew he was coming, and there being no hotel in the town, he climbed through a window in the old church, wrapped himself in a buffalo robe and slept all night in the sacristy. The following day he attended to the mission, fresh and bright as though he had slept in the best of beds. Dr. Smith, a man of means, and a resident of l'Isle de la Motte, having heard of the Bishop's " accommodations," met him at the next visit and insisted that he should make his home at his (the doctor's) house. The Bishop accepted the kindly extended hospitality, not only on that occasion, but on all subsequent visits to the mission. In six months after first meeting this good gentleman, who was a Protestant, the Bishop brought him and his entire family into the true Fold. The above-mentioned places he attended regularly from October, 1870, till some time in 1874. For the most part the Catholics residing here were the poorest of the poor, often unable to purchase even the necessaries of life. His heart went out to them ; his purse was open for them. For many a poor family he bought food and clothing out of his own means, and in like manner erected schools, chapels, and churches. At Enosburg he built a school ; at Franklin he enlarged the church and built a school; at Alburg he built a church and school, and the same in l'Isle de la Motte ; at Swanton and St. Johnsburg he introduced teaching communities and donated a house for their use in each of these two places. In 1874 Bishop de Goesbriand relieved his overburdened friend and co-laborer of a part of his work, permitting Bishop Rappe to retain charge of l'Isle de la Motte and Alburg, which he continued to visit monthly till 1877. Meanwhile, he also gave retreats or missions in the dioceses of Ogdensburg, Albany, Springfield, Portland, Sherebrook, St. Hyacinth, and Montreal. In the diocese of Burlington he preached missions in about thirty parishes. He also conducted a very successful mission in the great parish church of Notre Dame, Montreal, preaching the entire course of sermons himself. Immense audiences heard his eloquent and impressive sermons, and thousands took from him on that occasion the pledge of total abstinence. He was the Father Mathew of Montreal. Thus this holy and apostolic old man was engaged in doing good up to his seventy-sixth year, and within a few days of his death; never idle, always busy; never considering self, always mindful of the wants of others. The last mission he gave was at Grand Isle, near St. Albans. Although seriously ailing of what proved to be his last and fatal illness, he closed the mission exercises, after one week of intense pain and suffering, September 7, 1877. On the same day he left for Milton, twelve miles from St. Albans.

The following particulars of Bishop Rappe's fatal illness and death were given to the writer by the Very Rev. Father Druon, in a letter dated September 20, 1888: "He arrived at Milton in the morning (Friday, Sept. 7th), when Father Cardinal telegraphed to me. I reached Milton at 12.30 P.M. and found Bishop Rappe a little delirious, though he had taken a good fish dinner. I brought him to St. Albans without any trouble, in the afternoon, when I telegraphed to Bishop de Goesbriand, who arrived in the evening. He heard his confession, for at that time he had entirely recovered his consciousness. Dr. Fasset, who came to see him in the afternoon, found him pretty well, so that he had then hope of his recovery. After the Bishop's arrival at St. Albans, when he was still a little delirious, he wished to start for his missions, and it was then that he said: '*I have a grand mission to perform; I want to go to Cleveland by the way of Buffalo.*' On the following day he fell into a comatose state from which he never recovered; he died peacefully that night at 11.30 o'clock." The last words he breathed were: " *I have prayed for my friends; I have prayed for my enemies; now may God bless them all!* " Words of apostolic benediction, of forgiving and loving charity; an echo of the Last Words on Calvary!

His remains were brought to Cleveland—to the city he loved so well.* On arrival Thursday evening, September 13th, they were met by an immense concourse of people, Catholic and Protestant, all vieing to do honor to the dead Bishop whom in life they loved and venerated. By torchlight the immense funeral cortège passed from the Union Depot to the cathedral, where, on a magnificent catafalque, Bishop Rappe's mortal remains were placed in state for the night. Next day a Pontifical requiem Mass was celebrated by Bishop Dwenger, of Ft. Wayne. Bishop Ryan, of Buffalo, preached the panegyric, pronouncing a beautiful tribute to the memory of the sainted dead. The remains of Bishop Rappe were then enclosed in a vault beneath the cathedral he had built, and beneath the altar at which for eighteen years he had offered up the divine sacrifice.

Tuesday, October 16, 1877, the Rt. Rev. Bishop Gilmour preached in the cathedral at the Month's Mind of Bishop Rappe. From his sermon on that occasion we quote the following: "Bishop Rappe came as a missionary, he abided as a missionary, he persevered as a missionary. The same brave old missionary bishop! Seeking his people far and wide; preaching incessantly to them from the pulpit, day after day,

---

* Through the courtesy of Superintendent Payne of the Lake Shore Railroad an elegant car draped in mourning was placed at the service of the committee appointed to go to Buffalo to meet the remains of Bishop Rappe.

and year after year; patiently awaiting them in the confessional; by the bed of the dying, consoling and exhorting, or by the side of youth, guiding and protecting, encouraging or chiding, he was ever the same—the indefatigable bishop, who knew no self, only God and the things of God. Preaching retreats, erecting temples, founding convents, giving instructions in his universal character of missionary, he died as he had lived—a true soldier of Christ, a man of God. . . . . His last public act was to celebrate Mass and ask the prayers of the people for the grace of a happy death; his last words were an invocation of charity. It was meet that he should have been brought here to repose under the altar that he built; it was right that he should have come among his own for their prayers—those to whom he had given a life's earnest labors. It was fitting that his virtues and his memory should be placed before the people whom he so loved, for whom he had so labored."

The following communication to the "Cleveland Leader," September 10, 1877, was written by one of the ablest lawyers of the Cleveland bar, and by one who had and has no "church affiliations." It voiced the kindly feeling universally entertained toward Bishop Rappe on the part of non-Catholics:

"The Dead Bishop.

"And so the good Bishop has gone. Permit one who is neither Catholic nor Protestant, but who knew him well during all the long period of his ministry in Cleveland, to pay a tribute to his memory. Whatever were his personal accomplishments they were far surpassed by the qualities of his heart. All who knew him will concur in praises of his candor, his inviolable fidelity, his courtesy, his frankness, his freedom from the least tincture of unkindness or uncharitableness, his attachment to his friends, his gratitude, his deeds of charity, his patience amid the trials and perplexities of his charge, his mildness, his purity of life and manners, his fervent and unfeigned piety. Born a gentleman, he possessed in an eminent degree all the personal graces and suavity of manner which such birth implies. He was modest and unobtrusive. He preferred retirement and peace to the tumult and strife of the world. In the performance of every duty he was energetic, faithful, and cheerful. In a word, he was a great and good man; but because he was great and good, envy and jealousy conspired to drag him down. Relentless opponents, while they attempted to despoil him of his exalted office and good name, were totally unable to charge him justly with a single moral stain; and though he suffered much, he was certainly exempted from that most merciless of all sorrows, the anguish of remorse. His name will be enrolled with the names of other good and worthy men who by their lives and example have contributed to the culture, prosperity, and happiness of the human race. I think I see the good Bishop at the approach of the last mortal pang, closely embracing the crucifix, his gaze steadfastly fixed upon the world beyond the stars, with the words upon his lips, 'Into Thy hands, O Lord, I resign my spirit.' And though he died in a distant State, who can doubt that in the moment of dissolution he breathed forth a sweet and holy benediction for the diocese for which he had done so much!

"Faithful and loving hands have borne back to our beautiful city the remains of the beloved Bishop, and they shall repose in a crypt beneath the dome of the Cathedral which he erected for a people he loved so well.

"S. E. ADAMS."

The "Cleveland Leader," well known for its hostility toward the Catholic Church, had this to say of Bishop Rappe in its issue of September 10, 1877: "A dispatch from St. Albans, Vermont, announces the death of Rt. Rev. Amadeus Rappe. Bishop Rappe was of French birth and education. . . . . His fine qualities as a courteous, cultivated man made him many friends among people of all classes and religions, and many well remember the indignation of his American friends when

.... he was elbowed out of the diocese which he had so laboriously created. .... Few Catholic prelates have shown such a broad, intelligent liberality and so many winning qualities as a public-spirited citizen. Though always a zealous and aggressive Catholic, he had a manly respect for the rights and opinions of others."

In 1887, Bishop Gilmour authorized his Vicar-General, Mgr. Boff, to raise a fund by collections in the churches of the diocese, for a monument to be erected to the memory of Bishop Rappe. The response of the diocese was most generous. Since then a fine marble bust of the deceased Prelate has been executed and placed in the Bishop's residence and in October, 1888, a life-size statue in bronze of Bishop Rappe in full pontifical robes was cast in Rome. It will be placed either in the vestibule of the cathedral or on a large pedestal on the cathedral grounds facing Superior Street.

To continue the pen-picture of Bishop Rappe's character and description of his labors as priest and bishop, we can do no better than again quote from Bishop de Goesbriand's sermon referred to on page 246 of this memoir. Portraying Bishop Rappe's piety, love for souls, and apostolic zeal, he said: "Bishop Rappe drew his love for souls from the words and example of his Christian mother. He frequently used to say: 'What a treasure is a good mother!' Later on when a seminarist, under the guidance of a pious master, this love for souls increased; his zeal continued to develop by exercises of piety. During the seven years we lived together he rose daily at 5 o'clock, made his meditation, said Mass, went to confession every week, and made an annual retreat, either with his priests or privately. He had received in an eminent degree the gift of the fear of God, and this was the favorite theme for his sermons. He cherished those priests who taught their flocks how to pray, and how to fear and obey God."

.... "Shall I describe Bishop Rappe in the exercise of his zeal for souls? Of the following scene I have been a witness many a time: If this man of God met a stranger who was abashed at the sight of a priest he would stop him, call him. His keen, apostolic eye had discovered in this man the characteristic mark of Baptism. He would ask him in rapid succession: 'My good friend, are you a Catholic? Do you go to confession? Do you go to Mass? I see you drink to excess.' The answers might be inferred; severe reproofs would then follow; the guilty man chafed; covered with confusion, thunderstruck, he would fain withdraw. But now the tender-hearted missionary would speak words of heavenly comfort to the poor culprit, assuring him that it is possible, nay easy, to lead a virtuous life; he would speak in loving words of the Good Shepherd bearing on His shoulders to the fold the strayed sheep. The result of the interview would be a sincere promise of amendment, reception of the sacraments, and avoidance of evil occasion. The worthy deceased prelate, as priest or bishop, never wearied in seeking the wandering and stray sheep. Far and wide he sought souls estranged from God.

"But who can recount the number of souls this good Bishop brought back to the fold of Christ? Never was he unmindful of sinners; ever was he ready to go to their aid. Zeal for God and for souls was *his* predominant passion. I remember a certain night when he was called to a sick person. My bed was near to his. He returned after having fulfilled his ministry. Generally his sleep was profound, but on this occasion, during the few remaining hours of the night, he was restless and agitated. His sighs and pitiable moans impressed me so sadly, that they have ever remained vivid in my memory. The good priest feared that the person whom he saw die was little prepared to appear before God.

"During a great part of his priestly life, Bishop Rappe was obliged to exercise the sacred ministry in stations far removed from Catholic centres. Under these circumstances it was often necessary to exercise his holy functions in shanties or hovels, which often were low, open on all sides to the inclemency of the weather, and filthy to a remarkable degree. Bishop Rappe, before and even after his episcopal consecration, [never failed to meet his appointments at the time he set for them.] He was punctuality personified. At these stations all assembled in the evening, either in the open air or in one of the cabins. The sermon was always on the commandments of God, or on the dispositions necessary for confession. Never did he fail to excite these good, simple people to contrition, and kneeling down in their midst he would breathe for them a heartfelt, earnest prayer. A great part of the night he spent in listening to their confessions. Before daybreak he offered the holy sacrifice of the Mass and again gave them paternal instructions. I remember on one occasion, when visiting a 'Station,' he said Mass in the doorway of a log-cabin; the dwelling was too small to erect an altar. This log-cabin was in the woods near the railway then in course of construction. It had rained, and the mud on all sides was deep. At the sound of the bell for the elevation of the Sacred Host, every knee bent in profound adoration. A worthy priest who was there present, penetrated with deepest emotion, remarked: 'Paris I have seen; its grand religious ceremonies I have witnessed, but never did I behold anything so touching!' This visit was indeed most consoling. Ah! the reason was evident. These good, simple laborers had not abused the grace of God. After the exhortations of the venerable missionary, after the confession of their sins, these devout people withdrew, bearing in their hearts the precious treasure, Peace, blessing the apostle who left them but to continue elsewhere the work of his divine Master. Divine Providence, which had destined Bishop Rappe for so many and such noble works, had given him a remarkably vigorous and strong constitution. He could accommodate himself to the coarsest food; he could sleep in the open air or on an uninviting couch in the most miserable hut, and willingly did he put up with frequent and protracted fastings. During the space of three consecutive months, I witnessed his unremitting labors in the confessional, from the beginning of Lent to Trinity

Sunday. Thirteen hours daily did he listen to the confessions of all who presented themselves. In Cleveland he usually preached four or five times every Sunday, either in churches or to communities. A sick-call at a distance of sixty miles would make him mount his horse, without a thought for his own physical necessities. One night he had to travel twelve miles to reach a certain village church * in which he was to administer the sacrament of confirmation. He availed himself of a wagon belonging to some good man. The roads were muddy in the extreme; the wagon broke down, and still the distance was some nine miles. The undismayed missionary bishop picked up his valise, continued his route on foot, and at 1 o'clock in the morning reached the church. He entered it by opening one of the windows, (for he would not disturb the slumber of the pastor,) and sought three or four hours' rest in the confessional. At 5 o'clock the expectant pastor found him engaged in prayer before the altar. He was then sixty-seven years old; of them he had passed twenty in the episcopacy."

The following is taken from Dr. De Wulf's letter, previously mentioned in this memoir: † "During Bishop Rappe's short visits to Europe, after his departure for America, it may be truly said that his heart and his thoughts left not his country of adoption. He displayed an unbounded activity in the search for young missionaries. He travelled indefatigably through Switzerland, Germany, Belgium, France, collecting resources from all sides to build and adorn churches, to erect school-houses, found monasteries and hospitals in his new diocese.

"Many were the letters which he wrote to me. I think I cannot find one in which he does not charge me with commissions, either for his cherished flock in America, or for the securing of passages for his missionaries, or for ornaments and sacred objects for the altar.

---

* At Archbold, Ohio; Rev. Peter Becker was pastor of the village at the time.
† Page 227.

"He used to say to me, 'You are my coadjutor in the work of my Father.' Happy was I to be able to assist him in a way, how trifling soever, and to give him an assurance of my lasting and profound affection.

"I mention these facts only the better to make known the intimate nature of our relations, and the burning charity with which he was animated for his cherished children. In speaking of his charity, suffer me to advert to a recollection of past days. One day, in the course of conversation, he observed: 'I have no merit in being charitable; I came thus into the world. In my early boyhood days, when a poor man presented himself at the farm, I used to entreat for the poor mendicant. I would cling to my good mother's apron and would not desist, until she gave him an alms.'

"During his stay in Rome in 1870, he was attacked with a serious disease of the eye. In one of his letters he inquired what he should do. Ignorant of the nature of the malady, I could only advise him to consult a skilful physician; he probably neglected to do so, or it was too late. When he came back to Paris, he had completely lost the use of one eye. Two years after, the other eye was threatened in a similar manner. When I saw him, I greatly feared that an operation would be ineffectual; that he would become blind. This affliction he also feared. His resignation and his submission to the will of God greatly edified me.

"I took him to one of our most skilful specialists, Dr. D. Weaker, who, on seeing him, immediately said: 'It is not to-morrow, but to-day that the operation must be performed.' A few days after, he left my colleague's sanitarium—he was cured.

"His letters, which I religiously keep, I have just read and re-read, impelled by the recent request to forward any interesting document concerning the life of our saintly departed relative and Bishop.

"I cannot express the happiness I feel in reading these letters; they are full of fire, overflowing with sentiments of the love of God, with love for our holy Religion, for the Holy Father, for his beloved children of America, for poor deluded France which he still ardently loved, for his family and his friends. In one of his last letters he said: 'Oh! it seems to me that the older I grow, the more intensely do I love you all.'"

The Bishop was not a polished orator, but he was singularly expressive in his language, in which there was a vein of sympathetic poetry. This, coupled with his peculiar pronunciation and emphasis made him a most interesting speaker. Though his diction was far from pure English, it was plain, his delivery animated, and his appearance in the pulpit full of deep earnestness. While preaching he had a habit of brushing his brow and gesticulating freely, without much regard for "the rules of gestures." He never preached for effect; his aim at all times was "to preach Christ," not himself. He was also a ready speaker and on short notice would preach a sermon full of emotion and spiritual food, evincing the fact that he was a man given to reflection and mental prayer. He was perfectly at home in the pulpit. His sermons had these very desirable qualities—they were understood and remembered; they never failed to win the attention of his hearers. One of his favorite themes was Total Abstinence, of which, as has already been remarked in this memoir, he was a consistent and practical advocate for many years and up to the time of his death. He had a horror of saloons, or "grogshops," as he called them, and in sermon or lecture would attack them in scathing language.

Bishop Rappe was most courteous in manners; every act and motion indicated grace itself. Tall in stature, erect and rapid in his gait, he walked, cane in hand, with the agility of a young man of twenty, and with the air of a soldier. Approachable to all without distinction as to age, creed, or social condition, he was universally respected by those who had the good fortune of his acquaintance. The prominent Protestant gentlemen of Cleveland, Toledo, and elsewhere in the diocese, with whom he had business or social intercourse, had for him the highest esteem, which was based on his integrity, affability, and tolerance. In a word, he was acknowledged to be "every inch a gentleman."

He had a tender love for the orphans of his diocese, and frequently visited them in their respective asylums, entertaining them with anecdotes, and instructing them by plain and fatherly explanations of Christian doctrine and morals. His visits to the orphanages were the delight of the inmates.

Bishop Rappe possessed remarkable business ability, and his work in this direction gave unmistakable evidence of his practical knowledge of financial affairs. He would have become a millionaire had he been a banker or merchant. He could see things clearer and more quickly than some of the sharpest and keenest business men; the result of his early investments proves this. The purchases of the Ursuline Convent property, the lots on which Charity Hospital stands, the seminary grounds on Lake Street, were all made at times when ordinary business prudence would not have ventured to invest, but which, long since, have increased a hundredfold in value over first cost.

In disposing of his little savings in his last will and testament, Bishop Rappe did not forget the diocese of Cleveland. Charity Hospital, the Orphan Asylum, the Ursuline Convents of Cleveland and Toledo, and a number of poor churches were the recipients of his generosity now, as they had been so often whilst he was their spiritual head. He also left to his successor, for the benefit of a reform school for boys—a project he had long desired to realize—his house on Bond Street, which for so many years had been his residence. The land for the reform school is secured, but lack of means has thus far prevented the erection of the buildings necessary for the purpose. It is hoped that generous hearts will respond to the realization of this long-cherished hope and project of Bishop Rappe.

Few men on the missions of America ever excelled Bishop

Rappe in the line of his work. Untiring in zeal, patient in hardship, generous, unselfish, no labor seemed to weary or exhaust him. Good his aim, suffering and sorrow the objects of his charity, he lived for religion and his kind. Defective in early education, ill-versed in English, because learned late in life, yet by nature's gifts and his own energy of character, he ranked as an orator of more than ordinary powers. He was great as a missionary rather than as a bishop, and excelled as a pioneer who explored and outlined, leaving to others to shape and consolidate. A lover of his native land, he gave not only his allegiance but his most ardent support to his adopted country. A true patriot, a Christian man, tolerant of dissent, conceding to others what he asked for himself—religious and civil liberty—he died at the ripe old age of seventy-six, thirty years of which he had spent as priest and bishop on the missions of Ohio. He died amid the tears of his people and the respect of his fellow-citizens, with the well-merited reputation of a life spent for God and the good of his fellow-men.

ADVERTISEMENT OF THE FIRST CATHOLIC BIBLE.—"Gazette of the United States," Dec. 1, 1790:

This Day is published

BY CAREY STEWART AND CO.

No. 22 Front-street

The First American Edition of the

Doway Translation of the

VULGATE BIBLE.

Containing 790 pages in Quarto (Price six Dollars).

☞ Subscribers are requested to send for their books Nov. 29.

HISTORICAL SKETCH OF THE REV. JOHN THAYER, BOSTON'S FIRST NATIVE-BORN PRIEST.

BY THE REV. ARTHUR T. CONNOLLY, OF ROXBURY, MASS.

[Read before the United States Catholic Historical Society, October 18th, 1888.]

To the historical student who is conversant with the intolerant laws enacted by the early New England Colonists against the Jesuits, or as the law reads, any " eclesiasticall pson ordayned by ye authoritie of the pope," it will be interesting to hear that one of the first Catholic priests who exercised the duties of his divine ministry in the Puritan city of Boston, was a descendant of these same Puritans and a Bostonian by birth, the Rev. John Thayer.

This worthy pioneer of Boston's native-born priests was born about the year 1760. His parents, Cornelius and Lydia Thayer, were in easy circumstances, and strict members of the Presbyterian or Congregational Church. As the hostility of the Presbyterians to the Catholic Church was most bitter, we can naturally conclude that he was reared with all that intense hostility to Catholics so common to his parents' sect. In his early boyhood he refused to study, but at the age of sixteen, moved by a desire of improvement, he entreated his parents to send him to school. By dint of application, as he himself tells us, he soon repaired lost time, and acquired quite a knowledge of the Latin and Greek languages. Feeling now that he was prepared to enter college, he went to New Haven and made application for admission to Yale. When examined by the tutors he gave such proofs of talents that his request was immediately granted.

At the conclusion of his college course he was made a minister of the Puritan sect, and such was the high esteem in which his family was held, that he was appointed chaplain to Governor Hancock.

When he had filled this position about two years, he felt a secret inclination to travel. He nourished the desire and formed a resolution, as he himself tells us, of passing into Europe to learn the languages which were most in use, and to acquire a knowledge of the constitution of States, of the manners, customs, laws, and governments of the principal nations, in order to acquire, by this political knowledge, a greater consequence in his own country, and thus become more useful to it.

Such, he adds, were his human views, without the least suspicion of the secret design of Providence, which was preparing for him more precious advantages.

He embarked for Europe and arrived in France toward the close of the year 1781. Here he remained ten months totally, taken up in studying the languages, reading the best authors, and instructing himself in the principles of the government.

While thus engaged he was suddenly taken sick, and so opposed was he to all sects, and especially to the Catholic faith, that he gave strict commands that no priest should be allowed to visit him.

After his recovery he spent three months in England, occupied as he had been in France in observing the manners and customs of the country. Leaving England he returned to France with the intention of proceeding to Rome.

As yet no change had taken place in his feelings, for he was still strongly prejudiced both against the nation and the religion which from his youth had been represented to him in the most odious colors. On his way from Marseilles to Rome the vessel on which he sailed was wind-bound for several days at a little port called Port-Ercole. Here he formed the acquaintance of the Marquis D'Elmoro, an Italian nobleman, who treated him with the greatest hospitality. "His house, his table, his library," says Mr. Thayer, " were at my service, and he treated me with the kindness and affection of a father. Such goodness, such cordiality to a stranger, to an avowed Protestant, at once touched and surprised me. This religion, said I, is not, then, so unsociable, and does not, as I have been told, inspire sentiments of aversion and intolerance to those of a different persuasion."

Still, the prejudices in which he had been educated had too much influence over his mind to allow any great change in his sentiments toward the Catholic Church.

On his arrival at Rome he was still a Protestant; but as he was at last in the very city of the Popes, he resolved to instruct himself thoroughly in the principles of the Catholic Faith.

It was not through a suspicion that his own religion was false, nor with any intention of embracing another that he was impelled to pursue this study: but for the same reason that he would have been impelled to study the tenets of Mohammedanism had he been in Constantinople.

With regard to priests, and especially the Jesuits, he was deeply imbued with the opinion entertained by most Protestants, namely, that they were men of deep cunning, political craft, and subtle reasoning. He had never seen a member of this illustrious society, and knew the Jesuits only through the calumnies of their bitterest enemies.

In one of his rambles around Rome he fell in with two ecclesiastics whose courteous manners, simplicity, and conversational powers charmed him. Great, indeed, was his astonishment when they avowed themselves Jesuits. Soon, at his own suggestion, the Catholic religion became the topic of conversation. Shortly after he was introduced by these ecclesiastics to another member of their society, who kindly volunteered to give him all the information that he sought.

How far he was from the thought of changing his belief, will be easily seen from the following words that he addressed to this latter ecclesiastic on the occasion of his first meeting:

"Sir," said he, "I may possibly have conceived some false notions of your religion, as all the knowledge I have of it is taken from the report of its enemies; if this be the case, I wish to be undeceived, for I would not entertain a prejudice against any person, not even against the devil. Yet do not think of converting me, for certainly you will not succeed."

The examinations that he made of the dogmas of the Catholic Church were most searching and serious, and considering on the one hand, that unerring sameness through the long ages of the Church of Rome; and on the other, the constant instability of all other sects, especially the Protestant, he was forced to admit that Protestantism was not the religion of Jesus Christ.

Though convinced of this fact, he was not yet certain that the Catholic was the true religion. He still harbored a deeply-rooted prejudice against all miraculous events since the time of the apostles. This prejudice, however, was soon to be removed, for at the very time that he was present in Rome, the venerable, now sainted, Benedict Labre, died in the odor of sanctity. Like most of God's saints he was poor and despised during life, and God deigned to glorify him after his death.

Many miracles were wrought through his intercession, and all Rome spoke his praises and proclaimed his glory and sanctity. What Mr. Thayer had thus far refused to believe on hearsay, he was now forced by ocular demonstration to admit.

Among the multitudes that flocked from all sides to the tomb of the sainted Benedict was a poor woman suffering from some incurable disease. Mr. Thayer saw her piteous condition, and witnessed her miraculous restoration to health by the mere touch of the saint's holy relics.

"My God, I believe!" were the words that he insensibly uttered. He was convinced he must believe in the truths of the Catholic Church. In an instant he saw all that such a step would cost him. If he became a Catholic he must renounce all his ambitious projects of a bright earthly career;

he must dissolve all connection with loving parents and friends. He who had been the respected minister of Puritan Boston must become by embracing Catholicism only a despised and hated *papist*.

Whether he would or not, faith at last prevailed, and on the 25th of May, 1783, he publicly abjured Protestantism in the presence of a large assembly of former friends, whom he had specially invited to the solemn ceremony. Subsequently he resolved to consecrate himself to God, fully persuaded that he was called to the ecclesiastical state to labor for God's honor and glory, and the salvation of his own and his countrymen's souls.

He returned to France and entered that world-renowned school of learning and piety, the Seminary of St. Sulpice, at Paris.

After due preparation he was ordained to the priesthood, and soon after set sail from Havre de Grace. He reached Boston on the 4th of January, 1790. Boston at this period contained only 18,036 souls, and of this number about 100 were Catholics. There stood on School Street, between Washington and Tremont Streets, on the site now occupied by the Five-cents Savings Bank, a small brick chapel, built in 1716 by some French Huguenots, who had taken refuge in Boston at the revocation of the Edict of Nantes. This society after the death of its minister, Mr. Mercier, had gradually dwindled away to nothing.

In this small brick house where these Huguenot refugees had worshipped, and, as tradition says, the British in 1775 stabled their horses, the little Catholic congregation assembled.

From the close of the year 1788, when they first began to assemble together for religious service, until Fr. Thayer's arrival on the 4th of January, 1790, the members of the infant congregation had been ministered to by two ex-chaplains of the French Navy, the Revs. Claudius Florent Bouchard de la Poterie and Louis de Rousselet. A few months before Fr. Thayer's arrival, that is, on the 29th of May,

1789, the Abbe La Poterie was withdrawn from Boston by Rev. Doctor Carroll, at that time the Superior of the Missions in the United States. Although little, if anything, is known about Rev. Louis de Rousselet, still it is certain that he was a co-laborer with Fr. Thayer at least for a short time. On examination of the baptismal records I find that he administered baptism in Boston on the 21st of February, 1790, almost two months after the arrival of Fr. Thayer.

Although, as I have stated, the Catholics had been called together and ministered to by the Revs. Father La Poterie and Rousselet; still, strictly speaking, Rev. John Thayer was the first regularly appointed missionary rector of the Catholic church at Boston.

Finding on his arrival that the infant church had not made much headway under the administration of his predecessors, he immediately set to work to infuse new life into his little congregation. In order that he might be free and without danger of molestation in the exercise of his ministry, he secured from the Perkins family, the owners of the old Huguenot chapel, a lease of the building. Money was soon raised by subscription, and everything procured that was necessary for the adornment of the church and the respectability of Divine worship.

The Sunday following his arrival he offered up the Holy Sacrifice, and preached the word to a large assembly which was composed of persons of different persuasions.

Thus, says a Protestant, commenting on Father Thayer's first mass, was mass publicly said in a town where, only thirteen years before, the Pope and the devil were according to annual custom promenaded through the streets on the 5th of November, in commemoration of the famous gunpowder plot, and after serving as a spectacle of ridicule and scorn were burnt together, leaving it doubtful in those days which of the two were most hateful. Thus, too, might the same person have said, was mass offered publicly and by one who thirteen years before had himself joined with his neighbors in ridiculing the Catholic Church.

According to an account given by Fr. Thayer himself, he was received by all classes with the greatest kindness; still, I do not think it unchristian to say that in some instances this show of kindness was more apparent than real. The best criteria that we possess at the present day of the feelings that animated the minds of New Englanders at that time, are the expressions of the press on the occasion of his arrival in Boston.

No one can deny that the New England press was strictly Protestant at that day, and as a consequence any article relating to Fr. Thayer was a fair exponent of the public mind. I have examined many files of the early papers, and I have been able to find but two articles that exemplify, most conclusively to my mind, the feelings of New Englanders toward the Catholic Church in those early days. The sentiments expressed show, that while many still looked with deeply-rooted bigotry and hatred upon everything Catholic, there were many at the same time who evinced a true spirit of toleration.

The following articles I have taken verbatim from the "American Magazine" and the "American Museum."

In the September number of the "American Magazine," published in 1788, I find the following sketch. It expresses without any doubt the sentiments of a large number of New Englanders in relation to the Catholic Church:

"John Thayer was born of reputable parents in Boston about the year 1760. In early youth he discovered no inclination for books, and his father bound him an apprentice to a tailor.

"About sixteen years of age, he desired his parents to put him to school. He is careful to pass over the circumstances of his education. The truth is, by dint of application, with very little assistance of a teacher, he obtained some knowledge of the Latin and Greek languages. With this he went to New Haven, and by some means or other he introduced himself, for he possessed unparalleled impudence, to the acquaintance of some gentlemen, who recommended him to the notice of the President and tutors of college.

"He was accordingly examined in the classics, and gave

such proofs of talents that he was admitted a member of that society, and being a total stranger and without money the gentlemen of that town agreed to board and lodge him each a certain period, and the governors of college consented to give him his tuition.

"He thus subsisted upon charity till the last year of the usual term of residence at college when he was guilty of some disorderly conduct, for which he was dismissed with marks of disgrace. He soon fell upon a plan to get a living. He pretended he had been honored with the usual degree of bachelor of arts, and forged a license to preach. Notwithstanding this he found means afterwards to procure an appointment of chaplain to the garrison in Fort William, in Boston Harbor. The particulars of his history from this time to his leaving America are not come to hand. But about the year 1781 he found a passage to France. Here he was assisted by Dr. Franklin and Mrs. Wright, who were then in Paris; till his impudence and ill manners excluded him from further favor. He remained in Paris for some months and set out for Italy by way of Marseilles. At Rome he became acquainted with some ecclesiastics, with whom he had conversations upon the Catholic religion. After much inquiry and reading he was finally converted to the Romish faith by a miracle wrought on a sick woman by the relics of the Venerable Labre. He has abjured his former errors, and now lives in full communion with the votaries of St. Peter. This conversion of a little impudent fellow, who was often kicked out of good company in America, was despised by all who knew him—publicly disgraced, and guilty of every species of meanness, and of some crimes that should have cost him his ears—this conversion is celebrated by the Roman Catholics of Europe, and affords them a new and singular cause of triumph."

The sentiments of another class of New Englanders are clearly shown in the following article, which I copy, also verbatim, from the seventh volume of the "American Museum," published in 1790:

"PORTSMOUTH, NEW HAMPSHIRE,
"*Jan. 12th*, 1790.

"It must give pleasure to the public—it must clear the hearts of the oppressed in all places to be informed that as a Romish missionary has arrived and is exercising his office in Boston, it is the determination of that wise, politic, and prudent town, to conduct towards him as becomes advocates for religious liberty, and friends to the equal and just rights of mankind; and that he is to be protected, in common with all others, by government, and himself and his companion spared from that twin-brother to the inquisition—from that vulgar refuge of bad men, in a bad cause, the deceitful and persecuting tongue."

When Fr. Thayer had been in Boston about two weeks he was stricken down with the typhoid fever, and was confined to his house for nearly two months. In the month of March he was so far restored to health that he could resume his duties, for on the tenth of this month, about two months after his arrival, we find the record of his first baptism administered in Boston:

"Martii 10^a, 1790. Bostonii baptizata est Sarah filia Joanathan et Susanna Chapman ex legitimo conjugio Nata die 4^a Februarii, 1789. P. P. fuere Patritius et Maria Campbell.

"Am. J. THAYER, Miss. Apos."

During the whole of the year 1790 he appears to have remained constantly in Boston, for during this time we find in the Baptismal Register the records of several baptisms administered by him.

Prompted by a religious zeal for the conversion of his countrymen, he published in the beginning of the year 1791 the following advertisement in one of the public papers:

"Mr. Thayer, Catholic Priest of Boston, fully persuaded that he has found the inestimable treasure of the Gospel, is greatly desirous of imparting it to his dear countrymen. For this purpose, he offers to preach in the evenings of weekdays in any of the neighboring towns. If any persons desire to hear the exposition of the Catholic faith,—of which the majority of Americans have so mistaken an idea,—and will furnish any place for the accommodation of hearers, Mr. Thayer will be ever ready to attend them.

"He will also undertake to answer the objections any gentleman would wish to make, either publicly or privately, to the doctrine he preaches."

Shortly after the appearance of the above, a Rev. George Lesslie, pastor of a church in Washington, New Hampshire, looking upon the advertisement as a challenge, declared that he would take up the gauntlet and prosecute the controversy as long as he could hold a pen. He did so, but soon either his pen became too heavy or Fr. Thayer's arguments too conclusive, and his courage failing him he became silent. During this year Fr. Thayer delivered a series of controversial lectures, and invited all who loved the truth and sincerely desired their salvation to be present. His little chapel on the occasion of these lectures was crowded by many who came either through curiosity or a desire of hearing the exposition of Catholic doctrine.

Two years had now passed since his arrival, and owing to his untiring zeal and scholarly exposition of the Catholic religion, his little congregation began to gain some consideration, and the name of Catholic was no longer synonymous with ignorance as it had been in past days.

About this time France was in a state of revolution, and thousands of her best priests were exiled from their native land. On the 24th of June, 1792, four of her most zealous and pious priests landed in Baltimore: Rev. Francis Matignon, Regius Professor of Divinity in the College of Navarre; Rev. Ambrose Maréchal, Rev. Gabriel Richard, and Rev. Francis Ciquard, Director of the Seminary of Bourges.

What France lost America gained. Bishop Carroll was filled with joy at the thought of having four more priests to labor for the salvation of souls and resolved to send two of the number to New England, one to Boston and the other to the State of Maine. Dr. Matignon was sent to Boston, and after devoting some time to the study of English entered upon the duties of his ministry on the 20th of August, 1792. Filled with happiness at the acquisition of a co-laborer in the work of his Divine Master, Fr. Thayer now felt that he could give greater scope to his zeal by taking a wider range and extending his visits to other parts of New England.

Wrentham, Salem, Newburyport, Plymouth, Hanover, Braintree, Scituate, and nearly every town of importance in Massachusetts was visited by him.

He made missionary journeys also to Dover and Portsmouth in New Hampshire, to Newport in Rhode Island, and to Norfolk and Portsmouth in Virginia. Thus he travelled from town to town, from State to State, announcing the Gospel and restoring to God souls from heresy until the year 1799.

His zeal led him into many controversies with Protestant ministers, and although he often felt that he had convinced them of the truth of the faith that he preached, still he was forced at the same time to acknowledge that they were far from being converted.

Feeling probably that "no prophet is received in his own country," he left Boston, and after spending some time in Canada, offered his services to Bishop Carroll, in whatever mission he might see proper to place him. Bishop Carroll accordingly sent him to labor on the missions in Kentucky.

As he had been the first native-born priest who exercised his holy ministry in New England, so also he was the first native of America who exercised his priestly duties in Kentucky. Here he remained for about four years, and during two of the four labored most zealously on these wide-spread missions. It was while thus engaged that he often meditated on the advantages of a truly Christian education for the young, and finally conceived the design of establishing in his native city an institution similar to many that he had seen in France and Italy — a convent school for young Catholic females. In the year 1803, having obtained the approbation of Bishop Carroll, he went to Europe with a view of raising, by eleemosynary contributions, the necessary funds for si ch an establishment.

After spending some time on the Continent, he subsequently went to Ireland and exercised his holy ministry in the city of Limerick for several years.

I have been unable to learn the exact date of his death, which occurred in the last-named city, but I am sure it must have been some time previous to 1818. In his last will he left Dr. Matignon, his successor at Boston, between eight and ten thousand dollars, with instructions to carry out his design.

Rev. Dr. Matignon died on the 19th of September, 1818, and must have held these funds in trust quite a while, for so wisely had he managed the same, says one of his biographers, that they had almost doubled at the time of his death. The duty of fulfilling Fr. Thayer's pious intentions now fell to the lot of Dr. Matignon's bosom friend, the saintly Bishop, afterward Cardinal Cheverus. A lot of land adjoining the Church of the Holy Cross on Franklin Street was purchased, suitable buildings were erected, and on the 16th of June, 1820, at the invitation of the Bishop, two nuns and two sisters of the Ursuline Community of Limerick, arrived and took possession of this convent.

Mother Mary Ryan was the superioress of this little community, and to her was given the direction of the first Catholic school established for young ladies in New England.

After the sisters had occupied this convent for several years the health of several began to give way, and it was deemed necessary to remove the community to a less crowded locality.

Accordingly, in the year 1826 a site for the new convent and academy was secured in Charlestown Neck. Here the school for young ladies was reopened, and such was its popularity that for several years the daughters of Boston's most respected citizens, Protestant as well as Catholic, deemed it an honor to be numbered among the pupils of Mount Benedict

Academy. For the subsequent history of this worthy foundation of Father Thayer we must refer the reader to the history of "Mount Benedict, Charlestown," the 11th of August, 1834. In concluding this sketch of Rev. John Thayer, we can appropriately apply to him the beautiful words inscribed upon the tomb of his successor, the Rev. Dr. Matignon, by the good and loving congregation of the Church of the Holy Cross: "Far from the sepulchre of his fathers repose the ashes of the good and great Fr. Thayer; but his grave is not among strangers, for it is and will be watered by the tears of an affectionate flock, and his memory is cherished by all who value a manly, honest heart, honor a noble, sacrificing life, and love the true apostolic priest of God."

BISHOP CARROLL IN BOSTON.—"Boston, June 4. The Right Rev. Bishop Carroll of the Roman Catholick Church, arrived in town a few days since—and he confirmed the baptism of a number of Catholicks. This gentleman, justly esteemed for his piety, learning, and benevolence, will preach to-morrow at the Roman Catholick church."—"Gazette of the United States," June 15, 1791.

"Boston, June 7. On Sunday morning the Right Rev. Bishop Carroll preached an elegant and candid sermon at the Catholick chapel in School Street. His Excellency the Governor, and Lady, and the Hon. Edward Cutts were among a crowded and very respectable audience, who appeared highly gratified by the charity, the benevolence, the piety which graced the discourse of the Right Rev. preacher."—"Gazette of the United States," June 18, 1791.

CHURCH AT VINCENNES IN 1816.—"This was built by the French Roman Catholics, and in their own style. It is 68 feet in length, about 22 feet wide, and 9 feet from the ground to the eaves. It has a kind of steeple about 8 feet high, with a small bell. The Roman Catholics at present have no pastor."—David Thomas, "Travels through the Western Country in the Summer of 1816." Auburn, 1819.

EARLY CATHOLICS IN CONNECTICUT.

By Rev. Thomas J. Shahan, D.D.

[Read before the United States Catholic Historical Society, March 12, 1889.]

AMONG the English colonies on the Atlantic coast, the one in which the Catholic historian is least likely to find traces of his religion, or of its adherents, is, without doubt, Connecticut. Its thoroughly Protestant origin, the exclusive nature of the legislation which barred out from its limits all public worship not in accordance with Puritan law or usage, the constant wars with the great Catholic powers of Europe, together with its remoteness, and the few inducements it offered to strangers, made it no desirable home for even the most indifferent Catholics. Moreover, it was well known that there was a peculiar fierceness in the hate of its people for the Catholic religion, since they had left their own country because they could not abolish the last poor shadow of it as preserved by King and Parliament. Nor must it be forgotten that the people of Hartford and New Haven colonies were the kinsmen of those who fought at the battle of Worcester and followed Cromwell and Ireton on their bloody pilgrimage through Ireland. To them the Catholic religion was ever more the faith of a conquered and despised race.

There is therefore a certain pathos for the Catholic in the fact that the brother of John Davenport was the Superior of the English Franciscans, and the brother of the hunted regicide, Goffe, was the Superior of the Paris Oratory. It interests us also to know that among the oldest families there is one descended from an Irish Catholic lady, and closely related to a well-known Catholic family of Lancashire. This family preserves yet the rosary-beads and medal of Our Lady, heirlooms of a Catholic member, as far back as 1720, and a precious link in the chain of Catholicity where it was least suspected.

In the early period of its history, the emigration from the Old World brought few Catholics to Connecticut, and therefore it is almost vain to seek anything of interest in the rather dreary public records of the colonies. In answer to a query of the English Board of Trade in 1680, as to the "number of English, Scotch, Irish, or foreigners (who) have for these seven years last past, or any other space of time, come yearly to plant and inhabit within your corporation," the following reply was given:

"For English, Scotts, and Irish, there are so few come in that we cannot give a certain account. Some years come none; sometimes a family or two."

In answer to another query, "What persuasion in Religious matters is most prevalent?" the following reply was made:

"Our people in this Colony are, some strict Congregationall men, others more large Congregationall men, and some moderate Presbyterians; and take the Congregationall men of both sorts they are the greatest part of people in the Colony. There are four or five Seven-day men in o' Colony, and so many more Quakers."

However, the colonists were not averse to the opening of their ports to trade, and to tolerate for its sake men of other religions, provided they brought an increase of wealth to the coffers of the colony. In the same letter which contains the above replies to the circular of the Board of Trade, there was transmitted a petition that New London, Hartford, New Haven, and Fayrefield (Bridgeport), be made free ports, for, said they, "We are likely by reason of o^r losses at home, and the heightened price of goods from abroad to remain a poore but loyall people, and we humbly request your Hono^{rs} to represent vs so to his Sacred Matie, and if by your Lordship's mediation his Matie be pleased to cast any rayes of his favoure upon vs, and grant unto vs that New London and others of portes might be made free portes for 20, 15, or 10 years, it would be a great means to move men of estates to trade and settle there; it would bring trade thither, so that the wealth of his Maties Colony would be encreased, and his Matie in the conclusion receive no damage thereby." *

From this time forward we shall be more likely to find traces of Catholicity at New London than anywhere else in Connecticut, and it is a fact that the ancient port had always a poor reputation for true Calvinistic godliness, and in many respects was far more tolerant and easy than the other towns of the Commonwealth.†

In the records of New London for the year 1661, we find mentioned the names of William Cotter, and his wife, Elinor. Beyond the name there is no evidence that they were Irish or Catholics. However, at the very same period, we find mentioned at the capture of St. Kitts, in the West Indies, a Capt. Cotter, Irishman, and a Catholic, since he was suspected of friendship for the French, and a desire to go over to them.‡

At this period, too, the Irish Catholic settlers in the islands had grown so numerous that they were disarmed and put under surveillance. It is not improbable that some sought to escape from this tyranny, and may have made New London their home.§

From time immemorial a part of New London County, bordering on the sea, has been called Waterford. The earliest settlers here bore the names of Thomas and John Butler (1680),‖ and a portion of the town of Waterford was, until a recent date, known as Butlertown. To me this seems to indicate the Irish Catholic origin of a family which afterward became well known in the history of New London. This

---

* "Colonial Records of Connecticut, 1678–1689," pp. 292–301.
† Miss Caulkins' "History of New London," passim.
‡ "Calendar of State Papers, Colonial, An. 1667," p. 480.
§ "Calendar of State Papers, Colonial, 1660," pp. 486–7.
‖ Miss Caulkins' "New London," p. 264.

surmise borrows strength from the following entry in the marriage records of New London:

"April 18, 1725, Allan Mullins, Chirurgeon (Surgeon), son of Doctor Alexander Mullins, of Galway, Ireland, married to Abigail, daughter of John Butler, of New London."*

In the Circular of the English Board of Trade (1680), already referred to, there is a query as to the number of privateers or pirates that frequent the coast. "It is rare," was replied, "that ever there comes any here on these dangerous coasts; only about two years ago (1678) there came a French Captain called Lamoine wth three ships, one of which wintered at New London, and in ye spring went off to sea." These were Dutch prizes, of which one was sent to New York, the other was sunk, and were worth £100,000.†

As the large war-ships and frigates of the Catholic powers always carry chaplains, it is very probable that on this and similar occasions a Catholic priest visited New London. The only pirate mentioned in these ancient records is a certain Edward Ohely (O'Healy), who seems to have frequented the Connecticut shores of the Sound about the year 1682.

How many unfortunate Irish youths and maidens were scattered by Cromwell along the line of Connecticut seaports we shall never know, but it is more than probable that many were brought here, and adopted under changed names into the infant settlements. I quote a specimen of the way it was done from the Colonial State Papers, order of the Council of State, September 6, 1653. "Upon petition of David Selleck, of Boston, New England, merchant, for a licence for the Good Fellow of Boston, George Dalle, master, and the Providence of London, Thomas Swanley, master, to pass to *New England* and Virginia, where they intend to carry *four hundred Irish children*, directing a warrant to be granted, provided security is given, to pass to Ireland, and within two

---

* Miss Caulkins' "History of New London."

† "Documents relating to the Colonial History of the State of New York," vol. iii., p. 582.

months to take up four hundred Irish children, *and transport them to these plantations.*"

In the year 1706, there appears in New London one Simon Murfe (Murphy), a sailor on one of the transports sent against the French.

The Acts of the General Assembly for 1711 contain a very curious and interesting account of the reception of a French Embassy which passed through New London on its way to Massachusetts. I have made a copy of the minutes.

"At a meeting of the Council in New London, February 17, 17$\frac{10}{11}$. Two Frenchmen with six attendants who came from Canada, in company with Major Livingstone, with a message from the Governor of Canada to the Governor of Massachusetts, came to this place the last night; for whom it was ordered that eight horses be provided at the Colony's charge, to carry them into the Government of Rhoad Island, with two men for pilots, and to bring back the said horses, and that their necessary charge while they are in this place and upon the road, until they get into the Government of Rhoad Island be also defrayed by the Colony. On March 6, their expenses were ordered to be paid. Ordered that the treasurer pay out of the Colony's money unto Captain John Preutts the sum of nine pounds thirteen shillings, which is granted him upon the account of the French messengers from the Governor of Canada at their entertainment at his house. On their return they were entertained in Colchester by Joseph Chamberlin, for which, March 12, 1712, the Colony paid him one pound thirteen shillings. Finally they were accompanied to Hartford by the polite attention of New London, as the following item shows:

"Item paid on March 19, 1711, to Thomas Jiggels of New London, for the bearing and paying the charges of himself, John Plumb and the ten horses, they came hither with on the 11th instant, to bring the French gentlemen, viz., their charges in going back to New London, £0, 12, 0.*

---

* "Colonial Records, 1706–1716," pp. 197–8, 256.

The unmistakably Irish Catholic name of Owen McCarty occurs in 1693 among the inhabitants of New London, and from that time forward this name occurs in New London and along the Connecticut River. In 1738 appears on the roll of the State militia the name of Timothy Hierliby, and for many years afterward it is met with. During this period of the history of Connecticut many new Scotch and Irish names appear in the public records,—McDougall, McKenzie, McKnight, McIlroy, McEntyre, McNiel; undoubtedly the majority were Presbyterians, but it has occurred to me that perhaps some of these might have been Catholic Highlanders,* of whom many came to New York at this period, by invitation of the authorities to take up land in the northern part of the State.

In November, 1752, a Spanish vessel, having been disabled by shipwreck, put into New London for the winter. When ready to sail in the spring the captain found that a large amount of his cargo, which had been committed to the care of the customs officers, had disappeared. He refused to leave until his property, principally bullion, was restored, and remained with his crew in New London until January, 1755, when, finding his efforts fruitless, he left. This is the first permanent residence of Catholics in Connecticut. If there were no priest on the ship, at least the rosary was said, and the Mother of God honored with true Spanish devotion.†

Scarcely was the Spanish crew departed, when a sadder contingent arrived,—the Acadians, whom the English government had torn from their homes, as a hundred years before they had torn the Irish, and scattered them along the line of colonies, as a hundred years before they had scattered the Irish children. Verily,

" Exile is God's alchemy. Nations He forms like metals,—
Mixing their strength and their tenderness ;

---

* Dr. O'Callaghan gives somewhere a list of very similar names of Catholic Highlanders.
† Trumbull's "History of Connecticut," vol. I.

Tempering pride with shame and victory with affliction ;
Meting their courage, their faith, and their fortitude,—
Timing their genesis to the world's needs."

The history of their seizure and deportation is well known. On January 21, 1756, three hundred of these unfortunates were landed at New London. They formed so large an influx of aliens into the little colony that the General Assembly took cognizance of their arrival, and provided at a special session in the following manner:

"An Act for the *distributing* and well ordering the French People sent into this Colony from Nova Scotia.

"*Whereas*, there is a number of French people sent by Governor Laurence into this colony, and more daily expected, to be disposed of here, and supposed to be about four hundred in the whole, *It is therefore* resolved and enacted by this Assembly, That a Committee be appointed, and Hezekiah Huntington, Gurdon Saltonstall, Christopher Avery, and Pygan Adams, Esqrs., or any three of them are hereby appointed a Committee to receive said people and distribute them in the towns hereafter mentioned in the following manner, viz.:

"In New London, 12; Groton, 8; Saybrook, 7; Lebanon, 12; Pomfret, 6; Plainfield, 4; Hartford, 13; Norwich, 19; Preston, 6; Killingsworth, 4; Coventry, 5; Killingly, 8; Canterbury, 5; Windsor, 13; Stonington, 11; Lyme, 8; Windham, 8; Mansfield, 5; Woodstock, 6; Voluntown—; Weathersfield, 9; Middletown, 16; Tolland, 3; Colchester, 7; Symsbury, 6; Ashford, 3; Beauford, 8; Wallingford, 12; Woodbury, 9; Norwalk, 12; Danbury, 6; Glassenbury, 4; Haddam, 3; Hebron, 5; Suffield, 5; New Haven, 19; Milford, 9; Durham, 4; Fairfield, 17; Stamford, 9; Newton, 4; Farmington, 14; East Haddam, 6; Bolton, 3; Enfield, 8; Guilford, 11; Derby, 4; Waterbury, 6; Stratford, 14; Greenwich, 6.

"And the selectmen of each of said towns are hereby directed and required to receive of said Committee the number set to such towns as above, or as near as may be a like proportion of the whole number whether greater or less, and with the advice of the civil authority in such town to take care of, manage, and support them as though they were inhabitants of said town, according to the laws of this Colony. And if said Committee shall judge that any of said French people by reason of age, sickness, etc., shall be unable to travel or cannot be conveyed from the town where they are, or may be landed, that in such case said Committee shall provide for and support such aged, sick, or otherwise infirm persons at the charge of the Colony.

"And to prevent such French people making their escape out of the Colony, *It is resolved and enacted* that none of them be allowed to depart out of their respective towns without a writing under the hand of some of the civil authority of such town allowing of such departure. And if any of said French shall be found in any other town than that in which they were ordered to dwell, without liberty in writing as aforesaid, it shall be the duty of the civil authority where such person shall be found to confine such person, until upon examination it can be known from what town they departed, and when known, to convey them back from constable to constable, to the towns where they belong, there to be confined, and not suffered any more to depart without liberty as aforesaid. And said committee are hereby directed to take care in distributing said people that no one family of them be separated, and sent into two or more towns. This act to remain in force till that Assembly shall order otherwise."

In the following year, 1757, among the Acts of the General Assembly appears the following enactment, which recalls the wanderings of Evangeline: "Upon the memorial of Elisha Stoddard and others, Selectmen for the town of Woodbury, representing to this Assembly that there has lately come to said town of Woodbury, two families of the French Neutrals from Maryland, three persons in each family; and also shewing to said Assembly that said town of Woodbury had their proportionable part of the French Neutrals to support, sent to this Government by Governour Laurence ; praying to said Assembly to order concerning said Neutral families: whereupon it is resolved by this Assembly that one of said families be immediately transported to the town of Litchfield, and the other of said families to the town of New Milford, by the direction of the Selectmen of Woodbury, and that the Selectmen of said towns of Litchfield and New Milford are hereby ordered and directed to receive said French families and provide for their support and deal with them from time to time according to the directions of an Act of Assembly of this Colony, made respecting the French sent to this Government by Governour Laurence, and that the expence of transporting said French families from said Woodbury to said towns be at the expence of this Colony."

Four months after the arrival of the first body of exiles from Acadia, a second allotment appeared in the port of New London, May 22, 1756, under convoy of a man-of-war, and were distributed on the basis of the January enactment of the same year. It is difficult to trace the Acadian element in Connecticut. Doubtless they wandered about "in fruitless search and disappointed endeavor," seeking friends and acquaintances. Many must have died of a broken heart in a land where they were aliens in speech, religion, and custom.

Between 1760 and 1770, an occasional French name appears in the " Connecticut (Hartford) Courant." Among others, John Ledgerd, described as a French Neutral, and at a later date the name of Charles Ledyard, Frenchman, doubtless an Acadian.

By vote of town meeting December 6, 1757, the selectmen of Hartford were directed to build a small house for the accommodation of these people, as no suitable habitation could be hired ; and also to find business and employment for them, if possible. On December 26, 1759, Mr. Robert Nevins was granted 20s. for the portion of the rent and damages sustained while the French people lived in his house.*

---

* " Memorial History of Hartford County," vol. i., p. 302.

It is a tradition that many were employed in building the old Town Hall in New London. Another tradition yet lingers that there were two Acadian priests located at Hartford, one living on the Bloomfield, the other on the Windsor road. We know by a letter of Laurence to Captain Monckton, Aug. 26, 1755, that the priests of Mines, Piziquid, and Annapolis were put on board the transports. The priest of Chignecto, Miniac, if he could be caught was to go. On the other hand, it is far from improbable that some priest made his way to so great a body of the exiles, and Hartford was the most accessible spot in which to minister to them. This was told me by Mr. Henry Barnard, of Hartford, who had it from a contemporary of the Acadians, the grandfather of Admiral Ward of the war of 1812. This was related to Mr. Barnard while seeking information for Mr. Bernard U. Campbell, author of the "Life of Archbishop Carroll."

In Miss Caulkins' "History of Norwich," it is related that Captain Richard Leffingwell, in the brig "Pitt," carried 240 of these French people *with their priest* from Norwich to Quebec in 1767. Perhaps this is the same body referred to in the "History of New London."

In Litchfield, the name Shearway is said to be that of an Acadian family, perhaps a corruption of Chérier. In 1766 two hundred and forty of these unfortunates were allowed to embark at New London and return to their plundered homes. But an occasional one remained, as is evident from a poem printed in the "Connecticut (New London) Gazette," July 5, 1778. The writer celebrates the Declaration of Independence, and signs himself "A Nova Scotia Refugee." The following lines which occur in a description of the Acadian sufferings, seem to indicate that he still respected and loved his ancient faith:

> "The savage hordes invest a virtuous town,
> For zealous piety, high in renown,
> God's altars their first brutal rage receive."

In the year 1767, one Morte (Murtagh) Sullivan died in

New London, leaving in the hands of the friend at whose house he died, a note for £368,—owing to him in St. Eustatia. Considerable litigation followed the attempt to collect, and it is to this fact that this gentleman's name owes its appearance in the Acts of the General Assembly.

The following year (1768) the British man-of-war "Cygnet" wintered in New London harbor. When it sailed in the spring, it was minus the purser, Mr. John Sullivan, who had become enamored of New London society and stayed to marry Elizabeth, daughter of Gideon Chapman, of that town. Such incidents lead us to the belief that no inconsiderable number of Irish Catholics found a haven of refuge at one time or another before the Revolution, on the rocky but far from inhospitable shores of the Pequot Country.

In the famous butchery of Wexford by Cromwell, the Mayor, Robert Fanning, was among the murdered, and his head was stuck on a pole at the city gate. His nephew escaped later from Ireland, and settled close by New London, at Stonington, and became the ancestor of the well-known family of Fannings in Eastern Connecticut.

The custom of celebrating Guy Fawkes' Day, November 5th, by burning the Pope in effigy, was one of the ancient rites of the port, and was annually observed, until 1768, when an attempt was made to stop it, because of the abuses it gave rise to. A ridiculous figure of the Pope and another of the Devil were paraded up and down the principal streets, while the mob, at frequent intervals, demanded from the merchants or passers-by the price of refreshments. Towards midnight, when wearied with the sport, the poor Pope and Devil were burned in a bonfire. A general order of Washington, after the arrival of the French troops, did much to discourage this practice, but it did not entirely die out in New London for some years after the Revolution. In the end Benedict Arnold was substituted for the Pope.

During the years immediately preceding the Revolution a number of Irish names appear in the columns of the " New

London Gazette." Sometimes they are those of worthless outcasts, offenders against society, which is not to be wondered at, since it was a common thing to send the most abandoned characters from England and cast them on the shores of America. However, several names of respectable individuals are to be met with.

I have copied some from the lists of unclaimed letters in the "Gazette"—Daniel Burns, Anna Maloney, Patrick Robertson, Captain Callaghan. It is refreshing to find in the same paper, February, 1772, among the advertised sales of old cider, rum, and cognac, and the proposals for printing Calvinistic sermons, a solitary item of Catholic news—the Address of the Roman Catholics of Philadelphia to Richard Penn, Commander-in-chief of Pennsylvania.

I am all the more tempted to believe that a respectable number of Catholics either resided in or frequented New London at this time from the following advertisement which was kept in the paper for a long time:

FOR SALE.

A MASTER KEY TO POPERY, containing 300 large octavo pages.

By D. ANTONIO GAVIN,

Born and educated in Spain, some years a Secular Priest in the Church of Rome, and since 1715 a Minister of the Church of England.

The same book-store advertises also for sale O'Halloran's "History of Ireland," which they were not likely to sell to the natives. About this time the Quebec act, which guaranteed to the Canadians freedom of religious worship, met with considerable denouncement in communications to the "Gazette," which, however, seem to have been written by some ministers.

The colony of Connecticut, which had held itself strictly independent of king and parliament from the first day of its foundation, would not allow any one to the enjoyment of its liberties who did not first take the oath of allegiance and supremacy, which meant to renounce the Pope and deny the Blessed Sacrament. In May, 1778, an example of this act of naturalization occurred. The subject was a Spaniard, whose descendants still live in New London:

"Whereas Don Gabriel Sistera, a native of Barcelona, in the Kingdom of Spain, now resident in New London, hath by his petition preferred to this Assembly, prayed to be admitted to the privileges of his Majesty's subjects within this Colony; *Be it Enacted by the Governor, Council, and Representatives in General Court assembled, and by the authority of the same,* That the said Gabriel Sistera, having taken the oaths of allegiance, supremacy, and abjuration by law appointed, be, and he is hereby declared to be naturalized, and entitled to all the privileges, immunities, and advantages of his Majesty's English subjects, born within this Colony, as fully and effectually to all intents, constructions, and purposes whatsoever, as though he, the said Gabriel Sistera, had been born within the dominions of and subject to the King of Great Britain; Excepting only such privileges and immunities as by law are not competent to foreigners who have been or are naturalized." *

During the Revolution it was no uncommon thing to see the ships of France in the great harbor, and her sailors and soldiers in the streets of New London. I have copied from the pages of the "Gazette" several interesting items concerning the stay of the armed ship "Lion" at New London during the years 1777 and 1778. Occasionally her men deserted, and then an advertisement was duly put in the paper by J. Michel, Commander, offering a reward for their return. Much of their time was spent ashore, as may be seen from the advertisement of Thomas Allen's Coffee-house, which advertisement, neatly done into French, extols the merits of said establishment above all others.

---

* "Connecticut Col. Records," vol. xiv., p. 94.

There was, without doubt, one priest on board this vessel, perhaps more. From the issue of the "Connecticut Gazette" of May 28, 1778, I take the following curious item:

"Deserted from the French Ship 'Lion,' in the Harbour of New London, Labc (L'abbé) Galand, who was under the Character of a Priest on Board, and has taken with him a Quantity of Silver, Gold, and Paper Currency not his own. He has been missing about three weeks: Is a short, thick, well-built man, of light Complexion, large black Eyes, short strait black Hair, looks like a Jew. Speaks very little English. Can speak French, German, and Latin, has a good notion of Slight of Hand, rode a small black Horse, had on when he went away a brown Coat, black Jacket and Breeches, and blue Great Coat; has a small gold watch with a small bell to the chain, which he is very fond of showing. Whosoever will apprehend said pretended Priest and return him on board said Ship shall have a reward of TWO HUNDRED DOLLA(R)S paid by me. J. MICHEL,
"Commander of said Ship.
"New London, May 28, 1778."

During the first years of the Revolutionary war, a number of Irish names appear in the pages of the "Gazette" as deserters, among them Thomas Fitzgerald, James Maloney, and one William Foster, the latter described as an Irishman from Hebron. These deserters were often unfortunate redemptioners, or men sold into partial slavery,—perhaps, too, they were waifs of that great army of emigrants which poured from every port of Ireland during the eighteenth century into Pennsylvania and the South. An example of this is the famous Irishman, Matthew Lyon, the first Congressman from Vermont, who was sold into service at New London about this time, and redeemed himself for two bulls, whence his well-known oath: "By the bulls that redeemed me."

However, if the poor pay and bad treatment and the tradition of invincible England, made some desert, many others clung to the sad fortunes of the Continental troops, and in the attack on Fort Griswold by the traitor Arnold, at least two Irishmen laid down their lives for the defence of the Commonwealth,—Barney Kinney and Patrick Ward. Their names appear in the list of the killed, in the "Connecticut Gazette" of Sept. 21, 1781.

During the last half of the eighteenth century the mercantile ventures of New London were very extensive, and its carrying trade was hardly surpassed by any port of New England. There was a brisk demand in Europe for masts, shingles, lumber, etc., and a large trade in horses was done with the West Indies.

On the shipping lists of its merchants not a few Irish names appear. Foremost among these is Captain Michael Melally, sometimes spelled Mullaly, commander of various vessels engaged in the West India trade. During the Revolution he turned privateer, and commanded the brig "Nancy." In 1793 he married Miss Esther Prentis, of New London, and was for many years a respected citizen of the town. He died in 1812, at the advanced age of 77.

Captain Richard McCarthy was shipwrecked off Plum Island May 22, 1779, and his brother, Captain John McCarthy, died at sea in 1804.

Other well-known names among New London seamen of that day were Captains Michael Kelly, Murphy, and John Connor. Captains Francis Brady, Sheehan, and Charles O'Hara occur occasionally on the New London Marine List.

It was not strange that these names should be met with in New London, for during the days of that town's mercantile supremacy, and the brief period of Irish prosperity, a considerable trade had sprung up between them, and every season saw large invoices of Irish linens and paper-hangings brought up and distributed throughout the State. In the columns of the local paper already mentioned great sympathy is shown for the Irish in their struggle for independence. From New London passengers went frequently for business or pleasure to Ireland, as appears from the following advertisement which stood for years in the "Connecticut (Hartford) Courant," and the "Connecticut (New London) Gazette." I quote from the issue of the "Gazette" Dec. 15, 1783:

"FOR CORK AND BRISTOL.

"THE FAST-SAILING SHIP ANGELICA,

"Having excellent accommodations for passengers, will sail on the 1st Jan. 1784.

"Whoever wishes to engage a passage for the kingdom of Ireland may apply to Col: Joshua Huntington at Norwich, Mr. Peter Colt at Hartford, or the Commander on board the ship lying at Hallam's Wharf."

As a rule, these old colonial papers contain little local news of interest, but the following item reveals a detail of that implacable hatred with which the Irish exile has followed the enemy of his country. It is from the issue of the "Connecticut Gazette" for Sept. 7, 1781: "The whale-boat 'Privateer' has brought in to New York the well-known and violent persecutor of Loyalists, Old Murphy, who was found in one of the prizes she took in the Delaware."

Perhaps Old Murphy had a few wrongs to avenge. According to the old-fashioned American ideas he was a very good patriot.

Many of the British troops who fought on Long Island were Irish recruits, to whom great advantages had been offered to induce them to enlist. In fact, they had been promised a division of the land if the Americans were conquered. The prisoners made on Long Island were, therefore, in many cases Irishmen, and these were usually interned at Hartford, Litchfield, and other remote places. Farmington and Wethersfield received a number of these prisoners, as well as New Haven, and they were not unkindly treated, whence it is not improbable that some of them remained. In fact, the Rev. Calvin White, of Derby, Ct., an Episcopalian minister, whose conversion made a great deal of noise in the early part of this century, owed the grace of the faith to the conversation of one of these old soldiers.

When the old Newgate prison was destroyed in Dublin the government rid itself of many of the prisoners by putting them on transports and scattering them along the Atlantic coast. In June, 1778, the brig "Nancy," Capt. Robert Winthrop, brought 201 of these unfortunates into New London, where they were sold on the wharf as redemptioners to the farmers, and others sent on to the Southern markets. Hundreds were left exposed, to starve, on desolate islands in the West Indies, and one ship-load, between three and four hundred, were cast ashore in Machias Bay, Maine, whence they wandered through all the New England States, saying they had been shipwrecked. In the same year, 1778, a large number of Irish emigrants entered the port of New London. By an accident eleven of them perished off Fisher's Island.

For many years before and after the Revolution, the principal coffee-house in New London was kept by Thomas Allen, who, Miss Caulkins, in her admirable " History of New London," says, came from Boston, but according to the old traditions of the Episcopalians, with whom he worshipped, he was an Irishman from the Island of Antigua. His inn was the principal resort of New London, and in it was prepared the Weekly Marine List, setting forth the arrival and departure of vessels, or as the phrase of the day had it,—coming over or clearing the platform ; *i. e.*, passing the mouth of the Connecticut at Saybrook, bound in or out. Many of his clients must have been Irishmen, for he thus chronicles the departure of a ship for Ireland : " Sailed, Brig Patty, Josiah Lee, from New Haven, for *Dear Ireland.*" His antipathy to the British was abnormal, and he is remembered as one of those who took the Episcopalian minister from his pulpit and thrust him out of doors for attempting to pray for King George. When the feast of the Apostle of Ireland comes around, he marks against the date March 17,—*St. Patrick's Day!*

This Marine List is one of the most quaint and interesting

bits of nautical literature, and is frequently interspersed with wise saws, warnings against sin, good advice to Jack Tar, exhortations against too much liquor, etc.

A precious item is to be found under date of June 20, 1791, (a copy of this List was always published in the "Gazette" and in the "Courant.") It records the presence of the first Catholic Bishop in Connecticut, then a part of his vast diocese. "Sailed for New York, June 20 (Monday), Packet Hull, with whom went passenger the Right Reverend Father in GOD, JOHN, Bishop of the United States of America." He was on his way to Maryland from Boston, which he had left the previous Thursday, after having suspended the French missionary, M. Rousselet, and established in his place the famous Fr. John Thayer, as pastor of the Roman Catholic congregation. The fact that he timed his journey to stop in New London for Sunday is in itself evidence that the brethren of the faith were already there, and numerous enough to secure his presence for a Sunday.*

Two years later Father Thayer, the famous missionary, appears upon the scene. In the "Norwich Packet" for Nov. 14, 1793, there is the following notice of him: "On Friday evening last Mr. John Thayer, Catholic missionary, delivered to a large audience at the Rev. Joseph Strong's meeting-house in this city, a learned and ingenious discourse, in which he undertook to prove that the Catholic Church was the only true church of Christ. On Sunday evening following, at the same place, he delivered a discourse on the propriety and true piety of invoking departed saints, and the utility and efficacy of addressing prayer to them." †

This was in the First Congregational church of Norwich. The Rev. Joseph Strong referred to was a descendant on the mother's side of the Williams family carried off by the Indians at the massacre of Deerfield in 1704. Of the two children, Eunice and Esther Williams, Esther was ransomed

---

* The exiles from Santo Domingo alone would form a respectable congregation.
† Miss Caulkins' "History of Norwich," p. 472.

and brought home, but Eunice, having become attached to the Indians and the Catholic faith, refused to return, was adopted by the Indians, married a chief named Roger, and settled down at Sault St. Louis, near Montreal.

Very probably Fr. Thayer said Mass, for there was in Norwich at least one Irish Catholic—Edward Murphy. It is not improbable that some of the Santo Domingo refugees were there at the same time. Most likely, too, he visited New London, and consoled the faithful there, and, perhaps, preached in some meeting-house.

Between this time and the end of the century a certain number of Irish Catholic names are to be met with in the "Gazette." From the lists of unclaimed letters I quote the following:

Peter Doyle and Richard Kerney,* Patrick Lucas and James Mageness,† John Fogarty,‡ John Callahan and Henry McCabe.§ The above seem to be distinctively Catholic. There are others, perhaps, equally so, but being in doubt I did not copy them.

In 1795 there appears the advertisement of one John O'Brien, merchant tailor on Beech St. (now Water St.). For twenty years the same name recurs in the pages of the "Gazette." Mention is also made of the marriage of Miss Nancy O'Brien, and unclaimed letters belonging to Daniel O'Brien are advertised.

A family of Byrnes seems to have been domiciled in Waterford, but I have been able to learn nothing more of them than that the head of the family died June 12, 1811, at Waterford, aged 87, an honest and worthy citizen. Perhaps he was the father of John Byrnes,| a printer, who lived at Norwich about 1790, and founded the "Windham Phenix," which he edited for many years. He was postmaster of

---

* "Connecticut Gazette," Oct. 7, 1793.   † Ibid., Apr. 24, 1794.
‡ Ibid., July 14, 1794.   § Ibid., Jan. 16, 1795.
| In Miss Caulkins' "History of Norwich" there is nothing about this Byrnes.

Brooklyn in Windham County, a citizen of good repute, and a public-spirited individual.

In Feb., 1801,* Mr. John O'Brien offers one shilling reward for the return of his runaway apprentice, Francis Sistare, and at the same time the post-office held letters for Hugh McFadden, John McGinley, Michael Dawley, and Hugh Ward. In the issue of Nov. 18, 1801, John Maguire, of Pomfret, is declared insolvent. During the year 1805 † William Kelly, tailor, and William Burke, shoemaker, are among the advertisers in the "Gazette." Burke removed afterwards to East Haddam.‡ Joseph Healy, tanner in Angel Street near the college, Providence, R. I.,§ offers his business for sale, and letters are advertised belonging to Patrick Lucas, John Mynean (Moynihan), and Benjamin Sullivan. In 1807 James Riley, being confined in jail for debt, broke out. The sheriff, in advertising for his capture, says he was 28 years of age, and had a little of the Irish enunciation. During the last quarter of the 18th century Patrick and James Thompson were prominent merchants in New London; and in the beginning of this the names Grace and Butler recur with great frequency. In 1807 ∥ Michael Powers died at Waterford, aged 80, and I have already quoted the death in 1811 of Daniel Byrnes of the same place. Evidently this is a New Ireland in Connecticut long before we dreamed of it. On the lists of the fort at New London at this period are many names of Irishmen, and among the seamen who filled her ports not a few were Irish Catholics. Thus the names of O'Kelly, O'Laughlin, O'Brien, and Quinley, are to be seen in the columns of the paper between 1807 and 1812, in which year John McGinley advertises for sale his farm at the mouth of the harbor.

I will close this paper with an item copied from the "Connecticut Gazette" of Aug. 14, 1811. From time to time ships and brigs arrived in New London from Ireland, but

---

* "Connecticut Gazette," Feb. 5, 1801.   † Ibid., Oct. 9, 1805.
‡ Ibid., July 9, 1806.   § Ibid., Oct. 1, 1806.   ∥ Ibid., Sept. 9, 1807.

this is the only clue to the lists of passengers. There can be no doubt as to the religion of these emigrants:

NEW LONDON, Aug. 9, 1811.

SIR:

We the undersigned, being the entire of the passengers now arrived from Dublin on board your vessel, beg leave to request you and be pleased to accept our very sincere thanks for your polite, humane, and gentlemanly conduct to us during our voyage; a conduct the pursuit of which we are satisfied, will insure you success in your progress through life. We sincerely wish you success in all your undertakings, and are with esteem, sir,

Yr most obedient servants,

Marcus Moore,
Patrick Byrne,
Michael Byrne,
Michael Byrne, Jr.,
Patrick Maddison,
Denis Costigan,
John Smith,
George Mansell,
Thomas Boyd,
William Grigg,

Charles Smith,
Joseph Philipps,
Terence Maguire,
Patrick Reilly,
John Reilly,
Charles Callahan,
Thomas Ryan,
James McDonnell,
Wm. Campbell.

A FLEMISH HISTORY OF CANADA.—A history of Canada in Flemish is said to have been published in 1651 by Father Francis de Schmidt, S.J., who was born at Antwerp in 1576. He is also said to have issued "Verhael van d' Indien," Antwerp, 1635. It is possible that these works were translations of some of the Jesuit Relations; but they are unknown to collectors, not being mentioned by Dr. O'Callaghan, Dr. George H. Moore, or Henri Harrisse, the bibliographers of the Jesuit Relations.

INDIANS ON THE ENGLISH COAST IN 1508.—Bembo, in his "History of Venice" (vii., p. 257), mentions that in 1508 a French vessel met a boat full of American Indians not far from the English coast.

THE BEGINNINGS OF THE CAPUCHIN MISSION IN LOUISIANA.

As early as 1717, Bishop Duplessis Mornay, Coadjutor of Quebec and Vicar-General for Louisiana, arranged with the Company of the West, which had control of the province, to send Capuchin missionaries to attend the settlers. No account has yet been found of the voyage of the first Fathers or their early labors. The oldest known date is the entry of the Capuchin Father, John Mathieu, in the parish register of Mobile, January 18, 1721, and his assumption of the title of Vicar-Apostolic seems to indicate that he was Superior.

In a recent French catalogue, several letters of Capuchin Fathers relating to the Louisiana mission were offered for sale. One was secured by the writer, but the rest were reported sold. A second one, however, was purchased by a New Orleans dealer, and before it passed out of his hands, Dr. G. Devron copied it carefully, and has since published it in the "Comptes Rendus de l'Athenée Louisianais," restoring words cut off or worn away.

These letters throw new light on the early history of the Church in Louisiana and are here given in English:

I.

LETTER OF BRUNO DE LANGRES, CAPUCHIN, SUPERIOR OF THE LOUISIANA MISSION.

SIR:

We are extremely sorry to have left Paris without paying you our respects; the gentlemen with whom we treated never spoke to us about you. Apparently, sir, it was by our order, and not to withdraw you from your serious occupations. But we have not been less sensible of the fault which we have committed, when we recognized it at Orleans, where Monsieur de Madier informed us that you were the head of the Company of the Indies, for whose service we are going to Louisiana, and it is to repair this fault that I do myself the honor to write to you in the name of our Reverend Fathers, missionaries, to make our apologies, to assure you of our duty and of our prayers for you to our Lord.

We reached Nantes only on the 3d of March, because our boatmen were detained a long time in the public offices. On arriving, we found Mr. Fourtat laid up with gout, but his wife, who is a woman of ability, accustomed to business, has labored so attentively to expedite matters for us, that we have found everything arranged to our wish, according to the statement we have forwarded. If the agents who have charge of the rest are as punctual or as charitable, we shall have reason to be well satisfied. Recollect, if you please, sir, that we have not yet the King's patents for our establishment in Louisiana, and that we need it in duplicate, one for the Reverend Father Provincial, to be kept in the archives of the province, and the other to serve as our authority in Louisiana. You will also oblige us, sir, if in the orders you give the Governor of that country to receive us, you beg him to supply some little necessaries which we shall undoubtedly need in those new establishments, which are trifles, such as kitchen cranes, bedsteads, paper, tables, chairs, and some other small articles of furniture of that nature, of little consequence, and yet very useful.

Excuse me for dwelling so long on such trifles; the situation in which we are placed seems to require it.

Our Reverend Fathers, missionaries, present you their homage, wishing you the blessings of heaven, and I, who am more particularly with a very profound respect,

   Your very humble and very obedient servant,
     F. BRUNO DE LANGRES,
   Capuchin, Superior of the Louisiana Mission.

NANTES, March 5, 1722.

This would seem to indicate that Father John Mathieu was simply a pioneer, and that Father Bruno de Laugres was the first Superior of the Mission and took out several Fathers in 1722.

II.

NEW ORLEANS, this 7th September, 1723.
(Rec'd March 8, 1724.)

By the "Galatée."

SIR:

I flatter myself that you will not find it amiss if I take the liberty of exposing to you the condition in which my companions and myself have been since our arrival in this colony, and if I ask you to continue to honor us with your protection at this time when we feel only too sensibly how much we require it. We are here without church and without residences, and it does not seem that any exertion is made to erect any, although the orders of Messeigneurs, the Superior Councillors, are formal. Every man thinks only of his own comfort, which he finds means to obtain, while the establishments are entirely neglected. For six months we have had at New Orleans only a small room, which served us as chapel and kitchen, another to lodge four religious, and a third to store our provisions and other effects. I will not tell you, sir, what inconvenience we suffered during the sickness which attacked us at that time. We have recovered from it only a few days, and we are in a cabin, where I have arranged two cells, which are not even as large as the ordinary Capuchin cells in France. We have besides this a kitchen where one of our religious sleeps, and another room which serves as a sacristy, where a fourth is lodged. The house which we have converted into a church holds only about —— persons, which is only half a quarter of the inhabitants of New Orleans. It will be difficult for us to remain long in this state, our ministry becoming almost useless for want of a church in which we can assemble the people to instruct them, without which we cannot hope for any fruit of our mission. Almost all the inhabitants live in the most scandalous conditions, and in such a profound ignorance of the truths of our holy religion, that they may be said to be ignorant even of the first elements. No Easter Communion, no attendance at divine service, although we do all we can to attract them, both in public and private. Those who wish to keep up a show of religion, content themselves with a low mass on Sundays and holidays, and carefully avoid any where there is a word of preaching. The example of those who are at the head of the colony encourages this disorder. They ask us for a low mass after the high mass, which they attend, followed by a part of the people who have retained some religious principles, the parochial mass being so neglected that generally scarcely thirty or forty persons are found there. A better example on the part of the authorities could not but produce a good effect. I hope, sir, that you will endeavor to have our provisions increased, it being almost impossible for us to maintain ourselves on what is given us in a country where there is no other resource. The ministry gives very little, and even that little can be expected only at New Orleans, where there are a few offerings for masses, some (fees for) parochial functions in copper coin, which is valued so low that during our sickness I sent everywhere to get a couple of eggs, offering as much as —— sous apiece, but could not find them. Those who sold them replied that they could do nothing with our copper, and that if we had white money to give them, they had eggs to sell us. We have bought a few hens, which will be some help to us in future needs. For the rest, we have for our ordinary only a little pork, half a pound of bread, and the third of a chopine of wine, after supplying that for mass. The fatigue we endure running night and day to visit the sick and carry the sacraments to them, generally in mud knee deep, does not accord with such scanty nourishment. Here at New Orleans we can pay at the rate of France in copper money for a few bottles of wine and some quarters of flour, which out of consideration they are willing to grant us, but in the other posts, where our missionaries have no resource but the ration they receive from the Company, it will be absolutely impossible for them to live, unless the Company has the goodness to grant them this allowance gratis. I beg you to consider, sir, that our case is not like that of the missionaries who preceded us. These often had three times as much as we have, and when they were reduced to —— livres' allowance yearly, they found also means of subsistence by the traffic they carried on; they obtained from the storehouses goods which they then sold at threefold and fourfold, which gave them means to visit these same storehouses, where nothing was refused them for copper money, three and four times the amount of goods, which they had obtained for their original sum. We are not capable of such peddling, which we regard as ruinous to the colony. Hence, it seems to me just that we should be assisted from some other quarter.

You will have the goodness, sir, to remember that at Paris you promised us two cows and a bull. If you will kindly give orders that these cattle be delivered to us, we shall be deeply obliged to you, for a little milk with our bit of pork and the rice that we can find here will render our life less hard.

I take the liberty, sir, to address you papers in regard to a cask of wine, of which we were deprived by an act of bad faith on the part of the captain and —— of the vessel "l'Alexandre," who for five casks which have been delivered to us, put six in the original of their manifest, and to deceive Father Bruno, then Superior, noted on the copy delivered five casks, although in the body of the copy there seem to be due us only three out of the nine which the Company assigned us, and of which we then received only five. I am convinced, sir, that you will have the goodness to see justice done us.

Although it is foreign to my ministry to mingle in affairs, I nevertheless think that I shall not overstep the bounds which I draw for myself in this respect by informing you, sir, that it is very necessary that some water-mills should be erected in places adapted for them, or wind-mills where proper streams are wanting. Such mills will dispense with half the French flour sent over, and will prevent the frequent bread famines which now happen, for the common people will be content with rice or Indian corn bread, and many even of those better off will be glad to mix half French flour and half rice or Indian corn meal, which makes very good bread. Bread of this kind is made but by pounding the rice or Indian corn in a mortar, which is very laborious and repulsive work, because it takes a person a whole day to crack enough for one or at most two days. Moreover, the laborer loses a considerable time at this task, when he could be more usefully employed in the Company's establishment, and as the sick cannot be employed, they are left without food or provisions.

Suffer me, sir, in finishing my letter, to recommend to the honor of your protection the Mayor, who will have that of presenting this to you. He has rendered us an essential service by ceding to us his house, to afford us a little better lodging than that we occupied, as well as to afford us a larger and less unbecoming chapel. He obtains no rent, but a free passage to France, and some repairs that have been made there, the whole not amounting to half the rent the Company had previously paid for us. He desires permission to ship some provisions on a vessel when he returns to this country. I trust you will not refuse him this favor, nor me that of believing myself with all possible respect and gratitude,

  Sir,

    Your most humble and obedient servant,

      F. RAPHAEL DE LUXEMBOURG,

        Capuchin, Superior of the Mission.

ROBERT WALSH.

By Henry C. Walsh, of Philadelphia.

Duyckinck, in the sketch of Robert Walsh which appears in his "Cyclopædia of American Literature," says: "No adequate memoir has yet appeared of his career, which is well worthy of being written of with minuteness, for it would embrace a great part of the political, literary, and social history of America, with much of interest relating to the savants and statesmen with whom he freely mingled in the French capital." In answer to the kind request of the Editor of this magazine to supply a sketch of my grandfather, I should like to have been able to have drawn upon, or furnish some such memoir, but unfortunately nearly all the private papers, etc., belonging to the subject of this sketch were, by mistake, destroyed shortly after his death, which occurred in Paris in 1859. And as the present writer was born during the same year, he cannot of course give any personal reminiscences. I have before me, however, several sketches which appeared in French and American papers at the time of my grandfather's death. As he was eminently a man of his time, and worked for his time, thinking little and caring little for future fame, perhaps no better estimate can be formed of him than that given by his contemporaries. I have omitted such parts of the notices as go over the same grounds, in order to avoid tedious repetitions. The first sketch is translated from a French journal, and was written by M. Jomard, the celebrated Egyptologist, and a member of l'Institut:

"The United States has met with a severe loss in the person of Robert Walsh, who died recently in Paris, where he had held the position of Consul-General. The intelligence, impartiality, and lofty character of this learned man of letters made him a sort of connecting link, *a trait d'union* between three great nations, the United States, England, and France. His consummate experience in European and American affairs enabled him to regard political events in their true light, and his wide information made him rightly appreciate the progress of useful knowledge. In listening to him one learned thoroughly to understand the union of States, which justly or unjustly received from us an unfavorable and even severe judgment. Loyal and true above all, and especially just toward the French nation, he defended his country without bitterness, taking pains to direct attention to the services of those of his countrymen who, from Washington to the present time, have led the way in America in public affairs, science, and political economy, and have raised their country to the rank of the greatest nations.

"Robert Walsh was born at Baltimore in 1785, of an honorable family, originally from Ireland; his father, Count Walsh, Baron Shannon, came to America while quite young; he was of the elder branch of the family, the younger branch of the Walshes having come to France with James II.

"Robert Walsh was educated at two Catholic colleges in America, where he devoted himself with assiduity to literary studies. In 1801, at the age of sixteen, he studied law; at the same time he was a contributor to several journals. Three years later, having already received the degree of LL.D., he set out for Europe, and spent one year at Paris, during which time he made the acquaintance of many distinguished savants. He published several articles in the journals of Paris, in order to make the institutions and laws of America better known and appreciated. While he lived at the capital he put himself *en rapport* with M. Joubert, of the *Conseil d'Etat*, who was engaged upon the Code of Napoleon, and furnished him with much information upon the English and American laws. Afterward he went to England, visiting also Scotland and Ireland. At this time he was twenty years old. This tour occupied two years. In London he published in the press a series of political articles which attracted much attention; also some articles on conscription in France, and others of modern French biography. At the age of twenty-three (1808) he returned to America, and was admitted to the bar of Philadelphia, and subsequently to the Supreme Court of the United States. One year later he wrote his 'Letters on the Genius and Dispositions of the French Government,' which were reprinted in London, and ran through eleven editions, being afterward translated into almost all the languages of Europe.

"In 1810 a like success crowned his 'Appeal from the Judgments of Great Britain respecting the United States,' a work which went through several editions in England, and which obtained for him the thanks of the Pennsylvania Legislature. It was at this time that his health commenced to fail, and he was obliged to abandon the career of the law and devote himself entirely to letters and politics. To him is owing the establishment of the first quarterly review in America, 'The American Review of History and Politics,' which made its appearance in 1811. At this time he contributed all the articles on American biography in the 'Encyclopædia Americana.'

"In 1821, at the age of thirty-six, he founded the 'National Gazette,' and continued for fifteen years connected with its editorship. This journal was of a lofty character, and was a model in the art of criticism, embracing politics, science, letters, and the fine arts. He prepared in 1820 a complete edition, in fifty volumes, of the English poets, accompanied with biographical sketches, which labor, however, did not prevent his writing at the same time occasional articles for various journals. In 1836 he published two volumes of essays, entitled 'Didactics.' The following year Robert Walsh returned to Paris, at the age of fifty-two, as Consul-General of the United States. He found some of his old friends of 1805 still living there, and formed new ties with the savants, the littérateurs, and political characters of the day. His salon, open to a host of men of mark in the political, scientific, and literary world, was an especial attraction to his compatriots, and it was a priceless privilege for his friends in Paris to meet there distinguished Americans, and to form with them relations both useful and agreeable. These meetings were calculated to dissipate the prejudices so at variance with that mutual sympathy which should unite civilized peoples. Robert Walsh contributed much to these friendly relations by his unfailing courtesy, his kindly spirit, his happy disposition, and his refined wit. It was truly a great service which he rendered to two nations, and one which is not likely to be forgotten.

" For seven years he held the position of Consul-General of the United States, during which time he was a frequent contributor to leading American journals, among which were the 'National Intelligencer' and the 'New York Journal of Commerce,' and so kept his countrymen *au courant* with the current events of France and Europe. In addition to the fact that by his position and various connections he was most favorably situated to gain a knowledge of the true state of affairs, he was endowed with a natural perspicacity and keen discernment, and at the same time was possessed of unfailing kindliness and untiring courtesy, all the more praiseworthy, because he was afflicted with partial deafness which required of him great patience and attention. He took pleasure in introducing Americans, who had come to France to inform themselves upon European affairs, to French savants, who seconded him in his kindly intentions. Nor were the services less which he rendered to his countrymen by obtaining for them useful information, and by replying to their questions in regard to France. . . . . He took pleasure in spreading in France a knowledge of the works of his compatriots, of their recent scientific discoveries, their explorations, their astronomical researches, their progress in navigation, and their inventions and improvements of all kinds. As soon as any responsible account reached him touching the arts or sciences in his country, he communicated it without delay to the Institute, or to other learned societies. Nor was he less eager in transmitting to America the latest productions of French savants and men of letters.

"Robert Walsh was as simple in his tastes and habits as he was distinguished by his manners and understanding. He never assumed the titles of Count and Baron, although he held them from his father, but preferred his literary titles, of which he held many, being a Doctor of Harvard University, a member of the Academy of Turin, of the Academy of History of Madrid, and of almost all the learned societies in America."

I have some other notices before me from French journals, but as they are really embodied in the obituary above quoted, it is needless to give them. The following extracts are taken from various American papers of that day.

This is from a letter to one of the New York papers from a Paris correspondent:

"The life of Mr. Walsh in Paris, apart from the performance of official duties and his political and literary correspondence, has been a type of that social and intellectual enjoyment which is, perhaps, nowhere in the world to be met with in the same completeness and perfection as in the French capital. 'There exists among us here,' I remember to have heard M. Guizot once say, 'an absolute necessity, *soif*, or thirst, for mental intercourse, which is neither felt nor satiated anywhere else as it is in Paris.' The salons of Mr. Walsh were for nearly three-and-twenty years the scene of this intellectual learning in its happiest form of development. 'They were,' said to me the other day one of his oldest friends, now a Judge in the Supreme Court of Cassation, 'a sort of neutral ground, on which French, English, and American met to converse and interchange ideas and opinions with equal pleasure. It was, too,' he added, 'a ground which our friend was peculiarly fitted to occupy, from his almost equal intimacy and familiarity with all those countries alike. We have no one left to supply his place. M. ——,' naming one of the oldest members of the Institute, 'receives many foreigners in his salon, but then his knowledge of the world is almost exclusively French, and he is wholly wanting in that perfect acquaintance with English and American politics and literature which made him we have lost so complete in the requisites for his social position.'"

The Paris correspondent of the "Philadelphia North American," among other things said: " . . . . I am not myself acquainted with all the particulars of Mr. Walsh's career in the United States, but I have always understood that his native country stands indebted to his talents and intellectual energy for the very foundation of literary journalism. I mean of that class of newspapers and public writers whose aim and business it is not merely to chronicle events, but to seek to lead, elevate, and instruct their fellow-men, by the instrumentality of a press whose noblest privilege it is to be in the van of civilization and progress. In Paris, almost his adopted country, for a period of twenty-two years, Mr. Walsh has occupied a distinguished position in political society, and has enjoyed the familiarity of a great number of eminent Frenchmen. For many years his kindness, urbanity, intelligence, and keen enjoyment of conversational and social pleasures caused his salon to be the rendezvous of all that was most celebrated both of his own countrymen and of the country he had chosen for his retreat."

Extract from the Paris correspondence of the "Intelligencer":

" . . . . Robert Walsh's decease will carry your recollections far back into past years and his name will be refreshed in the thoughts of many, many contemporaries at home. Mr. John Quincy Adams used to think him the best American belles-lettres scholar. He founded the first American Quarterly Review, and instituted a journal in Philadelphia which our people may well remember with respect. Various literary performances independent of these, distinguished their author as one of the most remarkable publicists of his time."

Extract from the New York "Journal of Commerce":

". . . . Our first acquaintance with Mr. Walsh was in Philadelphia, when he was editor of the 'National Gazette,' established in 1820. The journal was *sui generis*. It is not too much to say that for the union of political sagacity and independence with literary fulness, taste and skill, this newspaper has never been surpassed in America. Its high moral tone, unconstrained dignity, varied learning and frequent wit and sarcasm, made it welcome to the doors even of opponents. It was less common in that day than it has since become, for daily journals to contain reviews of books and literary discussions, but these were frequent in the 'Gazette.' The editor moved in the best circles of scientific and lettered society, and kept open house for savants, authors, and gentlemen of taste and travel. No soirées of that period were more illustrated by the presence of celebrities than those given by Mr. Walsh. It was here that one might meet men as unlike as Bishop White, Bishop Cheverus, Dr. Channing, Mr. Duponceau, Dr. Chapman, Mr. Biddle, Mr. Binney, Charles Bonaparte, the diplomatic gentlemen of foreign name, and the most brilliant of female authors. We remember that our present plenipotentiary in China, Mr. Reid, made some of his earliest adventures in authorship in the columns of the 'National Gazette'; and that other persons beginning to try their newly-fledged wings, were cheered on and sustained by Mr. Walsh's helping hand and unenvying cordiality."

From the Boston "Transcript":

"The late Robert Walsh, whose death at Paris in the seventy-sixth year of his age has recently been announced, was a man of such peculiar and superior character, that the mere dates and facts of his career give but an imperfect notion of his influence and traits of mind. On the score of mere literary distinction, the noble and copious 'Appeal' to the trials and triumphs of American statesmanship, letters and science, with which he met forty years ago the sneers of the British public press, entitle him to grateful respect. It was of this work that Jeffrey, then the critical autocrat, wrote in the 'Edinburgh Review': * 'We must learn to love the Americans when they send us such books as this.' But it was to Mr. Walsh's brave example as an editor—ere that profession had assumed its due rank on this side of the water—his successful efforts in the establishment of the first able critical quarterly in the Middle States—the vast knowledge and disciplined taste he brought to the discussion of the drama, literature, education, and political questions, both in the 'American Review' and the 'National Gazette,' which gave the earliest impulse in a high direction to journalism among us.

"As a cultivator of English literature he was almost alone, for years, in Philadelphia—where the educated men were chiefly devotees of science; his house was for years the most delightful resort in that city for Boston visitors; every scholar and writer of distinction who visited the country found there a congenial welcome and atmosphere; what of the genuine literary tone, feeling, taste, and knowledge, Philadelphia could boast, either in her society, her press, or her hospitality, was thus long centred in the person, the writings, and the home of Robert Walsh; many is the discouraged young votary of letters he has cheered onward; many the dormant literary aptitude he has elicited; many the memorable intellectual conversations of which he was, then and there, the animating genius. Nor is this all. Mr. Walsh introduced the love of English literature as an element of education; to smatter French and thrum a piano, used to be the standard of education in the City of Brotherly Love, until he invited

---

* This is a mistake. It was of the " Letters on the Genius and Disposition of the French Government," that Jeffrey wrote the above. He naturally did not take kindly to the " Appeal," and attacked it in a lengthy review in the " Edinburg Review" for May, 1820. See Jeffrey's collected " Contributions to the Edinburgh Review."

teachers, promoted lectures, readings, criticisms, and so created an interest in and respect for the classic authors of our vernacular. . . . .

"His writings, though voluminous, were too desultory and occasional to make a great name; yet their usefulness can scarcely be overestimated; no man scattered more widely the seeds of liberal knowledge or fostered more successfully the appreciation of beauty and truth in letters. He loved literature for its own sake; an incessant reader, he gleaned the choicest of fruit of books with tact and ardor; he sought information from all; he improved every possible occasion to learn; in conversation, letters to the press, articles in reviews, pamphlets, etc., he threw off from time to time the results of his studies. He was not ambitious; he read and wrote to be useful and give pleasure, not to make a name.

"Probably no citizen of the United States of his age, ever personally and intimately knew so many celebrated men and women. Secretary of Legation with Pinckney in London, when a young man, and familiar with all the leading Englishmen of that day, he returned to the United States to cultivate the society of the learned and distinguished in every sphere, and then went again to Europe, to become a resident of Paris, and habitually associate with the authors, statesmen, and scholars who rally around the Institute, the Academy, and the libraries, lectures and salons of that brilliant capital. It was the social worth and enjoyment of literature that he chiefly prized; a more distinguished votary of knowledge it would be difficult to find in our day. His vivacity of mind, his intellectual zeal, his interest in politics, literature, science, and cultivated society never flagged.

"Within a few weeks of his death, he wrote a masterly analysis of the new publications, and a fond tribute to the casual literary labors of an old friend at home. He rose at four o'clock, kindled his own fire, made himself a cup of coffee, wrote until eight, passed the morning with his books, took a walk of observation, welcomed a circle of savants or friends after dinner, and retired early. Apt, quick, inquiring, eager, omnivorous in his mental appetite—for years his frail body seemed to be kept alive by his active, zestful intellect; and when he died the expression of his face was youthful. His last words were, 'I die in the faith of my ancestors—in the faith of the Holy Catholic Church.'"

I close with some extracts from a lengthy notice, headed "The Death of Robert Walsh," which appeared in the New York "Tribune," and signed by Wm. Henry Fry. After some general remarks upon " the neglect of the great men of this country, otherwise than senatorial, which characterizes us," Mr. Fry goes on to say :

" Robert Walsh was the literary and historical link between Jefferson, Madison, and Hamilton, and the men of the present day.*. . . . He was the most elaborate, polished, and elegant type of a literary man, who wrote chiefly from the historico-political point of view, in the United States. . . . . So precocious was his genius that at the age of sixteen he became a brilliant writer. His fecundity of genius was unrivalled by any American contemporary ; and in the race for renown, he preceded as to time even Irving and Cooper. The first work which gave him renown was one 'On the Genius and Dispositions of the French Government,' published in London about the year 1809 or '10. As a magnificent piece of diction, as a crushing array of facts against the sanguinary desolation of the hearts and homes of Europe, it must ever remain unsurpassed. There is a freshness in the word coloring, a massive arrangement of phraseology, that at once placed it in a classical niche. So profound was the sensation produced by this work, that twelve editions were printed in six weeks in London; and the learned, polite, and political world were entranced with it. Lord Brougham, through the 'Edinburgh Review,' did especial homage to the author, and the young

---

* Biographical details are not quoted, because they have been already given sufficiently.

American found himself the observed of all observers; the petted, flattered, and exalted among our Anglo-Saxon kinsmen. It was universally conceded in England that Napoleon I., and his policy, had never hitherto been so vigorously handled. . . . . When the 'Edinburgh' and the 'London Quarterly'; when the 'British Critic' and the 'Oxford Press'; when the 'Thunderer' and its echoes, and society public and society private, growled throughout England with contempt of everything American and everybody American, Mr. Walsh electrified the world with his 'Appeal from the Judgments of Great Britain on the United States.' This work produced a profound impression throughout the country. It was published in Philadelphia, in which city Mr. Walsh had settled; and so delighted and grateful were the Senate and House of Representatives of Pennsylvania, that on joint ballot they voted the illustrious author their thanks, couched in language of the most devoted admiration. The publication of this volume drew forth letters of congratulation from Thomas Jefferson, John Adams, John Quincy Adams, and many of the most eminent politicians, as well as from learned bodies. I know of no superior storehouse of gallant and glowing American facts, arranged in the most dazzling rhetoric, and with a fecundity of illustration hitherto unequalled or unapproached in American literature. I remember reading an old tattered copy of it with the passionate tears of boyhood, and finding in it the commonplaces of diction—the same dreary adjectives qualifying the same nouns—the same worn-out adverbs, the same verbs, which distinguish writing in ordinary, and, above all, those things uttered at bars and in senates, and quoted in school-readers as masterpieces of American eloquence. It is not within the limit of this letter to give a synopsis of such a remarkable work, which became a reservoir for future historians and even poets—the 'Evangeline' of Longfellow being suggested by a portion of the historical matter, either read by the poet in the original or in sources derived therefrom. It was said that Dr. Johnson, single-handed, did more for the English language than all the French Institute, with its forty members, for the French. Equally true was it that Mr. Walsh was, single-handed, more than a match for all the literary assailants of his country.

"The period of the agitation of this work was also that of the agitation of the Missouri Compromise. The respectable paper of the city of Philadelphia—then the centre of the commerce, finance, letters, and sciences of the Union—was neutral. It became, therefore, necessary to have a newspaper which would speak in the tones of liberty for the North. At the instance of a number of gentlemen, headed by Robert Vaux, a partnership was formed between the subject of our notice and the late William Fry, and the result was the 'National Gazette,' which at once became the organ of the Northern Liberals, and besides, the arbiter in matters of art and literature. Mr. Walsh's superior knowledge of European affairs was constantly exhibited; and without him, it may truly be said that many a Congressional speech would have been wanting..... The lingual accomplishments of Mr. Walsh, his European associations, and his elegant manners—his *savoir faire*—made his house the headquarters of fashionable life, and of exotic interest, including diplomatic adornments. Then the foreign ministers affected Philadelphia, for the metropolitan supremacy of New York was not then achieved. Mr. Walsh was a passionate lover of music, his soirées were the rage, and not to know them was to be yourself unknown. I have many pleasant recollections of boyhood in recalling these evenings where shone every celebrity who visited our shores. No such reunions had ever been possible before in this country, because the magnet of attraction —literary, artistic, and domestic—was wanting..... Some twenty years ago Mr. Walsh repaired to Paris, and there he resided up to the period of his death. Being, as we have seen, an accomplished scholar, and speaking French fluently and vernacularly, of course he could not receive the appointment of American Minister to France, the chief, if not sole qualification for that office being the inability to utter one word of Parisian, or the language of diplomacy. It is also the business of editors to supply erudition to statesmen, and then be rewarded with the lowest or lower order of appointments, and even that seldom. Mr. Walsh was 'honored' with the place of Consul-General. By this exquisite arrangement, due to the low tone of our national politics, we had the spectacle of 'the Commercial Agent' of our country, the Nestor of the literati, the victor in the great battle with the defamers of his country, being the cynosure of such men as Dupin, Thiers, Guizot, Molé, Michel, Chevalier, and other magnates, when they wished to confer with an American on American affairs—the American Embassy offering them the same facilities of intercourse as a deaf and dumb asylum. . . . . Mr. Walsh wrote a great number of letters to the 'National Intelligencer' and the 'Journal of Commerce' during his sojourn in Paris. He died in harness. I have written earnestly about him, knowing well his genial nature, the splendor of his literary achievements, his patriotic services, and the tendency of the public to forget the names and works of such characters."

NOTES ON OLD CHURCHES NEAR WASHINGTON.—Queen's Chapel, erected in Colonial times, with a large chimney, is about two miles northeast of the Capitol at Washington. The church was abandoned about 1820, when St. Peter's church was erected. It was, however, repaired about 1826, and Mr. Callan, a cabinet-maker, made a tabernacle for it about that time. The Jesuit Fathers then visited it about once a month. In the year 1844 Rev. John Donelan visited the church, and found the tabernacle used in former days in some old building. With the consent of the Queen family Mr. Donelan had it brought to Washington and placed in the sanctuary of St. Matthew's.—Letter of Mr. N. Callan, Washington, Aug. 31, 1876.

St. John's church is near the Washington and Rockville Turnpike road, and is eight miles from Washington, and near the dwelling of F. P. Blair.—Letter of same.

TO THE HON*ble* THE UPPER HOUSE OF ASSEMBLY OF THE PROVINCE OF MARYLAND.

THE PETITION OF SUNDRY RO. CATHOLICS ON BEHALF OF THEM-
SELVES AND OTHERS OF THE SAME COMMUNION RESIDING
IN THE PROVINCE AFORESAID,

HUMBLY SHEWETH:

That several of your Petitioners jointly and Charles Carroll Esqr seperately, preferr'd a Petition to your Hon'ble House in the year 1751 against a Bill then laying before you by which they would have been depriv'd of their Civil and Religious Rights had the same passed into a Law, to which Petitions your Pet^r humbly beg your Hon^{rs} will be pleased to be referr'd.

That yor Hon^{rs} actuated by Justice and as We humbly conceive being convinced that the Ro. Cath^s in this Province did not deserve the Hardships and Penalties that would be inflicted on them by the said Bill, were pleased to reject it, as you have some others since brought before you.

By so doing your Hon^{rs} have repeatedly given us the greatest satisfaction and pleasure as you thereby sufficiently manifested Your Opinions that we did not deserve the Hardships which those Bills would have expos'd us to.

That several Malicious Lies and Groundless Clamours continuing still to be spread against us, among others, *That Persons of the Ro: Cath persuasion had misbehaved in such a manner in some Counties as to give his Majesty's Loyal Subjects just cause to fear an insurrection and further it was intimated that some Ro: Cath Priests of this Province had been lately absent from their usual Place of Residence a considerable time.* The Clerk of the Council by direction of his Excell^y Hor^o Sharpe Esqr and Yo^r Hon^{rs} Wrote on the

15th of Augt 1755, to the Justices of the several County Courts of this Province, directing them to bind over such turbulent Ro: Cat to the next Assizes if any such should be found and that if any absenting Priests should be found who could not give a satisfactory acct of himself during his absence: They had also directions to commit such Priests to the Sheriffs custody unless he gave good security for his immediate appearance before the Governr & Council.

That your Petrs have not heard that a single Ro: Caths in the Province has even been accused, nor that any Priest has been mentioned as an Absentee.

That from these instances yor Petrs think it reasonable to conclude that all other reports tending to defame them, are equally false and malicious, since it's natural to believe that the Persons who forge such lies want nothing but Power or Proof to support them.

That the aforesaid Reports are groundless is manifest from the Answers of the Justices of St Mary's and Charles Counties where almost all the Ro: Cat of the Province reside to the Clerk of the Councils letter aforesd as well as from the Answers of several Justices of each County Court within this Province—

That moreover the Justices of St Mary's County Court moved as We have the greatest reason to suppose with indignation against our Slanderous Accusers, in their Answer to the aforesd letter, say: *We are not yet informed who have been the Authors of those reports mentioned in your Excellrs letter which have been in some Places so industriously spread, if We should discover them, We should take proper Measures for their being brought to Justice, as enemies to their Countrys peace & Friends to a Faction who labour to foment animosities among us to the endangering our common Security.*

That We behave as good and peaceable Subjects the above letters evince, and our Conduct has been so irreproachable, that our most inveterate enemies have not been able to prove any thing criminal against any one person among us.

That the unhappy defeat of General Braddock gave us a melancholy opportunity to convince all men open to conviction that we had the Welfare of our Country and the defence and protection of our Protestant fellow subjects as much or may be more at heart than the warmest of Our Patriots or the most inveterate of our Enemies. We need not lay before your Hon^{rs} the deplorable state and Circumstances of our Inhabitants on the frontiers from the last summer to the present time, nor that as no provision was made for their protection by the legislature, a subscription for that purpose was set on foot nor that by the money arising from that subscription the Govern^r has been enabled as we suppose to keep Capt Dagworthy and his company in pay to erect Block Houses & to garrison them &c. &c. Nor that without that subscription our Settlers on the frontiers must have been entirely abandoned to a savage and merciless enemy. The Ro: Cath. were not the men who opposed this subscription, on the contrary they countenanced it, they promoted it, they subscribed generously & paid their subscriptions honorably and if our numbers are compared with the numbers of our Protestant fellow subjects and if the sum paid on this occasion by the Ro. Cath. be compared with the sum Total collected, it may be said, the Ro: Cath contributed prodigiously beyond their proportion to an aid so seasonable and necessary.

That notwithstanding our irreproachable conduct, our peaceable behaviour and our readiness on all occasions to contribute and bear in common with our fellow subjects any loads or taxes that may be laid to defeat the ambitious views and prevent the unjust encroachments of the French on any of his Majesty's Dominions, we are informed a Bill is now before your Honours by a clause of which the Lands of all Ro: Cath. are doubly taxed.

That we conceive such a Tax or any particular Tax on us to be unjust and unreasonable.

That we hope, and we ground our hope on your Hon^{rs} Justice and moderation, that your endeavours will always be exerted to distress his Majesty's enemies, not to punish his innocent subjects & Therefore

We Humbly pray that your Hon^{rs} will not pass any Bill whereby our Lands may be doubly Taxed or any particular or partial Tax be laid on us or any of our Communion residing within this Province.

And Y^r Pet^{rs} as in Duty bound will pray &C.

Endorsed,

Petition of the Roman Catholics to the upper House presented April 10, 1756.

THE POOR CLARES AT GEORGETOWN.—In the "Sentinel of Liberty," Feb., 1799: "Madame de la Marche (Georgetown Academy) thanks the public for the encouragement she has received, and announces that she will be assisted by a lady educated in London, recommended to her by Mr. Leonard Neale and several other respectable gentlemen. Has waters for the cure of sore eyes, also salves."

March 8, 1799: "She expected next week a French clergyman, very eminent in science, who will teach French, etc."

June 18, 1801, in the "Museum and Washington and Georgetown Advertiser," she offers for sale two handsome dwelling-houses, lately occupied by her, near the College, 182 feet on Fayette and 192 on Third Street.

GENERAL DESCRIPTION OF THE METROPOLITAN PROVINCE OF BALTIMORE IN THE UNITED STATES OF NORTH AMERICA.

[Translated from a Latin manuscript of Archbishop Maréchal, prepared in 1821-2, between the time of the erection of the See of Cincinnati and the translation of Bishop Kelly to Waterford.]

SEE, Baltimore. Bishop, Ambrose Maréchal; number of secular priests, 40; number of churches, 52; number of the faithful, at least 80,000; Seminaries, Colleges, Monasteries. Greater Seminary for Philosophy and Theology, 15 students; Lesser Seminary for Classical Studies, 75 boarders, 12 day scholars; Sulpitian College, Baltimore, 68 boarders, 120 day scholars; Jesuit College, Georgetown, 50 boarders, 12 day scholars; where they have also a novitiate, 24 novices; Scholasticate, 10 scholastics; Regular priests, 18; Monastery of the Visitation of St. Francis de Sales, 70 in community; Carmelites, 27; Sisters of Charity of St. Vincent de Paul, 52. Present condition of religion, Peace, and by God's blessing, great prosperity.

See of Boston. Bishop, J. Cheverus; number of secular priests, 4; number of churches, 3; number of faithful, at least 3,500; Seminaries, Colleges, Monasteries, Ursuline Convent, 4 religious, no pupils. Present state of religion, All prosperous.

See of New York. Bishop, Dr. Connelly; number of secular priests, 5; number of churches, 4; number of Catholics, at least 24,000; Seminaries, Colleges, Monasteries, none; Regular clergymen, 1. Present state of religion, Grave dissensions.

See of Philadelphia. Bishop, Dr. Conwell; number of secular priests, 11; number of churches, 16; number of Catholics, at least 30,000; Seminaries, etc., none; Regular clergymen, 6. Present state of religion, The utmost confusion.

See of Virginia. Bishop, Dr. Kelly; number of secular priests, 2; number of churches, 2; number of Catholics, at least 2,400; Seminaries, etc., none. Present state of religion, Confusion.

See of Kentucky. Bishop, Dr. Flaget; number of secular priests, 15; number of churches, I do not know, but about 20; number of Catholics, at least 20,000; Seminaries, Colleges, Monasteries—greater seminary for philosophy and theology; Lesser Seminary for Classical Studies; Monastery of Dominicans; House of Sisters of Charity, 25 sisters; of the Mother of Dolors, 30; number of regular priests, 8. Present state of religion, Peace and increase of religion.

See of Charleston. Bishop, Dr. England; number of secular priests, 6; number of churches, 3; number of Catholics, at least 3,600; Seminaries, etc., none; Regular clergyman, 1. Present state of religion, Peace and hope of future prosperity.

See of Ohio. Bishop, Edward Fenwick; number of secular priests, etc. I can say nothing of this recently erected diocese.

Total Sees, 8; Bishops, 8; secular priests, 83; regulars, 34,—Total, 117; Churches, 100; number of Catholics, at least 163,500; Seminaries, Colleges, Monasteries, 15; Pupils—Boarders, 279; Day scholars, 144; Religious women, 208.

N. B.—In the United States of America in 1783 there were only 17,000 faithful and 15 priests, and no religious institution of any kind existed.

N. B.—In the probable number of Catholics which I give, I have reckoned only those belonging to congregations or parishes. But besides these there is in every diocese a great multitude of Catholics who, scattered in the villages, are destitute of churches and pastors, and if these are taken into account, it may be said that there are perhaps 60,000 Catholics in the diocese of Philadelphia; 50,000 in New York. The same can be asserted in proportion of the total number of Catholics in other dioceses, Baltimore excepted.

Moreover, the greatest part of the citizens of Louisiana and Florida, which this description does not include, profess the Catholic religion. Now, by adding their number to the Catholics of the province of Baltimore, it can be said without risk of error that there are at least a million of Catholics in the United States of North America.

THE CATHOLIC LAITY'S DIRECTORY TO THE CHURCH SERVICE, with an Almanac for the year 1817. Price 25 cents. Contents. New York: Published and sold by M. Field, 177 Bowery.

In his "Address to the Catholic Public," the editor "is sorry to observe that, as the present edition is the first, he had not sufficient time to collect more information respecting the colleges, churches, and institutions."

The following from pp. 34-5 is really all, with the obituary notes, that relates to the condition of the Church in this country at that time:

Catholic Churches, etc.—New York: St. Peter's Church, St. Patrick's Cathedral, New York Roman Catholic Benevolent Society. This Society was founded by a few individuals, in the month of April, 1816. A concert was given for its benefit in the month of June following. The rapid increase of the members and several donations, have enabled them to purchase a house for the reception of poor and destitute orphans, their principal object being to take care of, clothe, and give both a moral and religious education to such of the above description as are left without parents or guardians to shelter them from vice and immorality, etc. A petition is presented to the Legislature for their incorporation. Meetings are held once a month, at which time a discourse is pronounced by one of the members. Subscription, $3 per annum. The following gentlemen are elected officers for the first year: S. P. Lemoine, President; John Brennan, J. B. Dasege, Charles Delvecchio, Vice-Presidents; John White, Treasurer; Mark Desalrayd, Secretary; John O'Connor, Hugh Sweeny, Assistant Secretaries.

Catholic Benevolent Institutions, etc.—Baltimore: St. Peter's, St. Patrick's, and St. Mary's. One or more at each of the following places, viz.: Philadelphia, Washington, Norfolk, Richmond, Albany, Boston, Kentucky, Charleston (South Carolina), New Orleans, Alexandria, East Port (Maine), Lancaster (Penn.), Emmettsburg, Hagerstown, Conewago, Newtown (St. Mary's County), Fredericktown, Pittsburg, St. Inigoes, St. Thomas (Maryland), Halifax, St. Croix.

Colleges.—St. Mary's, Baltimore; Jesuits', Georgetown, District of Columbia; Jesuits', Emmettsburg, Maryland; Dominicans', Kentucky.

Nunneries.—Baltimore and Georgetown, Columbia.

Lower Canada.—As this country is about nine-tenths Catholic, it contains a considerable number of churches, colleges, nunneries, and benevolent institutions. Only the following came to our knowledge: At Montreal, Church of Notre Dame, a college, and the Ursuline Convent, and a seminary of Sulpitians.

Obituary (p. 28).—" It is a holy and wholesome thought to pray for the dead " (1 Macc. xii. 46).

Most Rev. John Carroll, Archbishop of Baltimore, 3d December, 1815.

Rt. Rev. Mich. Egan, Bishop of Philadelphia, 1814.

Rev. Carolus Franciscus Nagot, Superior of the Seminary of St. Sulpitius, Baltimore, 9th April, 1816.

Rev. Matthew O'Brien, formerly Pastor of the Church of St. Peter, Baltimore, Oct. 20, 1815.

Rev. Mich. Delacey, Pastor of the Church of Norfolk, 26th Feb., 1815.

Rev. Robert Plunkett and John Fenwick, 1815.

Rev. James Griffin and Peter Helbron, 1816.

Rev. Patrick O'Connor, 19th July, 1816.

Rev. Wm. O'Brien, 14th May, 1816.

At the end Mr. Field announced his intention to publish, by subscription, an edition of Butler's " Lives of the Saints," and also a Catholic magazine, a prospectus for which he had issued.

MEETINGS OF THE UNITED STATES CATHOLIC HISTORICAL SOCIETY.

At a meeting of the Executive Council of the United States Catholic Historical Society, held on the 3d day of September, 1888, it was moved and seconded that an address in the name of the Society be presented to the Honorary President, His Grace Archbishop Corrigan, on the occasion of his Silver Jubilee.

Charles Carroll Lee, M.D., James Fairfax McLaughlin, and John G. Shea were appointed a committee to prepare and present the address. It was duly presented to His Grace.

ADDRESS:

"MOST REV. ARCHBISHOP:

"At the last regular meeting of the United States Catholic Historical Society of New York, the near approach of the Silver Jubilee, or twenty-fifth Anniversary of your Grace's Ordination to the Priesthood, formed the most interesting subject of debate, and it was the good pleasure of the Society to appoint the undersigned a Committee to communicate to your Grace the hearty congratulations of every member of our body upon this joyous event. We now discharge that agreeable duty with unfeigned pleasure, and while your associates in the hierarchy and priesthood, together with the laity throughout the Churches, are tendering their respects and homage to their beloved spiritual leader, be ours the task of saluting you as President of this Catholic Historical Society and as the friend and patron of letters, and more especially as one worthy to lead our organization in the mission which it has set for itself to carry out. During the twenty-five years that have now elapsed they feel that you have cultivated letters with a zeal only less than that with which you have pursued your sacred office; that you have fostered learning; and that, by precept and example, you have instilled into those under your charge a love of literature and a reverence for the past.

"They deem it, therefore, peculiarly appropriate that an Association devoted to these ends, to which you have uniformly extended your kindly sympathy, and of which you are the honorary head, should, on such an auspicious occasion, assure you of its devoted loyalty. Your eminent standing in the Church, and personal influence as an American citizen, are both unerring harbingers for the future welfare of our young Society, in whose success you have so often expressed your deep interest.

"We have been instructed by our Society to convey to your Grace the unanimous expression of their love and respect, and to mingle with our congratulations upon this bright epoch in your career, earnest wishes that you may live to celebrate your Golden Jubilee with equal if not greater lustre and joy. The United States Catholic Historical Society, through its Committee, salutes most profoundly its President upon this day.

"We remain,
"Your Grace's Faithful, Obedient Servants,
"FREDERICK R. COUDERT,
"CHARLES CARROLL LEE,
"JOHN GILMARY SHEA,
"J. FAIRFAX MCLAUGHLIN,
} *Committee.*

"NEW YORK, *September* 19, 1888."

At a meeting of the United States Catholic Historical Society, held at the rooms of the Society, No. 20 West 27th Street, New York, on the 18th day of October, 1888. Present, the Vice-President, Charles Carroll Lee, M.D.; Recording Secretary, F. D. Hoyt; Corresponding Secretary, Marc F. Vallette; members of the Council, Trustees, and individual members of the Society.

An Historical Sketch of the Rev. John Thayer, "Boston's first native-born priest," prepared for the Society by the Rev. Arthur T. Connolly, of Roxbury, Mass., was read by Marc F. Vallette, the Corresponding Secretary.

On motion of John G. Shea the thanks of the Society were tendered to the Reverend author of the paper.

At a meeting of the United States Catholic Historical Society, held at No. 20 West 27th Street, December 5, 1888, the

Vice-President, Dr. Charles Carroll Lee, in the chair. A memoir of the Right Reverend Amadeus Rappe, first Bishop of Cleveland, by the Rev. G. F. Houck, was read.

The thanks of the Society were tendered to the Reverend author for his able and interesting paper.

The librarian reported the following contributions to the Library:

Reports of the Commissioner of Indian Affairs, giving a considerable number of those volumes so necessary for the study of the History of our Indian Missions.

13 Reports of the Smithsonian Institution, containing many important articles.

5 Volumes from the Record Commissioners of Boston.

The Life of the Illustrious Catholic Soldier, Col. Julius P. Garesché, current volume of Hoffmann's Catholic Directory; but we still lack some of the earlier numbers of the Catholic Almanac, and will feel grateful to any one who will send any from 1832 to 1870.

From Miss Mary J. Onahan, "The Social Question, its Gravity and Meaning," by the Abbé Winterer.

The Ave Maria for 1887 and 1888.

10 Reports of the Board of Indian Commissioners.

"Ecclesiastical History of Newfoundland." By Mgr. M. F. Howley.

Supplement to the Library Catalogue of the Dominion of Canada.

"Sullivan's Campaign against the Six Nations."

Poore's Index to Government Documents.

Publications from the Buffalo, Iowa, and N. E. Historic-Genealogical Societies.

The annual meeting and election of the United States Catholic Historical Society was held at 8 o'clock, March 12, 1889, in the parlors of the Catholic Club, No. 20 W. 27th Street. The President, Mr. Frederick R. Coudert, being in the chair. The paper of the evening, "Early Catholics in

Connecticut," prepared by Rev. T. J. Shahan, LL.D., of Hartford, was read by Rev. James J. Dougherty.

At the conclusion of the reading a vote of thanks was passed to Dr. Shahan, the writer, and to Father Dougherty, the reader, of the interesting paper.

The election of officers, trustees, and councillors of the Society was then held, and resulted as follows:

Honorary President, Most Rev. M. A. Corrigan, D.D.
President, Hon. Morgan J. O'Brien.
Vice-President, Charles Carroll Lee, M.D.
Cor. Secretary, Marc F. Vallette, LL.D.
Rec. Secretary, Francis Deming Hoyt.
Treasurer, Patrick Farrelly.
Librarian, Rev. James J. Dougherty.

TRUSTEES:

Rev. James H. McGean,
Thomas Addis Emmet, M.D., LL.D.,
Charles W. Sloane,
John Gilmary Shea, LL.D.,
R. Duncan Harris,
J. Fairfax McLaughlin,
John D. Keily.

COUNCILLORS:

Rev. Patrick F. McSweeny, D.D.,
Joseph J. Marrin,
Edward J. McGean,
James S. Coleman,
Joseph Thoron,
Joseph F. Mosher.

The following gentlemen were elected members of the Society:

Rev. William Daly, New York; John J. Morrissey, M.D., Greenpoint, L. I.

On motion of Dr. Lee, the thanks of the Society were tendered to the President retiring from office, for his services in behalf of the Society. Mr. Coudert acknowledged the compliment, and expressed his good wishes for the continued and increased prosperity of the Society, in his usual happy vein.

The Treasurer's report was presented and read, showing cash on hand to be $3,069.18—of which there is in the Building Fund $2,849.05 ; and subject to appropriation, $220.13.

A public meeting of the United States Catholic Historical Society was held June 3, 1889, in the Hall of the De La Salle Institute, W. 59th Street. The exercises were opened by an address from the President, Hon. Morgan J. O'Brien.

The paper of the evening, prepared by Dr. John Gilmary Shea, on "Why Canada is not a part of the United States," was read by Mr. Charles W. Sloane. It was well received and thoroughly enjoyed by an audience of about two hundred ladies and gentlemen. Rev. James H. McGean read the following resolutions, and moved their adoption :

WHEREAS, God in His Divine Providence has taken to Himself our late fellow member and esteemed friend, Franklin H. Churchill; and,

WHEREAS, From the beginning of the U. S. C. H. Society he was an earnest member, and a faithful and efficient officer, who by his counsel and experience was a helpful worker in the cause of Catholic History; and,

WHEREAS, His connection with this Society as well as with the many societies in union and sympathy with the Church and its objects, has made his name worthy to appear with honor on the page of Catholic history relating to our times; therefore, be it

Resolved, That in his death, the U. S. C. H. Society has lost a most useful and honored associate.

Resolved, That we hereby render testimony to our appreciation of his marked ability in the legal sphere of life in which he moved, and in the many and varied positions of trust and confidence which were ceded him by the Catholic societies of which he was a member.

Resolved, That we recall with pleasure the Christian spirit which actuated him in the performance of his life duties.

Resolved, That we, in the communion of the Church, mourn his life to us—and rejoice with him that he has been called from his labors to his reward.

Resolved, That in that same communion we extend our sympathies to his immediate relatives in grief, and assure them that our prayers will be united with theirs, that eternal rest be given and that perpetual peace may shine on the soul of Franklin H. Churchill.

Mr. Francis D. Hoyt presented the following resolutions upon the death of Commendatore Hickey, late editor of the "Catholic Review," and moved their adoption:

WHEREAS, It has pleased Almighty God to remove from our midst our friend and fellow-member, Patrick Valentine Hickey, one of the founders of the United States Catholic Historical Society, and one of the most earnest workers in the cause of American Catholic History; and,

WHEREAS, Mr. Hickey, by his unselfish devotion, his intelligent labor, and his Christian courage in the defence of Catholic truth, in the refutation of error, and in the promotion of the best and noblest works of Christian charity, won for himself a distinguished place in the foremost ranks of the Catholic laymen of his adopted country and of his time; be it

Resolved, That in the death of Commendatore P. V. Hickey, this Society has lost one of its worthiest and most esteemed members, the cause of Christian education an efficient and fearless defender, and the Catholic Church of this country a devoted and loyal son, whose zeal and good work were gratefully recognized and signally approved by the Supreme Pontiff.

Resolved, That we extend to the family of Mr. Hickey our earnest sympathy in their bereavement, assuring them that we shall cherish with pleasant memory the virtues of one who so truly merited the esteem and love of all who knew him, and that our prayers shall be united with theirs for the eternal rest of his soul.

Both series of resolutions were passed as read.

On motion of Father Dougherty, a vote of thanks was passed to Dr. Shea for the scholarly historical paper which the Society had just listened to; and to Mr. Sloane, for reading the same.

The thanks of the Society were also tendered to the Christian Brothers for their courtesy in granting the use of the Hall for the occasion, and to the gentlemen of the Institute Orchestra for the music which they had kindly furnished, and which added much to the enjoyment of the evening.

NOTES.

BANCROFT'S FALSE CHARGES AGAINST THE CATHOLICS OF 1776.—
The following appears in the Portland "Daily Press" of May 8, 1889:

"As an historical scholar I am astonished to see a respectable journal speak of 'the very dubious record of the Catholic Church in the days of the Revolution,' and cite a passage of Bancroft's 'History of the Constitution,' as though it were decisive. Mr. Bancroft's statement, so far from being supported by historical evidence, is a tissue of misstatements and incorrect inferences.

"The Quebec Act, October of 1774, aroused an anti-Catholic feeling in the thirteen Colonies. There is evidence of this feeling in the expulsion of the Catholic Scots from the Mohawk Valley and of Catholics individually in the Middle Colonies, but no evidence has been adduced that Catholics then, or later, voluntarily joined the English side against their fellow-colonists.

"Now, to take up Mr. Bancroft's statements. He says the Catholics 'were chiefly new-comers in the Middle States.' Is this true? Where is the proof? It is not true, and is not even probable. The wars between England and France from 1744 to 1763, interrupted the tide of immigration. An examination of the Colonial newspapers, published in various parts of the country, will show that the great immigration was prior to 1740.* The Catholics were a small percentage of this body. There was no general immigration of Catholics as such. Those who came settled mainly in Pennsylvania, and at the period of the Revolution the original immigrants had been mainly a generation in the country, and their children were born and reared as Americans. Maryland gained nothing by Catholic immigration after 1688, as penal laws prohibited the introduction of 'Irish servants.' The Catholic population there was almost

---

* Vessel arrived at Portsmouth, N. H., with 120 Irish passengers. Vessel at Charleston, S. C., with 250 Switzers.—" New York Gazette," Aug. 18, 1735.

Captain Bromadge, from Bristol, at Philadelphia, Sept. 2d, with passengers and 40 servants. Sunday—"Snow," from Ireland, with passengers. Monday—large ship from Holland with 388 passengers.—" New York Gazette," Aug. 30; Sept. 6, 1736. New York, Sept. 13th, 345 passengers from Ireland. "One thousand souls in twenty-four hours."—Same, Sept. 18-20.

exclusively American born. The Catholics in Indiana and Illinois were born on the soil. The Catholics were not chiefly new-comers; many could trace an American lineage almost as old as any man in Massachusetts Bay. Here is one misstatement of Mr. Bancroft.

"His next assertion is that the mass of the members of the Catholic Church, chiefly new-comers, followed the influence of the Jesuits. From the settlement of Maryland the Catholics in Maryland, Virginia, Delaware, and Pennsylvania had no priests except Jesuits, aided for about fifty years by Franciscans. They had grown up under their direction, and showed the good effects in their piety and zeal. The new-comers, as any one familiar with the history of the Catholic Church knows, did not take to the Jesuits at all. Many were from Ireland, where the Jesuits never have exercised any great influence over the people at large. Those from Germany came imbued with the literature created to crush the Jesuits. To talk of the new-comers as being influenced by the Jesuits is absurd. The writings of La Poterie in Boston, Smyth,* the German opponent of Graessel in Philadelphia, all show that the new-comers were strongly prejudiced against the Jesuits.

"Mr. Bancroft's next assertion is that the Jesuits cherished hatred of France for her share in the overthrow of their order. The Jesuits in this country belonged to the English province. That body had not suffered specially at the hands of the French Government. In all the documents published by Henry Foley, in his voluminous records and in all the unpublished writings, it is impossible to find any denunciation of France or anything to show any such hostility as Mr. Bancroft alleges. In fact his own volume shows that his only authority for this and his other charges against his Catholic countrymen was a despatch of Barbé Marbois, who was scheming to have the Catholics in the United States placed under a French bishop, to be nominated by the King of France and the Continental Congress, and who was to reside in France. And Mr. Bancroft makes that despatch an authority.

"The next statement is: 'In Philadelphia Howe had been able to form a regiment of Roman Catholics.' This is historically false. Howe had been unable to do so. He made the effort to raise a regiment of Roman Catholic volunteers, and found some gentlemen

---

* See La Poterie, "Resurrection of Laurent Ricci; or, A True and Exact History of the Jesuits." Philadelphia, 1789.

Rev. Patrick Smyth, "The Present State of the Catholic Mission conducted by the Ex-Jesuits in North America." Dublin, 1788.

willing to take the temporary American commission which alone could be granted to Catholics. Alfred Clifton, John Peter Eck, and some others, have been identified as members of St. Mary's church. Bancroft says Howe raised the regiment. Howe himself says that when he left America in May, 1778, Clifton, the lieutenant-colonel, had raised only 180, rank and file. By July the recruiting was transferred to New York, as appears by the 'New York Gazette,' published in that city; but Captain McKennon and Major Lynch showed their guineas in vain. 'The British and American Register for 1779,' published in New York at the close of 1778, heads the list of officers of that organization thus: 'Late Roman Catholick Volunteers.' The regiment, so far from having been raised by Howe, was given up as a failure by Clinton.*

"Where, then, is the proof that during the Revolution 'the Catholic Church showed an unhappy tendency'? Of all the Catholic priests then in this country, not one has ever been accused of sympathy with England against their fellow-citizens. Not one has ever been accused of being a Tory, or is claimed by loyalist writers of the time as being on their side. Even those English by birth took the oath to the new constitutions. The effort to place the Catholic Church in this country under foreign and royal influence emanated from Barbé Marbois, and was opposed steadily and successfully by the Catholic clergy of the United States, whose memorials show the most intense American feeling.

"JOHN GILMARY SHEA."

NEW MEXICAN ANTIQUITIES.—"Tourists visiting New Mexico find some interest in the fact that they are freely shown places, as well as edifices, to which considerable age (not to say antiquity) is attributed, by writers as well as by the people of the country in general. It may not be out of place to establish the correct dates of such points and structures, since, in regard to accuracy in this respect, considerable looseness has been and is displayed, in type as well as in words. Thus, Santa Fé is variously stated as having been founded in 1550 and 1583. The Chapel of San Miguel is often reckoned as being over three hundred years old; it is even stated by one writer

---

* "And Mr. Clifton, the chief of the Roman Catholic persuasion, of whom there were said to be many in Philadelphia, as well as in the rebel army, serving against their inclination; these gentlemen were appointed commandants of corps, to receive and form for service all the well-affected that could be obtained. And what was the success of these efforts? In May, 1778, when I left America, Col. Allan had raised only 152 rank and file; Col. Chalmers, 836; and Col. Clifton, 180."—Howe's "Narrative," p. 49.

on the past of New Mexico as being a relic from Coronado's expedition, and as dating, therefore, as far back as 1543, although Coronado (notwithstanding the misstatement made by Castañeda) evacuated the country in the spring of 1542. As to the ruined churches of Pecos, San Diego de Jemez, and others, dates are sometimes assigned to them coeval with, if not preceding, Columbus's discovery of America. As far as I know, Mr. John Gilmary Shea was the first to approach accuracy on the subject of dates of New Mexican Spanish structures.

" The first Spanish settlement in New Mexico has completely disappeared from the surface. I doubt very much if excavations even would yield any traces of the few buildings that constituted the hamlet of San Gabriel de los Españoles, or Yunque, on the site where now stands the station of Chanita (Denver and Rio Grande Railroad), opposite the Indian pueblo of San Juan, and about thirty miles north of Santa Fé. That first permanent establishment made by Spaniards on New Mexican soil was founded in 1598, in the months of August and September, and was completely abandoned in 1605. Thence the Spaniards moved over to the site where Santa Fé now stands, selecting that spot for its central position with respect to the most powerful tribes of sedentary Indians, and also for the reason that there was no (inhabited) pueblo in its neighborhood. The former Tano-village of Oga-P'oge was already in ruins in the sixteenth century. The foundation of Santa Fé, therefore, dates back to the year 1605. It remained the only Spanish town north of Parral (in Chihuahua) until after the uprising of 1680. Only after the reconquest, and in 1695, was the second 'villa' founded, Santa Cruz de la Cañada, twenty-five miles north of Santa Fé. Albuquerque dates from 1706. Other settlements are of much later date.

" In regard to single edifices, the oldest ones have completely disappeared. Not a vestige is found of the old churches of San Felipe, Santo Domingo, and of the parochial church of Santa Fé, finished about 1627. The first two churches named (both after Indian villages) existed certainly in 1605 and 1607. As to the chapel of San Miguel at Santa Fé, it is posterior to 1636. It was the chapel of the Indian families brought up from Zacatecas, who settled on the south side of the Santa Fé River. Burned down in 1680, it was fully restored only in 1710. The so-called palace stands very nearly on the site of the old one, but its restoration is posterior to 1697.

" In 1617 there were eleven churches extant in New Mexico, and some of these may be identified as still extant in ruins. They are:

The old church of Pecos, dedicated to 'Nuestra Señora de los Angeles'; the church of San Diego de Jemez, near the Jemez hot springs; the church of San Joseph de Jemez, reduced though to a mere heap of rubbish, five miles north of the pueblo of Jemez. Of the remaining eight, barely the sites are approximately known. The first parochial church of Santa Fé has completely disappeared; so have the churches of San Felipe, Santo Domingo, San Juan, Sandia, Taos, Picuries, and Santa Clara. The churches now in use at the pueblos are all modern, the one of Zia, perhaps, excepted. That of Santa Clara dates from 1760, the church at Zuñi from 1780.

"The ruins of churches and chapels in the villages around Zuñi are those of structures reared after 1629. Of still more recent origin are the stately and picturesque edifices, equally deserted, that stand in the ruined pueblos about the salt lagunes of the Manzano, south of Santa Fé. It may be affirmed that the churches of Cuaray, Abó, and of Tabirá (erroneously called Gran-Quivira), are the most striking monuments in New Mexico. Built of stone, with walls still erect to a height of from ten to twenty feet, and mostly in a location wild and picturesque, not only have they attracted the attention of the traveller, but considerable mystic lore has been attached to them and to their environment. Still, their past is well known. Ere I became connected with the Hemenway Southwestern Archæological Expedition, and while yet travelling under the direction of the Archæological Institute of America, I explored Cuaray, Abó, and Tabirá. Subsequent documentary researches, mostly for the new enterprise above mentioned, have developed the simple story of these forgotten missions. Cuaray (dedicated to the Immaculate Conception) was founded after 1630, Abó and Tabirá between 1630 and 1644. The large church at Tabirá, concerning which so many fabulous stories of hidden treasure, etc., have been circulated, is posterior to the latter date, and it was never finished. All these missions were abandoned about 1670 on account of the Apaches, and have never been reoccupied since. There are also rubbish piles denoting the site of the old church at Tajique, in the same region. The edifice dates from the same period.

"It may be asserted that there is in New Mexico no architectural vestige of Spanish origin that antedates 1605. Lapidary inscriptions, however, exist of older dates. Mr. F. H. Cushing found, while at the so-called 'Inscription Rock' last October, the name of Francisco Sanchez Chamuscado and of three of his companions, together with the year of their excursion into New Mexico—1581; and I also found at the same spot the inscription of Juan de Oñate

—1605, April 16. Some of the numerous hieroglyphs at the rock named have been read as giving much older dates, but I can positively assure that there is none anterior to the time of Chamuscado. Neither is it likely that any older one will ever be found at the 'Morro,' since Coronado and his men took a route which led them far to the south of the place, and at least thirty miles below it.

"AD. F. BANDELIER.

"Santa Fé, N. M., March 5th."—"Evening Post," March 28, 1889.

QUERIES.

HISTORY OF CHURCH ORGANS.—Can any of our readers give any facts in regard to the date of introduction, sizes, builders, etc., of the earliest organs used in the Roman Catholic Church in this country, whether in Mexico, Florida, Maryland, Michigan, or New York?

LEBANON, PA. T. E. S.

CHRONOLOGY OF CATHOLIC CHURCHES.—Is there any chronological list of the erection of Catholic churches in New York State?

M. E. W.

CATHOLIC NEWSPAPERS AND PERIODICALS.—Can any reader furnish a list of Catholic newspapers and periodicals printed in the United States before 1830? H. J. K.

SAN MIGUEL DE GUANDAPE.—When was this attempted Spanish settlement made? J. O'C.

[On the James River, Va., where Jamestown was subsequently begun by the English. The Spanish settlement was begun by Lucas Vasquez de Ayllon in 1526, accompanied by the Dominican Fathers Antonio de Montesino and Antonio de Cervantes.]

"TRUE TRANSLATION OF THE POPE'S ABSOLUTION" was printed and published by J. Parker, New York, in 1751. What was the work?

NOTICES OF RECENT PUBLICATIONS.

THE AUSTRALIAN BALLOT SYSTEM, as embodied in the legislation of various countries. With an historical introduction. By JOHN H. WIGMORE. Boston : C. C. Soule, 1889.

This is a very clear and lucid account of the system of voting planned by Francis S. Dutton and introduced in South Australia in 1857-8. Time has shown that its operation is simple, inexpensive, and conducive to honest elections. This has led to its adoption in some of the United States. The work of Mr. Wigmore is clear, definite, and timely.

HISTORY OF THE CATHOLIC CHURCH. For use in Seminaries and Colleges. By Dr. HEINRICH BRUECK, Professor of Theology in the Ecclesiastical Seminary of Mentz. With additions from the writings of Cardinal Hergenrother. Translated by Rev. E. PRUENTE. With an introduction by Rt. Rev. Mgr. JAMES A. CORCORAN, S.T.D. 2 vols. 8vo. Benziger Bros., New York, 1889.

It is very creditable to Catholics in this country that they have afforded those who read English, Church histories like those of Darras, Alzog, and Pruente. The first of these is especially popular and for general readers ; the second and third are intended rather for Seminaries. Alzog is, however, loaded up with references to German works, many of an ephemeral character, which are inaccessible here. Dr. Brueck's work, less extended, has in the translation references to works easily obtained, for further study of the subject treated. For the general reader, and for the student, this work is the best yet presented by the Catholic press. It is not too extended, the different subjects are carefully studied and clearly handled, making it a handy book of reference, and a work to be perused with pleasure and profit. That it is sound from a Catholic standpoint is evident from the endorsements given, and the part taken by the late Mgr. Corcoran shows that it is eminently fitted for Seminary use ; but it can be also commended to every college student and every gentleman who wishes on his library-shelves a safe guide in the annals of the Church.

LEAVES FROM THE ANNALS OF THE SISTERS OF MERCY. Volume III., containing sketches of the Order in Newfoundland and the United States. Catholic Publication Society Co., New York, 1889.

This third volume of an interesting series gives in most readable and authentic shape the labors of the daughters of Catharine

McAuley in the United States from 1843, when Bishop O'Connor obtained the first colony of the Sisters of Mercy, for the diocese which the will of Pius IX. had compelled him to accept. No modern sisterhood has grown so rapidly, or effected as much, and the volumes of this annalist of the Order afford not only matter for the student of history, but a volume of most edifying and interesting reading for all.

BIRTHDAY OF THE STATE OF CONNECTICUT. Celebration of the four hundred and fiftieth anniversary of the adoption of the first Constitution of the State of Connecticut by the Connecticut Historical Society, and the towns of Windsor, Hartford, and Wethersfield, Thursday, January 24, 1889. Hartford, 1889.

A HISTORY OF THE EQUESTRIAN STATUE OF ISRAEL PUTNAM, AT BROOKLYN, CONN. Hartford, 1888.

These volumes give in their titles all that is needed to explain their bearing. New England has been the great field for the collection of local and family annals, and there is scarcely an active historical society in the country in which you cannot ascribe the activity to New England blood in some of the members. These volumes give not only an account of the proceedings, but therein show how widely the descendants have departed from the faith and ideas of the ancestors whom they honor.

CHURCH HISTORY, by Professor KURTZ. Translated from the Latest Edition with approval of the author, by Rev. JOHN MACPHERSON, A.M. Vol. I. Funk & Wagnalls, New York.

This is a well-printed text-book for Protestant institutions, based on a German work so successful as to have run through nine editions in the original. It is well arranged and clearly written, and is likely to attain popularity here. In some respects it is a great advance on the older Protestant Church histories. A Catholic writer takes up century after century from the time of the Mission of the Apostles ; in the New Testament, the writings of the Fathers, early church historians, and acts of councils, he sees the progress of his Church, he sees heresies rise and fall condemned by the authority of the Church, and among the whole, Protestantism is but a matter of three centuries, like many other revolts from the Church. To the Protestant writers, a church history has been generally a plea for the separation from the Church in the 16th century. The old scheme used to be to attempt to show that the hierarchical government of the Church, the Pope as primate and ultimate judge of the faith, the real presence, communion with the blessed in heaven by prayer, a belief in an intermediate state, sacramental forgiveness of sins, etc., were not to be found in the primitive church, but were novelties gradually introduced, and that Protestantism was merely a return to the primitive type. The works of infidel and rationalistic investigators in our day have, however, forced an admission that this theory is untenable. The earliest records and monuments of Christianity betray evidences of doctrines, worship, practices still held by Catholics. Hence recent writers like Kurtz admit all this, but ascribe it to heathen influence on the disciples of the apostles, if not on the mistaken ideas of the apostles themselves. But this is to undermine all Christianity, for if Christ's commission to teach all nations, with a promise of personal guidance through all time, the matter taught to be believed and observed being all that he had confided to them, failed in the very days of the apostles, there can be no Christianity.

MEMORANDA.

Hon. T. A. E. Weadock delivered in February, 1889, an eloquent and well-conceived Lecture on Father Marquette, the explorer of the Mississippi Valley.

The Jesuit Fathers of the New York and Maryland province are preparing a history of Georgetown College. It will be a handsome quarto volume, richly illustrated.

"The History of the Carmelite Nuns in the United States," by the Rev. Charles W. Currier, C.SS.R., will be published by the Messrs. Murphy & Co., of Baltimore, Md.

Mr. James Bernard Cullen, of Boston, has in press, and will shortly publish, a "History of the Irish in Boston," in which the history of the Catholic Church in that city will be given at length.]

INDEX.

"Acadians before their Dispersion" The. By the Abbe' H. R. Casgrain............8, 100
Acadians.... 279
Adventures of a Jesuit Lay brother who set sail for Maryland in 1657............. 212
Aix-la-Chapelle, Treaty of...... 18
Albany, N. Y., Early Priests at..103
Anderson, Marshall............229
Antigua... 209
Armstrong, Governor........... 10
Assumption, (Sandwich) 183
Astor, John Jacob............. 59
Auriesville, N. Y. 183
Australian Ballot System......334

Baltimore, First Diocesan Synod of, 218; Second Provincial Council of, 77; Province of...318
Bandelier, A. F..............330
Barbaba................ 209
Bancroft's False Charges against the Catholics of 1776 328
Barbelin, F. Felix J.......... 78
Beginnings of the Capuchin Mission in Louisiana, The........295
Belanger, Andre 62
Bellamy, Rev. J..... ......150, 152
Bertrand, Rev. Mr.. ......144, 146
Benac, Portier............115, 118
Biography of Lieut. Col. Julius Garesche, U. S. A.... 223
Birthday of the State of Connecticut 335
Blanchet, Most Rev. F. N....... 75
Bonneville, Captain 63

Boston, 278; Pope Day in.....2, 214
Bradford, Br. Thomas.........212
Bressani, F. Joseph..........188
Briand, Rt. Rev. Dr... 98
Brute, Rt. Rev. S. G. 103, 224
Bruyas, F. James.............188
Bulger, Rev. Richard...........105
Burke, Rev. Edmund......117, 119
Burke or Bushe, Rev. James ...103
Burtsell, Rev. R. L........... 99

Cahokia... 89
Cake, Adam................... 81
Canada, Flemish History of.....294
Cane, James 87
Capuchins.... 295
Carroll, Most Rev. John..120, 90, 137 138, 217, 275, 278, 291, 321
Casgrain, Abbe' H. R.........8, 100
Catechism printed at Lancaster, Pa......................... 54
Catholic and Anti-Catholic Items from New York Papers....... 93
Catholic and Anti-Catholic Items from New York and Pennsylvania Papers, 1775—1782.,. 199
Catholic Laity's Directory, 1817..320
Catholic Newspapers and Periodicals 333
Cerfoumont, Rev. Mr..........103
Cerre, P. L.................... 42
Challoner, Rt. Rev. Richard..... 87
Chaudiere tribe....... 58
Charleston, Pope Day in........ 6
Cheverus, Rt. Rev. John 272
Chippewas.................. 124
Chouteau, Peter.............. 38

Chronology of Catholic Churches
  in N. Y. State............333
Church History by Prof. Kurtz.. 335
Church and State in the United
  States, by Philip Schaff, D. D..110
Churchill, F. H 327
"Church in Northern Ohio, and
  in the Diocese of Cleveland,"
  The. By Rev. G. F. Houck...109
Church Organs..............333
Ciquard, Rev. Francis..........270
Cleveland, See of 232, 236
Coeur d' Alene............ 58
Congress' Own ...,........177
Clarke, Richard H 245
Coleman, James S.........100
Collet, Oscar W........85, 101
Columbus and the Men of Palos.
  By John G. Shea 164
Condamine, Rev. Matthew....70, 78
Conewago, Mission of St. John
  Francis Regis............ 83
Connecticut, Early Catholics in..274
Connolly, Rt Rev. John.......105
Connolly, Rev. Arthur T...261, 323
Cornwallis, Edward........... 25
Corrigan, Most Rev. M. A..100, 322
Coudert, Frederick R.. 99, 322, 324

"Davenport, Christopher. The
  Brother of New Haven's Foun-
  der, a Franciscan Friar. By
  Rev. T. J Shahan......153
De Carheil, F. Stephen......... 13
De Goesbriand, Rt. Rev. Louis 231,
                          244. 245
Dela, Jonquiere, Gov.......... 18
Dela Poterie, Rev. C. F. B....265
De la Tour d' Auvergne Lau-
  ragais, Cardinal 227
De les Derniers. Moise......12, 24
De l' Isle Dieu, Abbé.......... 27
Demers, Rt. Rev Modeste....66, 75
De Miniac, Abbé........... 16

Denaut, Rt. Rev. Peter........183
Denonville, Marquis de.......183
De Smet, Rev. P. J.......56, 66. 78
D' Estaing, Admiral, Tory, ver-
  ses on...................203
Devereux, John C............105
Dieskau, General............. 5
Dilhet, Rev. John 122, 139
Doe Run 52
Donnelly, Rev. Arthur...... 99
Dougherty, Rev. James J...100, 324
Druon, Rev. Z.........240, 248, 249
DuBois, Rt. Rev. John.........103
Dufaux, Rev. Mr...........114, 116
Dunkers 49
Duplessis Mornay, Rt. Rev.....295
Ducouvray, Rev. J. B.........179
Du Vivier............. 14
Dwenger, Rt. Rev. J. F........245

Early Catholics in Connecticut.
  By Rev. Thomas J. Shahan....274
Early Notice of Catholics in Bos-
  ton......................220
Eckerline, Gabriel............ 50
Egan, Rt. Rev. Michael.....81, 321
Ehrenfried, Joseph............ 51
Emmet Thomas A............ 99
Ensyla, Chief................ 83
Ephrata Community........... 49

Farmer, F. Ferdinand. Memoir
  of by F. R. Molyneux......103
Farrelly, Patrick 100
Fenwick, Rt. Rev. E. D...... 148
First Catholic Bible in the United
  States...................260
Fisk, Rev Wilbur 71
Fitzsimmons, Thomas......... 81
Fitzsimmons, Rev. Mr........ 53
Flaget, Rt. Rev. B. J......143, 147
Flathead Mission.......55, 85
Florida..................... 208
Fort Frontenac......... 184. 185

Foxes............................124
Frambach, Rev. Mr............103
Franchere, Gabriel...........59, 62
Frechette, Rev. Peter......115, 119
Frederick, Md., Priests at.....103
French Canadians.............. 61
Further Notes on Pope Day. By
   Rev. T. J. Shahan, LL. D......214

Gallitzin, V. Rev. Demetrius A..104
Gandawague 183
Ganiltz, Rev. Anthony.....143, 149
Garakonthie 183
Garnier, F. Julian..............183
Gass, Sergeant Patrick..... 56
General Description of the Metropolitan Province of Baltimore, 1821-2. By Archbishop Marechal.....................318
Georgetown, D. C..............317
Gilmour, Rt. Rev. R...........250
Girard, Abbé................. 19
Gosselin, Major Clement........176
Gouentagrandi... 190
Goupil, Br. Rene..............168
Granadine..... 210
Grey Nuns....................241
Guy Fawkes' Day............. 1

Haestricht..... 86
Haffreingue, Abbé............227
Harding, F. Robert............ 31
Harris, R. Duncan 100
Healy, Rev. Gabriel A.......... 99
Hemes language, Catechism in..105
Hennepin, F. Louis............114
Herbermann, Charles G.......100
Hickey, P. V................ ..327
Hill, Judge William B 224
Historical Sketch of Rev. John Thayer, Boston's first native-born priest. By Rev. Arthur T Connolly..............261, 323
History of the Catholic Church.
   By Dr. H. Brueck...........334
"History of the Catholic Church in Monroe City and County, Mich." By Rt. Rev. Camillus P. Maes, D.D., Bishop of Covington................. ...113
"History of the Rise and Progress of Catholicism on Wallingford. By John G. Phelan.108
Holland, Rev. John Joseph..... 53
Holmes, Emmanuel. 201
Holy Man of Tours.... 106
Houck, Rev. George F.109, 225, 324
Houdin, Rev Mr. Apostate..... 95
Howard, Rev. Maurice 236
How Father Harding's Deed of St. Mary's Church Property came to be recorded by Bishop Egan 31
Howley, V. Rev. M. F.........106
Hoyt, F. D... .... 99, 323
Hubley, Bernard. 52
Hudson Bay Company......... 59
Hurley, Rev. Mr...............103
Hurons..... 124
Hyvon, Joseph................116

Indians on the English Coast in 1508.......................294
Iowa Historical Record... 108, 222
Iracque, Joseph..... 117

Jamaica.....................209
James, Sir John, of Crishall, Essex, Bart................... 86
Janvier, Rev. Mr..........144, 147
Jesuits 94
Jogues, F. Isaac........ 183

Kaskaskia Church. The old Bell of.......... 221
Keily, John D..................100
Kelly, Rev. Patrick............105
Kempker, Rev. John F......... 48

Index

Kootenais or Flat Bows 66

Labre, St. Benedict............264
Laclede... 36
Ladies of the Sacred Heart of
  Mary........................239
Lajoie, Louis........ 116
La Mousse, Ignace.. ....72, 74
Lancaster, Pa 49, 88
Langres, F. Bruno de ... .295
Lansingburgh, N. Y...........105
La Prairie..... 195
La Verendrye, Chevalier........ 55
Lee, Rev. Jason..............64, 71
Le Gardeur de St Pierre, Jacques.180
Lee, Charles C..... 99, 322, 323, 324
Le Loutre, Abbe......14, 16, 21, 28
Lesslie, Rev. George...........270
Letter of Rt. Rev. John Carroll,
  D.D., to Hon. Samuel Dexter,
  Secretary of War......... .. 217
Levadoux, Rev. Michael 120
Lewis and Clark Expedition.. . 56
Life, Journals and Correspon-
  dence of Rev. Manasseh Cutler
  L.L., D 222
London, Vicar Apostolic of 211
Lotbiniere, Rev. F. L. C.......178
Louisiana 208, 295
Luxembourg, F. Raphael... ...297

McCarty, Rev. Mr............. 222
McGean, Rev. James H.....99, 326
McLaughlin, J. Fairfax.   100, 322
McLaughlin, Rev. Peter.......237
McQuaid, Rev. Paul 103
Maes, Rt. Rev. Camillus P......113
Maillard, Abbé...............17, 28
Mallet, Edmond.......55, 176, 180
Malone, Rev. Mr. 52
Manchot, Chief..... 185
Manual of Catholic Prayers..... 98
Marchand, Rev. Mr..... 188
Marchena, F. Antonio de...164, 175

Marechal, Most Rev A........ 318
Marrin, Joseph J..............100
Maryland Catholics during the
  Revolution..................228
Maryland........ 208
Mascarene, Governor........... 10
Mathieu, F. John 295
Matignon, Rev. Dr. F..........270
Memoir of the Life and Labors
  of the Rt Rev. Amadeus Rappe
  first Bishop of Cleveland. By
  Rev. G. F. Houck....... ...225
Mengarini, F. Gregory.......... 79
Mickmaks................... . 98
Milet, F. Peter, Captivity among
  the Oneida Indians, 1689-1694.183
Molyneux, F. Robert....... 53, 103
Mommini, Mr 116
Monroe, Mich., History of the
  Catholic Church in..........113
Montour, Madam and her family.220
Mooney, John A........ 100

Nadeau, Martin..... 119
Nagot, Rev. C. F............. .321
Neale, F. Francis 32
Neale, F. Henry............... 88
Neale, Rt. Rev. Leonard........317
Newburyport, Pope Day in..... 5
New England and New York...207
New England 2, 204
"Newfoundland, Ecclesiastical
  History of." By V. Rev. M. F.
  Howley..... ....,....106
Newfoundland   ... .207
New Mexican Antiquities.......330
New Orleans..................297
Nez Perces 58
Nicollet 38, 48
Northwest Company 59
Notes on Parkman's "Conspiracy
  of Pontiac." By Oscar W. Collet 35
Notre Dame de Guiaudet..... 106
Nova Scotia or Acadia.........217

Index. 341

O'Brien, Morgan J............326
O'Connor, Rt. Rev. Michael.....104
O'Fallon's Colonies..........106
Onnonaragon................ 187
O'Reilly, Rev. F. Luke........ 95
Origin of the Mission to the Flat Head Indians. By Edmond Mallet....................... 55
Otasseté................... 193
Otonniata...............187, 189
Ottawas.................... 124

Pacific Fur Company........... 60
Pain, Rev. Felix............... 10
Palos 164
Pambrun, P. C................ 68
Parker, Rev. Samuel........64, 72
Payet, Rev. Mr...............188
Pellentz, Rev, F............... 53
Pend d' Oreilles 58
Pennsylvania.................208
Perez, F. Juan 164, 175
Petition of Catholics to Upper House of Assembly, Md.1756..314
Phelan, John G...............108
Phillips, Gov. Richard.......... 9
Plessis, Rt. Rev. J. O 119
Pinzon. Martin A.............166
Point, F. Nicholas............ 79
Pontiac's Death............... 85
Poor Clares, Georgetown, D. C..317
"Pope Day in America"..1, 214, 284
Port Royal.................11, 14
Pottawotamies...............124
Pré Ronde.................... 10
Priests in Virginia in 1678.....222
Princeton, N. J., Priest at......104
Purcell, Most Rev. John....228, 232

Quebec, Bishop of.....206, 210, 211
Quebec Bill................... 96

Raisin River, Mich............113

Rappe, Rt. Rev. Amadeus..225, 260, 324
Rawson, Keating..............105
Reaume, Charles..........116, 118
Richard, Rev. Gabriel..... 120, 139, 144, 150, 151, 270
Rosati, Rt. Rev. Joseph.....67, 76
Rousselet, Rev. Louis.........265
Roux, Rev. Benedict.......... 69
Roy, Olivier.................. 62
Ryan, Mother Mary...........272
Ryan, Rev. Mr................103

San Miguel de Guandape, Va....338
Saulnier, Rev. E.............. 69
Schaff Rev. P................110
Schmidt, Rev. Anthony........104
Sener, S. M.................. 49
Shahan, Rev. Thomas J....112, 158, 214, 274
Shanahan, Rev. John, Reminiscences of....................105
Shea, John Gilmary ..1, 86, 99, 164, 322, 328
Shirley, Governor 15
Silver Chalice found in Pennsylvania....................220
Silver Cross found near Montpelier, Iowa................. 48
Sloane, C. W.................326
Sloane, W. A................. 99
Smyth, Rev. Patrick.......... 89
Some Lancaster Catholics and other Historical Notes. By S. M. Sener................... 49
Spalding, Rev. H. H......65, 73, 74
Spokanes..................... 58
St. Albans, Vt...........244, 247
St. Ange..................39, 48
Sisters of Charity of St. Augustine....................239
Sisters of Notre Dame of Namur.232
Sisters of the Good Shepherd. 241
St. Genevieve, Mo............ 101

St. Kitts.................... 209
St Louis, Mo............ 35, 67
St. Mary's Church, Philadelphia. 81, 88
St. Mary's Mission............ 84
St. Mary's River............. 56
Summary on the Catholic Religion in the English Colonies in America.....................206

Thayer, Rev. John. 261, 273, 291, 323
Thoron, Joseph................ 99
Timon, Rt. Rev. John 237
Tjolizhitzay................. 80
Toledo, O 229

United States Catholic Historical Society, Meetings...... 99, 322
Ursulines, Cleveland, 239. Boston. 272
Utica, N. Y..................105
Utrecht, Treaty of.......... 9, 28

Vallette, Marc F.........100, 323
Valley, Rev. Francis. 221

Van Quickenborne, F. Charles, 77, 78
Vetch, Governor 11
Vincennes Church, 1816.......273
Virginia.....................208
Vissani, Rev. Charles A. .. 99, 206

Wadding, F. Luke............158
Walker, William.............. 70
Wallingford, Conn, Catholicity in.........................108
Walsh, Henry C...............301
Walsh, Robert. By Henry C. Walsh.......................301
Washington, George, suppresses Pope Day in Camp........... 7
Washington, D. C., Notes on old Church......................313
Whelan, Rt. Rev. Richard V....233
When was St. Genevieve founded?.........................101
Whitman, Dr. Marcus..... . 72, 4
Wood, Most Rev. J. F......... 92

Zarate Salmeron, F. Geronimo..105

Google

Google

THE HISTORY

OF

ANCIENT VINLAND

BY

THORMOD TORFASON.

Translated from the Latin of 1705 by

Prof. Charles G. Herbermann, Ph. D., LL. D.,

With an Introduction by John Gilmary Shea.

New York:
Press of the Society,
1888.

Google

INTRODUCTION.

The work of Torfaeus, a learned Icelander, which is here presented was the first book in which the story of the discovery of Vinland by the Northmen was made known to general readers. After the appearance of his work, the subject slumbered, until Rafn in this century attempted to fix the position of the Vinland of Northern accounts. Since that time scholars have been divided. Our leading historians, George Bancroft, Hildreth, Winsor, Elliott, Palfrey, regard voyages by the Norsemen southward from Greenland as highly probable, but treat the sagas as of no historical value, and the attempt to trace the route of the voyages, and fix the localities of places mentioned, as idle, with such vague indications as these early accounts, committed to writing long after the events described, can possibly afford. Toulmin Smith, Beamish, Reeves and others accepted the Norseman story as authentic, and Dr. B. F. De Costa, Horsford and Baxter are now the prominent advocates and adherents of belief in the general accuracy of the Vinland narratives.

As early as 1073 Adam of Bremen spoke of Vinland, a country where grape vines grew wild, and in 1671 Montanus, followed in 1702 by Campanius, the chronicler of New Sweden, alluded to its discovery. Peringskjold in 1697 published some of the sagas and thus brought the question more definitively before scholars; but Torfaeus, a man well versed in the history of his native island, in the book here given collected from the priestly and monastic writings all that was accessible in his day. Produced now in English, his History of Vinland will add to the literature of the subject, and with the volume of Dr. De Costa give the student almost all the

INTRODUCTION.

material for examination. Torfaeus first proposed the statement of the length of the day as a means of fixing the position of Vinland which he believed to be near Newfoundland.

Dr. Winsor says: "Of the interpreters of this ancient lore Torfaeus has been long looked upon as a characteristic exemplar."

Some of the earlier advocates of the Vinland story found corroborative evidence in the stone mill at Newport, the inscriptions on Dighton rock, and the bronze or copper found with a fair haired skeleton. These have been wisely abandoned as utterly untrustworthy.

The narratives are vague, and it has been made an objection that the only natives described are evidently men of of Esquimaux race, not our Indians. This is really an evidence in favor of the accounts. The country of Vinland was known and referred to before the days of Columbus. If the narratives had been invented after the exploration of our coast, and with knowledge of its actual inhabitants the writers would have placed Algonquins there, not Esquimaux.

We know too little of the movement of the great American nations to be able to write the whole story, but we know some facts. The early settlers in Greenland found no Skraelings, or Esquimaux there and they did not appear till near the middle of the fourteenth century. They were evidently forced northward. Jacques Cartier found at Gaspé and in possession of the valley of the St. Lawrence tribes of the Huron Iroquois family. All the vocabulary and words given by him are of their language. He gives no Algonquin or Esquimaux terms. Yet when Champlain settled Quebec less than a century afterwards these Huron Iroquois had fallen back up the St. Lawrence to Lake Ontario and were in possession of the territory south and west of the lake. The whole valley of the St. Lawrence and the Atlantic Coast to Chesapeake Bay were held by Algonquin tribes. These at the north warred with a tribe to whom they gave the name of Esquimaux or Raw Meat Eaters. The Esquimaux held their own in Labrador in 1612(Biard, "Relation de la Nouvelle France,") and in 1659 were still at war with the

Micmacs of Gaspé, (Relation, 1659). That they occupied the coast lower down before they were forced northward into Greenland, would seem therefore most probable. Yet if these accounts of voyages to Vinland were invented or built up on a few vague indications, the inventors could not have been such philosophic ethnologists as to place Esquimaux in New England. The accessible material at their hands would have led them to place Algonquins on the coast.

Rude implements found in the interglacial Jersey drift have been held by C. C. Abbot to have been associated with a people of the Esquimaux stock, so that Esquimaux may have occupied the coast below Sandy Hook.

Christian Irish had preceded the Northmen to the Faroe Islands, as Dicuil, an Irish monk, makes clear, and to Iceland; but the Scandinavians who settled Iceland and Greenland, who made voyages thence southward were just emerging from heathenism into the light of Christianity. Catholic bishops and priests, the mass and prayers are mentioned in the narratives, and one of the heroines makes a pilgrimage to Rome.

This fixes to a certain extent the time of the alleged voyages, for the time of the introduction of Christianity into Iceland and Greenland is fairly well authenticated.

JOHN GILMARY SHEA.

TRANSLATOR'S PREFACE.

Thormod Torfason, or as he latinized his name, Thormodus Torfaeus, the author of our History of Vinland, was born on the island of Engoe on the north coast of Iceland, in 1640. At this time Iceland formed a part of the kingdom of Denmark. Accordingly Torfason went to Copenhagen for his education. There the young man's brilliant abilities soon found recognition. He was hardly twenty years of age when the Danish King, Frederick III, who took a deep interest in the early history of the Northmen, appointed him *interpres regius* for northern antiquities. Two years later (1662) he was sent to Iceland, partly to perfect his knowledge of the ancient language of his native land, partly to gather Icelandish manuscripts for the royal library at Copenhagen. With the aid of Bishop Brynjolf Sveinsson, whom Torfaeus himself calls the most learned of all the bishops of Skalholt up to his time, he carried out his commission successfully; as a reward he was appointed secretary of the bailiwick of Stavanger in the south of Norway (1664). But Torfaeus was not destined to bury his talents in the administration of a small Norwegian country place. He remained there only three years; then he was recalled to Copenhagen and appointed Curator of the Royal Cabinet of Antiquities. While holding this position he again visited Iceland and subsequently made a voyage to Holland. During this voyage he proved that he had not only the love of learning of his Icelandish forefathers, but also the violent spirit of the old Vikings. Attacked by a man Torfaeus struck him down and killed him. He was tried and condemned to death. His distinction as a scholar however, led the King to pardon him, though he was obliged to pay a heavy fine and lost his place as the head of the royal Cabinet (1673. He went to

Norway and became more absorbed than ever before in the study of the Eddas, of the Sagas and of Northern Antiquities in general. On the death of Frederick III, his successor, Christian V, named Torfaeus Royal Historiographer of Norway and made him a member of the commission on education. The fruits of his studies now appeared in rapid succession. His History of the Faroe Islands appeared in 1695, and was followed (1697) by the History of the Orkneys, and the Table of the Chiefs and Kings of Denmark (1702). In 1705 was published the History of Vinland, which now for the first time appears in an English dress. The History of Ancient Greenland (1706) and the *Trifolium Historicum* (1707) led up to the publication of his principal work, the History of Norway in four large volumes (1711). This was the last of his works that appeared during his lifetime. But so great was the esteem in which he was held by Northern scholars, that many years after his death, in 1777, his unpublished miscellaneous papers were printed by his admiring countrymen. Torfaeus died in 1719.

All Torfaeus' works were written in Latin. Hence, while John Peringskjold was perhaps the first to revive the memory of the Norse discovery of America in his Swedish translation of the Heimskringla, (1697) yet Torfason's History of Vinland first made known the claims of the Northmen to European scholars. The body of his history, as he himself tells us in his preface, is based on two old Icelandish manuscripts, the celebrated Flatey Book, known as No. 1005 fol. of the Old Royal Collection in Copenhagen, and on a paper manuscript, No. 678 in the same collection. On the former are based Chapters I to VHI, of the History of Vinland, on the latter Chapters IX to XIV. The Flatey Book, so called because it was long preserved on the island of Flatey, near Iceland, is a remarkable work. It is in the main a history of the Kings of Norway, written on vellum, and fills 1700 closely packed pages of print at thirty-nine lines per page. Two priests, John Thordsson and Magnus Thorhallson, undertook this encyclopaedic work for an Icelander named John Haconson. Like most mediæval records, therefore, the story of the finding of Vinland by the Northmen has been preserved for us by Catholic priests. The Flatey Book was probably written at Widedals-tunga, near the monastery of Thingeyrar, whence the authors probably drew many of the manuscripts from which the material for their work was drawn. The learned Norse scholar Gudbrand Vigfussen, in the preface to his edition of the Orkneyinga Saga (Vol. I, p. XXV) has proved by an ingenious course of reasoning, that the manuscript was finished in 1387, about three hundred and seventy-five years after the discovery of Vinland. The version of this discovery, found in the Flatey Book, usually called the Saga of Eric the Red, was, however, taken from older manuscripts, so that we cannot say, when it was first written down from tradition.

The second account of the discovery of Vinland, taken by Torfacus from N. 768, O. R. C. of Copenhagen, is usually entitled the Saga of Thorfinn Karlsefne. Torfason's manuscript is much younger than the Flatey Book. But since his death another parchment manuscript was found in the Arne-Magnaean Collection of Copenhagen, being No. 544 of that collection, which seems to be the original of Torfaeus' paper manuscript. This old parchment proved to be even older than the Flatey Book, being ascribed by palaeographers to the end of the thirteenth or the beginning of the fourteenth century. Accordingly, if age is to decide, this version should be even more authoritative than the Flatey Book.

Torfaeus' narrative is based upon the manuscripts he had before him. Indeed, it may be said without exaggeration, that whole pages of his History are fairly literal translations of the Flatey Book, or of the Karlsefne Saga. He makes no attempt to reconcile nor to explain the discrepancies of the two versions of his story, though the differences are neither slight nor unimportant. To him the account of the discovery of Vinland, and found in the Saga of Eric the Red, seemed preferable to that of the Karlsefne Saga, because it is simpler and more probable. Perhaps his judgment may have been influenced by his own connection with the Flatey book, for it was by his hands that Bishop Brynolf

Steinsson sent the royal volume to King Frederick III (1662). Still his opinion has been endorsed by many scholars since his time and especially by Carl Christian Rafu, the editor of the *Antiquitates Americanae*, who first printed the Icelandic originals of the two Sagas. Of late, however, there seems to be a turn in the tide and Mr. Reeves, the author of 'The Finding of Wineland the Good," (Oxford, 1890) is outspoken In his advocacy of the Karlsefne Saga, as contained in the very old parchment Codex, A. M. No. 544. He supports his views by showing that other Icelandic manuscripts, containing brief accounts of the discovery of Vinland, or allusions thereto, agree with this version rather than with the story of the Flatey Book. However that may be, the reader after carefully perusing the two versions will see the importance of reconciling or at least explaining their discrepancies; and this may not prove impossible. At all events, so much is certain: Thormod Torfason has given a fairly full and correct, and an honest history of the discovery of Vinland, as given in the old Norse records. He has concealed no difficulties, nor omitted to present his readers with all the evidence available in his day. Nor has much been added to this evidence since, except a few extracts from Are Thorgillson's Islendingabok and from the Landnamabok, which confirm Torfaeus' documents, without adding anything essentially new. Our History of Vinland, therefore, has not outgrown its usefulness, though it is the earliest work, that made known to modern scholars the tale of the discovery of America by the Northmen.

Google

Google

Google

HISTORY OF
ANCIENT VINLAND,
OR OF
PART OF NORTH AMERICA.

In which is reviewed the Reason of the Name; the Position of the Land is determined from the length of the Days in winter; the Fertility of the Soil, and the barbarous character of the Inhabitants, the temporary sojourn of its Discoverers and their Exploits, the Name of the adjacent Lands and their Appearance, are set forth from ancient Icelandic Sources brought to Light

BY

THORMOD TORFAEUS,

Royal Historiographer of Norway.

Copenhagen :
Printed at the press of his Royal Majesty and of the University
1705
At the Author's Expense.

APPROBATION.

The character of our age is to extol what is new, neglecting the old. Therefore not so much the indulgence as the applause of the public is due to those who, like the most noble author of this work, rescue from darkness and bring to light ancient history and geography. Copenhagen, Sept. 2nd, in the year 1705.

P. VINDINGIUS.

To the most Illustrious and most Excellent
Hero
LORD FREDERICK DE GABEL, LORD OF BREGENTUED,
Golden Knight
of the Order of the Danebrog,
Secret Counselor of State and Justice
of His Sacred Majesty of Denmark and Norway,
Lord Lieutenant of Norway,
Royal Governor
of the District of Aggershus and Ferroe.

MOST ILLUSTRIOUS AND EXCELLENT LORD.

The year, immediately preceding the present, the fourth of this century, has been everywhere consecrated in eternal records as most memorable, the year when the most august sovereign of these realms and their hereditary King, our most clement Lord, Frederick the Fourth, accompanied, among other most illustrious, most noble and great ministers by your Excellency also, most illustrious Lord Lieutenant, most mercifully deigned after the example of his great father, of most glorious memory, Christian the Fifth, to visit his realm, from its easternmost boundaries even to Nidarosia, and was universally received with the most marked enthusiasm of the whole people and of all classes, with festive acclaim and the most earnest wishes, the most ardent prayers and supplications for the perpetual safety and lasting prosperity of his Majesty. Surely parts of the fifth and sixth days of July, and the intervening night which was turned into bright sunlight, more than other times, shone upon me most auspiciously, when on that royal visit our Sovereign permitted this obscure and humble village to be selected for his stopping-place, where it was our privilege to behold with due reverence the most kind and gentle features of his father and grand-father, so to say, revived in his most serene countenance, and after a long interval to recall them more clearly than in any mirror that glitters with bright colors. But when at the same time your Excellency brought up the questions of the exploration of ancient Greenland, and of the establishment of trade in Davis' Straits, I answered to the first part only and disapproved of a route so often passed over as little fit for reaching the end aimed at; being bidden to point out one more suitable, I put off the expression of my opinion, being hindered by the presence of his Royal Majesty. On the following morning I set it forth to your most illustrious Excellency most briefly, owing to your haste. So far was your Excellency from finding fault therewith, that you even deigned to publish, and afterwards to praise it, when not so long ago I explained it more fully in a letter to your Excellency; finally I inserted it in my Preface to Ancient Greenland. The second question, on exploring Davis' Straits, is sufficiently answered both by home precedents known to many and by foreign precedents; for it is proved that it has been visited long ago by vessels from Holland, and according to the testimony of Arngrim, from England also.

Finally, I humbly offer to your Excellency the present treatise on VINLAND, in order to testify and express most positively my feelings of most submissive devotion and outspoken respect. For as the superintendence and supreme government of all Norway, which you administer with the greatest care and success, has been intrusted to your Excellency, you are wont to enquire most carefully, among other things which relate to its welfare, what fame this people has attained in past ages. Although the most flourishing realms of our part of the globe bear complete witness to our fame, yet this is crowned by the glory of first opening through its colonists parts of the New World, among which this (Vinland) is by no means the least. I admit indeed, that the record thereof which has come down to us is very scant; for though mention is made therein of a great number of wild beasts and of traffic in their skins, yet there is no specific account, so that they note neither the varieties of birds nor of fishes, mention very few species of trees and none at all of plants, nor any other things relating to the description of the countries. But in as much as it does not lie in the power of any historian to furnish himself with richer materials than have been handed down to him, your Excellency will pardon my deficiency in this respect; for I know the moderation of your Excellency's mind to be such, that even if I had made a rather thoughtless mistake, you would yet extend to me your kind indulgence for my rashness. But as the mistake is not mine, trusting in your Excellency's kindness, of which I have heretofore received various marks, I most humbly submit to the patronage of your Excellency my work, such as it is, as well as myself, and request for both your favor, kindness, good will and protection. That the Lord of Heaven may plentifully grant your Excellency all prosperity in the fullest measure worthy of Heaven, I sincerely pray with suppliant mind, hand and pen.

Your most illustrious Excellency's

    Most humble servant,

        T. TORFAEUS.

PREFACE TO THE READER.

From the creation and renovation of the world, if you accept the Sacred Record, up to the present time, I know not what more important event has been handed down in history than the discovery of the New World ; though some ascribe the glory thereof to the ancient Phoenicians and their descendants, the Carthaginians, yet they lack the undoubted testimony necessary to convince all fully of its correctness; but even if this were completely admitted, yet they achieved no less glory, who restored it to perpetual light after being buried in oblivion for so many centuries thereafter. The fame of that immense achievement for a long time appeared to have been won by a man who has never been sufficiently praised, Christopher Columbus, a Genoese, who in the year of grace, 1492, discovered a part thereof. Nor did Americus Vespucius, of Florence, who set foot on it four years after, under the auspices of Emanuel, King of Portugal, carry off less renown; nay, he gained even greater glory. Some, however, claim for themselves the honor of discovering those countries in former ages; the Venetian brothers, for instance, Nicholas and Antonio surnamed Zeni, in the year 1380 after Christ, the last year of the Norwegian King Haco, the Sixth of that name, as he insisted, in truth the Seventh; and two centuries before these Madoc, son of Gwineth, (brother of the Prince of Wales) who is said to have led colonies to Canada and Florida, about the year 1170. But from the present work it will be clear that none of these (even should what is related of the Zeni be true, whereof hereafter) could claim for themselves the glory of first discovering America, nor could posterity justly and fairly claim it for them. The Greenlanders, colonists of Iceland and to some extent the Icelanders themselves, first of all snatched this glory from both, and indeed from Madoc, 150 years and more before his time. They did this in such a way that they have not only secured for themselves the undying honor and glory of discovering and of hastily settling Vinland, but also that of finally making it known far and wide and of publishing the Christian religion throughout the neighboring Albania or Great Ireland, (for this could not have been done before by others.) Therefore, kind reader, behold these two accounts of the discovery of Vinland, which for the present I offer you, not such as I should wish them to be, but such as they have been handed down to me, and as I can repeat them. Both are scant and slight; neither is entirely consistent with the other. I repeat them rather to strengthen my present thesis, and to leave the position of the country(Vinland) to be investigated by others from the facts here set down, and to reclaim for the descendants of the first occupants any right that may have accrued to them from that occupation than from a hope to satisfy you, even by both stories together. The first narrative, extending from the beginning to Chapter VIII is found in the Codex Flateyensis, in the history of King Olaf Triggvin, and, as it seems, in some other old manuscripts also. Having borrowed it from some one of these, the most distinguished head of the Royal Swedish Archives, John Peringskjold, inserted it in the history of the Norse Kings, the Heimskringla, from chapter 104 to chapter 112, whilst they do not exist in the manuscripts commonly ascribed to Snorro Sturleson, to wit: the Kringla or Jofraskinna, which I have borrowed from the Library of the Church of the Most Holy Trinity, at Copenhagen.

The second narrative, a most famous antiquary of the last century, the Icelander Bjorn of Skardsa, collected from ancient documents, and chiefly from that most perfect book on the Origins of Iceland, by the jurist Hauk, who died in the year 1334, and from various traditions of later times. Both agree in saying that at the end of the tenth century after the birth of the Saviour, or at the beginning of the following century, Vinland was seen and soon after discovered; and hence all doubt on this question is dispelled. Their differences in other particulars are so far from destroying the fundameutal parts of the story, that they rather strengthen them : for in as much as they agree in essentials, their differences in regard to details, and those more minute details, readily show that the different writers did not conspire to hand down falsehood, and moreover that they did not copy each others' writings. On this argument that most distinguished man, Olaf Rudbecke in the second paragraph of the first chapter of his Atlant. discourses learnedly : from him I shall cite a few words. For after promising a short dissertation on the abstruse method of writing, involved in fables and riddles, he adds : "But indeed, others, too, may be found who will regard not only this abstruse method of writing, but history setting forth everything in the plainest language, as fiction, especially if it happen that different writers disagree in some particulars. But if such writers are compelled at different times to relate one and the same event, do we believe that they will always use the same order, the same number of words, and precisely the same enumeration of the minutest particulars? By no means! Truly not even the four Evangelists agree thus among themselves, however wonderful may be their agreement in truth and on all the chief points of the heavenly teaching. The books of Kings also and the so called Paralipomena in the Old Testament, although they relate the events of the same period, yet so differ in language and at times in the fulness of the facts, that to obtain a complete and perfect version of the history, they must sometimes mutually complement and help each other. Therefore to attain the truth, it will certainly suffice to trace out the essential features of the story ; the disagreement of writers in lesser particulars, is too unimportant to obscure the truth, when it shines by its own light, a principle which will be illustrated more fully by a famous example. Moses has given us by far the most accurate account of the deluge and has set forth most carefully its occasion, causes, details, chronology and the story of the men that survived it ; the same event was afterward, by the faith of tradition, made known to the pagans also ; but both on account of the length of time and the somewhat doubtful good faith of the writers, the story has many and considerable breaks, some interpolations, as well as many changes." Then after setting forth the various versions of the catastrophe he finally adds: "What of the fact that any one who is willing to consider these things carefully, will see clearly this inference, which while it was not before thought of by any one, yet exceeds all mere probability: that there underlies the narrative of these writers, though they differ from one another, a certain most undoubted substratum of agreement and truth, placed there so to say by divine Providence; for as we regard those who relate the same fact in precisely the same words and according to the same arrangement and style, as pilferers of other's work (except one who precedes the rest in time) so also, had the Chaldeans, Scythians, Greeks and Egyptians agreed entirely with Moses or any other historian of the deluge, both in language and details, they could never have escaped the same criticism, and in that case the whole story would seem to depend on the testimony not of many but of a single witness. But whenever different writers differently set forth the same event, in regard to which they agree with one another, it is evident at once that the same fact was beheld or perceived by several persons, but was not handed down to posterity by all with equal truth in all respects nor with the like care. Meanwhile however, the pith of the story will be confirmed by several and will not admit of doubt on our part."

But I am excusing the variations of the present narratives in a larger preface than is necessary, for they are very slight and can be examined with very little trouble.

I. The CODEX FLATEYENSIS relates that the new countries were seen, but not entered, by Bjarne, the Icelander, that they were explored and endowed with names by Leif. Bjorn of Skardsa is silent concerning Bjarne, but the rest he admits; there is a slight difference of opinion whether Leif came to the new lands when returning from Norway, or whether he sailed from Greenland especially, in order to explore them.

II. The Codex Flateyensis says that Thorvald, the son of Eric the Red, next visited them and was finally pierced with an arrow by the Skraelings. Bjorn tells a far less probable story, for he introduces the fabulous country of the unipedes.

III. The Codex Flateyensis says that after Thorvald's death, his brother Thorstein undertook a voyage thither: Bjorn places that voyage before Thorvald's death The Codex is more trustworthy, for it first tells of his wife's death, of the marriage contract, and lastly how she married Karlsefne.

IV. The Codex Flateyensis describes a third expedition to Vinland under the leadership of Karlsefne: the third, for Thorstein had not reached Vinland. Bjorn recounts the story more simply, yet he errs in counting Thorvald among his companions, for he had been previously slain; nor is it more worthy of belief, that he gave their names to Markland and Helluland; to other places he certainly appears to have given names.

V. The Codex Flateyensis alone relates the fourth voyage to Vinland, which Bjorn did not find mentioned in Hauk's book; and yet it is quite probable, for it was the last; and Freidis, the daughter of Eric the Red, seems to have been present with both, and during the last to have become mad and to have acted in a ferocious way. The minute details I shall not examine, for it is not of such importance whether the discovery of those countries or the death of Eric the Red is placed one or two years sooner or later, and the like. What may be a matter of controversy regarding the position of Vinland I have discussed in a note with all possible diligence. For it must be sought in that part of the North American continent where the productions here described grow or which the descriptions fit, and where the character of the country is found agreeing therewith; but whether these suit the character of the climate in which Estotiland lies according to the common opinion, I greatly doubt.

I am not unaware that Buno in his notes to Philip Cluverius' Introduction to Universal Geography, book VI, chap. 12, denies that Estotiland is to be found in those parts of America (he describes Canada), as well as that the island of Frisland ever existed in the adjacent part of the ocean.

PREFACE.

Henry Kipping, Pol. Institutes, book I, chap. 20, p. 173., not only supports him, but denies that they are located anywhere, in the following words: "Frisland and Estotiland exist nowhere, whatever the Venetian Zeni in their Sea Voyage may have wished to make us believe;" but Buno in the notes of the afore-mentioned work, book III, chap. 20, paragraph 4, page 209, contradicts himself and says that Greenland is separated by Davis' Strait from the American Estotiland. For my part I have no quarrel in regard to the name, since Sanson d' Abbeville and more recent geographers regard the new land of Labrador, adjoining Hudson Bay as identical with Estotiland; that it is not the same, however as the Estotiland, which the Zeni describe, I suspect from the fact that they state that it (Estotiland) lies more than a thousand miles to the west of Frisland. Since Frisland however is usually placed in 62^0 latitude and about 342^0 of longitude, whilst Estotiland is placed 58^0 of latitude and about 290^0 of longitude, they (the Zeni) must have proceeded farther towards America and have found there the Estotiland which they describe. This land without doubt was large, since it was little smaller than Iceland, but superior in fertility, inasmuch as it was situated in a milder climate, very rich, and abounding in all kinds of products, even gold and various metals; remarkable for its cities, castles, towns and splendid structures. But I do not know whether this fits those barbarous tribes in those times. There is besides the published description of the island of Drogio and of the vast country extending thence towards the south and southwest, which present the features of another continent; these statements suggest the opinion that they were carried to parts of North America, and that those who afterwards discovered the furthest parts of North America, convinced that they had reached the same Estotiland, of which they (the Zeni) speak, adopted the name, though the position was different; certainly the construction of boats, quite well known to those tribes (the Skraelings) and described exactly in this document, an art perhaps wholly unknown to such distant nations at that time, would also convince me that those brothers were carried to that part of the ocean and reached some part of America; if I were sure that their book was printed before the knowledge of those tribes (the Americans) was wide spread and furnished impostors full material for fiction and the power of inventing fables. Above all, on account of the gross and unskilful concoction and wonderful stories with which it is filled, I think that the book was compiled in more recent times under the name of such distinguished men, for the purpose of gaining authority. I think this is so because I know the bare-faced impudence of Bleyker and the shameless boldness of Martinerius, not to mention other names; both of these, with astounding temerity, printed and published their travels, itineraries to Iceland and Greenland, (and the latter pretends that in the time of Frederick the III, of most glorious memory, he traveled thither, though I am not certain that the one ever saw Iceland and either of them Greenland), they were believed by many and the latter to no slight degree gained credence with that most distinguished man, Olaf Rudbecke, and won his respect. It is miraculous that the chief city of Frisland should have abounded in such quantities of fish, that Flemings as well as Britons, besides English, Scots, Norwegians and Danes imported them in great numbers, and the islanders accumulated immense wealth therefrom; that in the annals of these nations there is no mention of them, and not even a trace of Frisland and of the trade with its inhabitants; that not even the Norwegians and Icelanders, who, frequently stopping in their country and at their courts, fought in their wars while others were engaged in commerce, have any knowledge that Frisland was ever under their power, and that it was wrested from them by Zichinnus, and that—a thing unusual with kings—it was never, I shall not say, recovered, but not even sought after or attacked with a view to restore it to its allegiance. You retort that it is mentioned by geographers, for Johannes Laurentius Ananias in his FABRICA DEL MONDO, informs us that in his day it greatly abounded in fish and for that reason was frequented by Scotch and British merchants, and that he was informed by Jonas, the Breton, a relative of Jacques Cartier, who first discovered New France in the year 1554, that he (Jonas) had himself entered it and that its inhabitants are very polite and kind towards foreigners; and this is confirmed by John Boterus. Moreover, John Antony Maginus bears witness that in his day the English traded there to the great advantage of the islanders, and that they called the island West England. Ortelius also mentions it on page 90, Berti on page 56, as well as John Miritius in a geographical treatise published in the year 1590; whose words Arngrim Jonas quoted on page 190 of book III, of his CRYMOGAEA adding his own opinion on the several points. But Mercator and Hondius going further, set down the cities of Frisland with their proper names: 1° the capital of the same name as the island. 2 Sorand; 3 Ocibar; 4 Sanestol; 5 Crodme; 6 Doffais; 7 Campo; 8 Rane; 9 Bondendon; 10 Rovea; 11 Andefort; 12 Cabaru. Small islands near Frisland are also enumerated: 1° Ilofo; 2 Jedeve; 3 Venai; 4 Monaco; 5 Spirige; 6 Streme; 7 Ibini; 8 Duime; 9 Porlanda. That these statements were read by those most learned men Buno and Kipping, I have not the slightest doubt: still they could not be induced to attach any importance to them; nor were more recent geographers moved to give them a place in their descriptions. For my part, I who have gathered the history of Norway from all kinds of documents worthy of credit, have certainly nowhere found any mention of this Frisland, and therefore deny that it was ever subject to the Norwegians; whatever is there (in Zeno) recounted of Zichinnus' war with the Norwegians, must therefore be placed among the myths Nor is what he wrote of Iceland and the neighboring islands, more probable; for it is contrary to the experience of all ages. On these points the reader may consult Arngrim Jonas, in his description of Iceland, part 2, memb. 2, page m. 140 and ff., as well as Theodore Thorlake's Dissertation on Iceland: these will fully satisfy him.

Therefore, passing over the absurdities, which that writer has published about Greenland. so different from the description of Ivar Berius, a man most familar with those matters, and ignoring the other tales which he added, for example, concerning Grisland, Estland and Icaria and the unknown and never discovered situation of those lands, we conclude that the glory of first discovering Vinland belongs, whole and undiminished, to the Greenlanders and Icelanders, the descendants of the Norsemen, and we award to them not only the glory of discovering it but also of making known the Christian religion to those peoples. For Are Marson is said to have been driven by storms to Great Ireland near Vinland, which (Great Ireland) they otherwise call ALBANIA or HVITRA MANNA LAND, and is distant from Ireland a voyage of six days towards the west according to the Book of Origins of Iceland, part 2, chap. 22, page 64. This distance does not differ greatly from the computations of Philip Cluverius, who reckons the distance thence to Canada at 200 miles (Book VI, chap. 2, p. 419). He (Are Marson) is there said to have been converted to Christianity. This happened before the year 1000 after Christ, and before Christianity was introduced into Iceland, for he was the great grandson of Ulf Skialg, who first settled Reikyanes and as at that time neither Greenland nor much less the above mentioned Great Ireland was Christianized, the sacred mysteries of Christianity which he then embraced must have been taught him whilst he was detained there (in Great Ireland) but he was detained there as long as he lived. This, I conjecture, was done by Jones, Jonas, or John, an Irish Bishop, who whilst Isleif, the first Bishop of all Iceland, was presiding over the Cathedral of Schalholt, came thither between the years 1056 and 1080 and is said to have gone thence to Vinland, to have preached the Gospel, and having gained over many to Christ, to have finally been tortured and killed; on this subject, see chap. XVI, of our Vinland. At that time therefore, not only Vinland, which was then found worthy to be spoken of by Adam of Bremen in his writings, but also this very Great Ireland became known, so that this story of the aforesaid Are, which we have just recounted was taken by Icelanders from the Relation of Thorfinn, Earl of the Orkneys, who died in the year 1064, published in Iceland and adopted into literature. Hence, we readily infer that even more Christians from Ireland and elsewhere went thither from the time those lands first became known, to propagate their religion, though the Icelanders and Greenlanders were not aware of this. This, however, has been recorded by them, that subsequently in the next century, that is to say in the year 1121, Eric, the first Bishop of Greenland, visited Vinland, as a place well known at that time, (for what other purpose, I ask, except to labor there for Christ ?) and that the opinion prevailed that he perished during that visit. But in the chapter quoted above, it is mentioned, that long before him, Bjarn the champion of Breidavik reached, if not Vinland, certainly some other part of North America, and that by his aid and influence, his countryman Gunnlaug Gudleifson with his whole ship's company was saved from imminent danger of life. These are the men, who, as Sanson d'Abbeville in his description of Virginia, page 14, suggests, were taken by a certain Gascon for Gascons; for he writes that he (the Gascon) assured him (Sanson) that he would prove that Gascons had been in New France four or five hundred years before Baron de Lery or John Verazzani came there ; now, the former came there in 1518, the latter in 1542. As this time agrees precisely with the period when those countries were first discovered, the story adds great authority to our story. I shall say nothing of the part of New France bordering on the sea, called Norumberga, as Cluverius thinks, from the city of the same name, which name Buno in his notes to the same passage interprets to mean Norway or a colony led thither from Norway. It is clear that after the time of Christopher Columbus, no part of New France was settled by the Norse; perhaps the name given to the land in ancient times was preserved, but whether the city was built before the arrival of the French, I have not yet ascertained; certainly if it was founded before their time, it seems to imply the origin of the name from the tribe, if afterwards, from the country in which it lay, and that again derives its name from the old colonists. Thus it has been fully proved that that part of America became well known throughout the North and West in the eleventh century of the

Christian era. I do not know any more than others, how, during the succeeding centuries up to the time of Columbus it was plunged into the densest darkness and became again unknown. That Harold (the Bold or Imperious), the most skillful chief of the Northmen, who, as Adam of Bremen says, was about to explore it, was carried by storms to the icebound ocean of Greenland, and returned without achieving his plans, I gather from his story: had he examined its character and products more carefully, he would no doubt, after settling his quarrel with the Danes, have there found richer booty, and that too entailing neither loss nor danger; and he would have acquired wealth and power formidable to the whole North. But engaged in lengthy wars, he had no time for so great and unknown an undertaking. To explore it and Vinland as a part of it, a certain Rolf was sent in the 88th year of the thirteenth century, by Eric, the second of that name, King of Norway, surnamed PRESTAHATARA, the Priest-hater, (the Greeks would translate it μισόκληρον and supplies for that voyage were exacted in the following year from the Icelanders, according to the conjecture of Arngrim (Crymogaea, Book III, p. 119 and ff.); this took place only two centuries before Columbus discovered a part of South America. What we have related above of Madoc about the year 1170, is therefore nowise absurd; for that several nations at this period sent colonies thither is probable; and I know not how Thorfinn, Earl of Orkney, otherwise acquired his knowledge of those countries, even as regards minute details, (as appears in the story of Are). On the other hand, if in those centuries (for we speak of the thirteenth century under Eric II, king of Norway) the knowledge of those lands still existed, how did it wholly escape the knowledge of Henry VII, King of England and of all his ministers two centuries later? For it is proved that Columbus first made known his plans and offered his services to this king, which he would surely not have refused, if he had known of the lands and of their vicissitudes. I am convinced that all the settlers were killed or conquered by the barbarians there; that the rest were debarred from the use of ships and unable to leave, and that if there were any additional visitors, they were treated in the same way, and that for this reason the memory of those countries and peoples, consecrated among the Icelanders only, suddenly vanished. That the Greenlanders and Icelanders fearing the violence and number of the natives, gave up the occupation of the land, not of their own accord, but against their will, we read here, and Ivar Berius bears witness that all the Western District (Vestri Bygd) of Greenland was laid waste by the Skraelings. I shall not thence conclude with the distinguished Grotius, that these tribes (the Skraelings) were the descendants of the Greenlanders, but I rather consider them the offspring of the Samoyeds, whose customs and mode of life are proved by a comparison of both to resemble those of the Skraelings; their physique and character also is very similar: both are slim of build, nor do they differ in form and features, both cover their tents and bodies with the skins of wild beasts, both alike adore the sun, both value highly the cheapest goods, mirrors, fish-hooks, knives and rattles; both are equally skilled in the use of the spear, and in unfailingly striking the mark; both eat raw flesh, whence both have a fetid stench; I shall not speak of other points of resemblance. Nor is the passage (from Asia to America), however much obstructed by the intervening mountains and deserts. entirely barred, especially to men pursuing wild animals; this passage, moreover, is afforded by bays and straits which are spanned with ice by the constant cold, as if by a bridge. Nor is there a boundless distance between the two peoples, for in the far North the degrees of latitude are smaller and the distance too, broken by the intervention of tribes near Sualbardus, as is shown in the 5th chapter of my Greenland towards the end. This origin is, furthermore proved by the animals common to both, which differ from the horses and oxen, for example, that have been brought to Greenland. These were unknown in America before the arrival of the Spaniards, and the natives were frightened by their lowing and neighing. Therefore, in conclusion, those barbarians seem to be the offspring of the Samoyeds, carried to the furthest ends of America either by some land route hitherto unknown, or in the little boats invented by themselves, (which were not endangered by the sea). And yet I should not forthwith think that the other parts of America were peopled by them, and that nations differing from them in appearance and customs were descended from them; the difference (in physique and customs) of these tribes implies a difference of origin also, and of them, I must not discourse, as they lie outside of the scope of my work. But if anyone thinks the same of the last chapter of this book which deals with the prodigies of Froda, let him know that we were led by the incidents there related to refresh the wearied spirits of our readers with a certain variety, and everybody can fix their value according to his disposition without any objection on our part. As nothing further that is worthy of mention suggests itself, do you, kind reader, read and judge kindly of these pages, whatever their value. Farewell.

HISTORY OF

ANCIENT VINLAND.

Google

CONTENTS OF THE CHAPTERS OF THE PRESENT HISTORY OF VINLAND.

	page
Approbation.	2
Dedication.	3
Preface to the Reader.	6

Chapter I.
Of the occasion of first noticing and then Discovering Vinland. 25

Chapter II.
Of the Discovery of Vinland by Leif. 27

Chapter III.
Of the Discovery of Vines and Wild Grapes and of Leif's Return. 28

Chapter IV.
Of the Voyage of Thorvald to Vinland, and his Expeditions to parts of it; of the findings of some persons of an unknown race; of the Murder of Thorvald and the return of his companions to their native country. 30

Chapter V.
Of the toilsome and fruitless voyage of Leif's brother, Thorstein, who intended to visit Vinland, of his forced return to Greenland, when the plague had broken

out, of his death and the prodigy connected with it. . 32

Chapter VI.

Of the Voyage of Karlsefne to Vinland, of his traffic with the Skraelings and of the disputes thence arising, which resulted in open war. . . . 34

Chapter VII.

Of the fourth Expedition to Vinland, under the leadership of Thorvald, the husband of Freydis and two Icelanders, Helge and Fimbog, of the inhuman cruelty of Freydis, of Karlsefne's return to Iceland and of his family. 37

Chapter VIII.

Of Leif's journey to Norway to King Olaf Tryggvin, of his discovery of Vinland on his return, and of the successful preaching of the Christian religion in his native country. 41

Chapter IX.

Of the fruitless attempt of Leif's brother, Thornstein, to explore Vinland, of his return to Greenland, of his marriage with Thorbiorn's daughter, Gudrid, of her education and ancestors in Iceland. . . 42

Chapter X.

Of a certain prophetic woman, of her appearance and of skill in the magic (seidic) art. . . . 44

Chapter XI.

Of the infectious disease that arose among Thorstein's crew, of his death and of a prodigy, of the ancient

mode of burial in Greenland, of the arrival of Karlsefne, and his marriage with Gudrid. . . . 47

Chapter XII.

Of Karlsefne's Voyage to Vinland, of his companions on
that Expedition, viz: Bjarue, Thorhall, and Thorvard, the son-in-law of Eric the Red, and his son
Thorvald. 51

Chapter XIII.

Of Thorhall, the Hunter, who is driven by storms to Iceland, and there held in bondage to the end of
his life, of the further Expioration of Vinland by
Karlsefne and his companions, of the land and water
products there, of the dress of the Skraelings, of their
traffic and of the disputes and wars thence arising,
which however end in the Skraelings sustaining
greater loss. 53

Chapter XIV

Of the slaying of Thorvald, the son of Eric the Red, by
a one-footed man, of Karlsefne's sojourn at Straums-
fiord for three winters, of the birth of his son Snorre,
of the captivity of two Skraelings, of the dangerous
voyage Bjarne Grimolfson in the Irish Ocean, of his
honorable conduct towards a certain Icelander in extreme peril of life, of Karlsefne's return to Iceland,
and his descendants. 57

Chapter XV.

Adam of Bremen's Story of Vinland, consistent with the
above, and his great mistake regarding its position,
whilst Olaf Rudbeck no less erroneously identifies

CONTENTS.

Vinland with Finland, and the story of the position of Great Ireland and of Are, the Icelander, and of the pitch of the Greenlanders. . . . 60

Chapter XVI.

Of the voyages to Vinland, of the Saxon Bishop Jones and of Eric, Bishop of Greenland, and concerning Gudleif Gudlangson. 62

Chapter XVII.

Of the prodigies of Froda. . . 65

Addenda. . 74

CHAPTER I.

OF THE OCCASION OF THE FIRST NOTICING AND AFTERWARDS DISCOVERING VINLAND.

The well-known Herjulf, who accompanied Eric the Red in the year 985 from Iceland, and settled Herjulfsnes, by his wife Thorgerde had a son, named Bjarne, who going in tender youth to foreign parts, acquired wealth and experience ; his winters he spent alternately either abroad or with his father, and he had resolved to pass the present winter at his father's home. But when on his return to his native land he learned that his father had gone to Greenland the same summer and there settled, being a stubborn observer of customs he had once adopted, he declared, he would spend the winter in his father's house even in Greenland, though unknown to him and recently discovered; therefore he entrusted his ship to an unknown sea, unploughed by any of his sailors before him. Three days were passed in sailing, during which he saw nothing except the sky and the water, and then a northwind blowing, darkness for several days prevented his seeing anything, and made it impossible to direct the ship's course; the darkness being dispelled, they sailed a whole day and night with sails set, until an unknown land came in view. When on approaching it, they found it bare of mountains, covered with forests and low hills, they turned their ships and left it. For two days after they sped along before a south south-east wind, until another country came in sight, level, and full of woods; when the captain recognized that it differed from the mountainous and snow-clad landscape of Greenland, though the sailors begged him to land and take in water and wood, and though the wind was still, he yet did not permit himself to be prevailed upon, for which he even incurred some blame. When he had departed thence, taking advantage of a south-west wind, which for three days filled his sails, he found still another land with lofty mountains and white peaks. This, too, when on approaching it he had found it an island, he passed by as useless. And now as the breeze grew strong, he ordered the sails to be partly furled; four days were passed on this part of the voyage; then at last a fourth time land was seen, which from the description of others he judged to be Greenland, and directing his ship towards it, he reached towards evening Cape Herjulfsnes, where his father lived; and having been more lucky in finishing his voyage, than he was wise in undertaking it, he ceased henceforth to travel and remained with his father as long as the latter lived, and after his death took possession of his estate.

CHAPTER II.

OF THE DISCOVERY OF VINLAND BY LEIF.

When Bjarne Herjulfson crossing over from Greenland came to Eric Hacon's son, the Earl of Norway, he was at first hospitably received by him and then enrolled in the number of his courtiers, and related what lands, until then untrodden by any one, as far as he knew, he had seen; in the opinion of the crowd, he was partly condemned, because he lacked ambition to explore them. The next summer he crossed to Greenland and there was repeatedly question of seeking those countries. To him, therefore, came Leif, the Lucky of Brattahlide, bought his ship and having hired thirty-five sailors, asked his father to become their leader for the purpose of looking up the lands recently seen. Eric excused himself on account of his old age, which made him less fit to bear the hardships of sea and tempest than he was in his youth. At last he yielded to the importunities of his son, and trusted to fortune which had favored him beyond the rest of his family; but setting out from home, when not far from the ship, he was thrown off his horse, which had grown restive, and sprained his foot; regarding this as an unfavorable omen he declared that fate had not ordained that he should discover more lands than the one they inhabited, and returned home, whilst Leif with his associates carried out their plans; among these there is said to have been a certain southerner (for by his name our ancient writers understand the Germans), Tyrker by name. The country last seen by Bjarne, first met their view, and approaching it, they sent out a boat; climbing up mountains covered by perpetual snow, they noticed that below as far as the sea, the land was covered with continuous rock, and was therefore utterly uninhabitable. Then said Leif: Bjarne's listlessness, at least, we have made amends for by exploring the country. I shall therefore, give it a name to match its character, and it shall be called HELLULAND, that is to say, rocky land. Starting thence they found another land; landing here, likewise, they found it flat, and without harbors, here and there green with woods, and again covered with white sand. This Leif called MARKLAND from its flatness (hence it is clear that the word MARK means not as some say "country," but "plain" or "flat land.") Sailing thence after a short delay, a north-wind filling their sails for two days; they again saw land, along whose northern side stretched an island. They brought their ship close up to this and disembarking in clear weather, they observed grass dripping with dew and vying even with honey in sweetness. Returning thence to their ship they brought it to the sound, which lay between the island and the cape, that stretched northward from the mainland: when sailing past the cape they veered towards the west. the water ebbed away, and the ship struck on the quick-sands, and was separated from the sea by great shallows. But so great was their eagerness to see the newly found land, that without waiting for the tide, they left the ship behind and immediately entered the land by a river which flowed from a lake; when the tide rose, they brought the ship by the river into the lake, and after fastening it by casting anchor they established huts on the bank and then built commodious winter quarters. Both river and lake abounded in great shoals of salmon, larger than any they had seen before. So great is the fertility of the soil and the mildness of the climate, that cattle did not seem to need hay in the winter season; there is no winter cold; the grass did not wither. In winter the days were longer than in Iceland or Greenland, the sun rose about nine o'clock at the time of the winter solstice and set at three o'clock. (That they were not very exact in this observation, is proved by the fertility of the country and the character of the climate; for nowhere else at 50° 26´, from the equator, where the longest day is eighteen hours and the shortest six, is such fertility known to prevail. For with them the parts of the day consisted of three hours; but they did not accurately distinguish them in these parts.) Then, their dwellings being completed, they were divided into two parties, some were kept home, others having drawn lots, were sent out to explore the country in a body, lest being scattered they be exposed to danger; but they were instructed not to explore it further than they could go and return in one day; Leif alternately joined each party, being everywhere welcome on account of his prudence and skill.

CHAPTER III.

OF THE DISCOVERY OF VINES AND WILD GRAPES, AND

OF LEIF'S RETURN.

Now it happened that when the exploring party returned, the German Tyrker alone was missing. Leif forthwith sent twelve men to seek him, for he was very anxious on his account, inasmuch as the man had lived a long time in his father's house, had been fond of himself from childhood and his devoted follower; they had not gone far from the winter quarters when they met him in a jolly frame of mind, and looking like a drunken man, who, rolling his eyes hither and thither, excited their laughter, being a man small of stature, but exceedingly skilled in all kind of mechanical arts. Asked for the reason of his delay and chattering for a long time in

German, a language unknown to the rest, he finally answered that he had gone a little further than Leif and found vines and grapes; when they expressed doubts, he assured them that he had been born where grapes grew in plenty. Therefore, dividing the work among his sailors, Leif set some to gather grapes and others to cut vines, and filled the boat with the former and the ship with the latter. The fields there produced wheat of their own accord, and the trees called MAUSUR; of each they took some to carry home, and some timbers of such size that they could be used to build houses. Leaving the newly found country in the beginning of spring, Leif called it, from the vines and grapes, Vinland or Wine Land. Then returning to Greenland with favorable winds, when its snow-clad mountains were in sight, he turned his ship from the straight course: when one of the crew asked the reason, whether he noticed a cliff or a ship, he answered that he was not clear about it. When all thought the object seen to be a cliff, he saw also some men wandering on them, for he was keener sighted than all the rest. But when they had all seen the shipwrecked men, he declared that if they were peaceful, he would take them out of danger, but otherwise he would bring them under his power; having despatched a smaller boat, he took off fifteen, together with their Norse captain Thorer, and received all, together with as much merchandise as they could take, into his ship, and brought them to the bay of Eriksfjord and to his paternal estate Brattahlide. Thorer with his wife Gudrid, Thorbjorn's daughter, and three sailors, he himself entertained; the rest he distributed among his neighbors, who gave them hospitality. Thereafter he received the name of the Lucky or Fortunate; this however, the manuscript Chronicle as well as the Codex Flateyensis, on page 233, contradicting itself, referred to the year 1000. Henceforth he is reported to have grown in wealth and reputation. But to his brother Thorvald the new country did not seem to have been sufficiently explored. Therefore he borrowed his brother's ship, on condition however, that he should first bring home the timber which Thorer's wrecked ship had carried, and which had been left on the cliff. The same winter disease breaking out among Thorer's crew, carried him off, with a great part of the men: Eric the Red, a man famed for discovering Greenland, died the same year. I cannot find the exact year either of the Christian era or of the reign of Yarls Eric and Sven who at that time ruled Norway.

CHAPTER IV.

OF THE VOYAGE OF THORVALD TO VINLAND AND HIS EXPLORATION OF PART OF IT; OF THE FINDING OF SOME PERSONS OF UNKNOWN RACE; OF THE SLAYING OF THORVALD, AND THE RETURN OF HIS COMPANIONS TO THEIR NATIVE COUNTRY.

Thorvald, having engaged thirty sailors, started off to Vinland and spent the winter in fishing, in the winter quarters of his brother Leif. The following spring, keeping back a light boat, he put a part of the sailors on board the ship and sent them to explore the western parts of the country, throughout the summer. The land seemed pleasant, being covered with woods that were at a short distance from the sea; the shore was covered with white sand, lined everywhere with many islands, separated from one another by extensive shoals: no human dwellings were found there, nay not even the dens of wild beasts: only in an island towards the west, wooden structures were found, pyramid-shaped, such as are used instead of barns, to store corn (the Codex Flateyensis calls them KORNHIALM AF TRE), but no other traces of man. And so they returned the same autumn to their winter quarters. The following summer the ship steering towards the eastern and northern shores was overtaken by storms and running on a headland, broke its keel and underwent repairs there for a long time. Hence Thorvald called the headland KIALARNES, that is to say, Cape Hull.

Then turning eastward they came to the entrance of a bay and steering the ship to the nearest headland, all covered with forests, brought her to a harbor. Then Thorvald, with all his crew, landed on the cape and was taken by the beauty of the spot: "Here," said he, "it is beautiful, and I should like to fix my home." And returning to the ship they beheld three hills on the sand below the headland: on betaking themselves thither they noticed three boats of leather or hide, and under each boat three men, one of whom escaped with his boat: the remaining eight were seized and slain, with great thoughtlessness, for it would surely have been better to humor them rather than frighten and exasperate them. Returning thence to the headland they saw within the bay some hills which they judged to be inhabited. Then a sudden sleep fell upon them all, so deep that it could not be shaken off even for the appointed watches; it was broken by a voice suddenly heard which called out as follows: "Awake, Thorvald, I beseech thee, with all thy companions, if you intend to save your lives: embark all of you with the greatest speed and depart hence." Aroused by these words, they behold the entire bay covered with boats; Thorvald, therefore, advises his men in this sudden emergency, to protect themselves by defences, made up of twigs and logs, but not to be forward in attacking the enemy. Then there arose a great crowd and poured upon them javelins and arrows right and left; but after a short hour they scattered in flight and disorder. These men the Norsemen called SKRAELINGS, in contempt, that is to say, DWARFS. Then Thorvald asked his men whether any of them had been wounded; when they told him that no one was hurt, he said, that he himself had been wounded, having been struck by a missile, which passing his shield, had lodged underneath the armpit, and that the wound no doubt was mortal; he therefore ordered himself to be carried to the headland, where he had intended to settle and bade them bury him there; adding that his intentions had not been frustrated, for that he would dwell there for a long time. He commanded two crosses to be erected, one at his head, the other at his feet, and the headland in future to be called KROSSANES, or "the headland of the crosses," and he ordered the men to hasten thence speedily. Here the Codex Flateyensis states, that at this time Greenland was converted to Christianity, though Eric the Red died before its conversion, whilst on page 233, it (the Cod. Flat.) stated, that in consequence of Leif's exhortations, Eric, with the whole population of Greenland had been baptized. There (at Krossans) Thorvald was buried, as he had instructed his men; but the sailors having returned to their companions, remained there the following winter. But in the ensuing spring, having laden their ship with vines and grapes, they weighed anchor and came to Greenland, to Leif, on the estate of Brattalihde.

CHAPTER V.

OF THE TOILSOME AND FRUITLESS VOYAGE OF LEIF'S BROTHER THORSTEIN, WHO INTENDED TO VISIT VINLAND; OF HIS FORCED RETURN TO GREENLAND WHEN THE PLAGUE HAD BROKEN OUT; OF HIS DEATH AND THE PRODIGY CONNECTED WITH IT.

Whilst these events took place in Vinland, Thorstein the third son of Eric the Red, married Gudrid, the wife of the Thorer, whom Leif had saved when Thorer was shipwrecked. Having now learned of his brother's death, he resolved to sail over to Vinland, in order to bring home Thorvald's remains. In the same ship, therefore, in which his brother had sailed, he weighed anchor, having shipped a crew of 25 chosen men, and obtained the winter-quarters of his brother Leif, not as a present but for use; he took his wife, to share not only his couch but also his voyage. Having been tossed about by storms all summer, he was carried one week after the beginning of winter into the western bay of Greenland, called Lysufjord: there he distributed all his sailors in winter-quarters in the neighborhood, but he alone with his wife, being without quarters, remained in the ship for some days: finally at the invitation of a certain Thorstein, surnamed Surt, or the Black, who was the only man there, who with his wife, called Grimhilde, inhabited a house without family; he staid with him and considering the means of the master, was entertained, if not sumptuously, at least kindly. In the beginning of winter a disease attacking all Thorstein's sailors, carried off many of them; their bodies he placed in coffins and put on the ship, intending to take them to Eric's bay and bury them in the spring. At that time Christianity was new in Greenland, and Thorstein the Black and his wife Grimhilde had not yet adopted its doctrines. The woman, in size and strength was a match for the strongest man: at length' the same plague attacked her as well as Thorstein Ericson, and they lay ill at the same time. But she having died first, according to the custom of the less wealthy in those places, was to be placed on a bier: but whilst her husband Thorstein was busy in procuring it, Grimhilde, in presence of Thorstein Ericson, who was ill at the same time and of his wife Gudrid, began to look for her shoes, intending to rise; but going back to bed as her husband returned, she struck it with a great thud; her husband with great exertion and difficulty carried her out and buried her. Afterwards Thorstein Ericson died. Now Thorstein, the owner of the farm, to console his (Thorstein Ericson's) widow, promised to take her to Eriksfjord, with the corpses of her husband and his companions, and to bring many to his house, lest she would waste away there through dulness. Meanwhile the dead Thorstein sitting up in bed said: "Where is Gudrid?" and he thrice repeated this question. She, dazed by this prodigy, asked her host whether she must answer, and was prevented by him from doing so. But he went up to the bed and took a seat near it; then he enquired what he (Thorstein Ericson) wished. The latter answered that though he had reached a beautiful place, he desired to comfort his wife and make known to her her future destinies; he foretold that she would marry an Icelander, would live with him in his country for a long time, and that from him would spring a noble family; that she would visit Rome, would become a nun, near the church which was building in Iceland, and would peacefully die there in advanced old age. Whether this story be true, or was concocted and corrupted to flatter the bishops who were descended from her, I leave to the reader's judgment. After saying this Thorstein sank back into his bed. His corpse and those of his companions the other Thorstein honestly took where he had promised to bury them, and selling his farm emigrated with all his property to Ericsfiord, and lived there, but much more respected than before. The corpses were all buried near the Church, which had then been built; but Gudrid departed to her husband's brother, Leif.

CHAPTER VI.

OF THE VOYAGE OF KARLSEFNE TO VINLAND; OF HIS TRAFFIC WITH THE SKRAELINGS, AND OF THE DISPUTES THENCE ARISING, WHICH RESULTED IN OPEN WAR.

In the same year a very wealthy man, Thorfinn, surnamed Karlsefne, an Icelander, son of Thord of Hesthofde, grandson of Snorre by Thorhilde Riupa, daughter of Thord Geller, great grandson of Thord, of the estate Hofde, called also Spakonufellzhofde, starting from Norway to Greenland was hospitably received by Leif, and having gained his consent married Gudrid. He, with sixty sailors formed a partnership to colonize Vinland, the profits to be shared equally. Karlsefne was accompanied by his wife, took with him various kinds of animals, crossed over to settle Vinland and arrived in safety near Leif's tents, which he had received for a loan; there he found stranded on the coast a whale, of the species called REID, and considered one of the largest (being 100 and sometimes even 130 cubits long). This was a matter of much importance for their household stock; but the small and large cattle, and among them a fine bull, having found rich pasture, began to thrive greatly. Then Karlsefne ordered trees to be cut down and polished, and then to be placed on the rocks and dried. And they harvested all the products of the earth and sea, now gathering grapes and again fishing; (I am less convinced of what Bjorn of Skarzda, a distinguished Icelandish historian, inserted into his history, and which was no doubt copied from an ancient manuscript, that wheat grew there.) When the first winter was past and the summer had come, they saw the dwarfs, whom they called Skraelings, rushing in great numbers from the woods, not far from the place where the bull was grazing with the cows; frightened at his dreadful lowing the Skraelings turned to the house of Karlsefne, with their packs, which were filled with various kinds of furs, especially of the sable and of white mice. When they were about to enter at once by the door, they were kept back by the orders of the owner, who differed from them not only in bodily appearance, but also in language; nevertheless, putting down their packs, they exposed their goods for sale, wishing to exchange them for arms, which Karlsefne forbade as dangerous to himself and his men; instead of them he commanded the women to offer them food and refreshments, prepared from milk; having tasted these, they desired only them and nothing else and bartering food for their merchandise, they departed, gorged with food. Meanwhile Karlsefne repeatedly fortified his wooden structures. But in the beginning of winter when his wife had brought forth his son Snorre, the Skraelings returned in much greater numbers than before, provided as on the former occasion with wallets; again milk preparations were given them and paid for with packs thrown over the fences. Perchance Gudrid, who was seated in the house near the infant's cradle, remarked a shadow in the entrance: then a woman attired in a great black cloak, her head covered with linen, dark haired, pale faced, and with eyes of unusual size, too large for one head, entered and approaching addressed her in these words: "What is your name?" Having given it and asked the woman's name in return, she learned that she too was named Gudrid: but when she invited her to be seated, a great sound and noise was heard outside, for one of Karlsefne's servants killed one of the Skraelings, who was about to steal some arms, and immediately the woman, who had been seen by Gudrid alone and by no one else, disappeared. The Skraelings also, betaking themselves to flight, left behind them their wares and their garments. But Karlsefne, thinking that they would return in greater numbers, to avenge the death of their countryman, sent all his men to clear the interior of the woods, that the cattle might the more readily be concealed there, and he ordered ten men to show themselves on the headland, to entice the Skraelings more easily; for the battle-field he selected a spot between the wood and the water, lest his force be surrounded by numbers: the bull was placed before the line of battle. Nor was he mistaken; for the Skraelings flocked thither in great numbers, to their marked loss, for many were slain in the conflict. The bull too which was strange to them, greatly frightened them by his lowing, which was unpleasant to their ears. Among them one man, handsome in build, taller than the rest, was conspicuous and seemed to be the chief. When perchance one of the Skraelings, after seizing an axe that was lying by and looking at it for a while struck it into the head of a comrade and killed him by the blow, the tall man seeing this took it into his hands and examining it for a short time hurled it very far into the sea, seemingly detesting the iron that was forged to slay men. Immediately thereafter, all fleeing in disorder hid in the woods; but Karlsefne after passing the winter, the next spring loaded his ship with vines and other products that grew there, and returning to Greenland, reached the bay of Ericsfjord and wintered there.

VINLAND.

CHAPTER VII.

OF THE FOURTH EXPEDITION TO VINLAND UNDER THE LEADERSHIP OF THORVARD, THE HUSBAND OF FREYDIS, AND TWO ICELANDERS, HELGE AND FIMBOG, OF THE INHUMAN CRUELTY OF FREYDIS AND OF KARLSEFNE'S RETURN TO ICELAND, AND OF HIS DESCENDANTS.

In the very summer that Karlsefne returned to Greenland, two brothers, born in the eastern district of Iceland, landed there from Norway and wintered there. Meantime Freydis, the daughter of Eric the Red, (a bastard according to Bjorn of Skardza), considering at Gardar the plan of revisiting Vinland in the following spring, went to them and invited them to join her in partnership; this was agreed upon with a fixed apportionment of gain and loss, the condition being added that the members of both parties should be equal and consist of thirty men only, fit for bearing arms, besides the women. Then she, having borrowed her brother Leif's tents, immediately broke the agreement about the number of the sailors, embarked five more men on her ship and concealed them until they had reached Vinland. The brothers, who had reached Vinland a little sooner, were bringing their effects into Leif's tent, which she on her arrival indignantly declared to be against the agreement, because it (the tent) had been loaned to her, not to them. They retorted that, an agreement having been made for the common advantage, they had supposed that the use of the tent also was common; nevertheless they declared that they would give way to her frenzy; for that they would not contend with her malice; and taking away their effects, they built another house on the shore. Now she ordered trees to be cut, vines perhaps (for so they are called in the account of the departure), with which she intended to load the ship. At the approach of winter the customary games were begun, but quarrels arising the games did not last long, all intercourse between the brothers and Freydis and her sailors, being for a long time broken off. On a certain morning Freydis, rising from bed without shoes, having put on only her husband's over-garment and having walked unaccompanied to the brothers' tents over the dew-covered ground, stood silent for a while in the doorway, which a sailor who had just gone out had opened; when Fimbog, who alone was awake, remarked this, he asked what was the matter. She called him out to a private conference and led him to a block of wood placed at the side of the tent for use as a bench and there they sat down. Then in answer to her question, how he was pleased there, he replied that he liked the land very well, but that their quarrels without any previous cause displeased him greatly; when she had declared that she too was displeased for the same reason, she stated the cause of her coming: for as she intended to return to Greenland, she said, she wished to exchange her ship for his as being larger, and he promised to give it to her, to please her. After this conversation they parted, Fimbog returning to his bed, she to her husband's. When the latter felt her feet, chill with cold and dripping with moisture, he asked the reason. She, seething with grief and rage, mingled reproaches with wailing, complaining that having gone out to the brothers' tents and asked for an exchange of ships, she had been overwhelmed with blows and covered with lashes, and saying that on account of his listlessness she would be exposed to the insults of all in the future, for that he had not the spirit to avenge her; therefore she had good reason to be homesick after her own country, where owing to the protection of her own family, she had always been and would thereafter be free from every insult and safe; moreover she threatened that if he delayed avenging this most foul insult, she would dissolve her marriage with him. Having embittered her husband by these and similar words, she suddenly stirred him up to call out all his men forthwith to take arms; entering the huts of the other party who were asleep, they bound them, led them forth, and beheaded them. All the men being slain, when the women only (they were five in number) remained and no one wished to slay them, she herself demanded an axe and killed them all with her own hand. Whilst all loathed her deed, she appeared as if triumphing over some exploit, threatened them one by one with death, if they made the matter known in Greenland, and ordered them to say, that the men who had been slain, were living in Vinland. On the approach of spring, she loaded the ship of which she had robbed the brothers with the products of Vinland and prepared it for her return to Greenland; they arrived there in the beginning of summer, while Karlsefne, in the bay of Eriksfiord, was waiting for favorable winds with a well equipped ship, the best that had left Greenland up to that time. But when she (Freydis) felt that the murders could not be kept hidden by fear and threats only, she generously divided the booty among her companions, and moreover bribed every one of them with gifts, because, besides the shame of their infamous gains and the fear of punishment, for they had all a share in the crime, the obligation incurred by accepting her gifts would more efficiently prevent their making known her misdeeds. Trusting to these wily expedients, she staid at home secure and quite wealthy, with her husband, Thorvard by name, who was subject to her orders. But not even so could the dreadful crime be kept concealed, without its being made known to her brother Leif, by the very men who had obeyed her in perpetrating it; he having examined three of them drew out the truth, and cursing his sister, declared that, though he did not wish to put her to death, he prophesied that her offspring would be unlucky. Thereafter Freydis, hated by all as long as she lived, passed a life infamous and devoid of all respect. Karlsefne, having weighed anchor with his wife Gudrid after a prosperous voyage reached Norway, plentifully provided with means; he was greatly honored by the chief men of that country and passed the winter there. But when his ship lay in port ready to sail to Iceland, a certain man of Bremen offered to buy its cornice (it is called HUSASNOTRA) for a quarter of a pound of gold: when he had sold it, he saw that it was made of the wood called MAUSR, previously unknown to him, although brought from Vinland.

(Arngrim thinks that the wood was the MAFHOLTERBAUM, or butcher's broom, (MEUSDORN) which, when used as a binding keeps off the mice, how correctly I know not; that this kind of wood was very precious appears from the life of Harold the Haughty, who presented a drinking bowl (of this wood) as a magnificent gift to Thorer of Steige who called it the Royal Cup. When he had afterwards arrived at the bay in Eastern Greenland called Skagafjord, and there passed the winter he bought the estate of Glaumba, and erected a building that was magnificent considering the place, and dwelt there: as long as he lived he was respected among the foremost men, and from him thereafter sprang a famous line. After his death his wife, after long presiding over the house, with her son Snorre, born in Vinland, went to Rome. On her return thence she learned that he, (Snorre) had built a church at home. Free from worldly cares henceforth, she devoted herself to God, having become a nun, and to the end of her life worked for holier ends. Snorre's son Thorgeir was the father of Ingveld, the mother of Bishop Brand, and Snorre's daughter Hallfrid was the mother of Runoff, the father of Bishop Thorlak. Snorre's own brother was Bjorn, the father of Thoruna, who begot Bishop Bjarne. Now what has been here related, as the Cod. Flat. page 288, declares, was copied down from the lips of Karlsefne. But it differs greatly from the story followed by Bjorn of Skardza, although the latter is redolent of the spirit of antiquity, and interspersed with very ancient verses, which Hauk, the judge (lagmare, nomophylax) collected: he flourished in 1406; it will be worth while to give a summary of this version.

CHAPTER VIII.

OF LEIF'S JOURNEY TO NORWAY TO KING OLAF TRYGGVESON; OF HIS DISCOVERY OF VINLAND ON HIS RETURN, AND OF HIS SUCCESSFUL PREACHING OF THE CHRISTIAN RELIGION IN HIS NATIVE COUNTRY.

He, Hauk, calls the wife of Eric the Red Thorhilde, and their sons Thorstein and Leif, uncommon men, of whom the former always remained with his father; and never was there in Greenland any man who excelled him in endowments of mind and body. Leif, on the contrary, he tells us, sailed away from Greenland, and first came to the Hebrides; there, having tarried a long time in summer, he kept company with Thorgunna, a woman of noble descent, but skilled in occult arts, or rather a sorceress. When she wished to accompany him, as he was leaving, Leif is reported to have asked whether this could be done with the consent of her relatives. She replied that she did not care for this; whereupon he replied, that with so small a retinue, he could not carry off so noble a lady. She declared that she was pregnant by him and would undoubtedly give birth to a son, whom she promised or threatened to send to him, as soon as his years would permit, saying that she would follow herself; moreover she foretold, that this son would one day be no more useful to him, than his departure at that time was agreeable to her. And Leif departing presented her a finger-ring as well as a cloak of Greenland stuff, and a belt adorned with animal's teeth. That boy, called Thorgils, subsequently came to Greenland and Leif recognized him as his son. He is also said to have come to Iceland in the summer, which preceded the prodigies of Froda (which cannot at all be correct, for these, according to the Eyrbyggva Saga, fall in the year of our Lord one thousand, which is the year in which the boy was born.) Having thereafter lived in Greenland, he is said before his death, to have seemingly performed some prodigy. What this was, I find nowhere explained more in full.

Leif sailing in autumn from the Hebrides to Norway, was held in high honor by King Olaf Tryggveson, and was commissioned by him to plant the Christian Religion in his native country in the following summer; for Leif is said to have been regarded by the King as a remarkable and a lucky man. On that voyage, going astray for a long time from the right course, he is said to have come upon unknown lands, in a situation where no one before had suspected that there was land. The soil spontaneously produced wheat; vines also grew there as well as the trees called MAUSR: now those trees are said to have been so large, that timbers fit for house-building were taken from them. On that voyage, it is related, he rescued a shipwrecked man, and on his return he made known the Christian Religion and exhibited letters of King Olaf, sure proofs of his royal will, and published the glories of the new faith in many words. His father, (Eric the Red) refused to embrace it, but his (Eric's) wife Thorhilde immediately accepted it and had a church built, where she with those who were converted, devoted herself to prayer. Afterward that church was called Thorhilde's Church. Having become a Christian she separated from her husband's bed and board, at which the latter was vexed. In the following winter Leif converted fifty Reppas or villages to Christ: Bjorn of Skardza relates that this event took place in the eastern district of the country.

CHAPTER IX.

OF THE FRUITLESS ATTEMPT OF LEIF'S BROTHER THORSTEIN TO EXPLORE VINLAND; OF HIS RETURN TO GREENLAND; OF HIS MARRIAGE WITH THORBJORN'S DAUGHTER GUDRID, OF HER EDUCATION AND ANCESTORS IN ICELAND.

Afterwards several Greenlanders were seized by the desire to explore the country found by Leif, the chief of whom was Thorstein Ericson, a wise and popular man. However the eyes of all were turned to Eric to be the leader of the expedition, for he was a lucky man as his discovery of Greenland proved and moreover distinguished by his experience: after long refusing he finally yielded to the requests of his friends. The ship of Thorbjorn Vifillson, (of whom more hereafter) was selected for the purpose and fitted out with twenty sailors and scant provisions. Early on a certain morning Eric rode away from home and first hid a box full of gold and silver; but on his way he fell from his horse, broke two ribs and severely injured his arm where it joined the shoulder. He therefore bade his wife Thorhilde to raise the hidden treasure, for he owned that he had met with the accident as a punishment for hiding it. Then they sailed from Ericsfjord amid great joy; but for a long time and wearily they strayed from their course, for they had Iceland in sight and also saw Irish birds; after being driven across the ocean they again arrived at the bay of Ericsfjord towards winter, and all the sailors, who had no homes, were liberally supported by Eric the Red during winter. In the same winter Thorstein, the son of Eric the Red, with the consent of his father married Gudrid, the daughter of Thorbjorn Vifillson: of her parents and her education as a girl a short account must be given. Vifill, the father of this Thorbjorn, was one of the companions of Queen Audr, an immensely rich woman, the mother of Thorstein the Red, and in fact Vifill was sold into slavery among the Irish captives before Audr restored him to freedom. But when she divided estates among her nautical followers and had passed him by, he is said to have asked why she did so; but she answered that it did not matter, for that wherever he would be, he would be a great man. However she gave him a valley called after his name Vifilsdal, where he afterwards dwelt to the end of his life. His sons were Thorgeir and Thorbjorn; they married the daughters of Einar of Laugabrekka, the son of Sigmund, the grandson of Ketil, Thistel, who gave his name to a bay, (Thistilsfjord): the former married Arnora, the latter Hallveiga, by whom Thorbjorn begat the above-mentioned Gudrid, of whom we are speaking, a maiden of wonderful beauty; her Orm, a wealthy man, of the estate of Arnestap, in the western quarter of Iceland, and his wife Halldise brought up. Her hand was refused to a certain Einar, in spite of his wealth, which he had made by trading, merely because he was born of a freedman, though the girl's father Thorbjorn, greatly needed means to support the expenses of his family. When Thorbjorn saw that his means were reduced, and his family could not be maintained with the same splendor as before, he preferred to plough the soil rather than give up his accustomed magnificence. He therefore departed to Greenland to his friend Eric the Red, whom he had helped in Iceland with money and men. For when Eric left Iceland he promised his friends that he would not fail to help them in need, if the occasion to do so should ever present itself. With thirty sailors and among the number Orm and his wife and family, who could not bear to desert him, Thorbjorn left his country and was borne to Cape Herjulfsnes, and there hospitably received and generously supported with all his sailors, by a wealthy man, the foremost of the place, Thorkel by name. But a sickness arose on the voyage and spread among the sailors, and Orm, as well as his wife, was carried off thereby.

CHAPTER X.

OF A CERTAIN PROPHETIC WOMAN; OF HER APPEARANCE AND OF HER SKILL IN THE MAGIC (SEIDIC) ART.

At that time a dreadful famine afflicted Greenland and many desired to know how long it would last and hoped that they would easily find this out during the winter, from a certain prophetic woman, Thorbjorg by name. She was wont to stop in that country with those who, eager to know the future and their own fortunes, invited her to stay with them. But as Thorkel was looked upon as by far the most prominent man of the district, it seemed incumbent on him to take this burden upon himself and satisfy the wishes of the people. Thorkel therefore invited her to his home, and, as usual, treated the woman with respect; she was the sole survivor of nine sisters, all prophetesses. A lofty seat on a platform was prepared for her and a pillow filled with cock's feathers placed under her; the appearance of the wise woman is described as follows: She put on a dark blue cloak tied with thongs (they call them TINGLA MOTTUL) adorned down to its lowest border with little stones; around her neck hung little glass balls; on her head she wore drawn up a cowl of black lambskins and white catskins; in her hand she carried a staff, crowned with a brass globe studded with little stones; she wore a girdle (Thomas Barthol translates "HUNLANDICD" according to the words of the copy, which he followed; this reads HYNDSKAN LINDA; mine reads HNIOSKU LINDA. i. e. 'dry girdle or zone' which makes no sense: I conjecture that it should be written HUNDSKINS LINDA, i. e., 'a dogskin girdle,' for the various other skins suggest this selection;) from it hung an immense pouch, in which were stowed the instruments of her magic art; to her feet she attached shaggy calfskin shoes with long latchets, at the ends of which were large tin balls: on her hands she wore catskin gloves, shaggy and white on the inside. All saluted her respectfully, but she received their greetings, according as she favored them. Thorkel having taken her hand led her to the seat prepared for her, and begged her to look at his house, family, flocks and herds with care; but she in reply to most of his remarks was silent. The dishes served to her were porridge of goat's milk, and the hearts of all the kinds of animals that were found there; she used a brass spoon, a knife with its point broken off, whose handle was made of whale's teeth, and which was encircled by two brass bands. When the meal was ended, the tables were removed. Thorkel went up to her, asking whether she had had an open view, how she was pleased with the house and the ways and dispositions of its inmates, and how soon she could know, what was to be investigated. She answered that she could give no reply, till she had slept there a night. On the following afternoon, all things necessary for magic (seidic) incantations were furnished. But first of all she asked for women, who knew a song called Vardlokr, which was absolutely necessary to practice the Seidic art; but no one was found that knew it. Then Gudrid, Thorbjorn's daughter, answered: "I am not a sorceress and know nothing of the magic art; however Halldise, my teacher in Iceland taught me a song called Vardlokr," "Indeed" said Thorkel, "you are blessed for your knowledge." Then Gudrid replied: "Magic is the only thing I will in no wise abet; for I am a Christian." From this remark, compared with what has been said above, it follows that Vinland was discovered after the year 1000. But the wise woman suggested that she could oblige her friends without offense to her religion. Overcome by this temptation of Satan, the tender maiden sang a magical song with a sweet melody to the admiration of all: meanwhile the women stood around the platform on which the sorceress sat. The song being ended the sorceress thanked Gudrid, saying that many and various spirits, who were before about to leave and refused to obey her, allured by the song and the sweet notes of the songstress had approached, and that many things that were before concealed, had become manifest to her. She foretold to Thorkel that the corn famine would not last beyond winter and that it would be relieved when the weather would grow mild, that the disease which had thus far harrassed them would cease faster than they thought; that she would recompense Gudrid for the aid given her, that she (Gudrid) would soon marry the greatest man in Greenland, that the marriage would not last long however, as the fates recalled her to Iceland, that there a great and distinguished offspring would be born of her, which was illumined by brighter rays than she could bear to look upon; having then saluted Gudrid in a friendly way she dismissed her. Afterwards persons, who wished to know certain matters, consulted her, each for himself; and she, freely answering the questions, unravelled what she was asked. Then she was called by messengers to other estates: on her departure, Thorbjorn, Gudrid's father, who had refused to be present at the impious ceremonies and the magic rite and had gone to another estate, was recalled. The words of the witch were verified in every respect, for both the famine and the death ceased on the approach of spring, as well as the plague that had begun with Thorbjorn's sailors. Thorbjorn, therefore, taking his vessel from Cape Herjulfsnes, came to the bay of Ericsfjord and when his arrival had been celebrated with great joy by Eric, was entertained hospitably with all his family during all the winter or rather during the rest of the winter, (for the ancients reckoned the early part of spring as winter); but the following spring Eric pointed out to Thorbjorn some land in Stockanes, where he built quite a roomy house and laid out a magnificent estate, where he dwelt as long as he lived. Then Thorstein, the son of Eric the Red, married Gudrid with Thorbjorn's consent; the Codex Flateyensis says, that she married Thorstein, as a widow, having previously been married to Thorer whom Leif saved when shipwrecked. The nuptials were celebrated with great pomp at Brattahlide, during Eric's lifetime, contrary to the report of the Codex Flateyensis.

CHAPTER XI.

OF THE INFECTIOUS DISEASE THAT AROSE AMONG THORSTEIN'S CREW; OF HIS DEATH AND A PRODIGY, AND OF THE ANCIENT MODE OF BURIAL IN GREENLAND; OF THE ARRIVAL OF KARLSEFNE AND HIS MARRIAGE TO GUDRID.

The half of the estate called Lisufjord (I should prefer to read "of a certain estate in Lisufjord") Thorstein owned, the other half a namesake, who had also a wife, named Sigrid (Grimhild in the Cod. Flat.) Thither Thorstein, the son of Eric the Red, betook himself with his wife, at the beginning of autumn, and there he passed the winter; but an infectious disease invaded the entire house. A steward named Gard, a man disliked by many, fell a victim and then the rest, and finally the plague seized Thorstein Ericson also, and Sigrid the other Thorstein's wife, and they lay ill at the same time. But Sigrid, who was ailing, accompanied by Thorstein Ericson's wife one evening retired to a privy where, the ailment increasing in violence, she was unable to repress her wails. Having heard her wails, Gudrid regretted that they had gone too far to be heard, when crying for help, and urged her to return in haste; Sigrid answered that she was stopped by ghosts, that were standing at the door and that among the number she recognized herself and Gudrid's husband Thorstein. After a while she advised that they return, for the ghosts had vanished; but she said that she saw Thorstein holding a scourge, about to lash the rest. After they had returned home, she died the same night and a coffin was prepared to bury her corpse. But as her husband Thorstein had taken some oarsmen to the harbor, who were about to go on a fishing expedition, he was hastily recalled by a messenger from the sick Thorstein, who feared danger from his (the other Thorstein's) wife Sigrid, lately deceased; she had risen from the dead and harassing him seemed to be about to get under his bed-clothes. Thorstein (Sigrid's husband) returned, and finding that she had entered Thorstein's bed buried a large axe in her breast. But Thorstein Ericson died towards nightfall. But when night had worn on a little, he raised himself and bade his wife Gudrid be called, declaring that this hour was allowed him by God to settle his affairs. The host, therefore, roused her from sleep, made known to her her husband's commands, and said, he did not know what to advise her in the matter. But she answered that this prodigy would be memorable. that trusting to the Divine Mercy, which had always been kind to her, she would go to her husband and learn what he had to say; for, if any danger threatened, she would not escape it, nor would she be the cause why her deceased husband should wander about after death; that there was great reason to fear that this might happen, if she proved faithless to him. On approaching the dead man, it seemed to her, she saw him pouring forth tears; afterwards he whispered some words in her ear privately, known to her alone. But in public he spoke as follows : Blessed are they who embrace the Christian religion, for it is based on Divine grace and mercy; few however religiously observe it ; moreover, from the very establishment of religion in Greenland, the dead have been sinfully buried in unconsecrated ground, the funeral rites being scantily celebrated. He, so he continued, wished to be carried to church with the others who had died there, except Gard alone, because he had troubled those who had died thus far during the winter. That man, he warned them, ought to be burned as soon as possible in the avenging flames. Then he foretold some of his wife's future destinies and bade her to beware of marrying any Greenlander and to give her money to the Church, and partly also to the poor. Having said this he again fell asleep. A similar story is told in the seventh book of "Chronicles" by Dithmar of Merseburg. It was customary in Greenland, and in other half-christian or even uncivilized lands that were visited by ships, to bury the dead in unconsecrated ground, to place sticks over their breasts for the purpose of marking the grave of the buried man; after a lapse of time, however long, the priest pulled out the sticks, poured some water into the hole by way of lustration and performed burial songs. Thorstein was carried to the church along with the other dead. But Gudrid went to her husband's father, Eric the Red, who treated her as a daughter. Shortly after her father Thorbjorn of Stockanes died; as she was his sole heir, Eric took upon himself the whole care of her patrimony and administered it faithfully. At the same time two ships from Iceland came to the bay of Ericsfjord : the one was commanded by Thorfinn Karlsefne, accompanied by Snorre Thorbrandson, of the estate of Skogastrand on Alftafjord bay in Iceland, and forty sailors ; the other was commanded by Bjarne Grimolfson, from the district adjoining Breidafjord Bay, together with Thorhall Gamlason from the eastern part of the island, and carried as many sailors; (the Cod. Flateyensis says that Karlsefne came from Norway.) Now Eric the Red setting out with several natives to trade with these was received kindly and invited to take as a gift all he wished, of the goods for sale. Unwilling to be outdone in generosity, he invited the entire crews of both ships to his house to pass the winter, and they, pleased with his generous hospitality, took all their merchandise thither: and they found buildings large enough to receive them and everything was furnished generously. As Christmas approached, Eric grew sad. Karlsefne remarking this, asked the cause of this sudden change, promising to pay liberally for what Eric had with great generosity spent on them. The latter replied that they were most welcome guests, inasmuch as they received what he offered them with grateful hearts; but that he was not disposed to cause loss to his friends; he regretted that when after leaving him they would come to other lands, they might justly complain, that nowhere did they rembember the Christmas or Yule festival to have been celebrated more scantily than at Brattahlide, in Greenland with Eric the Red. Karlsefne saw that this trouble could be easily dispelled, for he had corn and barley in plenty to furnish the banquet with all the generosity Eric wished, and he allowed Eric to bring it home. Eric did this and nowhere is a more splendid festival said to have been celebrated in a poor country. At the end of the feast, Karlsefne spoke to Eric of marrying his daughter-in-law Gudrid, for he was her guardian, and easily obtained her hand; the wedding was celebrated with great splendor at Brattahlide, and there the winter was passed. And this is the story of Gudrid and her parents; let us return to Vinland.

CHAPTER XII.

OF KARLSEFNE'S VOYAGE TO VINLAND AND OF HIS COMPANIONS ON THAT EXPEDITION, VIZ: BJARNE, THORHALL AND THORVARD, THE SON-IN-LAW OF ERIC THE RED, AND ERIC'S SON THORVALD.

During the same winter the conversation often turned upon a voyage to Vinland (according to these documents, however, Leif is not reported to have given it this name). In the beginning of spring Karlsefne and Snorre fitted out their ship for the expedition; Bjarne and Thorhall, whom we have mentioned before, embarking in their own ship, were taken as partners in the undertaking. A third ship was commanded by Thorvard, the son-in-law of Eric the Red, who had married his illegitimate daughter Freydis, and by Eric's son Thorvald, and these were accompanied by Thorhall surnamed the hunter. This man tall in stature, of great strength, gigantic build and dark complexion, rudely and sharply spoken and of gloomy and forbidding appearance, had long followed the family of Eric the Red and spent his summers in hunting and his winters as steward. This man always suggested dark plans to Eric, for he was careless in practising the Christian religion, but very well acquainted with pathless and desert places and solitudes. One hundred and forty, (but as has been often said, the hundred consisted of twelve tens) sailors took part in this expedition. They sailed in the first place to the western part of inhabited Greenland, thence to the Bjarney Islands, for a night and a day (TVO DAEGR), thence southwards, till land came in sight. There many large cliffs projected twelve cubits broad; there was also a large number of foxes; this land they called HELLULAND. Thence they sailed for a day and night toward the southeast by east, until they saw a wooded land abounding in animals; southeast by south of this main land lay an island. There they killed a bear and from this circumstance called the island Bjarney and the main land Markland:

thence they sailed southward until they reached a certain headland: there the hull of a ship was found and the cape was therefore called Kjalarnes and they named the shore FURDUSTRAND, or wonderful, or wonderfully vast strand. Then the land was indented with bays, and after entering one of these Karlsefne sent forth a man and woman of the Scotch race, so swift in running that they outran wild animals; these King Olaf Tryggvason had presented to Leif when departing. The man's name was Hake, the woman's Hekja. He gave them a night and two days to explore the land and ordered them to start southward; at the appointed time they returned, the one bearing a cluster of grapes, the other an ear of wheat. Their garment, called KIAPAL which was sleeveless and open at the sides, was at the same time a covering for the head, and a clasp fastened it between the thighs. Then setting sail they entered another bay, near whose entrance lay an island, surrounded by currents, and thence called Straumsey: there they wintered and landed their cattle. The land was very fertile but produced neither vines nor grain. Here forgetting the things necessary to support themselves during the winter, which must be collected in autumn, they occupied themselves in exploring the country. But in the island there was so great a number of the ducks, whose feathers are most prized and which are called by the Norse AERD or contracted AER, that they could hardly walk over it without destroying the eggs. But winter coming on and fishing and hunting being impossible, a dearth of provisions followed. They therefore prayed to God; but when their prayers were not heard as soon as they wished, Thorhall the hunter set out; after seeking him two days and a night, they at last found him lying on a steep ridge, with mouth wide open and murmuring something: to their questions, what he was doing there, he made no reply; however, he went home with them. Shortly after a sea-monster was cast on the shore, but no one knew what kind of fish it was; when they cooked and eat it, it seemed not to agree with them. Then said Thorhall, the Red one (he meant Thor) is after all more powerful than your Christ, for with this did he reward the song which I sang in his honor; for he has seldom failed me. Having learned this, they threw the fish into the sea and committed themselves and all they had to God. Soon the weather grew mild and the sea, now quiet, was fit for fishing; thenceforth they had enough of food by land and sea, for there was also abundance of game.

CHAPTER XIII.

OF THORHALL THE HUNTER, WHO IS DRIVEN BY STORMS TO IRELAND AND THERE HELD IN BONDAGE TO THE END OF HIS LIFE; OF THE FURTHER EXPLORATION OF VINLAND BY KARLSEFNE AND HIS COMPANIONS; OF THE LAND AND WATER PRODUCTS THERE; OF THE DRESS OF THE SKRAELINGS AND THEIR TRAFFIC, AND OF THE DISPUTES AND WARS THENCE ARISING, WHICH HOWEVER END IN THE SKRAELINGS SUSTAINING GREATER LOSS.

Thorhall the hunter, with nine sailors, passing Furdustrand with ship turned northward, sought Vinland. Two pieces of verse are extant, sung by him whilst he brought water into the ship, which have the true flavor of antiquity and in fact are marked by the genius of that age. Having doubled Kialarnes whilst he was sailing westward, a storm arising from the west drove him to Ireland, where he and his men passed a wretched existence, being kept in cruel bondage, until they were punished with death on account of their hatred of Christianity and their impiety. This story is reported to have been brought to Iceland by merchants. But Karlsefne with Snorre and Bjarne, sailing southward, in order to seek in the opposite direction, after a long voyage came to a place where a river rising in a marsh emptied into the sea; but his ship could not enter the river, because long estuaries intervened and the tide was running low: therefore they moored her at the mouth of the stream; there the level country produced wheat, the hills native vines; all the streams were full of fish, which, when ditches had been dug to the verge of the sea, so as to receive the tide water, were carried into these and caught with the hands whilst the tide lasted or receded; this kind of fish they called SACRED because they were caught without labor, I fancy. Many and various kinds of animals wandered over the fertile meadows and through the woods. After passing there two weeks spent in refreshing their bodies by sports without a sign of human cultivation appearing, they beheld one morning approaching them many boats covered with hides: in them javelins were raised as signals and whirled around, following the motion of the sun and creaking with the friction. Snorre Thorbrandson and Karlsefne interpreted them to be signs of peace and advised that they should, carry a white shield at their head and go to meet the strangers; when they saw this they rowed up vigorously and landed, wondering at the Greenlanders; nor did the latter wonder less at them, for they were swarthy, of ill-favored appearance, with short hair, broad cheek bones and large eyes; then after a short delay, having passed the headland, the strangers turned their boats southward. Thorfinn with his companions had passed a winter without snow, in huts, which he had erected in different places nearer to or farther away from the sea; the cattle feeding on grassy fields needed no other fodder. But in the beginning of spring, hide-covered boats, swarming in the bay, brought parties of Skraelings with signals of peace: they were received with white shields and induced to land. Then they bartered on the one side pieces of red cloth a span broad, with which the strangers were wonderfully pleased and which they wrapped about their heads, on the other side fur skins; when the red cloth proved insufficient to satisfy the wishes of those who asked for them, pieces of a finger's breadth were given them; Karlsefne's bull, perchance rushed out from the wood and so frightened them with its horrid bellowing, that they forthwith betook themselves to flight and staid away for three weeks. When these were passed an immense number of small skiffs arrived and seemed almost to cover the whole sea; and they whirled their signals not as before, when they meant peace, in the direction of the sun's motion, but in the opposite direction. Karlsefne recognizing this as a declaration of war ordered a red shield to be raised and went to meet them with an armed force. But the Skraelings rushing out of their ships, assailed them at a distance with missiles hurled from slings, and then threw a dark blue ball, not unlike a sheep's stomach stuck on a spear, on the ground above Karlsefne's soldiers, but kept back the spear; this ball striking the earth with great noise, caused such dread and terror, that Karlsefne with his companions saw their only safety in flight. They rushed along the upper river bank in a disorderly manner and seemed to be surrounded on all sides, both on land and sea, by the numbers of the enemy; nor could their flight be stayed until they reached some steep rocks. There recovering their courage, they resisted bravely. But Freydis, seeing her countrymen fleeing, came up fearlessly and cried out: "How do you, warriors, flee from those dwarfs, whom you can slaughter like sheep: forsooth had I arms, I should hack them into pieces more boldly than any of you." Her words nowise encouraged the panic-stricken fugitives. Therefore, as she could not follow them, when they fled to the woods, (for she was pregnant) it seemed wholly unlikely that she would escape the Skraelings. While she was pursued by them she came upon the corpse of one of her countrymen; it was Thorbrand Snorreson, whose skull had been crushed with a stone. Having seized his sword, she prepared to fight. But when she saw several running up to her, she uncovered her breast and approached it to the sword. Frightened by this, the Skraelings fled to their boats and departed in great haste. Karlsefne, having praised Freydis, began to consider what men they were that had rushed forth from the woods; at last it was found that they were pure illusions, and that there were no forces except those which had been in the boats and attacked them. Then he took to bandaging the wounded. Two Norsemen were lost in that battle, but many Skraelings. One of the latter, when he had come upon the corpse of a Greenlander and picked up his axe that lay next to him, struck it into a block of wood; but when the

Skraelings noticed that the axe was fit for cutting and sharp, one after the other tested its sharpness by cutting wood. But when one man made the same experiment on a stone, he broke the axe. Now when it was not found as fit to cut stone as wood, it was looked upon with scorn and thrown into the sea with a great effort. Karlsefne foreseeing that there would be constant danger from the natives, decided to abandon the land, however pleasant it might be. Intending therefore to return to Greenland, as he sailed northward, he came upon five sleeping Skraelings, dressed in garments of skins. Next to them lay hollow pieces of wood, like reeds, filled with animal marrow mixed with blood. Conjecturing by this sign that they had been driven into exile, the Norsemen killed them. Afterward they were borne to a headland so full of wild beasts, that it was almost entirely covered with their excrements, for there the beasts stopped over night. The Norsemen called it MIKIUNES from the manure. Thence they came to the bay of Straumsfjord, where plenty of all kinds of necessaries were found. Others relate that Karlsefne, together with Snorre, when he landed the first time at Straumsey, set sail southward from that harbor with one ship manned with forty sailors, for the purpose of seeking Vinland; that he left behind him the hundred others, including his wife and Bjarne; that not quite two months passed before their return and that he brought them thence to Vinland, where the winter was passed. Then Karlsefne, setting out with a single ship to find Thorhall the hunter, by sailing northward doubled Cape Kialarnes, and changing his course slightly towards the west, coasted along the land that lay on his left, which was an unbroken desert interrupted by no cultivated district, until entering the mouth of a river that flowed from east to west, he found a suitable harbor for his ship.

CHAPTER XIV.

OF THE SLAYING OF THORVALD, THE SON OF ERIC THE RED, BY A ONE-FOOTED BEING, OF KARLSEFNE'S SOJOURN AT STRAUMSFJORD FOR THREE WINTERS, OF THE BIRTH OF HIS SON SNORRE, OF THE CAPTIVITY OF TWO SKRAELINGS, OF THE DANGEROUS VOYAGE OF BJARNE GRIMOLFSON IN THE IRISH OCEAN, OF HIS HONORABLE CONDUCT TOWARD A CERTAIN ICELANDER IN EXTREME PERIL OF LIFE, OF KARLSEFNE'S RETURN TO ICELAND AND OF HIS DESCENDANTS.

One morning on the shore something was seen to move; when they had shouted at it, a one-footed being, rising up near the bank of the river, where the ship stood at anchor, rushed forth and immediately buried an arrow in the flank of Thorvald Ericson. When Thorvald had drawn it out and seen his own fat clinging to it, he said: "Fertile indeed is the land we have found, though we are hardly allowed to enjoy it." Shortly after he died of this wound, Karlsefne with his companions pursuing the unipede as he swiftly ran towards the north, at times had him in view, until he rushed headlong into a certain bay. This adventure one of them celebrated in a song, which exists to this day. Thence sailing northward they thought they saw the country of the unipedes and deemed it useless to run further risks. But the mountains that begin at the harbor in Vinland called Hoop, they found were continued in an uninterrupted range by the very mountains in the place where they were staying, and that in the middle was Straumsfjord, equidistant from there and from Hoop. Then they passed the first winter in Straumsfjord, (whither they seem to have been driven back by the winds) where a dangerous dispute arose about the common use of the women which the unmarried men claimed should be promiscuous. At the beginning of autumn Karlsefne's son Snorre, who had been born there and was now three years old, set sail from Vinland. Thence, their sails filled with the south wind, they came to Markland; here they found five Skraelings, one bearded, two women and as many boys; the rest got off and escaped into the earth (where perchance they had haunts;) but the boys were caught. Being afterwards brought away and taught the language of Greenland and made acquainted with Christian rites, they said that their mothers name was VETTHILDE, and their fathers name VAEGE. Two kings, they reported, ruled the Skraelings, one called AVALLDAINNA, the other VALLDIDIDA. Among them there were no houses, their place being supplied by caves and dens; facing their country was another, which was inhabited by men dressed in white garments, and terrible on account of the noise they made, before whom spears were born, from which hung cloths. It was believed that they described HVITRA MANNA LAND or White Man's Land, or HIBERNIA MAGNA. Bjarne Grimolfson was swept away by a tempest to the Irish Ocean. When the sea, which was full of worms, that gnawed and pierced the ship, foiled the efforts of the men that baled out the ship, and the water filled it, it began gradually to sink in the waves. They had a boat covered with a tar made from seal's grease: that kind of boats the worms never perforate (they are called SELTJORU.) As this could contain only one-half of the sailors and all had not the means of escaping, Bjarne ordered them to determine by lot, without regard for any one's rank, who were to go in the boat. No one opposed so fair a proposal. The lot favored him among others. As he entered the boat an Icelander, who by lot was left behind, cried out: "Will you abandon me here?" Bjarne said that it was done by the decision of the lot. "And yet," answered the other, "you promised my father in Iceland that we should share the same lot." "Be it so," answered Bjarne, since you cling so desperately to life, enter the boat, for I shall willingly yield you my place." And so returning to his ship he preferred to life faith and honor, the loss of which he dreaded much more than present death that stared him in the face. The skiff arrived safe with Bjarne's companions at Dublin, a celebrated city of Ireland. But Bjarne with the rest, all think, was swallowed up in the waves, for nothing further was heard of him. By what right he sacrificed his life, granted to him by God, I shall not discuss; but surely he left to all posterity a remarkable example of good faith, which he would by no means have imperilled, had he taken advantage of the favors of fortune. In the following summer Karlsefne is reported to have crossed to Iceland with his wife and to have betaken himself to his mother, on the estate of Reinarnes. Hauk, NOMOPHYLAX or chief judge of Iceland, about the year 1294, compiled the book of which the above are extracts, and which is called HAUK'S BOK or Hauk's book after his name, from the writings of the monk Gunnlaug, who died in the year 1219, and from several other old chronicles, both pagan and Christian. He enumerates his ancestors from Thorfinn Karlsefne, beyond the genealogy contained in the Codex Flateyensis, as follows: Karlsefne's son Snorre had a daughter Steinvor, the wife of Eniar of the manor of Grund, the grandson of Ketill, the great-grandson of Thorvald Krok, the great-great-grandson of Thorer, of the manor of Espishol. By her he begat a son Thorstein, called Ranglat, or the wicked, the father of Gudrun, the wife of Jorund, of the manor of Kelldum. Their daughter Halla bore Flose; the daughter of Flose, Valgerdis, was the mother of the chief judge Erlend the Strong, the father of our chief judge Hauk who is the ninth from Karlsefne. Another daughter of Flose, who was sixth from Karlsefne, was Thordis the mother of Ingibjorg, called the Rich, whose daughter was Hallbera, Abbess of the monastery of Reinenes. Many other distinguished families in Iceland are said to have been descended from Karlsefne and Gndrid. And this is the story the Antiquities relate of Vinland; many details, it is true, contradict one another; but I abstain from examining these.

CHAPTER XV.

ADAM OF BREMEN'S STORY OF VINLAND CONSISTENT WITH THE ABOVE; HIS GREAT MISTAKE REGARDING ITS POSITION; OLAF RUDBECK NO LESS ERRONEOUSLY IDENTIFIES VINLAND WITH FINLAND; THE STORY OF THE POSITION OF GREAT IRELAND; OF ARE THE ICELANDER AND THE PITCH OF THE GREENLANDERS.

"Moreover," says Adam of Bremen, he (*i. e.*, Sven Astritharson, King of Denmark) spoke of one other island found by many in that ocean, (which washes Norway and even Finnmark) an island called Winland, because vines grow wild there; that corn also abounds there without being sown, we have found to be proven, not by some storied opinion but by the undoubted history of the Danes." This statement compared with our narrative proves that the report about Vinland seemed at that time not idle, but to merit undoubting belief, because it was supported by the experience and testimony of reliable men; for Adam of Bremen lived at the time of Harold the Haughty, King of Norway. Now Harold began to reign in the forty-sixth or rather the forty-fifth year after Vinland was first discovered and afterwards settled. Concerning these events he adds to his recital: "Beyond this island (he has been speaking of Vinland) no other habitable land is found in that ocean; but all beyond is full of intolerable ice and unbounded darkness; this fact Marcianus mentions, saying that after one day's sail beyond Thyle the sea is frozen solid. This was lately tested by Harold, the most experienced chief of the Northmen; for having explored with ships the latitudes of the northern ocean, when the limits of the ceasing world were wrapt in darkness before his eyes, he escaped with difficulty the immense depth of the abyss by retracing his steps." Olaf Rudbeck, in chapter 7, paragraph 8, page 291 of his *Atlantica*, writes as follows on this passage: "Something like this no doubt had of old persuaded Adam of Bremen that in the extreme north, near the sea of ice, was situated an island that produced the vine, and was for that reason called Vinland. This he believed on the authority of the Danes, however, as he himself does not hesitate to state on page 37 of his work on the situation of Denmark; but that he was deceived either by the credulity of the Danes or by his own, is clearly shown by the similarity of the name of Finland, a province belonging to our kingdom, for which in Snorro and the History of the Kings the name of Vinland occurs more than once, and whose headland stretches into the extreme north and even to the sea of ice." He thinks that by Vinland Adam of Bremen understood Finland, and that he took the Finnish ale for wine, though that drink is common to the Fins and other northern nations and can hardly be mistaken for grapes and vines, which, Adam of Bremen thinks, grow wild in Vinland. And that he was not deceived by the Danes, as Rudbeck supposes, is plain from the facts we have stated. But where the name of Vinland occurs in Snorro and the Histories of the Kings, I have not up to this time found out.

Concerning the Great Ireland spoken of, which the ancients call White Man's Land, or Albania, the Origins of Iceland say, that it is separated from Ireland or Hibernia by a distance which you can measure by a six day's voyage towards the west, and they place it near Vinland. Thither, as the same book relates, Are Marson, the great-grandson of Ulf Skialg, who first settled the district of Reikjanes, in the western districts of Iceland, was driven by a storm: there he was first initiated into the mysteries of Christianity, and there although he was not allowed to depart, he was well treated and held in great honor. Hrafn, called the Limerick-trader, from his frequent voyages to Limerick, a city of Ireland, first brought this report to Iceland, and Thorkel Geiterson affirmed, that the same story was afterwards related in the Saga of Thorfinn, Earl of the Orkneys. This Are was the cousin of Thorhild (whom others call Thiodhild) the wife of

Eric the Red, who discovered Greenland. For Jorund, the other son of Ulf Skialg, and the brother of Mar by his wife Thorbjorg, called Knarrabringa, begat this Thorhild. The genealogy of Ulf Skialg we have traced from Hjorleif the Gallant, king of Hordia, as set down in his life. Pitch from seal's fat is said to be used by the Greenlanders alone; they hang up oil fried from seal's fat, and put it into boats of skin to dry, until it thickens, then color it black and besmear the ships. This method Bjorn of Skardza described; to me it seems more likely that it can be dissolved, unless something else be added to the seal's fat.

CHAPTER XVI.

OF THE VOYAGES OF THE SAXON BISHOP JONES, AND OF ERIC, BISHOP OF GREENLAND, TO VINLAND, AND OF GUDLEIF GUDLAUGSON.

The appendix to the Landnama Book relates that Jones or Johannes, a Saxon Bishop, (the Hungrvaka book, which is written on the history of the bishops of Iceland, asserts that he was an Irishman, or Hibernian,) after first preaching the Christian faith for four years in Iceland, set out thence for Vinland, in order to convert its people, and finally sealed his mission there by suffering torture and death.

In the year 1121, Eric, bishop of Greenland, visited Vinland. His family, the book on the Origins of Iceland, part 1, On the general occupation, chapter 13, page 15, traces back to the first settlers of Iceland. Eric's father being Gnup, Gnup's Birning, Birning's Gnup, Gnup's Grimkel, Grimkel's Bjorn, surnamed Gullbera or Gold-bearer, who first settled southern Reykjadal, a district of Southern Iceland. Grimkel's wife was Signya, Valthiof's daughter, who occupied the whole district called Kios; his father was Aurlig, who occupied a great part of Kjalarnes; his father was Hrap, the son of Ketill Flat-nesi or Flat-nose, the grandson of Bjorn Buna.

I know not whether this Vinland or some other uncertain part of America is meant by the land, to which, as the Eyrbyggja Saga reports, Gudleif Gunnlaugson of the province of Straumfjord in the western district of Iceland, sailing from Dublin, a city of Ireland, towards the end of St. Olaf's life, was driven on his return to Iceland by east and north winds. On this occasion he fell into great danger of death or of lifelong slavery, after losing his way and roaming for a long time over the western ocean without meeting any land. But then an extensive country which they saw, attracted the sailors, who were worn out with hardships and weak with long sea-sickness, to a safe harbor by the hope of refreshment. When they had reached shore, the inhabitants started up by hundreds, dragged them all from their ship and threw them into chains. The language of these people was unknown to the Northmen, and yet seemed to resemble most the Irish tongue. They understood that thereupon the people of the country deliberated, some condemning the Northmen to death, others to slavery, until an old man of lofty stature and with venerable white hair and a great retinue, before whom a standard was borne, rode up and like a prince was received with the utmost respect. To him thereupon were submitted the opinions of those who had been debating. Having summoned the sailors he addressed them in Danish and asked, whence they came. Having learned that most of them were Icelanders, he asked Gudleif, from what part of Iceland they came. When the latter had mentioned Borgarfjord, he enquired concerning the state and condition of the several nobles there and extending his conversation enquired for Snorre the priest, his sister Thurid and her son Kjartan. When the crowd thereupon interrupted him, demanding that some decision should be come to regarding the ship, he selected twelve men as his council and retired. After considerable delay he addressed Gudleif in the following words: "I have pleaded your cause before my fellow citizens, who consider it a favor that they have left your fate to my decision, and accordingly I grant you permission to depart. Indeed, though summer is far advanced, I advise and urge you to sail hence as soon as possible, for this people is unmanagable and faithless, and will soon be angered on account of the violation of its laws." Then said Gudleif: "What shall I report in my native country? Whom shall I declare my deliverer to be?" "To know that is unnecessary," he answered, "for I do not wish my friends and relatives to be drawn hither through affection for me, lest perchance the same fortune awaits them which you would have met with, had I not intervened; moreover, I am already of such an age that death may overtake me at any moment; but even if it be put off ever so long, there are far away in this land other men more powerful than I, who will certainly not send off strangers unharmed." Thereupon he remained with them, until a favorable breeze sprang up, and to Gudleif, as he departed, he gave a golden ring and a sword, the former to be delivered to Thurid, sister of Snorre the priest, the latter to her son Kjartan, who after his father's death held the manor of Froda. In reply to the question, by whom he should say the gifts were sent, he replied: "by one to whom the sister of the priest Helgafell was dearer than the priest himself had been." But if any one should think that from these words he knows who I am, do you repeat my words that I forbid any one to journey hither; for this land for the most part is harborless, and the people hostile to strangers, no matter where they land, unless perchance as in your case, accident has brought them. Gudleif having taken his ship out of the harbor the same autumn, reached Dublin, whence he had started and there he spent the winter. It is plain that the man was Bjorn, called the champion of Breidavik, who, recorded history relates, served under Palnatoke, then under Stjrbjorn, chief of Suecia (Sweden,) and after his murder a second time under Palnatoke, though in accordance with the established custom of Icelandish writers, the chronology is not treated with care. As a young man, he had fallen in love with Thurid, and was for that reason pursued by her brother, in order to put him to death; after courageously escaping him by his wiles, he permitted himself to be prevailed upon by entreaties, to leave his country;

but to what place the ship which bore him was borne, no one had determined with certainty, before it became known that he had been driven to the place where Gudleif found him; but how this happened has never since been found out. That this country was some part of America, is made likely by the winds which Gudleif met with, by the direction of his voyage and by his departure from and return to Ireland. But as I have made mention in Chapter 8 of the prodigies of Froda and of the woman from the Hebrides by whom, according to the book which Bjorn of Skardza followed, Leif the Lucky is falsely reported to have had a son, and as we have now come to the same manor where these incidents are said to have occurred and the same persons among whom they happened, it is proper to copy the story of them from the history of the Eyrbyggians, and add them here as a finishing touch to our history.

CHAPTER XVII.

OF THE PRODIGIES OF FRODA.

In the first year of the reign of the Jarls Eric and Sven, sons of Hakon, Jarl of the Hladae, prodigies were remarked on a manor in the western quarter of Iceland, called Froda; their cause and origin I shall relate in order. The manor was occupied by a wealthy man called Thorodd, surnamed SKATTKAUPANDI, or the tribute-buyer. For he sold his boat to some shipwrecked men of Orkney who were in danger of life on the coast of Ireland, while bringing tribute money from the Hebrides and Mona (Man) to Earl Sigurd about the year 980, and took for pay a part of the tribute, as has been recounted by us in our History of the Orkneys, chapter 10. His wife was Thurid, the sister of the famous Snorre, priest of Helgafell, whose authority was very great in that part of the island. Thorodd had received in his house a woman, Thorgunna by name, who had come the same summer from Dublin on the invitation of his wife. She was led by the hope of getting possession of the many and valuable treasures which the stranger possessed. This woman was a native of the Hebrides, and was at this time more than fifty years old. However, she would not pay a large sum for Thurid's hospitality, nor sell what was dearer to her than gold, even at the greatest price, though she was worried ever so much by her hostess; she said, she would earn her living by work, but not by low and servile work. On these conditions she was received as a guest. The bed assigned to her she covered with spreads and blankets so precious that nothing more valuable was ever seen in that place. Thurid all the more inflamed with the desire to possess them, offered Thorgunna an immense price, but in vain. She would not sleep on the ground, she answered, even for the sake of Thurid, however respectable a lady she might be. Whenever the weather was unfavorable to drying hay, she worked at embroidery, at other times using her own mattock, she worked at the hay. Her form was tall and she was proportionally stout; her complexion was slightly dark, her eyes large, her hair also was dark and long, and her manners graceful. There was in the same house a certain Thorer Vidlegg, (Wooden-leg) with his wife Thorgrima, called GALDRAKINN, or of the magic chin; he was to be supported at the host's expense by right of relationship, at that time, I believe, still in vogue. Thorgunna and Thorgrima forever quarrelled. Young Kjartan was passionately loved by the stranger Thorgunna, but her passion was unreturned, and she was vexed that she did not please him equally. A rainy summer was followed by a dry autumn. The sky was clear, undotted by even a single cloud, when all bent upon gathering hay, performed each the duty assigned to him by the master. Thorgunna on that day was to dry and gather into sheaves as much hay as would suffice to feed an ox throughout the winter. At one o'clock in the afternoon a cloud arising in the north moved over Thorodd's house and the manor of Froda. From it fell so much rain that it saturated all the hay which had not been put into sheaves, and the sky became so dark that the workmen could not see one another. But when the cloud passed away it was seen that it had rained blood. Then the weather grew clear, and all the blood which had fallen on the hay, dried, except that on Thorgunna's sheaves; nor could the blood which stained the mattock she held, and her garments, be cleansed off. When Thorodd enquired of her, what this prodigy meant, she said she did not know, but that it foreboded the death of somebody who was close to him. Having gone home the same evening and put off the garments that were dripping with blood, she went to bed, repeating that she saw she was detained by sickness. On that evening she would take no food. Early the following morning Thorodd went to her and asked, what she thought would be the issue of her illness. She answered that she would not suffer from disease thereafter, for the present would be her last sickness; that she considered him the wisest man of the manor, and for that reason warned him after her death to dispose of the property owned and left by her, according to her testament or last will; that if this were disregarded it was much to be feared farther prodigies would follow the one that had been seen. But he promised to recognize her as a prophetess and not to disobey her instructions or last will. "My corpse," she replied, "I order to be taken to Skalholt, where I foresee will be for a long time the foremost place in the island; for I hope that the ministers of the gospel are already assembled there, who will perform my obsequies according to the sacred rite. As a reward for your trouble and the outlay which you will make for this purpose, you will take in advance as much of my property as I shall order and with this you can be satisfied. Your wife will take from the undivided property my purple cloak which I dispose of in this manner, that she may submit with equanimity to whatever I provide regarding the rest. My ring the church of Skalholt shall have in payment for my burial; but the coverings of my bed, and my girdles, and all my possessions I command to be burned, for I do not foresee that they will be of any service to any one; and yet I do not do this, because I envy mankind the possession of my property, but because I do not wish men on my account to suffer and be overwhelmed by the many hardships and afflictions which I foresee will follow, if my directions will be disobeyed." Thorodd repeated his former promises. Then her illness began to grow more violent, and after the lapse of a few days it carried her off. The corpse was placed in a coffin and the next day taken to church. Then Thorodd bade all the equipments of her bed to be carried outside and a fire to be lit, into which they were to be thrown. When his wife saw this, she said that things so valuable should not be destroyed; for, said she, her old wives' talk is not of enough importance to make me willing to suffer the loss of these valuables through fear of her threats. And adding entreaties, she urged her husband with such earnestness to preserve the garments, that she saved all the girdles and coverlets from the fire, the neck-cloths, mattrasses and pillows only being consigned to the flames. And yet Thorodd's wife was not satisfied by this concession, though he was vexed at her excessively violent threats. Afterwards the funeral preparations were made and the corpse-bearers were taken to the bier, and men of distinction were selected for the office; special horses too were chosen, for a long journey of many miles was to be gone through. The corpse was wrapped in linen shrouds which were seamless. Straightway they passed through solitudes, nor was anything remarked that was worthy of mention, before they had passed the manor of Valbjarnarvall. There the mire, softened by the rain, hindered their progress. They had crossed with difficulty the river called Nordra in the Eyafjord, for it was filled by the streams which it receives, and which formed pools owing to the long rain storms, and could be crossed only with difficulty, if at all. One evening they came, tired by their long toil, to the manor called Nes, situated in the district of Stafholztung. There, as they were denied a lodging and yet could not proceed further on account of the approaching darkness, they set down their burden and carried the corpse into a house that lay apart. Having entered the dining hall, they intended to pass the night fasting. Though the servants had gone to sleep, they heard a sound as if of a

man walking in the store room. Suspecting that there were
thieves they ran in, and on opening the door, beheld there a
woman tall of stature and naked, and covered by no garment
whatsoever, who dealt out food; frightened thereby they
dared not approach, and going to the corpse-bearers they related what they had seen. When these had hastened thither
they recognized Thorgunna, whose corpse they were carrying,
and did not think it safe to meddle with her affairs. When
she had got as much food as she thought right, she brought
it into the dining-room and placed it on the table. Then the
corpse-bearers said to the host: "Perhaps you will regret
refusing us food and hospitable kindness." Then the host
and his wife replied, that they should have food and whatever
they might need. After this assurance Thorgunna departed
from the dining room and appeared there no more; but the
guests entering took off their wet garments and changed
them for dry ones; having signed with the cross the food
which Thorgunna had placed there, they partook of it without delay and without any harm to themselves. Having
spent the night there, they resumed their journey on the
following day, and, wherever they came, they spread the
report of this occurrence and obtained what they asked for,
as no one dared to refuse them what they needed. At last
they arrived at Skalholt and the ring and the other treasures
willed by Thorgunna, were delivered to the priests and
eagerly accepted by them, and the corpse was committed to
earth already consecrated, and the corpse-bearers arrived
safe at their homes without any damage.

On the manor of Froda there was an immense kitchen;
thence there was an entrance, always open, to the bedcham-
ber, the beds being shut in with hangings on both sides. For
after the manner of those times, those buildings were adjoining. Now next to the kitchen were two small buildings,
one on each side; in the one dried fish were kept, in the other
vessels filled with grain; every evening the hearth was lit
to cook food, and near it the household were wont to sit
together, before going to sup. Now on the evening when
the corpse-bearers returned, whilst the household sat near

the hearth, a large moon appeared on the kitchen wall, which moved leftwards through the kitchen. Nor did it recede while they were in the kitchen; it was seen by all alike. Thorodd, the host, asked Thorer Vidlegg what the prodigy meant. He answered that it was called VIDARMANA (which is translated "tree moon") and that it foreboded deaths. This marvel lasted a whole week. Then the shepherd, who had returned home unusually silent and more stern than was his wont, was thought to have come upon some prodigy, for he walked by himself and spoke to himself. This lasted till the first two weeks of winter had passed; then at last, having returned, the shepherd took to his bed, and the following morning he was found dead. After being buried near the church he troubled the living; for Thorer Vidlegg rising from bed one night, went outside; when about to return he noticed that the shepherd near the doors was about to prevent his re-entrance. Striving thereupon to escape he was pursued and seized by the shepherd and thrown down at the door with a great crash. Then taking to bed he lay ill for a long time until he died and was buried near the church. Afterwards he was seen in company with the shepherd to walk the night. Next one of Thorodd's servants after lying ill for three days died. Now the fast that precedes Christmas and begins with the first Sunday of Advent was approaching, although at that time Christmas was not celebrated in Iceland, and already six had died in the same house. One evening the heap of dried fish was heard to be upset, but when it was inspected, it was found in its usual condition. After the Yule feast Thorodd accompanied by five servants, sailed in a large ship to bring home fish; but on the same evening in the kitchen of Froda, a seal's head was seen to start up from the floor. When one of the servant-women saw this, she struck it on the head with a piece of wood, but with every blow it rose higher and turned its eyes towards Thorgunna's bed, which was covered with blankets. One of the hired men assailed the seal with repeated blows, but the seal emerged more and more, until it had stretched out its arms; at the same moment the hired man taken with a fit fell down, and great fear seized the rest. At last young Kjartan smote the seal with a powerful blow. Then it shook its head and turned its eyes hither and thither; thereupon he rained down blows without ceasing, and at each blow the seal sank down and appeared to be about to die, until it was wholly suffocated, and Kjartan struck the earth over its head. All these monsters seemed to fear Kjartan most of all. The following day Thorodd and his companions perished in the waves near the place called Enne, and the ship with the fish was dashed against the shore, but the corpses were not found. When this news was brought home, Kjartan and his mother invited their friends to a funeral feast: the provisions, now used for the funeral banquet, had been intended for the Yule feast. On the first evening of the banquet, when all the guests had taken their seats, Thorodd with his companions, all dripping, entered. This was regarded as a good sign, for the guests were thought to be hospitably received, whenever those who had been drowned came in to the funeral feast celebrated in their honor; for at that time there remained much of the pagan superstition, though the Icelanders were Christians and had been baptized. Thorodd with his men, having passed through the dining hall, made for the kitchen, without answering any one's greeting; finally they all seated themselves near the hearth, the servants fleeing. There these dead men tarried until the fire was covered with ashes; then they departed. On every evening, while the funeral feast lasted, this took place. The guests thought it would cease when the feast had ended. But it turned out very differently. After the guests left, when the servants came to light the hearth, Thorodd with his companions took their seats near it, for they were all dripping wet and with their hands wrang the water out of their clothes. As they sat there, Thorer Vidlegg came from the opposite side with his companions, equal in number to the others and all covered with dust, sat down and he shook the dust from his garments on Thorodd and his companions. But the servants were all driven from their seats on that evening and had no light. The following evening fire was lit in another house, for they hoped that the ghosts would not come there; but the ghosts behaved as before. On the third evening, at Kjartan's suggestion, an oblong hearth was built in the kitchen and a fire lit: but the food was cooked in the small house. This proved successful, for then the servants were not troubled. But Thorodd with his men occupied the kitchen. They heard that the fish in the fish heap were scaled off during the nights. On climbing up the fish heap they saw standing forth a scorched and black tail, like a calf's tail. One man leaping up seized it, and tried to draw it to himself, and called on the rest to do likewise. All the servants of the house, both male and female, ran to draw it out, but it did not permit itself to be stirred and seemed dead. When they used their utmost strength, however, it suddenly slipped from their hands and took the skin from their palms. Thereafter no trace of it was seen; but when they destroyed the heap of fish, they found the fish scaled off. When this was done, Thorgrima Galdrakinn, or of the magic chin, being seized by a sudden sickness, died, and she was seen seated in her husband's company. And now the disease was renewed a second time, after the tail appeared and more women died than men. Six of them were carried off at once by the disease and the ghosts of the dead drove the others away from the house. Of thirty domestics who were alive in the preceding autumn, seven survived in the month of Goa, (a part of which corresponds with February, a part with March.) In this condition of affairs, Kjartan visited his maternal uncle Snorre the priest, and asked his advice. He deputed a priest sent to him by Gissur the White along with his son Thord Kause, accompanied by six others to go with Kjartan and advised them to burn the girdles and all the bed-clothes of Thorgunna and to summon to judgment all the dead that were hostile to the living, and requested the priest to perform his sacred offices, to bless water, and to absolve the servants from their sins. On the eve of the feast of the Purification of the Blessed Virgin, they arrived at Froda, and the neighbors were gathered in the road and summoned to accompany them; on their arrival a fire was lit on the hearth to cook food. Thurid, the mistress of the manor, had at the time been attacked by the same disease of which the rest had perished. Kjartan having entered the kitchen took the coal from the hearth: there he saw his father Thorodd sitting as usual with his companions near the hearth; going out Kjartan destroyed Thorgunna's bed and all her furniture, and burned all her clothes and adornments; then he summoned Thorer Vidlegg to judgment, while Thord Kause called Thorodd, because they had invaded another's house without permission, and deprived the inhabitants of life and strength. Thereupon all that sat at the hearth side were summoned; then judges were appointed at the door and a law-suit instituted as in a law-court, witnesses and proofs were brought forward and repeated at the trial and a final decision given. This having been done, Thorer Vidlegg rising said: "I remained here as long as I was permitted," and he departed by the door where the trial had not been held. Then judgment was pronounced in the shepherd's case, and as soon as he had heard it, he rose and said: "I shall depart now, and I think I should have done so before." And Thorgrima Galdrakinn having heard her sentence answered: "We sat as long as we could," and having said this she left. One by one they were expelled in this way; after saying something, they went forth, unwillingly however, as their words showed. Thorodd, the lord of the manor was condemned last, and hearing the decision rose and said: "Few of us are left, let us all flee." And so he was the last to leave the house.

Then Kjartan with the rest entered the house; but the priest sprinkled the several parts of the house with holy water, and on the following day celebrated mass and the sacred rites, and thereafter the dead no longer infested it, and Thurid, the mistress of the house, recovered.

Here we may remark the devil's cunning and his power over those, who either do not know the true religion or are less instructed in the articles of faith; for nowhere do we read that anything similar happened on that island, after the true light of the Gospel rose and enlightened its inhabitants.

ADDENDA.

I translated that the sun at the time of the solstice, rose in Vinland about nine o'clock and set at three; I shall give my reasons for doing so. But as other reasons occurred to me afterwards, that stirred up doubt on this question, I shall leave both to be weighed by the unprejudiced reader. For after this History of Vinland was returned to me in print, I began to examine these points again and again, because the position of the land seemed to be nowise compatible with the fertility there described, and this was especially the case after the Swedish translation of the History of the Norse Kings called HEIMS KRINGLA, published by the distinguished John Peringskiold came into my hands. For following the interpretation of the learned Gudmund Olafson, he translated this passage differently; for both, adhering strictly to the rules of the grammarinns and translating word for word, understood it otherwise than I did, and yet did not catch the author's meaning any better. For the author, though he does not refer the latitude of the land to any precise degree of the equinoctial line, nevertheless left this to be clearly inferred from the rising and setting of the sun in winter and would have left it more clearly stated, if he had found it more carefully described. He certainly used clear language, as it appeared to me. The passage reads as follows in the 105th chapter of the Swedish edition, page 331 : *Meira var par jafndaegri enn a Graenlandi eda Islandi, sol hafdi par eyktarstad, og damalastad um Skammdeigi."* The meaning of these words the distinguished Arngrim Jonas, in the ninth chapter of his Greenland expounds as follows: In that place there is no such winter, or cold, nor is the winter solstice the same as in Iceland or Greenland, the sun remaining above the horizon about six hours (for they had no sun-dials.) This meaning I found myself long before seeing the work of Arngrim Jonas, firstly from the information of Brynjolf

Svenonson (if I understood him correctly), the most learned of the bishops of Skalholt up to his own time, a man without peer, to whom as a youth I was sent in the year 1662 with royal letters by my most clement Lord, the best of Kings, Frederick III, to learn the true signification of the most difficult ancient words and phrases, and secondly from the relation of sunrise to sunset as will be shown presently. Now I shall examine Peringskjold's interpretation. "The day too," says he "is longer than in Greenland and in Iceland for the sun there had periods of increase, and day-light appeared about breakfast time (six or seven o'clock) when the day was shortest." From this explanation we learn nothing certain of the position of the country. Peringskjold was led astray by the word EYKT, which usually means a space of three hours, but in another sense expresses the third hour after noon, which is also called NON. Explaining the author in the first sense, he showed nothing peculiar: for no longer periods of increase belong to the sun there than elsewhere. Nor have we here a single word about day-light, that is to say, dawn, but there is question of sunrise and sunset; nor, in my opinion, did the Icelanders breakfast at six or seven o'clock, but at nine o'clock, which they call DAGMAL. I should translate the author's words as follows: "There (in Vinland) the winter days are always longer than in Greenland or Iceland, the sun there touched the third hour afternoon and the ninth before noon." Here the words sunset and sunrise are so explained, that even if the word EYKT were unknown in the latter sense, yet its meaning could easily be deduced from its connection with the ninth hour before noon and the meaning of the word Dagmal, which always denotes that hour, as well as from the relation of sunrise to sunset and its connection with the third hour.

This view is confirmed from the ancient division of the natural day customary among the Icelanders: for the day is divided into eight parts according to the time the sun passes in each. For they call NATTMAL the part of the day while the sun is in the northwest, LAGNAETTE, while it is in the north, OTTA or RISMAL, *i. e.*, dawn or rising time, whilst it is in the northeast, MIDUR MORGUN, while it is in the east, DAGMAL, while it is in the southeast, HADEIGI, while it is in the south, NON, while it is in the southwest, MIDURAFTAN, while it is in the west.

Convinced by these arguments, I placed Vinland in Estotiland; but when I judged again and again that the products of the country (Vinland) did not suit the climate of Estotiland I began to examine the Swedish version more carefully, and especially to enquire more diligently into the meaning of the word EYKT, suspecting that this word led astray the Swedish translator. Finding it in no dictionaries, except that of Gudmund Andreson, and there set down only with the former meaning, I began to study the most ancient Canon Law of the Icelanders. From its ninth chapter I copy the following words: "*Ver skulum hallda Laugardag enn siounda hvern nonhelgan, sa er naest Drottinsdeigi firir, paskal ei vinna upp fra eykt, nema pat er nu man ec telia, pat a at, vinna allt er drottinsdag a at vinna. Pa er eykt er ut sudrs aept er deilld i pridiunga, og hefir Solinn geingna tvo luti, enn einn ogeingin.*" These words we translate as follows: "We shall hold sacred every seventh day, that is to say, the Sabbath, (Saturday) up to the Nona. This immediately precedes Sunday. Then from the EYKT hour it is not allowed to work, except for those things which I shall now mention: then all those things must be prepared which are necessary for Sunday. By EYKT is meant the time when the heavens between south and west are divided into three parts and the sun has completed two parts, whilst the third remains." I had written that the description of Vinland had explained this in clear words, but now I find that it has entangled that narrative, which the present passage made even more difficult. For the word NON denoted three o'clock after noon both in Iceland and formerly among the Anglo-Saxons; and from the establishment of the Christian religion or from the passage of this very law every generation in Norway so understood this word, and to-day in accordance with this rule the Norse rest on Saturdays. The present passage likewise illustrates it, inasmuch as it bids the sanctification to begin from NON and work to cease at EYKT; thence some may wish to infer that NON and EYKT are synonyms and that they designate the hour so often mentioned. But how far the very description of the same differs from this opinion, everybody sees. For the space through which the sun passes from midday to sundown, requires six hours, a third of which makes two hours. Two-thirds end at four o'clock after noon. If EYKT and NON are to be understood to mean this hour, in the first place the most ancient and most generally accepted division of hours falls to the ground, each of which, like the canonical hours, includes three common hours. The connection with the hour, DAGMAL, also disappears, for this designates nine o'clock before noon. Now it is not possible that on the day of the winter-solstice the sun should set at four o'clock in the afternoon and rise at nine o'clock in the forenoon; for it really rises at eight o'clock, and the day from sunrise to sundown is lengthened to eight hours. If then the words EYKT and NON mean the same thing, and signify the fourth hour, Dagmal is not nine o'clock, but must be advanced to eight o'clock, and consequently Vinland lies under the forty-ninth degree, and its shortest day measures eight hours; and this position certainly fits its products better than the position of Estotiland. We read that among the Romans NONA had not always the same meaning; for, as appears from the ancient manuscript of the Manerii, it sometimes meant midday. But the NONA of the clocks in most ancient times meant the last hour, when the sun was already setting (see Hofm. lex. at the word NONA); in like manner it might mean among us also, hours different from three o'clock after noon. As to the word DAGMAL, Gudmund Andreson in his lexicon supports our present view; for by Dagmal he understands, not nine o'clock before noon according to the received use of the word, but eight o'clock, which corresponds precisely with the sun's setting at four o'clock after noon; aud I doubt not that he wrote this supported by some authority; but whence he got, it I am not yet clear. However that may be, the explanation of our manuscript which translates the word EYKT by four o'clock, claims for itself undoubted authority, whether EYKT means the same thing as NON or not. As I said before, I leave these points to be examined by the judgment of the intelligent reader, and first of all he must decide, whether public prayers were said from three o'clock, that is to say, NON, to four o'clock, and then, whether the holiday began at four o'clock, *i. e.*, EYKT; this being settled, everything is consistent, and we recognize in the land, which to-day under the name TERRE NEUVE or TERRA NOVA on the adjacent continent on the coast of Canada has been reduced under the power of the French, the ancient Vinland. But if the position of the places which is here set forth, be compared more carefully with the character of those countries, I doubt not but that everything will be more clearly understood by those who either inhabit them or visit them purposely.

On page 61, after line 23, insert: After writing the foregoing I received Heimskringla, or History of the Norse Kings, translated by Joh. Peringskjold, printed at Stockholm, 1697, and find from chapter 103 to chapter 115 matter which is found in neither of the authentic copies of the Church of the Most Holy Trinity, the KRINGLA or the JOFRASKINNA. They are taken either from copies of the History of Olaf Triggeson or from some other source.

Google

INDEX.

Adam of Bremen...............60
Albania, or Great Ireland..7, 14, 61
Alftafjord.........................49
Ananías, J. L....................12
Andefort........................ 13
Are Marson................. 61
Arnestap.......................44
Arnora 43
Astrutharson, Sven 60
Audr, Queen 43
Aurlig...... 62
Avalldainna....................58

Barthol, Thomas................45
Berius, Ivar....................17
Bjarne..................25, 26, 53
Bjarne, Bishop..................40
Bjarn of Breidavik, ...15, 64
Bjarne, the Icelander..........9, 25
Bjarne Grimolfson..............49
Bjarney Islands................51
Bjorn of Skardsa ...7, 9, 10, 34, 37
                                40, 62, 65
Bjorn Buna 62
Bleyker... 12
Bondendon 13
Borgarfjord..... 68
Boterus, John...................18
Brand, Bishop................. 40
Brattahlide 29, 47, 50
Breidafjord.....................49
Bremen, Adam of.. 14
Buno....................10, 11, 18

Cabaru........................13
Campo.........................18
Canada........................10
Cape Hull......................30
Cartier, Jacques...............18
Cluverius, Philip...........10, 15
Codex Flateyensis..7, 9, 10, 29, 31,
                    32, 40, 47, 49, 50
Columbus, Christopher......15, 16
Crodme........................13

Dagmal................ ......76, 78
Davis' Straits.. ,.. 4
Dithmar, Bishop of Merseburg...64

Doffais.........................18
Drogio..........................11
Dublin............. ...... 63, 64
Duime............... 18

Einar of Langabrekka...........48
Enior...........................59
Eric II..........................16
Eric, first Bishop of Greenland.15,62
Eric the Red...9, 25, 30, 32, 41, 42,
                43, 47, 49, 50, 61, 65
Eric and Sven................30, 65
Eriksfjord....29, 33, 34, 39, 43, 47,
                                49, 65
Erlend the Strong..............59
Espishol........................59
Estland.........................14
Estotiland............10, 11, 77, 78
Eykt....................76, 77, 78
Eyrbyggva Saga................41

Flose...........................59
Frederick III................12, 76
Frederick IV.................... 3
Freidis.............10, 37, 38, 51, 53
Frisland.................11, 12, 13
Froda..................41, 65, 69, 72
Furdustrand....................52

Gamlason, Thorhall.............49
Gardar..........................37
Gissur the White 72
Glaumba........ 40
Gnup...........................92
Greenland...4, 17, 25, 26, 39, 41, 43,
                    44, 46, 49, 50, 51, 65
Grimhilde. 33, 47
Grimkel........................62
Grimolfson, Bjarne..... .....49, 58
Grisland...... 14
Grund..........................59
Gudleif Gunnlaugson...... 63, 64
Gudleif................. 65
Gudmund Olafson........ 75
Gudmund Andreson........ ...78
Gudrid.....29, 32, 33, 34, 43, 46, 47,
                        48, 49, 50, 65
Gudrun, wife of Jorund.........59

INDEX

Gunnlaug ... ... .59
Gunnlaugson, Gudleif ... ... .63, 64

Hacon, Eric 26
Hake ... ... .52
Hekja ... ... .52
Hako 6
Hakon, Earl ... ... .65
Halla ... ... .59
Hallbera ... ... .59
Halldise ... ... .44
Hallfrid 40
Hellveiga ... ... .43
Harold the Bold, or Haughty ... .16, 40, 60
Hauk 7, 40, 41, 59
Heimskringla ... ... .75, 79
Hebrides ... ... .65
Helluland ... ... .27, 51
Henry VII 16
Herjulf ... ... .25
Herjulfsnes ... ... .25, 26, 44, 47
Hjorleif ... ... .62
Hondius ... ... .13
Hrafn ... ... .61
Hrap ... ... .62
Hudson Bay ... ... .11
Hvitra Manna Land... ... .14, 58

Ibini 12
Icaria 14
Iceland ... ... .39, 44, 65
Ilofo ... ... .13
Ingibjorg ... ... .59
Ingveld ... ... .40
Ireland ... ... .53, 58, 65

Jedeve ... ... .13
Jonas, Arngrim ... ... .13, 40, 75
Jonas, the Breton ... ... .13
Jones, Jonas or John an Irish Bishop 14
Jones or Johannes, Bishop ... .62
Jorund ... ... .62

Karlsefne ... 10, 35, 36, 37, 39, 50, 51, 53, 54, 57, 59
Kelldum ... ... .59
Ketill ... ... .59
Ketil, Flatnesi ... ... .62
Kios ... ... .62
Kipping, Henry ... ... .11, 18
Kjalarnes ... ... .30, 52, 53, 54, 62
Kjartan ... ... .66, 71, 72, 73
Kornhjalm af tre ... ... .30
Kringla or Jofraskinna 7, 79

Krossanes ... ... .32

Lagnaette ... ... .76
Landnama Book 62
Leif 9, 30, 32, 37, 41, 42, 51
Leif of Brattahlide ... 26, 27, 29, 34
Lery, Baron de ... ... .15
Limerick ... ... .61
Lisufjord ... ... .47
Lysufjord ... ... .32

Madoc 6
Magin, John A ... ... .13
Mar ... ... .62
Markland ... ... .27, 51, 57
Marson, Are ... ... .14, 61
Martinerius ... ... .12
Mausur ... ... .29
Mercator ... ... .13
Mikiunes 54
Miritius, John ... ... .13
Monaco ... ... .13

Nattmal ... ... .76
Nes ... ... .68
Nordra ... ... .68
Norumbega 15

Ocibar ... ... .13
Olafson, Gudmund ... ... .75
Olaf Triggvin, Trygveson 7, 43, 52, 53
Orm ... ... .44
Ortelius ... ... .13
Otta or Rismal ... ... .76

Palnatoke 64
Peringskjold, John 7, 76, 79
Porlanda ... ... .13

Rane ... ... .13
Reid, Whale 34
Reikyanes ... ... .14, 61
Reinarnes ... ... .59
Reinenes Monastery 59
Reykjadal ... ... .62
Rolf 16
Rome ... ... .33, 40
Rovea ... ... .13
Rudbecke, Olaf 8, 12, 60
Runoff ... ... .40

Samoyeds ... ... .17
Sanestol ... ... .13
Sanson d' Abbeville ... ... ,11, 15
Schalholt ... ... .14
Sigmund ... ... .43

INDEX.

Sigrid..............................47, 48
Sigurd Earl......................65
Skagafjord........................40
Skalholt..........................69
Skialg Ulf........................14
Skogastrand......................49
Skraelings......10, 11, 17, 31, 35, 36
                              53, 54, 57
Snorre..............40, 51, 53, 57, 59
Snorre, priest of Helgafell...63, 64,
                                65, 72
Snorre Thorbrandson..............49
Sorand............................13
Spakonfellzhofde.................34
Spirige...........................13
Stafholztung.....................68
Steinvor..........................59
Stjrbjorn.........................64
St. Olaf..........................63
Straumsfjord......................54
Straumsey.........................54
Streme............................13
Sturleson, Snorro................7
Sven Astritharson................60
Svenonson, Brynjolf..............75

Terre Neuve......................79
Thistel...........................43
Thistilsfjord....................43
Thorer................29, 32, 47, 59
Thorer of Steige.................40
Thorer Vidlegg........66, 70, 71, 73
Thorana...........................40
Thorbjorg.........................44
Thorbjorg Knarrabringa..........62
Thorbjorn.................29, 43, 47
Thorbjorn of Stockanes.......49, 65
Thorbjorn Vifillson..........43, 47
Thorbrandson, Snorre.............49
Thord of Hesthofde...............34
Thord Kause......................73
Thordis...........................59
Thorfinn, Earl of the Orkneys....14
                                16, 61
Thorfinn, Karlsefne....34, 49, 59, 65
Thorgeir.....................40, 43
Thorgerde........................25

Thorgils..........................41
Thorgaima Galdradinn........72, 73
Thorgunna....66, 67, 69, 70, 72, 73
Thorhall..................51, 53, 54
Thorhall Gamlason................49
Thorhild or Thiodhild........61, 62
Thorhilde..................41, 42, 43
Thorhilde Riupa..................34
Thorkel...........................44
Thorkell Geiterson...............61
Thorlak, Bishop..................40
Thorlake, Theodore...............13
Thorodd........65, 67, 68, 70, 71, 73
Thorstein Ericson....10, 32, 33, 41,
                         42, 47, 48, 65, 69
Thorstein the Black..............33
Thorstein the Red................43
Thorstein Ranglat................59
Thorstein, Surt..................32
Thorvald Krok....................59
Thorvald........9, 10, 29, 30, 31, 32
Thorvald Ericson.................57
Thorvard..........................51
Thurid..............63, 64, 65, 66, 73
Tyrker........................27, 28

Ulf Skialg........................62

Vabjarnavall.....................68
Vaege.............................58
Valgerdis.........................59
Valldidida........................58
Valthiof..........................62
Venai.............................13
Vesputius, Americus...............6
Vestri, Bygd......................17
Vetthilde.........................58
Vifill............................43
Vifillson, Thorbjorn.........43, 47
Vifilsdal.........................43
Vinland......4, 7, 14, 16, 25, 29, 30,
                  34, 37, 39, 51, 61, 63, 77
White Man's Land.............57, 61
Winland..........................60

Zeni, the......................6, 11
Zichinnus........................12

Google

THE LATEST. THE BEST. THE CHEAPEST.

APPROVED TEXT-BOOKS
FOR CATHOLIC SCHOOLS.

KELLY'S UNIVERSAL SERIES OF SCHOOL BOOKS.

Edited by the Rev. HENRY A. BRANN, D.D., of New York.

These new Readers, soon to be ready for introduction, are the most beautifully illustrated series of Catholic Readers ever presented to the Clergy and Sisters of this country, and the only properly graded series for Catholic Schools ever published. They stand in the very front rank of excellence. Nothing that is important or useful in school-room methods in reading is omitted.

They have been prepared by practical teachers of long experience, aided in their work by suggestions and assistance from many learned clergymen and educators in our most noted colleges, academies, and schools.

No expense has been spared by the publisher to give our Catholic Institutions and Schools a series of Readers superior in every respect to any now published.

CAMPBELL'S READING SPELLERS.

A New Method of Teaching Spelling. Specimen Pages and Descriptive Circulars furnished on application.

CATECHISMS AT REDUCED RATES.

CORRESPONDENCE INVITED.

Address for Introduction Terms and other information concerning my publications,

THOMAS KELLY, Publisher, Printer, and Binder,
358 and 360 Broome Street, New York.

Specimen pages and books sent free, on application, to the Rev. clergy.

ST. JOHN'S COLLEGE,
FORDHAM, N. Y.

This College enjoys the powers of a University, and is conducted by Jesuit Fathers.

It affords every facility for the attainment of a complete Classical and Commercial Education.

French and German are taught without charge.

Spanish, Music, and Drawing are also taught by competent Professors. But for these branches there are extra charges.

For further information apply to

REV. T. J. CAMPBELL, S.J.,
PRESIDENT.

SETON HALL COLLEGE,
SOUTH ORANGE, N. J.

Conducted by secular Priests, aided by Lay Professors. Situated near the Orange Mountains, fourteen miles from New York. Buildings heated by steam, lighted by gas, and thoroughly ventilated. Course of studies—Classics or Commercial. Discipline strict, kind, and gentle, with the refinements of home. Domestic Department in charge of the Sisters of Charity.

For Catalogue, giving further information, apply to

VERY REV. J. H. CORRIGAN, A.M.,
PRESIDENT.

MANHATTAN COLLEGE,
GRAND BOULEVARD AND 131st STREET,
NEW YORK.

This College, organized in distinct departments, Collegiate and Preparatory, each embracing various grades, offers parents every facility for placing their sons, at any age, under its care.

The plan of studies is divided into three courses, Classical, Scientific, and Commercial, and thus secures to students a classification according to their aptitudes and probable future avocations.

Its healthy location and the conveniences for exercise at its command, guarantee that sound health and proper physical development which are at the base of all good education.

For Catalogue giving further information, apply to

THE SECRETARY.

A. M. D. G.

COLLEGE OF ST. FRANCIS XAVIER,

39 West 15th Street, New York City.

The College of St. Francis Xavier, conducted by the Fathers of the Society of Jesus, was founded in October, 1847, and in January, 1861, was endowed by the Regents of the University of the State of New York with full Collegiate powers and privileges ; it is intended only for day scholars.

The course of studies embraces Logic, Metaphysics, and Theodicy ; the English, Latin, and Greek languages ; Rhetoric, Poetry, and Elocution ; Mathematics and the Natural Sciences ; History, Geography, and Mythology. French and German are elective studies.

One of the principal objects ever kept in view in reading the Latin and Greek classics is to make use of them as an aid to the study of English. The plays of Shakespeare, the works of American and British poets, and the masterpieces of American and British orators and prose writers, are made the subject of critical study and analysis. Moreover, an English composition, in prose or verse, is written by every student once a week.

Three or four hours a week are devoted to Mathematics, besides an additional hour every month for review. The Physical Sciences are kept for the last two years ; Chemistry is begun in Rhetoric, and the Philosophers assist daily at lectures on Physics, and go through experimental work in chemical analysis.

Attached to the College is a complete Grammar Department, and a successful examination in the highest class of the Grammar Department admits the student into the College proper. There is also a Preparatory Department for such as are not advanced enough to enter the Grammar Department.

TERMS: PAYABLE IN ADVANCE.

Entrance Fee, $5.00.

	PER QUARTER.
Tuition, including use of Library,	$15.50
Dinner,	25.00
Drawing,	5.00

ST. FRANCIS' COLLEGE,

300-312 BALTIC STREET, AND 37-47 BUTLER STREET,
NEAR COURT STREET, BROOKLYN, N. Y.

Entrance at Butler Street.

CONDUCTED BY THE FRANCISCAN BROTHERS.

This Institution is chartered and empowered to confer such literary honors and degrees as are granted by the other colleges and universities of the United States.

The course of studies pursued in the College embraces English Literature, Rhetoric, Poetry, Elocution, History, Geography, Phonography, and the Science of Accounts; Mathematics; the Physical Sciences—Natural Philosophy, Chemistry, Physiology, Botany, Zoölogy, and Geology; the Greek and Latin, French and German Languages; Logic and Metaphysics.

Special attention is given to Grammar, Penmanship, Arithmetic, and Book-keeping in the Preparatory and Commercial Departments, and in the Primary, Spelling, Reading, Writing, Geography, and Arithmetic.

The College is situated in a healthy and retired part of the city. The building is large and commodious and well supplied with whatever is necessary for Geographical, Chemical, Astronomical, and Physical illustrations.

It has ample accommodations for over four hundred students, with neat and shaded playgrounds, arbored fountain, ball-alleys, and gymnasium.

The scholastic year for day-scholars is divided into four sessions of ten weeks each, and for boarding-scholars into two sessions of five months each, commencing the first Monday of September and closing the last week of June.

—————— TERMS: ——————

Day-scholars, per quarter, - - - - - - - from $8.00 to $15.00
Board and tuition per annum, payable half-yearly in advance, including washing, use of bed and bedding, - - - - - - - - 250.00
Boys under fifteen, - - - - - - - - 200.00

For further particulars apply to the President,

BROTHER JEROME, O.S.F.

D. F. MURPHY, Jr.,

PUBLISHER,

CHURCH STATIONER,

PRINTER, AND LITHOGRAPHER,

64 VESEY STREET.   56 BARCLAY STREET.

NEW YORK.

SPECIALLY EQUIPPED FOR HIGH-CLASS WORK.

THE AVE MARIA,

A CATHOLIC FAMILY MAGAZINE,

Devoted to the Honor of the Blessed Virgin.

24 pp. Imperial 8vo. Established in 1865.

PUBLISHED EVERY SATURDAY, AT NOTRE DAME, INDIANA.

THE "AVE MARIA" is the only periodical of its kind in the language. Its primary object is to honor the Blessed Virgin, and make Her better known and better loved. It commends itself, therefore, to all who venerate the Mother of God and wish to see Her patronage and devotion to Her extended.

It embraces the two great essentials of a popular periodical, viz.: Rational Amusement and Sound Instruction. There are articles on the Recurring Festivals, Essays and Short Articles, Stories, Sketches, Poems, Catholic Notes and Miscellany, Notices of New Publications, etc. There is also a YOUTH'S DEPARTMENT, which is made as entertaining and profitable as possible for younger readers.

The Holy Father has given his special blessing to all who, as subscribers, or in any other way, further the interests of this periodical.

The "AVE MARIA'S" staff of contributors includes some of the best Catholic writers, at home and abroad: The Rev. A. A. Lambing, LL.D.; the Rev. Father Edmund, C.P.; the Rev. Richard J. McHugh, the Very Rev. J. Adam, the Rev. Matthew Russell, S.J.; and others of the Rev. and Rt. Rev. Clergy; John Gilmary Shea, Kathleen O'Meara, Maurice F. Egan, Anna Hanson Dorsey, Brother Azarias, Christian Reid, B. I. Durward, Eleanor C. Donnelly, Charles Warren Stoddard, Eliza Allen Starr, Nugent Robinson, Clara Mulholland, the author of "Tyborne"; Marion Muir Richardson, T. F. Galwey, Margaret E. Jordan, Arthur J. Stace, "Marie," Anna T. Sadlier, William F. Dennehy, "Mercedes," Ella B. Edes, E. L. Dorsey, Octavia Hensel, W. D. Kelly, Angelique de Lande, Mary E. Mannix, and others.

TERMS OF SUBSCRIPTION.
POSTAGE FREE.

One Year.. $ 2.50
Clubs of Ten (and upward, at the rate of $2 each, with a Free Copy
 to the one getting up the Club).................................. 20.00
Foreign Subscriptions....... $3.00, or 12 shillings British.

Payments in advance. Procure Money Orders on NOTRE DAME, IND., or register letters containing money. Specimen copies FREE to any address. Subscribers are invited to send the names of friends in any part of the world who would be interested in the "AVE MARIA." All communications should be addressed to the Editor and Publisher,

Rev. DANIEL E. HUDSON, C.S.C., Notre Dame, Indiana.

PURE ALTAR WINES.

REVEREND SIR:—It is well known that at present it is difficult to procure an absolutely pure Wine for Sacramental use. Few, if any, of the present dealers, can tell you the maker of the Wine they sell, and few can offer with their Wine the endorsement of any ecclesiastical authority, from the place where the Wine is produced. This I have determined to remedy. FATHER PARISIS' FAMOUS Grape Mission Wine, BERNALILLO, NEW MEXICO; and JOHN MORAN'S LOS ANGELES, CAL., are acknowledged to be the best in this country. Both bear the highest testimonials from the Heads of their respected dioceses, viz.: Archbishops Salpointe and Lamy of the Santa Fe, Bishop Mora of Los Angeles, Archbishop Riordan, San Francisco, and a number of the Reverend Clergy where this Wine is made, and I supply these in original casks, as received, or bottled, in cases, if preferred.

My connection with the extensive firm of Messrs. Thurber, Whyland & Co., enables me to make all my purchases for Cash, otherwise I could not quote to the trade the following exceptionally low prices. The present season is an unusually advantageous one for shipping this wine to ensure its arrival in good condition:

REV. FATHER PARISIS' FAMOUS MISSION GRAPE WINE, WHITE.
By the barrel, per gallon.............. $1.50 | Per case of one dozen bottles.......... $5.00

JOHN MORAN'S FINE WHITE WINE.
By the barrel, per gallon.............. $1.00 | Per case of one dozen bottles.......... $4.00

ZINFANDEL CLARET.
By the barrel, per gallon .... .90 | Per case of one dozen bottles.......... $3.75
(Fully equal to superior Bordeaux.)

ORDINARY TABLE CLARET.
By the barrel, per gallon.............. .80 | Per case of one dozen bottles.......... $3.60
(Fully equal to good Bordeaux.) Five bottles to the gallon.

We sell in packages of one barrel and upward, not less, except in cases, as the quality is deteriorated by changing into kegs; and at least a barrel should be purchased and bottled at one time. Terms, free on board cars at New York, less 2 per cent. for cash in thirty days, *or if preferred, three months' credit.*

PURE BEESWAX CANDLES.
SPECIAL OFFER.

In order to utilize storage space, we wish to clear out a stock of Pure Beeswax Candles, white and yellow, at less than the actual cost to manufacture. In order to effect this your attention is invited to the following quotations:

HAND CAST.
Plain Yellow, unbleached, Tenebra, pure, *Non Plus Ultra*, per lb., (not less than a box of 36 lbs.).. .30
Plain White, 1, 2, 3, 4, 5 and 6 to pound, pure *Non Plus Ultra*, per lb............... .35

ALTAR CANDLES—HYDRAULIC PRESSED.
My Hydraulic pressed, extra hard Stearic Wax Candles are the very best of the kind manufactured. They are made expressly for Church use, and in hardness, whiteness, beauty of finish and brilliancy of light, are not excelled. *Full weight, sixteen ounces to pound.*

4 or 6 to lb., 30 lbs. per box, per lb.... .15 | 1 or 2 to lb., 25 lbs. per box, per lb..... .16

The Candles weighing one and two to pound, are specially made for occasions when services are long, such as Forty Hours' Devotion, Lenten Services, and during the Octave of the Solemnity of Corpus Christi.

PURE OLIVE OIL, FOR SANCTUARY LAMPS.
Imported direct from Mediterranean Ports, guaranteed pure, in 2½ and 5 gallon cans,
    patent stoppers, per gallon.. 1.50
In quantities of 10 gallons (no charge for cans), per gallon............................ 1.35
In barrel lots of 42 gallons, per gallon.. 1.25
Cotton Seed Oil, finest quality, put up in 5-gallon cans, patent stopper, per gallon..... .75
In barrel lots, per gallon... .60

WAX TAPERS, IN COILS.
1, 2, 3, 4, 6 and 8 to a pound, ornamented, per pound.................................... .75
1, 2, 3, 4, 6 and 8 to a pound, plain, per pound... .60

WAX GAS LIGHTERS.
Price per 5 pounds 2.25

FLOATING TAPERS FOR OIL LAMPS.
Nuremberg Tapers, price per dozen large boxes.. 1.50

M. SULLIVAN,
(In connection with Messrs. THURBER, WHYLAND & CO.),

A few doors from the General Post-Office.   **12 Barclay Street, New York.**

THE
UNITED STATES CATHOLIC HISTORICAL MAGAZINE
IS PRINTED BY
EDWARD O. JENKINS' SONS,
AT
20 NORTH WILLIAM STREET, NEW YORK.

ESTIMATES GIVEN FOR ANY CLASS OF
Printing, Electrotyping and Stereotyping.
FINE BOOK PRINTING A SPECIALTY.

WE PRINT ANYTHING FROM A POSTAL CARD TO A WEBSTER'S UNABRIDGED DICTIONARY.

EDWARD O. JENKINS' SONS, 20 NORTH WILLIAM STREET, NEW YORK.

COOGAN BROS.,

CARPET AND FURNITURE DEALERS,

Cor. Bowery and Grand St.

PUBLISHED QUARTERLY.　　　　　　　　　　$2.00 A YEAR.

UNITED STATES
CATHOLIC
HISTORICAL MAGAZINE.

PUBLISHED UNDER THE AUSPICES OF THE UNITED STATES
CATHOLIC HISTORICAL SOCIETY.

VOL. II.　NO. VII.

NEW YORK.
2 LAFAYETTE PLACE.
P. O. BOX 2078.
1889.

Entered at the New York Post-Office as Second-Class Matter.

CONTENTS.

	PAGE
A MEMOIR OF THE LIFE AND LABORS OF THE RIGHT REV. AMADEUS RAPPE, D.D., first Bishop of Cleveland. By the Rev. G. F. Houck	235
HISTORICAL SKETCH OF THE REV. JOHN THAYER, Boston's first native-born priest. By the Rev. Arthur T. Connolly, of Roxbury, Mass.	261
EARLY CATHOLICS IN CONNECTICUT. By the Rev. T. J. Shahan, D.D.	274
THE BEGINNINGS OF THE CAPUCHIN MISSION IN LOUISIANA. By J. G. S.	295
ROBERT WALSH. By Henry C. Walsh.	301
PETITION OF THE ROMAN CATHOLICS OF MARYLAND TO THE UPPER HOUSE OF ASSEMBLY IN 1756	314
GENERAL DESCRIPTION OF THE METROPOLITAN PROVINCE OF BALTIMORE IN THE UNITED STATES OF NORTH AMERICA. By Archbishop Maréchal	318
THE CATHOLIC LAITY'S DIRECTORY TO THE CHURCH SERVICE, with an Almanac for the year 1817	320
MEETINGS OF THE UNITED STATES CATHOLIC HISTORICAL SOCIETY	323
NOTES.—Advertisement of the first Catholic Bible, 260; Bishop Carroll in Boston—Church at Vincennes in 1816, 273; A Flemish History of Canada—Indians on the English Coast in 1508, 294; Notes on old Churches near Washington, 313; The Poor Clares at Georgetown, 317; Bancroft's False Charges against the Catholics of 1776, 328; New Mexican Antiquities, by A. F. Bandelier	330
QUERIES.—History of Church Organs.—Chronology of Catholic Churches.—Catholic Newspapers and Periodicals.—San Miguel de Guandape.—Pope's Absolution	333
BOOK NOTICES.—History of the Catholic Church, by Brueck—Brithday of the State of Connecticut.—History of the Equestrian Statue of Israel Putnam.—Church History, by Professor Kurtz	334
MEMORANDA	336

www.ingramcontent.com/pod-product-compliance
Lightning Source LLC
Chambersburg PA
CBHW031959300426
44117CB00008B/825